COMMUNICATION IN JAPAN AND THE UNITED STATES

SUNY Series, Human Communication Processes
Donald P. Cushman and Ted J. Smith, III, Editors

COMMUNICATION IN JAPAN AND THE UNITED STATES

WILLIAM B. GUDYKUNST, EDITOR

STATE UNIVERSITY OF NEW YORK PRESS

Published by
State University of New York Press, Albany

© 1993 State University of New York
All rights reserved

For information, address State University of New York
Press, State University Plaza, Albany, N.Y., 12246

Production by E. Moore
Marketing by Fran Keneston

Library of Congress Cataloging-in-Publication Data

Communication in Japan and the United States / William B. Gudykunst,
    editor.
        p.   cm. — (SUNY series in human communication processes)
    Includes bibliographical references and index.
    ISBN 0-7914-1603-8. — ISBN 0-7914-1604-6
    1. Communication—Japan. 2. Communication—United States.
I. Gudykunst, William B. II. Series.
P92.J3C65 1993
302.2'0952—dc20   92-27134
                                                              CIP

10 9 8 7 6 5 4 3 2 1

CONTENTS

PART III. COMPARING COMMUNICATION
IN SELECTED CONTEXTS

PART IV. CONCLUSION

PREFACE

Over the last two decades, extensive research has been conducted on communication in Japan and the United States. This research is published in a wide variety of sources, including books in English and Japanese, communication and area studies journals in the United States, as well as university annual publications in Japan. To date, much of this research has been inaccessible. No single volume contains a summary of the research conducted. One purpose of this volume is to fill this void by presenting a summary of current research on communication in Japan and the United States. Research conducted to date, however, has not been highly systematic. A second goal of the volume, therefore, is to establish a preliminary research agenda for future research on communication in Japan and the United States. My final goal in preparing the volume is more applied. In order to improve relations between Japan and the United States, members of both cultures need to better understand how each other communicate. The research presented provides a solid foundation for teachers and trainers to use in helping people in the two cultures better understand each other.

In preparing the volume, I had several audiences in mind. First, the volume is aimed at communication scholars and graduate students interested in how communication varies across cultures in general or how communication varies in Japan and the United States in particular. Second, the volume should benefit scholars interested in area studies (e.g., Japan experts). Area studies have become so specialized that often area experts are not aware of research conducted in their country of interest (e.g., Japan) within specific disciplines such as communication. Third, trainers conducting training for business personnel working in

Japan and the United States should find the research presented useful. The research presented provides a solid foundation for the development of culture specific training programs.

Editing a volume such as this is never accomplished without help. Many of the authors presented preliminary versions of their chapters at the Conference on Communication in Japan and the United States held at California State University, Fullerton in March 1991. Tsukasa Nishida coordinated the Japan side of the conference, and many colleagues and students at California State University, Fullerton helped in organizing the conference. I want to especially thank the authors for their cooperation in revising their chapters for the book and for their help in preparing the volume. Yuko Matsumoto, Seiichi Morisaki, and Hiroshi Ota provided invaluable assistance in ensuring that the Japanese terms used in the volume are correct. The series editor, Don Cushman, and the editor-in-chief at SUNY Press, Lois Patton, provided guidance and support in the preparation of the volume. My friend and colleague, Stella Ting-Toomey, provided support throughout the project and, in addition, she made many suggestions that improved the quality of the volume. Completion of the volume was facilitated by a General Faculty Research award from California State University, Fullerton.

Part I
THE STUDY OF COMMUNICATION IN JAPAN AND THE UNITED STATES

Chapter 1

INTRODUCTION

William B. Gudykunst

Prior to the Meiji Restoration, the Tokugawa shoguns placed severe restrictions on contact between Japanese and *gaijin* (foreigners). Japanese who left Japan were forbidden from returning under penalty of death. There were, however, many contacts between Japanese and the outside world before Commodore Perry "opened" Japan to outside contact in 1853. Frequently ships sailing off the coast of Japan were caught in storms and many were carried across the Pacific to North America. Japanese on these ships had contact with people in the United States, including prominent people such as Abraham Lincoln (Plummer, 1992). Many of these encounters were plagued by misunderstandings.

When Commodore Perry arrived in Japan, his sailors found the Japanese to be "the most polite people on earth" (cited in Dulles, 1965). Perry himself, however, reported that he was frustrated by the "lies" he was told and the "evasive" Japanese style of communication (Dulles, 1965). Dulles concluded that the opposing perceptions of Japanese courtesy and hypocrisy "helped set a pattern of American thinking about Japanese that has persisted for a century" (pp. 68-69). Virtually all accounts of the early contact indicate that cultural misunderstandings began with the first contact between people from Japan and the United States.

Current relations between Japan and the United States are complicated. In the United States, for example, there was only a handful of people involved in making U.S. policy toward Japan two decades ago. Today, however, there are at least three different groups concerned with U.S. policy (Friedman, 1992). First, there are those concerned mainly with issues of national security (i.e., State Department, Pentagon, National Security Council). Second, there are those whose main interest is in protecting production of U.S. goods and their sales around the world (i.e., Office of United States Trade Representative, Commerce Department). Third, there is the group concerned with overall U.S. trade policy (i.e., Office of Management and the Budget, Council of Economic Advisers). Friedman (1992) argues that one of the major problems confronting U.S. policy toward Japan is that each of these groups sees Japan differently. The situation in Japan may be more coordinated, but there are diverse views of the United States among the prime minister, the Diet, and the Foreign Ministry.

While the relations between Japan and the United States are complicated, people in the two countries tend to have positive views of the other country. A recent *New York Times*, CBS News, and Tokyo Broadcasting System poll (conducted in November 1991; see Wiseman, 1991, for results), for example, indicates that 77 percent of the people in the United States "say their feelings toward Japan are generally friendly," and 65 percent of the people in Japan hold a similar sentiment toward the United States.[1] Relations between the countries in recent years, however, have been strained. Many politicians in the United States have engaged in "Japan bashing" and Japanese politicians have criticized workers in the United States (e.g., Yoshio Sakurauchi's comments in January 1992). The main reason for the strain in Japan-United States relations appears to stem from the trade imbalance (e.g., see Friedman & LeBard's, 1991, *The Coming War with Japan*). Numerous fictitious books have been published in the United States in recent years on the theme of an economic war between the United States and Japan (see Reich, 1992, for an overview of these books).[2]

Clyde Prestowitz, President of the Economic Strategy Institute, argues that one reason for the difficulty in dealing with the frictions between Japan and the United States is that people assume a close alliance between nations is possible only if they are similar (cited in Chira, 1991). Prestowitz believes that it is the insistence on similarity between the two countries when none exists that is making it difficult to deal with the frictions between the two countries. In order to improve relations between the United States and Japan, citizens of the two countries must better understand each other (Luttwak, 1991; Miyoshi, 1991). Reischauer (1971) points out that

We in this country [the United States] have been very slow in becoming aware of the importance of Japan and the need for greater understanding of what Japanese feel and think in their relations with us. The Japanese too have been obtuse in their perceptions of American attitudes. On both sides we have let this thinness of understanding develop into a frightening crisis of confidence in each other. It is high time that we set seriously about trying to understand what the other is thinking. (p. v)

The need for understanding is even greater today (1992). A recent *Time* (10 February 1992) poll[3] indicates that only 13 percent of the people in the United States think they know "a lot" about Japan and its people (42 percent think they know "some things") (Murrow, 1992); only 5 percent of the people in Japan think they know "a lot" about the United States and its people (42 percent think they know "some things") (Hillenbrand, 1992).

Even though North Americans and Japanese do not think they know a lot about each other, they hold complex stereotypes about each other. The *Time* (10 February 1992) poll revealed that North Americans think that Japanese are competitive (94%), crafty (69%), devoted to fair play (35%), friendly (59%), hardworking (94%), lazy (4%), poorly educated (12%), prejudiced (53%), and violent (19%) (Murrow, 1992). The Japanese, in contrast, view people in the United States as competitive (50%), crafty (13%), devoted to fair play (43%), friendly (64%), hardworking (15%), lazy (21%), poorly educated (21%), prejudiced (41%), and violent (23%) (Hillenbrand, 1992). People in Japan admire the freedom of expression (89%), the variety of life-styles (86%), the treatment of women (68%), and the leisure time available to workers (88%) in the United States (Hillenbrand, 1992). North Americans, on the other hand, admire Japanese industriousness (88%) and educational institutions (71%) (Murrow, 1992).

Improving understanding between people in the United States and Japan requires that cultural similarities and differences be recognized, and that negative stereotypes become more positive. Kitamura (1971) pointed out that "we have come to a stage in our [U.S.-Japan] relations in which we need hard understanding based on recognition and appreciation of differences rather than easy understanding based on similarities" (p. 37). Cultural similarities and differences are created and manifested through communication. It is impossible to improve relations between Japan and the United States without understanding how communication patterns are similar and different in the two cultures. This is the first volume to summarize the state of our knowledge regarding communication in Japan and the United States. To place the volume in context, I briefly overview the approaches to cross-cultural research used to study communication in Japan and the United States.

CROSS-CULTURAL RESEARCH ON COMMUNICATION IN JAPAN AND THE UNITED STATES

The discipline of communication has existed for a relatively short period of time in the United States. In this short period, extensive research has been conducted on various aspects of communication. There is comprehensive research, for example, on interpersonal, mass, and organizational communication, to name only three areas. The vast majority of this research, however, has been limited to studying how Euro Americans communicate in the United States.

Recently, interest has increased in how communication varies across cultures. There appear to be several reasons for the increase of interest in cross-cultural variations among communication researchers. First, a specialized area of research focusing on the study of communication and culture has developed in the last twenty years. A large portion of the research conducted by scholars interested in international and intercultural communication involves comparisons of communication in different cultures. The researchers also study communication between members of different cultures.

Second, several theorists have included culture as one of the major components in their frameworks. Cronen, Chen, and Pearce (1988), for example, see "intercultural communication and comparative patterns of communication" (p. 67) as central to understanding communication in their "coordinated management of meaning" framework. Numerous researchers using this framework, therefore, have compared communication in different cultures. To illustrate, Nakanishi and Johnson (1993) examined the influence of self-disclosure on conversational logics (a central construct in the coordinated management of meaning framework) in Japan and the United States.

Third, some researchers have recognized that if they do not test their theories and/or hypotheses in other cultures, their generalizations are severely limited. Gudykunst, Yang, and Nishida (1985), for example, extended Berger and Calabrese's (1975) uncertainty reduction theory of initial interactions to developed relationships (e.g., friendships, dating relationships). They argued that if the theory was not tested in other cultures, the theory would have a restricted range. Their research, however, indicates that the theory generalizes to Japan and Korea.

Fourth, there has been an increase in the number of international students studying communication in the United States. Many of these students have conducted research comparing communication in their home culture with communication in the United States. This work appears to have stimulated interest in cross-cultural research by the faculty supervising the international students' work.

Fifth, the discipline of communication has began to develop systematically in other countries and professional associations focusing on communication are being formed in other countries.[4] The Communication Association of Japan, for example, has been formed in the last decade. It holds an annual conference at which research on Japanese communication is presented. Much of this research involves explicit comparisons with communication in the United States.

The combination of these factors has led to an increase in the cross-cultural communication research conducted in the last two decades. Of the cross-cultural communication studies conducted to date, by far the largest percentage compare communication in Japan and the United States. There appear to be at least four major reasons for the amount of research conducted in these two countries. First, there appear to be more Japanese Ph.D.s trained in communication in the United States than Ph.D.s from any other country. Second, there is extensive anthropological research on Japan that has examined some aspect of communication to provide a foundation for cross-cultural comparisons. Third, Japan's culture is very different from the culture in the United States and it is more accessible than other cultures which are very different (in part because the Ph.D.s trained in the United States are potential collaborators). Fourth, several conferences have been devoted specifically to discussing communication in Japan and the United States. The conference organized by John Condon and Mitsuko Saito held at International Christian University in Tokyo in 1974, for example, brought together scholars interested in communication in Japan and the United States and stimulated collaborative research by scholars who met at the conference. More recently, communication scholars from Japan and the United States met at California State University, Fullerton in 1992 for a conference attended by approximately 400 people.

There are several different types of research used to compare communication in Japan and the United States. Kohn (1989), for example, isolates four types of cross-cultural research: (1) studies where culture is the object of study, (2) studies where culture is the context of study,

(3) studies where culture is the unit of analysis, and (4) studies that are transcultural.[5] Each of these types of studies have different goals.

In the first type of cross-cultural study culture is the object of study. The researcher's primary interest is learning more about the specific cultures being examined. This approach is basically descriptive in nature, and is used widely in anthropology and area studies. Communication researchers, however, have conducted extensive descriptive research on communication that contributes to our understanding of the cultures in Japan and the United States. Barnlund's (1975, 1989) research is an example of this line of work. He has conducted large-scale surveys designed to describe communication patterns in Japan and the United States. Research describing communication in Japan and the United States implicitly provides information on the two cultures. The descriptive research presented in this volume, therefore, should be useful to area studies experts interested in Japan.

When culture is treated as the context of the study, researchers are interested in understanding how different aspects of cultures influence communication. Investigators, for example, can study how dimensions of cultural variability (e.g., individualism-collectivism; in individualistic cultures the focus is on the individual, while the emphasis is on the group in collectivistic cultures; this dimension is discussed in detail in the next chapter) influence communication in Japan and the United States. To illustrate, Gudykunst, Nishida, and Schmidt (1989) were interested in explaining how culture influences communication in ingroup and outgroup relationships. They compared communication in Japan and the United States. As predicted, they discovered that there are greater differences in ingroup-outgroup communication in Japan (collectivistic culture) than in the United States (individualistic culture). By comparing the results from Japan and the United States they drew conclusions about the influence of individualism-collectivism on ingroup-outgroup communication. To draw definitive conclusions, however, data from at least one additional individualistic culture and data from at least one additional collectivistic culture are needed (Gudykunst, Gao, Schmidt, Nishida, Bond, Leung, Wang, & Barraclough, 1992, added Hong Kong and Australia and the patterns were consistent).

Researchers using the culture as context approach might also be interested in testing the extent to which theories and/or hypotheses generalize across cultures. The goal of social science research ultimately is to develop theories that generalize across time and space.[6] Testing theories or hypotheses developed in one culture in another culture, is one way to extend their generalizability.[7] To illustrate, researchers might conduct research in the United States that supports the hypothesis that there is a positive association between gathering personal information about strangers and reducing uncertainty about strangers' behavior. If they are interested in generalizing their hypothesis, they might collect data in Japan to see if the hypothesis holds in a different culture (i.e., cross-cultural generalizability). The present volume, therefore, will be useful to communication researchers because it demonstrates how communication varies across cultures.

Kohn (1989) points out that often it is difficult to distinguish between studies that treat culture as the object of study and studies that treat culture as a context. Classifying a study depends on the investigator's intent. Research conducted for one purpose, however, can be useful to investigators interested in the other function of cross-cultural research. The research presented in this volume designed to treat culture (Japan and the United States) as a context for studying communication, for example, should be of interest to area studies experts whose main interest in Japan and the United States is as objects of study.

The third type of cross-cultural research focuses on culture as the unit of analysis. Kohn (1989) points out that "what distinguishes research that treats nation [or culture] as the unit of analysis is its primary concern with understanding how social institutions and processes are systematically related to variations in national [or cultural] characteristics" (p. 22). The most widely cited work in this area is Hofstede's (1980) work on deriving dimensions of cultural variability (discussed in detail in the next chapter). Research using culture as the level of analysis requires that data from large numbers of cultures be available for analysis.

The final type of cross-cultural research is what Kohn (1989) calls "transnational" or what I will call transcultural. This type of research treats cultures or nations as parts of larger international systems. This strategy for cross-cultural research often is used in international relations and diplomacy. The primary examples of this type of research in communication focus on the transmission of mass media messages across national borders.

The preceding discussion suggests that there are many types of cross-cultural research on communication in Japan and the United States. The types of cross-cultural research conducted often are aimed at different goals (e.g., learning about a culture, testing the generalizability of hypotheses). The most important reason for conducting cross-cultural research, however, was not addressed; namely, improving relations between Japanese and North Americans requires that we understand how communication patterns are similar and different in the two cultures. If members of the two cultures do not understand how communication is similar and different in Japan and the United States, they will not be able to accurately interpret each others' communication. If the research presented in this volume contributes to better understanding between the people of the United states and Japan it will have accomplished one of its major purposes.

OVERVIEW OF THE VOLUME

As indicated earlier, the goal of this volume is to summarize the current state of knowledge regarding similarities and differences in communication in Japan and the United States. The authors of the various chapters, therefore, present broad overviews of communication in particular areas. Overlap in the material covered across the chapters was unavoidable. Where overlap exists, however, it tends to be presented from the perspective of different disciplines (e.g., anthropology, communication, psychology, sociolinguistics).

The volume is divided into four parts. This chapter and the following chapter constitute part I—introductory material. In the next chapter, William Gudykunst and Patricia San Antonio review the major approaches used to study communication in Japan and the United States. They begin with a review of anthropological research on Japan, focusing on studies that contribute to our understanding of communication. Next, they discuss a line of research conducted in Japan known as *nihonjinron* (discussions of the Japanese). These two lines of research tend to treat culture as the object of study. Gudykunst and San Antonio also review research designed to treat culture as the context of study. They conclude with a discussion of the issue of equivalence (e.g., equivalence of meaning for concepts) in comparing communication in Japan and the United States.

Part II contains three chapters. The purpose of these chapters is to place the study of communication in Japan and the United States in context. The chapters in part II, therefore, focus on issues of culture and self, culture and language, and ethnicity and communication.

Takie Sugiyama Lebra discusses culture, self, and communication. She argues that understanding differences in self contruals is necessary to understand differences in communication in Japan and the United States.[8] She contends that the Japanese self is "socially contextualized, embedded, or situated." The self in the United States, in contrast, is viewed as "socially independent and internally consistent." Lebra examines the consequences for communication of these different self construals, focusing on the consequences for communication in Japan. She demonstrates how the self construal influences conversational features such as fragmentation, interruption, and the role of the listener.

Lebra also links self-conceptions to empathy and self-presentations. She argues, for example, that there is a paradox regarding self-presentations in Japan and the United States: "the [North] American self is so closed that it can afford to open up in communication, whereas the Japanese self, so exposed and subject to involuntary leakage, must be wrapped up." She goes on to point out that the more individuals unwrap within a boundary, the more wrapped they must be with outsiders. In discussing these subtle paradoxes regarding the self in Japan and the United States, Lebra responds to criticism of the *nihonjinron* approach to the study of Japanese society. Her position clearly suggests we must try to understand cultural differences *and* basic values shared in common when we study communication in Japan and the United States.

Kaoru Akasu and Kojiro Asao examine the sociolinguistic factors that influence communication in Japan and the United States. They discuss seven dimensions that influence the choices individuals make in selecting the linguistic expressions they use: (1) properties of the speaker such as sex, age, status; (2) the sense of relationship (e.g., belonging) the individuals have with their partners; (3) the relative power or social standing of the individuals communicating; (4) the roles that the individuals perform when they communicate; (5) the type of message being exchanged; (6) the degree to which the communicators invade each others' territory; and (7) context and interdependence. Akasu and Aasao's discussion of context and interdependence compliments Lebra's discussion of the self. They link several Japanese sociolinguistic patterns (e.g., the use of ambiguity and indirectness) to an interdependent conceptualization of the self.

In concluding, Akasu and Asao argue that there is a need for a general framework that will allow researchers to compare the influence of language on communication. They also suggest that while there are cross-cultural comparisons of Japanese and English, there is a need for research on language usage in Japanese-North American interaction. They contend that the two forms of research are complimentary, not different.

Harry Kitano focuses on Japanese American values and communication patterns. He does not focus on cross-cultural comparisons per se, but rather on how Japanese Americans are similar to and different from Japanese in Japan and Euro Americans in the United States. Kitano discusses the influence of acculturation and generation on Japanese American attitudes and communication. He concludes that Japanese Americans maintain some characteristics of Japanese in Japan and, at the same time, have assimilated the values of the mainstream culture in the United States.

Part III contains three chapters. The focus of these chapters is on comparing communication in Japan and the United States in different contexts. Specifically, the interpersonal and intergroup, organizational, and mass mediated contexts are examined.

William Gudykunst and Tsukasa Nishida summarize cross-cultural research on communication in interpersonal and intergroup relationships in Japan and the United States. They isolate similarities and differences in communication in initial interactions and developing relations, as well as communication in ingroup-outgroup and same-opposite sex relationships. They conclude, for example, that one of the major differences in communication in Japan and the United States involves how people communicate with members of their ingroups and outgroups. Since Japan is a collectivistic culture and people use mainly an interdependent self construal which is based on ingroup membership, there is a large difference in ingroup and outgroup communication. North Americans, in contrast, come from an individualistic culture and mainly use an independent self construal which is *not* influenced highly by ingroup memberships, and, therefore, there is not as large a difference (as in Japan) in ingroup and outgroup communication.

Gudykunst and Nishida also examine the encoding and decoding of messages (e.g., communicative style, predisposition toward verbal behavior, recognition and expression of emotions). The vast majority of the research discussed is consistent with the position Lebra and Akasu and Asao present in their chapters. Gudykunst and Nishida present a summary of research on communication in intercultural relationships between Japanese and North Americans. They conclude by outlining research issues that need to be addressed in future studies of interpersonal and intergroup communication.

Lea P. Stewart focuses on communication in an organizational context. She discusses alternative explanations for differences in Japanese and North American organizations (i.e., culture vs. structure). Stewart isolates differences in superior-subordinate relationships, including leadership, upward communication, downward communication, horizontal communication, and decision-making.

Stewart concludes by examining the shortcomings of current research comparing organizational communication in Japan and the United States and providing suggestions for future research. She argues, for example, that most research to date is descriptive. Stewart goes on to point out that cross-cultural researchers in the area tend to use cultural variables without clear conceptualization (including addressing issues of conceptual equivalence) and operationalization. One area where Stewart suggests future research is on the issue of convergence and divergence of organizational practices in Japan and the United States and how these practices are manifested in Japanese-North American operations.

Youichi Ito examines issues in mass communication in Japan and the United States. Ito begins by summarizing the major theoretical models of media influence. He argues that the "bipolar" models (i.e., models that focus on the sender/message and the receiving individual/society) do not adequately explain mass media effects in Japan. Ito suggests a "tripolar" model that incorporates mass media, government policies, and public attitudes to explain mass media effects in Japan. He outlines the mutual influences among these three factors. Ito argues that the mass media (especially newspapers) often serve as "opposition parties" in editorials discussing government policy in that the mass media locate "defects and mistakes" in government policy. Given that the general public frequently supports the government, there also often is disagreement between the media and general public. Ito argues that when one of the three (media, government, general public) disagrees, there is pressure for it come into compliance and join the consensus. He explains this process using the concept *kuuki*, the dominant air or atmosphere.

In order to illustrate his model, Ito applies the tripolar model to recent case studies. The two case studies involve the revision of the Japanese tax laws and Japan's response to the Gulf War. These case studies clearly indicate that "Western" theories cannot adequately explain mass media effects in Japan. While Ito does not focus on cultural differences, the cultural factors that influence mass media effects are reflected in the bipolar and tripolar models he presents.

The final part (IV) contains one chapter. In the final chapter, William Gudykunst, Ruth Guzley, and Hiroshi Ota suggest future directions for the study of communication in Japan and the United States. They begin by summarizing the major trends to emerge across the chapters. As should be clear from the preceding overviews of the chapters, there are numerous themes that are consistent across communication contexts (e.g., the influence of independent and interdependent self construals). Next, they examine critical methodological issues that need to be taken into consideration in studying communication in Japan and the United States. To illustrate, Gudykunst, Guzley, and Ota discuss issues of emic versus etic approaches, as well as the need to establish conceptual, functional, and measurement equivalence. They conclude by suggesting specific areas where additional research is needed. These suggestions provide a "blueprint" for future cross-cultural and intercultural studies of communication in Japan and the United States.

NOTES

1. A Gallup Poll conducted during the same time period, however, indicated that only 48 percent of the United States population hold a "favorable" attitude toward the Japanese. The differences may be due to wording of the questions. There also is rising "scorn" for the United States in Japan (see Helm, 1991). The figures have remained relatively constant over the years (see United States-Japan Advisory Commission, 1984, for figures in the 1970s and 1980s).

2. The U.S. Commission on Civil Rights (1992) argues that "Japan bashing" has triggered violence and bigotry toward Asian Americans in the United States. Improving relations between Japan and the United States, therefore, could have positive consequences for interethnic relations within the United States.

3. The poll was conducted in late January 1992 by Infoplan/Yankelovich International for *Time*.

4. Until recently, communication was not a separate discipline in most countries. Generally, interpersonal communication was studied in social psychology or human relations, while mass communication was studied in sociology. This is still true today, even in the United States (e.g., many sociology departments offer courses on mass communication and some offer courses on interpersonal communication).

5. Kohn uses the term nation. I have substituted culture for nation.

6. Blumler, McLeod, and Rosengren (1992) include temporal comparisons as part of comparative research when they extend Kohn (1989) types. I do not find their argument convincing. There are major differences between comparing data from three cultures and comparing data across three time periods. I, there-

fore, do not include temporal comparisons here. Temporal comparisons, however, must be made to establish generality of theories and hypotheses.

7. There are, of course, methodological issues which must be taken into consideration. Some of these issues are discussed in the second chapter and some are addressed in the final chapter.

8. For an alternative, but compatible, discussion of the self in Japan and the United States, see Markus and Kitayama (1991).

REFERENCES

Barnlund, D. (1975) *The public and private self in Japan and the United States.* Tokyo: Simul Press.

Barnlund, D. (1989). *Communicative styles of Japanese and Americans.* Belmont, CA: Wadsworth.

Berger, C. R., & Calabrese, R. (1975). Some explorations in initial interactions and beyond. *Human Communication Research, 1,* 99-112.

Blumler, J., McLeod, J., & Rosengren, K. (1992). An introduction to comparative communication research. In J. Blumler, J. McLeod, & K. Rosengren (Eds.), *Comparatively speaking: Communication and culture across space and time.* Newbury Park, CA: Sage.

Chira, S. (1991, December 8). Pearl Harbor's smoke, Hiroshima's fallout. *New York Times,* p. E5.

Cronen, V., Chen, V., & Pearce, W. B. (1988). Coordinated management of meaning: A critical theory. In Y. Y. Kim & W. B. Gudykunst (Eds.), *Theories in intercultural communication.* Newbury Park, CA: Sage.

Dulles, F. R. (1965). *Yankees and samurai.* New York: Harper and Row.

Friedman, T. L. (1992, June 28). Fractured vision. *New York Times Magazine,* pp. 24-25, 47, 51-52.

Friedman, G., & LeBard, M. (1991). *The coming war with Japan.* New York: St. Martin.

Gudykunst W. B., Gao, G., Schmidt, K. L., Nishida, T., Bond, M., Leung, K., Wang, G., & Barraclough, R. (1992). The influence of individualism-collectivism on communication in ingroup-outgroup relationships. *Journal of Cross-Cultural Psychology, 23,* 196-213.

Gudykunst, W. B., Nishida, T., & Schmidt, K. L. (1989). Cultural, relational, and personality influences on uncertainty reduction processes. *Western Journal of Speech Communication, 53,* 13-29.

Gudykunst, W. B., Yang, S. M., & Nishida, T. (1985). A cross-cultural comparison of uncertainty reduction theory: Comparisons of acquaintance, dating, and friend relationships in Japan, Korea, and the United States. *Human Communication Research, 11,* 407-455.

Helm, L. (1991, October 25). Japan's rising scorn for America. *Los Angeles Times,* pp. A1, A14-15.

Hillenbrand, B. (1992, February 10). America in the mind of Japan. *Time,* pp. 20-23.

Hofstede, G. (1980). *Culture's consequences.* Beverly Hills, CA: Sage.

Kitamura, H. (1971). *Psychological dimensions of U.S.-Japanese relations.* Cambridge, MA: Harvard University Center for International Affairs.

Kohn, M. L. (1989). Introduction. In M. L. Kohn (Ed.), *Cross-national research in sociology.* Beverly Hills, CA: Sage.

Luttwak, E. N. (1991, December 29). For Japan and the U.S., the choice is to fight or cooperate. *Los Angeles Times,* pp. M1, M6.

Markus, H., & Kitayama, S. (1991). Culture and the self: Implications for cognition, emotion, and motivation. *Psychological Review, 98,* 224-253.

Miyoshi, M. (1991). *Off center: Power and culture relations between Japan and the United States.* Cambridge, MA: Harvard University Press.

Murrow, L. (1992, February 10). Japan in the mind of America. *Time,* pp. 16-20.

Nakanishi, M., & Johnson, K. (1993). Implications of self-disclosure on conversational logics, perceived competence, and social attraction: A comparison of Japanese and American cultures. In R. Wiseman & J. Koester (Eds.), *Intercultural communication competence.* Newbury Park, CA: Sage.

Plummer, K. (1992). *The Shogun's reluctant ambassadors: Japanese sea drifters in the North Pacific.* Portland: Oregon Historical Society.

Reich, R. B. (1992, February 9). Is Japan really out to get us? *New York Times Book Review,* pp. 1ff.

Reischauer, E. O. (1971). Introduction. In H. Kitamura, *Psychological dimensions of U.S.-Japanese relations.* Cambridge, MA: Harvard University Center for International Affairs.

U.S. Commission on Civil Rights. (1992). *Civil rights issues facing Asian Americans in the 1990s.* Washington, D.C.: U.S. Government Printing Office.

United States-Japan Advisory Commission (1984). *Challenges and opportunities in United States-Japan relations*. A report submitted to the President of the United States and the Prime Minister of Japan.

Wiseman, S. R. (1991, December 8). Japanese think they owe apology and are owed one on war, poll shows. *New York Times*, pp. Y16.

Chapter 2

Approaches to the Study of Communication in Japan and the United States

William B. Gudykunst and
Patricia San Antonio

Lafcadio Hearn wrote popular descriptions of Japan and the Japanese culture for readers in the United States during the late nineteenth and early twentieth centuries.[1] Hearn's personal relationship with Japan and love for the Japanese culture struck a chord with his North American readers. His treatment of Japan as an exotic "other" for people in the United States held up Japanese culture as a mirror for the United States culture. Treating Japan as an exotic other, however, also obscured the commonalities between the United States and Japan.

While initial North American interest in Japan grew out of this fascination with the "other" (Cleaver, 1976), it has increased over the years as American military, political, and economic ties to Japan have grown in importance. Bernard Silberman (1962) isolated three reasons for the enduring interest in the study of Japan in the United States. First, Japan presents an "intriguing" culture and "personality puzzle" to North Americans. Japanese behavior during World War II, for example, was surprising to North Americans who could not predict Japanese actions or understand their motivations. Second, Japan is accessible because of its international position and technological advancement.

There have been no political or military barriers to the study of Japan since World War II. Third, Japan is culturally different from the United States, but is going through similar processes of modernization and industrialization which makes comparisons to the North American social situation instructive.

The purpose of this chapter is to overview the major lines of research that provide the foundation for research on communication in Japan and the United States. The studies which have been conducted are based on either an emic or an etic approach to the study of communication across cultures.

The distinction between the emic and etic approaches can be traced to Pike's (1966) discussion of phonetics (vocal utterances which are universal) and phonemics (culturally specific vocal utterances). Brislin (1983) argues that in current usage the distinction is employed basically as a metaphor for differences between the culture specific approach (emic, single culture) and general (etic, universal) approaches to research. Berry (1980, pp. 11-12) presented a succinct summary of the distinction:

Emic approach	Etic approach
studies behavior from within the system	studies behavior from a position outside the system
examines only one culture	examines many cultures, comparing them
structure discovered by the analyst	structure created by the analyst
criteria are relative to internal characteristics	criteria are considered absolute or universal

While the two approaches are different, they are not incompatible.

EMIC APPROACHES TO THE STUDY OF COMMUNICATION IN JAPAN AND THE UNITED STATES

In this section we examine the predominant emic approaches to the study of communication in Japan and the United States: traditional anthropological research on Japan and indigenous Japanese writing on Japan. While communication is not the focus of this research, most studies indirectly address issues of communication. This line of research on Japanese culture provides the foundation for much of the cross-cultural research on communication conducted to date.

Next, we overview the indigenous approach to the study of Japanese culture known as *nihonjinron* (literally, "discussions of the Japanese"). Most writers in this genre reject outsiders' analyses arguing that understanding Japanese culture requires an indigenous approach. *Nihonjinron* analyses of the Japanese culture provide a coherent description of the Japanese culture that must be taken into consideration in comparatively studying communication in Japan and the United States.

Anthropological Research on Japan

For the most part, anthropological research on Japan has taken place since the end of World War II.[2] Aside from many descriptions of the exotic aspects of Japan written for popular consumption in the United States (Cott, 1991), there was only one ethnography, *Suye Mura* (Embree, 1939), available before the Pacific War. Embree wrote a conventional village ethnography, common in anthropological research at that time. The social organization, institutions, and agricultural cycle of the village was described in detail as was kinship, family relations, and the importance of the household. Even in such a traditional village ethnography, the militarization of Japan was an obvious presence (Embree, 1939).[3]

At the onset of World War II and the cessation of relationships with Japan, United States military commanders could not find reliable information about Japan and the Japanese. In an attempt to correct for the lack of reliable information, anthropologists did "long distance" research about Japan. One of the most famous products of this line of work was Ruth Benedict's (1946) *The Chrysanthemum and the Sword*. Working from a variety of published materials and interviews with Japanese Americans and Japanese nationals in the United States, Benedict studied the national culture of Japan and the relationship between culture and personality. Her research focused on child-rearing practices, values and attitudes about proper behavior, and hierarchical organization in Japan. Benedict attempted to categorize and analyze the psychology of the Japanese people as an aid to understanding or predicting their behavior. Benedict's work, still well known and cited today though its limits are recognized, spurred the continuing interest in both the psychology and the culture of Japan.

The themes developed by Embree (1939) and Benedict (1946) set the stage for much of the anthropological research done after World War II. The goal of North American anthropological research in Japan was to describe and understand Japanese culture from an implicitly

North American cultural perspective. With the United States occupation of Japan many anthropologists began to work in Japan to do research on village life and customs. These ethnographies (e.g., Beardsley, Hall, & Ward, 1959; Cornell & Smith, 1956; Norbeck, 1954) established a body of ethnographic description of the Japanese population.[4]

In addition to studies of the village community and personality, the rapid modernization of Japan became an important topic for research. Another theme was the conflict between traditional and modern, as well as the emerging differences between urban and rural social organization. Anthropologists explored such topics by studying the emerging salaryman (Vogel, 1963) and city life in Tokyo (Dore, 1967; Plath, 1964). Abegglan's (1958) ethnography of a Japanese factory, for example, chronicled the emergence of several important themes. In describing the social relations in a modern Japanese factory, Abegglan described how the interaction in the factory was patterned on the conduct of traditional Japanese hierarchical relationships. The company was compared to the household, tying cultural tradition to success in a new environment.

In the 1950s and 1960s research on kinship and the study of the family and descent systems emerged (Tamanoi, 1990). The patrilineal and patriarchal Japanese family was studied as the preeminent socioeconomic and religious unit in Japanese society (Tamanoi, 1990). Interest focused not only the structure of the family and kin groups, but also on the nature of the family in terms of the various family roles. One example of such a focus was on the power of the wives and mothers in such a hierarchical, male-oriented family system (Tamanoi, 1990). Current studies of kinship and studies of the group in Japanese society grew out of such interests during the 1960s and into the 1970s (Nakane, 1967).

In the 1970s, the interest in tradition, structure, and social interaction meshed importantly in Nakane's (1970) *Japanese Society*.[5] Nakane combined two elements, an interest in the structure of Japanese organizations (based on the idea of the household) and an analysis of how such structural elements operate in a business environment. Clark's (1979) study of a Japanese company took a more historical viewpoint than Nakane.

During the 1970s there were many ethnographies which explored the major themes first studied in the 1950s, including the change from rural to urban organization and life-style. These ethnographies included studies of the traditional versus the modern, and agriculture versus business. As Japanese society became increasingly modern, the importance of tradition in modern social forms was of great interest to anthropologists. Rohlen's (1974) ethnography of a Japanese bank, for example, focused on traditional Japanese spiritual education in the training and integration of Japanese employees into a company. Cole (1971) studied Japanese blue-collar workers in a modern factory.

In discussing structure and tradition, much of the early ethnographies of Japan were static. With large-scale social change, anthropologists studied how change affected traditional Japanese villages and such research often took the form of restudies of ethnographies done earlier (e.g., Norbeck, 1976; Smith, 1978). Village life, however, was not the only focus for studies of change. The effect of modernization on other parts of Japanese society was also important. The study of "new religions" (e.g., Davis, 1980; McFarland, 1967) and their ties and differences with traditional religious beliefs and ancestor worship are examples of this line of work (Smith, 1974). The emphases of these ethnographies were on changing values and culturally meaningful coping mechanisms in the face of great social change and dislocation. There also were studies examining some of the "realities" of life in the Japanese work force for both men and women. Plath's (1984) *Work and Lifecourse in Japan*, for example, focused on such issues as career development, the place of women, and advancement in the Japanese work force.[6]

Another point of comparative interest was in the status of women in Japan. Studies of women in Japan focused on the traditional position of women in Japan and how the status of women changed with industrialization and modernization. Early work (e.g., Lebra, Paulson, & Powers, 1976) tends to show women dealing as best they can with the restraints imposed on them by the male-dominated system. Recent research (e.g., Bernstein, 1983; Dalby, 1983; Imamura, 1987; Lebra, 1984; Smith & Wiswell, 1982), however, demonstrates that traditional Japanese women's roles carry with them a certain type of power. To illustrate, Dalby (1983) argues that geisha are their own mistresses in a world of women. Lebra (1984) also shows how the sexual division of labor allows women mastery of their own sphere at home.

In the 1970s and 1980s, anthropologists began to look at Japanese society in terms of process and change. Instead of tradition and stability, the conflicts and problems of modern Japan became an important focus of research. The work of DeVos and Wetherall (1983), Krause, Rohlen, and Steinhoff (1984), Lee and DeVos (1981) and Wagatsuma and DeVos (1984), for example, provides a look at the problems within Japanese society and how such conflicts are resolved.

Modern ethnographies on Japan by North Americans often reflect concerns about their own culture and values (i.e., the United States).

One example of this type of work is research on Japan's schools (e.g., Rohlen, 1983; White, 1987). The organization and successes of Japanese schools highlight the problems and inadequacies of the educational system in the United States. To illustrate, Tobin, Wu, and Davidson (1989) conducted a comparative ethnography of Japanese, Chinese, and North American kindergartens. The researchers had the Japanese, Chinese, and American teachers watch videotapes of their students' behavior, comment on the behavior, as well as watch and comment on the behavior of the children and teachers from the other two cultures. The researchers also had a dialogue with the various teachers about why they behaved certain ways in the videotaped interactions. The interaction is reflected in the ethnography in a way that highlights the differences and similarities of the United States and Japanese cultures and the reaction of individuals in one culture to the other culture.

Another example of an explicit cultural comparison is seen in Bayley's (1976) *Forces of Order*. Bayley examined the problems and successes of Japanese police in order to shed light on the situation in the United States. Bayley is specifically comparative in his work, and takes the point of view that Japanese and North Americans have much in common in terms of the history of the police, the prevalence of violence in the media, and the degree of urbanization. From such similarities, he goes on to discuss the differences in such characteristics as gun control in Japan, the organization and deployment of the police in the two countries, and varying attitudes to and handling of different categories of crimes in Japan and the United States.

Recently, anthropologists have recognized the interest and importance of the interface of Japanese and North American culture. White (1988), for example, looks at the consequences for Japanese businessmen and their families who are sent abroad to work in the United States. Her research suggests that their contact with another culture "handicaps" them in their own.

Because of popular interest, increasing social and business interaction between Japanese and North Americans, and a new emphasis in anthropology on reflexivity, research on interaction between Japanese and North Americans is becoming more common.[7] In most cases, the work is based in business or company situations where Japanese and North Americans must work together (e.g., March, 1988; Tung, 1984). It is in such studies that anthropologists deal with the issue of Japanese and North American communication. Hamada (1991), for example, studied the communication of Japanese and North Americans in a joint-venture company in Japan.[8] She also has written about the problems and communication difficulties faced by English-speaking professional Japanese women who work in Japanese companies in the United States (Hamada, 1990).

Nihonjinron

Nihonjinron (literally, "discussions of the Japanese") is a genre of writing on Japanese society that focuses on the uniqueness of the Japanese. Other terms associated with this genre of writing include, but are not limited to *"nihon bunkaron,"* "the group model," and "the consensus model" of Japanese society. Sugimoto and Mouer (1989) suggest that

> although these terms have been used rather loosely, they have nevertheless come to designate a fairly coherent image of Japanese society. The image consists of a theory or set of theories which portray Japanese society as having exceptionally low levels of conflict. In these descriptions, importance is attached to the unusually strong emphasis in Japanese culture on group membership and on consensus. The Japanese have been presented as lacking a strong ego, and as being exceptionally homogeneous culturally and socially. National culture has often been the major variable of resort when explaining structures and behavior which seems to set Japanese apart from people in other societies. (p. 3)

They go on to argue that the approach is not based in social science, rather, it depends on "intuitive insight" and anecdotal evidence.

Dale (1986) isolates three assumptions that set *nihonjinron* writings on the Japanese apart from empirical research. First, writers using this approach "assume that the Japanese constitute a culturally and socially homogeneous racial entity, whose essence is virtually unchanged from prehistorical times down to the present day" (p. iii). Second, they assume that the Japanese culture is very different from all other cultures. Third, they are "consciously nationalistic, displaying a conceptual and procedural hostility to any mode of analysis which might be seen to derive from external, non-Japanese sources" (p. iii).

As one illustration of the *nihonjinron* approach, Dale (1986) quotes Hamaguchi's (1977, pp. 2-3) critique of the use of Western approaches to the study of Japan:

> Many of the authoritative theories and concepts employed in the national characteristics of the Japanese in research to date have

their provenance in the West. And yet, notwithstanding this, students of these problems have adopted and used these theories uncritically, even without scrutinizing them from a cultural perspective. . . . Hardly any investigation has been undertaken of the appropriateness or inappropriateness of these [Western theories]. (p. 28)

Dale points out that Hamaguchi is not an extremist and that Hamaguchi does see some value in Western work on Japan. Hamaguchi, however, also argues that Western theories do not coincide with how the Japanese view themselves and, therefore, a Japanese perspective on Japanese society is necessary. Dale contends that Hamaguchi does not identify the Western approach being criticized or make any attempt to logically refute it. Dale also believes that Hamaguchi's position does not recognize that different observers (either inside the system or outside it) can come to very different conclusions.[9]

The language used to analyze the culture assumes a critical role in the *nihonjinron* approach. Proponents of this approach believe that non-Japanese words cannot capture the Japanese experience. Ohno (1976), for example, argues that

each Western word is loaded with cultural and historical meaning and association. A word such as "hierarchy" means automatically an order of power relationships. It has a connotation of oppression, denial of individualism, its rights and freedoms which should lead to the equality of men [and women]. In Japan, hierarchy simply signifies ritual order. It defines neither the location of power nor responsibility. Thus Western words as such are not appropriate for describing non-Western reality. (p. 26)

Befu (1980a) takes a different position regarding the use of Western words. In discussing the example of social classes, he argues that

emically Japanese have a wide variety of native concepts referring to social classes. . . . Although these concepts are not identical to the classes conjured up in English (e.g. "upper class" etc.), the issue here is not whether Japanese have terms of stratification which are conceptually identical to those in the West, but instead whether Japanese conceive of their society as being made up of horizontal strata. The existence of these Japanese terms clearly indicates that the Japanese conception of society does include the notion of stratification. (p. 34)

Dale (1986) agrees with Befu that exact equivalence is not the issue. He goes on to ague that given the *nihonjinron* position, "outsiders" must avoid the use of simplistic translations in their analyses of Japanese society (see the chapter on sociolinguistics by Akasu and Asao in this volume for a more detailed discussion of language).

Sugimoto and Mouer (1989) point out that the *nihonjinron* approach has been challenged from the early 1950s. The challenges have been based on modernization theory (see Miyanaga, 1991, for a recent discussion) and the notion of cultural convergence, as well as critiques of Japan being a consensus-based society (e.g., Befu, 1980a, b; Lummis, 1982). They go on to point out, however, that the *nihonjinron* approach continues to be well received, citing work such as Amanuma (1987), Doi (1985, 1986), and Hendry and Webber (1986). Sugimoto and Mouer cite two important examples of recent work in this area: Sato, Kumon, and Murakami's (1979; summarized in Murakami, 1984) work on *ie* (the working group) as a cultural form, and Hamaguchi's (1977, 1982, 1983, 1985) work on contextualism in Japan.

Sato, Kumon, and Murakami (1979) argue that there is a fundamental continuity in the Japanese culture (i.e., the social structure before and after World War II is basically the same). The *ie* is viewed as the basis of Japan's society. They argue that uniqueness of the Japanese society is a function of their orientation to interpersonal relations (*aidagarashugi*) and the degree to which Japanese are aware of their relations to others. Kawamura (1989), however, points out that Sato, Kumon, and Murakami do not explain what the groups are that form the *ie*, and "as in other *nihonjinron*, they do not define key terms such as individualism (*kojinshugi*), groupism (*shudanshugi*), or the special relational orientation (*aidagarashugi*) in a way that allows the concepts to be clearly differentiated" (p. 222).

Hamaguchi's (1977, 1982, 1983, 1985) work focuses on the "contextual" orientation of the Japanese that sets them apart from others. Hamaguchi (1983), for example, summarizes the ways individuals view themselves in Japan and the United States (see also Lebra's chapter in this volume).[10] In the United States,

> an "individual" . . . holds a conviction that he [or she] is a firmly established substance which is solely independent, and, therefore, cannot be invalidated by others. Also, he [or she] is convinced that he [or she] is the master of himself [or herself], but at the same time he [or she] is liable for his [or her] own deeds. The indi-

vidual objectifies such an assertion (that he [or she] is undoubtedly himself [or herself]) and the sense of autonomy. (pp. 140-141)

Japanese, in contrast, view themselves contextually:

> For the Japanese, "self" means the portion which is distributed to him [or her], according to the situation he [or she] is in, from the living space shared between himself [or herself] and the other person with whom he [or she] had developed a mutually dependent relationship.
>
> A reason why this self-consciousness of the Japanese is formed this way is probably that self and others are in a symbiotic relationship, and that they believe that their beings depend largely on other beings. . . . This relativistic "self" can easily be mistaken for being unindependent. . . . However, here, selves are "mutually dependent," and their spontaneous fulfillment of the needs are intentionally controlled. (p. 142)

Sugimoto and Mouer (1989) point out, however, that contextualism "defies definition in an operational sense" (p. 7). While Hamaguchi does not use the terms, his descriptions of how individuals view themselves in the West and in Japan clearly reflect cultural differences in individualism-collectivism which are discussed below.

To summarize, Table 2.1 (adapted from Dale, 1986) contains the major contrasts that writers in the *nihonjinron* tradition tend to draw between Japan and "the West." *Nihonjinron* writers, for example, see Japan as a homogeneous, vertical society based on hierarchy, shame, duties, harmony, and dependence. The West, in contrast, is viewed as a heterogeneous, horizontal society that is based on egalitarianism, guilt, rights, rupture, and independence. Communication in Japan is viewed as being based on a language that prizes reticence, sentiment, silence, ambivalence, emotions, subjectivity, situational logic, and particularity. Communication in the West, on the other hand, is viewed as being based on languages that value rhetoric, logic, talkativeness, rationality, objectivity, rigid principles, and universality.

As indicated earlier, the *nihonjinron* approach to the study of Japanese culture has been criticized (e.g., Dale, 1986; Sugimoto & Mouer, 1986). Writers in this genre, however, have isolated numerous concepts important in the study of communication in Japan and the United States. These concepts must be integrated into comparative studies if we are to better understand cultural similarities and differences in communication in Japan and the United States.

TABLE 2.1
Selected Differences between the "West"
and Japan in *Nihonjinron* Writing*

"West" (United States)	Japan
Horizontal	Vertical
Egalitarianism	Hierarchy
Guilt	Shame
Rights	Duties
Independence (inner-directed)	Dependence (other-directed)
Unstable	Stable
Intolerant	Tolerant
Logic, either/or	Ambivalence, both/and
Rational	Emotional
Objective	Subjective
Rigid principle	Situational logic
Talkativeness	Silence
Universality	Particularity
Heterogeneity	Homogeneity
Rupture	Harmony
Donative/active	Receptive/reactive
Open	Closed
Elaborately expressive language (rhetoric favored)	Allusively laconic language (reticence prized)
Rational, impersonal language (adapted to logic)	Emotive and personal language (a vehicle of sentiment)
Insensitivity to dirt of others (impurity)	Sensitivity to dirt of others (purity)
Divisive	Harmony
Bellicose	Peaceful

*Adapted from Dale (1986), Tables 4, 5, 6, 7, 10, and 15.

ETIC APPROACHES TO THE STUDY OF COMMUNICATION IN JAPAN AND THE UNITED STATES

One objective of cross-cultural research is to theoretically explain similarities and differences in communication in interpersonal and inter-group relationships. In order to theoretically explain variability in communication across cultures, it is necessary to isolate dimensions on which they differ. Foschi and Hales (1979) succinctly outline the issue involved in treating culture as a theoretical variable: "a culture X and a culture Y serve to operationally define a characteristic a, which the cul-

tures exhibit to different degrees" (p. 246). There are several characteristics (i.e., dimensions of cultural variability that can be used to explain
etic similarities and differences in communication patterns in Japan
and the United States.[11]

Individualism-Collectivism

Individualism-collectivism is the major dimension of cultural variability
isolated by theorists across disciplines (e.g., Chinese Culture Connection,
1987; Hofstede, 1980; Ito, 1989b; Kluckhohn & Strodtbeck, 1961; Marsella,
DeVos, & Hsu, 1985; Triandis, 1988, 1990). Individualistic cultures emphasize the goals of the individual over group goals, while collectivistic cultures stress group goals over individual goals.[12] In individualistic cultures, individuals assume responsibility for themselves and their
immediate family only. In collectivistic cultures, individuals belong to
collectivities or ingroups which look after them in exchange for the individuals' loyalty (Hofstede, 1980). Following Triandis (1988), ingroups
are "groups of people about whose welfare one is concerned, with whom
one is willing to cooperate without demanding equitable returns, and
separation from whom leads to discomfort or even pain" (p. 75).

Triandis (1988) contends that ingroups are more important in collectivistic than individualistic cultures. Lebra (1976), for example, points
out that collectivism "involves cooperation and solidarity, and the sentimental desire for the warm feeling of *ittaikan* ("feeling of oneness")
with fellow members of one's group" (p. 25) and that this feeling is
shared widely in Japan (see Zander, 1983, for a discussion of the value
of belonging to groups in Japan). Triandis argues that the larger the
number of ingroups, the narrower the influence and the less the depth
of influence. Since individualistic cultures have many specific ingroups,
ingroups in individualistic cultures exert less influence on individuals'
behavior than ingroups do in collectivistic cultures where there are a
few general ingroups. Triandis' conceptualization also suggests that
members of collectivistic cultures draw sharper distinctions between
members of ingroups and outgroups, and perceive ingroup relationships to be more intimate than members of individualistic cultures.

Lebra's (1976) contention that *ittaikan* is shared widely in Japan
should not be taken to imply that Japan is a homogeneous culture.[13]
Miyanaga (1991) argues that there is

> antagonism between those from the eastern and western regions
> of Japan; those from the west often complain that they never feel

accepted in Tokyo, located in the east. In western Japan, people from the east are referred to as *bando mono*, literally "a person from the east," which carries a derogatory connotation of "uncivilized." In the same way that ethnic background carries associative connotations in [North] America, regional (prefectural) backgrounds are socially significant to the Japanese. (p. 12)

Miyanaga goes on to point out that all Japanese speak two "kinds" of Japanese: standardized and their own dialect or accent. Standard Japanese is spoken in social situations, but individuals use their own dialect or accent with members of their ingroups.

Most scholars agree that the United States is an individualistic culture and Japan is a collectivistic culture (Hofstede's [1980] scores for the United States [91] and Japan [46] are different on this dimension).[14] While these terms are not heavily value-laden in the United States, the translations of both terms are value-laden in Japan. Ito (1989b), for example, points out that Japanese scholars do not use the translation of the term collectivism, *zentaishugi*, because it often is used to refer to dictatorial political systems. Rather, they use terms like group oriented (*shuhdanshugi*; Nakane, 1970, among others), relationalism (*aidagarashugi*; Kumon, 1982), contextualism (*kanjinshugi*; Hamaguchi, 1982), or interindividualism (*saijinshugi*; Ito, 1989a). Ito (1989b) also points out that the term used for individualism in Japanese, *kojinshugi*, also has negative connotations (e.g., selfishness).

Critiques of the *nihonjinron* approach or the group model of Japanese society (e.g., Befu, 1980a, 1980b) suggest that acceptance of this model with its emphasis on harmony and *giri* (voluntary feelings of obligation)[15] leads scholars to overlook Japanese "personhood" (e.g., concepts such as *seishin* or *jinkaku*; see also Hamaguchi's, 1977, discussion of interpersonalness).[16] Befu, for example, argues that *seishin* deals with "individuals qua individuals." "*Seishin* has to do with one's spiritual disposition, one's inner strength, which results from character building and self-discipline" (Befu, 1980b, pp. 180-81; see Rohlen, 1973, for a discussion of this concept).[17] He further suggests that "behind the appearance of group solidarity one will find each member is being motivated more by personal ambitions than by his [or her] blind loyalty to the group. Put another way, Japanese are loyal to their groups because it pays to be loyal" (Befu, 1977a, p. 87).

Befu (1980b) contends that the concepts of *tatemae* and *honne* must be considered in explaining personhood in Japan. *Tatemae* refers to the principle or standard by which a person is bound, at least outwardly (a public presentation). *Honne,* in contrast, refers to a person's "real" or inner wishes (Lebra, 1976). Yoneyama (1973) also argues that the distinction between public matters (*oyake-goto*) and private matters (*watakushi-goto*) must always be taken into consideration when analyzing Japanese communication (see also Doi's, 1986, discussion of *omote* and *ura*). Befu (1980a, 1980b) contends that the group model can explain public matters, but not private matters. This contention is supported by two studies of value orientations in Japan. Caudill and Scarr (1961) and Nishida (1981) found that while collaterality predominates in Japan, the value orientation (collaterality, lineality, individualism) individuals select depends on the specific sphere of life being examined.[18] Finally, Befu suggests that Japanese interpersonal relationships can be explained from an exchange theory perspective (e.g., a theory similar to Altman & Taylor, 1973; see Nakamura, 1990, for a recent study using social exchange models to explain interpersonal relationship development in Japan).[19]

Before proceeding, it also should be noted that focusing only on the individualistic tendencies in the United States leads scholars to overlook collectivistic aspects of the culture (for a recent discussion see Bellah, Madsen, Sullivan, Swidler, & Tipton, 1985, 1991; Wuthnow, 1991). Kluckhohn and Strodtbeck (1961), for example, point out that while individualism predominates in the United States, collaterality and lineality (two forms of collectivism) also affect behavior.[20] Nishida (1981) found that while individualism predominates overall in the United States, the value orientation (individualism, collaterality, lineality) individuals select depends on the specific sphere of life being examined.[21]

Recent work (e.g., Gudykunst, Nishida, Chung, & Sudweeks, 1992; Miyanaga, 1991) suggests that individualism-collectivism is a dialectic. Altman, Vinsel, and Brown (1981) argue that there are three features of dialectics: (1) dialectics involve oppositions, (2) there is a unity to the opposites, and (3) there is a dynamic relationship between the opposites. With respect to individualism, this implies that both orientations coexist in Japan and the United States (and other cultures as well) and that the two orientations influence different aspects of behavior. A dialectical orientation suggests that neither North American nor Japanese behavior are totally unique. How these issues are manifested in Japanese and North American communication are discussed in detail in Gudykunst and Nishida's chapter in this volume.

A scheme of cultural variability closely related to individualism-collectivism is Hall's (1976) differentiation between high- and low-context communication. "A high-context (HC) communication or message is one in which most of the information is either in the physical context or internalized in the person, while very little is in the coded, explicit part of the message. A low-context (LC) communication is just the opposite; i.e., the mass of information is vested in the explicit code" (Hall, 1976, p. 79). While no culture exists at either end of the high-/low-context continuum, the culture of the United States is at the low end, slightly above the German, Swiss, and Scandinavian cultures. Japan and Korea, in contrast, fall at the high end of the continuum. Gudykunst and Ting-Toomey (1988) argue that low-context communication predominates in individualistic cultures and high-context communication predominates in collectivistic cultures. It must be kept in mind, nevertheless, that low- and high-context communication take place in all cultures.[22]

Uncertainty Avoidance

In comparison to members of cultures low in uncertainty avoidance, members of cultures high in uncertainty avoidance have a lower tolerance "for uncertainty and ambiguity, which expresses itself in higher levels of anxiety and energy release, greater need for formal rules and absolute truth, and less tolerance for people or groups with deviant ideas or behavior" (Hofstede, 1979, p. 395). In high uncertainty avoidance cultures, aggressive behavior of self and others is acceptable; however, individuals prefer to contain aggression by avoiding conflict and competition. There is a strong desire for consensus in cultures high in uncertainty avoidance, therefore, deviant behavior is not acceptable. High uncertainty avoidance cultures also tend to display emotions more than low uncertainty avoidance cultures. Low uncertainty avoidance cultures have lower stress levels and weaker superegos and accept dissent and taking risks more than high uncertainty avoidance cultures.

Hofstede (1991) points out that uncertainty avoidance should not be equated with risk avoidance. He goes on to point out that people in

> uncertainty avoiding cultures shun ambiguous situations. People in such cultures look for a structure in their organizations, institutions, and relationships which makes events clearly interpretable and predictable. Paradoxically, they are often prepared to engage in risky behavior to reduce ambiguities, like starting a fight with a potential opponent rather than sitting back and waiting. (p. 116)

He summarizes the view of people in strong uncertainty avoidance cultures as "what is different, is dangerous," (p. 119) and the credo of people in low uncertainty avoidance cultures as "what is different, is curious" (p. 119).

Hofstede (1980) compared scores on uncertainty avoidance with data from other large-scale cross-cultural studies. This comparison revealed that in comparison to members of low uncertainty avoidance cultures, members of high uncertainty avoidance cultures resist change more, have higher levels of anxiety, have higher levels of intolerance for ambiguity, worry about the future more, see loyalty to their employer as more of a virtue, have a lower motivation for achievement, and take fewer risks. In organizations, workers in high uncertainty avoidance cultures prefer a specialist career, prefer clear instructions, avoid conflict, and disapprove of competition between employees more than workers in low uncertainty avoidance cultures.

Before proceeding, it is necessary to point out that both low and high degrees of uncertainty avoidance exist in every culture, but one tends to predominate. There are differences between Japan (92) and the United States (46) on this dimension.

Power Distance

Power distance is defined as "the extent to which the less powerful members of institutions and organizations accept that power is distributed unequally" (Hofstede & Bond, 1984, p. 419). Individuals from high power distance cultures accept power as part of society and superiors consider their subordinates to be different from themselves and vice versa. People in low power distance cultures, in contrast, see superiors and subordinates as the same kinds of people with differences in power being due to the roles they are filling. Outside the role, superiors and subordinates are equal in low power distance cultures.

People in high power distance cultures see power as a basic fact in society, and stress coercive or referent power, while people in low power distance cultures believe power should be used only when it is legitimate and prefer expert or legitimate power (Hofstede, 1980). Hofstede (1991) also points out that

> in small power distance countries there is limited dependence of subordinates on bosses, and a preference for consultation, that is, *interdependence* between boss and subordinate. The emotional distance between them is relatively small: subordinates will quite readily approach and contradict their bosses. In large power distance countries there is considerable dependence of subordinates

on bosses. Subordinates respond by either *preferring* such dependence (in the form of autocratic or paternalistic boss), or rejecting it entirely, which in psychology is known as *counterdependence*: that is dependence, but with a negative sign. (p. 27)

The power distance dimension clearly influences the relationship between superiors and subordinates in organizations.

Low and high power distance tendencies exist in all cultures, but one tends to predominate. Hofstede's (1980) data suggest there are only minor differences between Japan (40) and the United States (54) on this dimension.

Masculinity-Femininity

High masculinity, according to Hofstede (1980), involves a high value placed on things, power, and assertiveness, while systems in which people, quality of life, and nurturance prevail are low on masculinity or high on femininity. Cultural systems high on the masculinity dimension emphasize differentiated sex roles, performance, ambition, and independence. Conversely, systems low on masculinity value fluid sex roles, quality of life, service, and interdependence.

Hofstede (1991) points out that this is the only dimension to emerge in his study that involved male and female differences across cultures. He found that males attach more importance than females to two work goals: "have an opportunity for high earnings" and "have an opportunity for advancement to higher level jobs." Females, in turn, valued two work goals more than males: "have a good working relationship with your direct supervisor" and "work with people who cooperate well with one another." Hofstede concludes that "the importance of earnings and advancement corresponds to the masculine, assertive, and competitive social role. The importance of relations with the manager and with colleagues corresponds to the feminine, caring, and social-environmental oriented role" (p. 82).

Hofstede (1980) compared masculinity-femininity scores with results of other cross-cultural studies. He found that, in comparison to people in feminine cultures, people in masculine cultures have stronger motivation for achievement, view work as more central to their lives, accept their company's "interference" in their private lives, have higher job stress, have greater value differences between men and women in the same position, and view recognition, advancement, or challenge as more important to their satisfaction with their work.

As with the other dimensions of cultural variability, both masculinity and femininity tendencies exist in all cultures. One tendency, however, tends to predominate. Scores for the United States (62) and Japan (95) differ on this dimension (Hofstede, 1980).

Confucian Work Dynamism

Hofstede (1980, 1991) observed the four dimensions discussed in this section (individualism-collectivism, power distance, uncertainty avoidance, masculinity-femininity) in his study of a large multinational company. The dimensions may have a "Western bias" because of the methodology used in collecting the data. The Chinese Culture Connection (1987; the Chinese Culture Connection is a group of researchers organized by Michael Bond at the Chinese University of Hong Kong) tested Hofstede's conclusions using a methodology with a "Chinese bias." They found four dimensions of cultural variability: Confucian work dynamism, integration, human-heartedness, and moral discipline. Three of the these dimensions correlated with dimensions observed in Hofstede's study: integration correlated with individualism, moral discipline correlated with power distance, and human-heartedness correlated with masculinity-femininity. The only dimension that did not correlated with one of Hofstede's dimensions was Confucian work dynamism.

In the Chinese Culture Connection's (1987) study, Confucianism work dynamism dimension involved eight values. Four values were associated positively with the dimension—ordering relationships, thrift, persistence, and having a sense of shame—while four were negatively associated with the dimension—protecting one's face, personal steadiness, respect for tradition, and reciprocation. The Chinese Culture Connection argues that the four positively loaded items reflect a "hierarchical dynamism" present in Chinese society, while the four negatively loaded items reflect "checks and distractions" to this dynamism.

The Confusian work dynamism dimension is consistent with Confucianism.[23] Hofstede (1991) summarizes the tenets of Confucianism by isolating four key principles:

1. The stability of society is based on unequal relationships between people. . . .
2. The family is the prototype for all social organizations. . . .
3. Virtuous behavior towards others consists of not treating others as one would not like to be treated oneself. . . .

4. Virtue with regard to one's task in life consists of trying to acquire skills and education, working hard, not spending more than necessary, being patient, and persevering. (p. 165, italics omitted)

The Confucian work dynamism dimension was isolated by asking Chinese respondents in different countries to indicate the extent to which the Chinese values applied in the country in which they resided.

Hofstede (1991) computed scale scores for countries as a whole on this dimension. The scores for the United States (29) and Japan (80) were different.

To summarize, it appears that Japan and the United States differ on the individualism-collectivism, uncertainty avoidance, masculinity and Confucian work dynamism dimensions of cultural variability. These dimensions can be used to provide plausible explanations for some of the cultural differences in communication observed in the two cultures, while power distance may explain some of the similarities. A full explanation of similarities and differences, however, cannot be based on these dimensions alone since they do not present complete pictures of the cultures of the United States and Japan.

NOTES

1. The first Japanese volume written for westerners appears to be Kazuko Okakura's (1991/1906) *The Book of Tea*. In this volume, the author attempted to explain Japanese aesthetics and philosophy to a western audience.

2. For recent descriptions of the "everyday life" in different spheres of Japanese life, see the special section in the Autumn, 1990 issue of *The Wilson Quarterly*.

3. Embree's wife, Ella Lury Wisewell, was present when he did his ethnography and she kept an extensive diary of her own on the life of village women. Her notes were edited and published in Smith and Wisewell (1982).

4. This research was implicitly comparative and aimed for both a cultural and psychological understanding of Japan in contrast to the United States culture. This line of research has continued into the present day. To illustrate, Doi's (1973) study of *amae* and research by DeVos (1973), DeVos and Wagatsuma (1966), Lebra and Lebra (1986), and Silberman (1962) focused on the raising and socialization of Japanese children, group behavior, and interpersonal interaction.

5. It is important to note that Dale (1986) sees Nakane's work as fitting into the *nihonjinron* tradition discussed below.

6. Other ethnographies in this vein include Beston's (1989) study of a Tokyo neighborhood, Edward's (1989) study of "wedding palaces," and Noguchi's (1990) study of the national railways.

7. The effects of identity on the fieldwork experience also is an important component in recent ethnographies. Kondo (1990), for example, discussed her identity in doing work in a small factory in downtown Tokyo. As a Japanese American, the anthropologist is aware of what she refers to as the "negotiations over her identity", how to act as a Japanese or an American. She sees her work as intrinsically bound up with this issue of her identity and how the Japanese she works with relate to her. In this way the communication between the Japanese and American fieldworker and her Japanese respondents is a major component of the research findings. Hamabata (1989) also was concerned with how his identity as a Japanese American male working with the women in powerful Japanese business families colored his relationships with them, and how he was constrained by a combination of the context and his identity.

8. Van Willigen and Stoffle (1984) also looked at this interaction between Japanese and North Americans in a work context.

9. Dale's (1986) example is that of Redfield's conclusion regarding Tepoztlan as an "amicable community" and Lewis' conclusion that it filled with factional strife and suspicion (see Murphy, 1972, for a discussion of opposing conclusions being reached by different observers).

10. The following translations of Hamaguchi's writing were presented by Miyanaga (1991, pp. 18-19).

11. Ito (1989b, 1992) discusses alternative explanations for cultural differences (e.g., homogeneity-heterogeneity, religion, population density, human relations vs. ideological societies). We believe that some of these may be highly related to those we present. We could, for example, argue that the human relations vs. ideological society explanation is a modified version of individualism-collectivism.

12. Lebra (this volume) argues that the major differences between Japan and the United States influencing communication is the way the self is conceived. This distinction obviously is linked directly to individualism-collectivism, but will not be discussed in detail here since Lebra examines the differences in depth. For recent discussions of individualistic and collectivistic differences in self-conceptions, see Trafimow, Triandis, and Goto (1991) and Triandis (1989). For other discussions of self-conceptions in Japan and the United States see Bond and Cheung (1983), Cousins (1989), DeGooyer and Williams (1990), Marcus and Kitayama (1991), and Yamaguchi (1991). See also Kimura (1988, 1989) and Plath (1980, 1989) for alternative discussions of the self in Japan.

13. *Nihonjinron* writers, however, do argue that Japan is a very homogeneous culture. It clearly is more homogeneous than the United States, but as Miyanaga points out, it is not as homogeneous as the *nihonjinron* writers would have us believe.

14. Triandis, Bontempo, Villareal, Asai, and Lucci (1988) tested several of the predictions regarding ingroups in Japan and the United States. They discovered that Japanese students only report that they would pay attention to the views of their co-workers more than students in the United States. They conclude that "the Japanese feel honored when their ingroups are honored and pay attention to the views of some, but not all, ingroups; they subordinate their goals to the goals of some ingroups, but they do not conform much" (p. 333). One partial explanation for Triandis et al.'s finding is that they did not take into consideration the degree to which the respondents identified with their culture. Gudykunst, Nishida, Chung, and Sudweeks (1992) found that strength of cultural identity and perceived typicality influence the individualistic and collectivistic values students in Japan and the United States hold. Hamaguchi (1980b) suggests that Japanese adults working in corporations tend to have a "human relations" (i.e., collectivistic) orientation (an English summary of this research is presented by Befu, 1990). Yamaguchi (1990) found that collectivism among Japanese is associated positively with sensitivity to rejection, affiliative tendency, and self-monitoring, while it is associated negatively with need for uniqueness and internal locus of control. For a recent discussion of how individualism-collectivism is manifested in elementary school classrooms, see Hamilton, Blumenfeld, Akoh, and Miura (1991). Schrag and Seichi (1991) demonstrate that individualism-collectivism appear as themes in the first stories that children are told in Japan and the United States.

15. See Minamoto (1969) and Nishida and Nishida (1978) for discussions of *giri*.

16. See Nakamura (1967) for an earlier discussion of the individual in Japanese society. See Ito (1989b) for a review of Japanese views on interpersonal communication; see Midooka (1990) for a recent discussion of Japanese styles of communication. Also see Dale (1986), Hamaguchi (1980a, b, 1985), Lummis and Ikeda (1985), Mito (1991) for alternative discussions of Japanese individualism.

17. Also see Murayama, Nojima, and Abe (1988) for a discussion of person-centered groups (i.e., groups based on the work of Rogers, 1970) in Japan.

18. Caudill and Scarr (1961), for example, found that collaterality predominates in Japan for family/work relations (Kluckhohn & Strodtbeck's, 1961, question R3) and personal property inheritance (R6), while individualism predominates for choice of delegates (R4) and wage work (R5). Nishida (1981) found that collaterality predominated for choice of delegate (R4), bridge build-

ing (R1), and wage work (R5), while individualism predominated in family/work relations (R3), property inheritance (R6), and land inheritance (R7). Kusatsu (1977) found that Japanese men valued an exciting life, mature love, pleasure, and true friendship.

19. See Befu (1989) for an application of social exchange theory in explaining Japanese behavior.

20. The issues raised here (i. e., personhood in Japan and collectivism in the United States) need to be addressed directly in future research. One possible way they can be addressed is by incorporating Triandis and his associates' (1985) idiocentrism-allocentrism personality dimension (which corresponds to cultural variability in individualism-collectivism) in future research. Gudykunst, Gao, Nishida, Nadamitsu, and Sakai (1992) included measures of this dimension and found that idiocentrism correlates with different aspects of self-monitoring in the two cultures (see the self-monitoring section of Gudykunst and Nishida's chapter in this volume for details).

21. Nishida (1981) found the same pattern for North Americans as for the Japanese (see earlier note). Kusatsu (1977) found that North Americans valued sense of accomplishment, wisdom, salvation, and national security.

22. The chapter on sociolinguistics by Akasu and Asao and the chapter on interpersonal communication by Gudykunst and Nishida contain discussions of how low- and high-context differences between Japan and the United States influence communication.

23. For a extensive discussion of the influence of Confucianism on communication see Yum (1988). While Yum initially draws a distinction between collectivism and Confucianism, this distinction gets lost in much of the discussion and, therefore, a portion of the discussion actually focuses on collectivism, not Confucianism per se.

REFERENCES

Abegglan, J. C. (1958). *The Japanese factory: Aspects of its social organization.* Glencoe, IL: Free Press.

Altman, I., & Taylor, D. (1973). *Social penetration processes.* New York: Holt, Reinhart, and Winston.

Altman, I., Vinsel, A., & Brown, B. (1981). Dialectical conceptions in social psychology. In L. Berkowitz (Ed.), *Advances in experimental social psychology* (Vol. 14). New York: Academic Press.

Amanuma, K. (1987). *Gambari no kozo* (The structure of "gambari"). Tokyo: Yoshikawa Kobunkan.

Bayley, D. H. (1976). *Forces of order*. Berkeley: University of California.

Beardsley, R. C., Hall, J.W., & Ward, R.E. (1959). *Village Japan*. Chicago: University of Chicago Press.

Befu, H. (1977a). Power in the great white tower. In R. Fogelson & R. Adams (Eds.), *The anthropology of power*. New York: Academic Press.

Befu, H. (1977b). Social exchange. *Annual Review of Anthropology, 6*, 255-281.

Befu, H. (1980a). A critique of the group model of Japanese society. *Social Analysis, 5/6*, 29-43.

Befu, H. (1980b). The group model of Japanese society and an alternative. *Rice University Studies, 66*, 169-187.

Befu, H. (1989). A theory of social exchange as applied to Japan. In Y. Sugimoto & R. Mouer (Eds.), *Constructs for understanding Japan*. London: Kegan Paul.

Befu, H. (1990). Conflict and non-Weberian bureaucracy in Japan. In S. Eisenstadt & E. Ben-Ari (Eds.), *Japanese models of conflict resolution*. London: Kegan Paul.

Bellah, R., Madsen, R., Sullivan, W., Swidler, A., & Tipton, S. (1985). *Habits of the heart: Individualism and commitment in American life*. New York: Harper and Row.

Bellah, R., Madsen, R., Sullivan, W., Swidler, A., & Tipton, S. (1991). *The good society*. New York: Knopf.

Benedict, R. (1946). *The chrysanthemum and the sword*. Boston: Houghton Mifflin.

Bernstein, G. L. (1983). *Haruko's world: A Japanese farm woman and her community*. Stanford: Stanford University Press.

Berry, J. (1980). Introduction to methodology. In H. Triandis & J. Berry (Eds.), *Handbook of cross-cultural psychology* (Vol. 2). Boston: Allyn & Bacon.

Bestor, T. C. (1989). *Neighborhood Tokyo*. Stanford: Stanford University Press.

Bond, M. H., & Cheung, T. (1983). College students' spontaneous self-concept: The effects of culture among respondents in Hong Kong, Japan, and the United States. *Journal of Cross-Cultural Psychology, 14*, 153-171.

Brislin, R. (1976). *Translation: Application and research*. New York: Gardner.

Brislin, R. (1983). Cross-cultural research in psychology. *Annual Review of Psychology, 34*, 363-400.

Caudill, W., & Scarr, H. (1961). Japanese value orientations and culture change. *Ethnology, 1,* 53-91.

Chinese Culture Connection. (1987). Chinese values and the search for culture-free dimensions of culture. *Journal of Cross-Cultural Psychology, 18,* 143-164.

Clark, R. (1979). *The Japanese company.* New Haven: Yale University.

Cleaver, C. (1976). *Japanese and Americans: Cultural parallels and paradoxes.* Tokyo: Charles E. Tuttle.

Cole, R. (1971). *Japanese blue collar: The changing tradition.* Berkeley: University of California.

Cornell, J. B., & Smith, R. J. (1956). *Two Japanese villages.* Ann Arbor: University of Michigan Press.

Cott, J. (1991). *Wandering ghost.* New York: Alfred A. Knopf.

Cousins, S. (1989). Culture and self-perception in Japan and the United States. *Journal of Personality and Social Psychology, 56,* 124-131.

Dalby, L. C. (1983). *Geisha.* New York: Vintage.

Dale, P. N. (1986). *The myth of Japanese uniqueness.* New York: St. Martin's Press.

Davis, W. (1980). *Dojo.* Stanford, CA: Stanford University Press.

DeGooyer, M., & Williams, J. (1990). *Self-concepts in Japan and the United States.* Paper presented at the Congress of the International Association for Cross-Cultural Psychology, Nara, Japan.

DeVos, G. A. (1973). *Socialization for achievement: Essays on the cultural psychology of the Japanese.* Berkeley: University of California Press.

DeVos, G. A., & Wagatsuma, H. (1966). *Japan's invisible race: Caste in culture and personality.* Berkeley: University of California Press.

DeVos, G. A., & Wetherall, W. O. (1983). *Japan's minorities: Burakumin, Koreans, Ainu, and Okinawans.* London: Minority Rights Group.

Doi, T. (1973). *The anatomy of dependence.* Tokyo: Kodansha.

Doi, T. (1985). *Omote to ura* (The revealed and unrevealed). Tokyo: Kobundo.

Doi, T. (1986). *The anatomy of self.* Tokyo: Kodansha.

Dore, R. P. (1967). *City life in Japan.* Berkeley: University of California Press.

Dore, R. P. (1978). *Shinohata: Portrait of a Japanese village.* New York: Pantheon.

Edgerton, R. B. (1985). *Rules, exceptions, and social order.* Berkeley: University of California Press.

Edwards, W. (1989). *Modern Japan through its weddings: Gender, person, and society in ritual portrayal*. Stanford: Stanford University Press.

Embree, J. F. (1939). *Suye Mura: A Japanese village*. Chicago: University of Chicago Press.

Foschi, M., & Hales, W. (1979). The theoretical role of cross-cultural comparisons in experimental social psychology. In L. Eckensberger, W. Lonner, & Y. Poortinga (Eds.), *Cross-cultural contributions to psychology*. Lisse, The Netherlands: Swets & Zeitlinger.

Gudykunst, W. B., Gao, G., Nishida, T., Nadamitsu, Y., & Sakai, J. (1992). Self-monitoring in Japan and the United States. In S. Iwaki, Y. Kashima, & K. Leung (Eds.), *Innovations in cross-cultural psychology*. The Hague: The Netherlands.

Gudykunst, W. B., Nishida, T., Chung, L., & Sudweeks, S. (1992). *The influence of strength of cultural identity and perceived typicality on individualistic and collectivistic values in Japan and the United States*. Paper presented at the Asian Regional Congress of the International Association for Cross-Cultural Psychology, Kathmandu, Nepal.

Gudykunst, W. B., & Ting-Toomey, S., with Chua, E. (1988). *Culture and interpersonal communication*. Newbury Park, CA: Sage.

Hall, E. T. (1976). *Beyond culture*. New York: Doubleday.

Hamabata, M. M. (1989). *Crested kimono*. Ithaca: Cornell University Press.

Hamada, T. (1990). Cultural dynamics, gender, and meaning of task in a Japanese high tech firm in the United States. In T. Hamada & A. Jordan (Eds.), *Cross cultural management and organizational culture: No. 42. Studies in third world societies*. Williamsburg: College of William and Mary.

Hamada, T. (1991). *American enterprise in Japan*. Albany: State University of New York.

Hamaguchi, E. (1977). *Nihon rashisa no sai-hakken* (Rediscovering "Japaneseness"). Tokyo: Nihon Keizai Shinbunsha.

Hamaguchi, E. (1980a). *Nihonjin no rentai-teki jiritsu-teki* (The "associatedness" of the Japanese self). *Gendai no Esupuri* (Contemporary Esprit), *160*, 127-140.

Hamaguchi, E. (1980b). *Nihonjin ni totte no shi geki* (Stimuli for Japanese). *Gendai no Esupuri* (Contemporary Esprit), *160*, 5-21.

Hamaguchi, E. (1982). *Nihonteki shuhdanshugi towa nanika* (What is the Japanese groupism). In E. Hamaguchi & S. Kumon (Ed.), *Nihonteki shudanshugi* (Japanese groupism). Tokyo: Yuhikaku (Sensho).

Hamaguchi, E. (1983). *Kanjin shugi no shakai Nihon* (Japan, society of contextual men). Tokyo: Touyou Keizai.

Hamaguchi, E. (1985). A contextual model of the Japanese. *Journal of Japanese Studies, 11*(2), 289-321.

Hamilton, V., Blumenfeld, P., Akoh, H., & Miura, K. (1991). Group and gender in Japanese and American elementary classrooms. *Journal of Cross-Cultural Psychology, 22,* 317-346.

Hendry, J., & Webber, J. (1986). *Interpreting Japanese society.* Oxford: Journal of the Anthropological Society of Oxford.

Hofstede, G. (1979). Value systems in forty countries. In L. Eckensberger, W. Lonner, & Y. Poortinga (Eds.), *Cross-cultural contributions to psychology.* Lisse, The Netherlands: Swets & Zeitlinger.

Hofstede, G. (1980). *Culture's consequences.* Beverly Hills, CA: Sage.

Hofstede, G. (1991). *Cultures and organizations: Software of the mind.* London: McGraw-Hill.

Hofstede, G., & Bond, M. H. (1984). Hofstede's culture dimensions. *Journal of Cross-Cultural Psychology, 15,* 417-433.

Imamura, A. E. (1987). *Urban Japanese housewives: In home and the community.* Honolulu: University of Hawaii Press.

Ito, Y. (1989a). A nonwestern view of the paradigm dialogues. In B. Dervin, L. Grossberg, & E. Wartella (Eds.), *Rethinking communication.* Newbury Park, CA: Sage.

Ito, Y. (1989b). Socio-cultural backgrounds of Japanese interpersonal communication style. *Civilisations, 39,* 101-137.

Ito, Y. (1992). Theories of interpersonal communication style from a Japanese perspective. In J. Blumler, J. McCleod, & K. Rosengren (Eds.), *Communication and culture across space and time.* Newbury Park, CA: Sage.

Kawamura, N. (1989). The transition of the household system in Japan's modernization. In Y. Sugimoto & R. Mouer (Eds.), *Constructs for understanding Japan.* London: Kegan Paul.

Kelly, W. W. (1988). Japanology bashing. *American Ethnologist, 15,* 172-176.

Kimura, B. (1988). *Aida* (Inbetweenness). Tokyo: Kobunsha.

Kimura, B. (1989). *Hito to hito no aida* (Between people). Tokyo: Kobunsha.

Kluckhohn, F., & Strodtbeck, F. (1961). *Variations in value orientations.* New York: Row, Peterson.

Kondo, D. K. (1990). *Crafting selves*. Chicago: University of Chicago Press.

Krause, E., Rohlen, T. & Steinhoff, P. (Eds.). (1984). *Conflict in Japan*. Honolulu: University of Hawaii Press.

Kumon, S. (1982). *Soshiki no Nihongata moderu to obeigata moderu* (Japanese and American models of organizations). In E. Hamaguchi & S. Kumon (Eds.), *Nihonteki shuhdanshugi* (Japanese groupism). Tokyo: Yuhikaku (Sensho).

Kusatsu, O. (1977). Ego development and sociocultural processes in Japan (in English). *Keizaigaku Kiyo, 3*, Part I, 47-109, Part II, 74-128.

Lebra, J., Paulson, J., & Powers, E. (Eds.). (1976). *Women in changing Japan*. Stanford: Stanford University Press.

Lebra, T. S. (1976). *Japanese patterns of behavior*. Honolulu: University of Hawaii Press.

Lebra, T. S. (1984). *Japanese women: Constraint and fulfillment*. Honolulu: University of Hawaii Press.

Lebra, T. S., & Lebra, W. P. (Eds.). (1986). *Japanese culture and behavior*. Honolulu: University of Hawaii Press.

Lee, C. & DeVos, G. (1981). *Koreans in Japan*. Berkeley: University of California Press.

Lummis, C. D. (1982). *A new look at the chrysanthemum and the sword*. Tokyo: Shohaku-sha.

Lummis, C. D., & Ikeda, M. (1985). *Nihonjinron no shinso* (The underlying assumptions of the theories of the Japanese). Tokyo: Haru Shobo.

March, R. (1988). *The Japanese negotiator*. Tokyo: Kodansha International.

Marcus, G. E., & Fischer, M. M. (1986). *Anthropology as cultural critique*. Chicago: University of Chicago Press.

Markus, H., & Kitayama, S. (1991). Culture and the self: Implications for cognition, emotion, and motivation. *Psychological Review, 98*, 224-253.

Marsella, A. J., DeVos, G., & Hsu, F. L. K. (Eds.). (1985). *Culture and self: Asian and Western perspectives*. New York: Tavistock Publications.

McFarland, H. N. (1967). *The rush hour of the gods*. New York: Macmillan.

Midooka, K. (1990). Characteristics of Japanese-style communication. *Media, Culture, and Society, 12*, 477-489.

Minamoto, R. (1969). *Giri to ninjo* (Obligation and human feeling). Tokyo: Chuo Koronsha.

Mito, T. (1991). *Ie no ronri* (The theory of *ie*) (two vols.). Tokyo: Bunshindo.

Miyanaga, K. (1991). *The creative edge: Individualism in Japan*. New Brunswick, NJ: Transaction.

Miyoshi, M. (1991). *Off center: Power and culture relations between Japan and the United States*. Cambridge, MA: Harvard University Press.

Murayama, S., Nojima, K., & Abe, T. (1988). Person-centered groups in Japan. *Person-Centered Review, 3*, 479-492.

Murphy, R. H. (1972). *The dialectics of social life*. London: George Allen and Unwin.

Nakamura, H. (1967). Consciousness of the individual and the universal among the Japanese. In C. Moore (Ed.), *The Japanese mind*. Honolulu: East West Center Press.

Nakamura, M. (1990). *Daigakusei no yujinkankei no hattenkatei ni kansuru kenkyu - Kankeikanyosei o yosokusuru shakai kokanmoderu no hikakukento* (A study of the development processes of friendship in college students: A comparative examination of social exchange models predicting relationship commitment). *Syakaishinrigaku Kenkyu* (Research in Social Psychology), *5*, 29-41.

Nakane, C. (1967). *Kinship and economic organization in rural Japan*. New York: Humanities.

Nakane, C. (1970). *Japanese society*. Berkeley: University of California.

Nishida, H. (1981). Value orientations and value changes in Japan and the U.S.A. In T. Nishida & W. Gudykunst (Eds.), *Readings in intercultural communication*. Tokyo: Geirinshobo.

Nishida, H., & Nishida, T. (1978). *Giri and its influence on Japanese interpersonal communication*. Paper presented at the Speech Communication Association Summer Conference on International and Intercultural Communication, Tampa, FL.

Noguchi, P. (1990). *Delayed departures, overdue arrivals*. Honolulu: University of Hawaii Press.

Norbeck, E. (1954). *Takashima: A Japanese fishing community*. Salt Lake City: University of Utah Press.

Norbeck, E. (1976). *Changing Japan*. New York: Holt, Rinehart, and Winston.

Norbeck, E. (1978). *Country to city: The urbanization of a Japanese hamlet*. Salt Lake City: University of Utah Press.

Ohno, S. (1976). Fragile blossom, fragile superpower—A new interpretation. *Japan Quarterly*, 23(1), 12-27.

Okakura, K. (1991/1906). *A book of tea*. Tokyo: Kodansha.

Pike, K. (1966). *Language in relation to a unified theory of the structure of human behavior*. The Hague: Mouton.

Plath, D. (1964). *The after hours*. Berkeley: University of California Press.

Plath, D. (1980). *Long engagements: Maturity in modern Japan*. Stanford: Stanford University Press.

Plath, D. (Ed.). (1983). *Work and lifecourse in Japan*. Albany: State University of New York Press.

Plath, D. (1989). Arc, circle, and sphere: Schedules for selfhood. In Y. Sugimoto & R. Mouer (Eds.), *Constructs for understanding Japan*. London: J Kegan Paul.

Rogers, C. (1970). *Carl Rogers on encounter groups*. New York: Harper and Row.

Rohlen, T. P. (1974). *For harmony and strength*. Berkeley: University of California Press.

Rohlen, T. P. (1983). *Japan's high schools*. Berkeley: University of California Press.

Sato, S., Kumon, S., & Murakami, Y. (1979). *Bunmei to shite no ie shakai* (Ie society as a pattern of civilization). Tokyo: Chuo Koronsha.

Schrag, R., & Seichi, C. (1991). *Peter Rabbit meets Gon-Fox together with mother on Sesame Street: An intercultural analysis of first stories told to American and Japanese children through books and television*. Paper presented at the Speech Communication Association convention, Atlanta.

Silberman, B. S. (1962). *Japanese character and culture*. Tucson: University of Arizona Press.

Smith, R. J. (1974). *Ancestor worship in contemporary Japan*. Stanford: Stanford University Press.

Smith, R. J. (1978). *Kurusu*. Stanford: Stanford University Press.

Smith, R. J., & Wiswell, E. L. (1982). *The women of Suye Mura*. Chicago: University of Chicago Press.

Sugimoto, Y., & Mouer, R. (1986). *Images of Japanese Society*. London: Kegan Paul.

Sugimoto, Y., & Mouer, R. (1989). Cross-currents in the study of Japanese society. In Y. Sugimoto & R. Mouer (Eds.), *Constructs for understanding Japan*. London: Kegan Paul.

Tamanoi, M. A. (1990). Women's voices: Their critique of the anthropology of Japan. In B. J. Siegel, A. R. Beals, & S. A. Tyler (Eds.), *Annual review of anthropology* (Vol. 19). Stanford: Annual Reviews, Inc.

Tobin, J. J., Wu, D. Y. H., & Davidson, D. H. (Eds.). (1989). *Preschool in three cultures*. New Haven: Yale University Press.

Triafimow, D., Triandis, H. C., & Goto, S. (1991). Some tests of the distinction between the private self and the collective self. *Journal of Personality and Social Psychology, 60,* 649-655.

Triandis, H. C. (1988). Collectivism vs. individualism: A reconceptualization of a basic concept in cross-cultural psychology. In G. Verma & C. Bagley (Eds.), *Cross-cultural studies of personality, attitudes and cognition.* London: MacMillan.

Triandis, H. C. (1989). The self and social behavior in differing cultural contexts. *Psychological Review, 96,* 506-517.

Triandis, H. C. (1990). Cross-cultural studies of individualism-collectivism. In J. Berman (Ed.), *Nebraska symposium on motivation* (Vol. 37). Lincoln: University of Nebraska Press.

Triandis, H. C., Bontempo, R., Villareal, M., Asai, M., & Lucca, N. (1988). Individualism-collectivism: Cross-cultural perspectives on self-ingroup relationships. *Journal of Personality and Social Psychology, 54,* 323-338.

Triandis, H. C., Davis, E., & Takezawa, S. (1965). Some determinants of social distance among American, German, and Japanese students. *Journal of Personality and Social Psychology, 2,* 540-551.

Triandis, H. C., Leung, K., Villareal, M., & Clack, F. (1985). Allocentric vs. idiocentric tendencies. *Journal of Research in Personality, 19,* 395-415.

Tung, R. (1984). *Business negotiations with the Japanese.* Lexington, MA: D. C. Heath.

Van Willigen, J., & Stoffle, R. (1984). The Americanization of *shoyu*: American workers and a Japanese employment system. In H. Serri (Ed.), *Anthropology & international business.* Williamsburg, VA: College of William and Mary.

Vogel, E. F. (1963). *Japan's new middle class.* Berkeley: University of California.

Vogel, E. F. (1979). *Japan as number one.* Cambridge, MA: Harvard University.

Wagatsuma, H., & De Vos, G. A. (1984). *Heritage of endurance: Family patterns and delinquency formation in urban Japan.* Berkeley: University of California Press.

White, M. (1987). *The Japanese educational challenge: A commitment to children*. New York: Free Press.

White, M. (1988). *The Japanese overseas: Can they go home again?* New York: Free Press.

Wuthnow, R. (1991). *Acts of compassion: Caring for others and helping ourselves*. Princeton: Princeton University Press.

Yamaguchi, S. (1990). *Empirical evidence on collectivism among the Japanese*. Paper presented at the Conference on Individualism-Collectivism, Seoul, Korea.

Yamaguchi, S. (1991). *"Jiko" no shitenkara no shudan oyobi bunkasa eno apurochi* (An approach to group processes and cultural differences from the perspective of the self). *Syakaishinrigaku Kenkyu* (Research in Social Psychology), *6*, 138-147.

Yoneyama, T. (1973). Basic notions in Japanese social relations. In J. Bailey (Ed.), *Listening to Japan*. New York: Praeger.

Zander, A. (1983). The value of belonging to a group in Japan. *Small Group Behavior, 14,* 3-14.

PART II
CULTURE, LANGUAGE, AND ETHNICITY

Chapter 3

CULTURE, SELF, AND COMMUNICATION IN JAPAN AND THE UNITED STATES

Takie Sugiyama Lebra

Political urgency for global communication and understanding is being voiced today in two opposite messages. We are warned, on the one hand, against overstating cultural differences but instead exhorted to see sameness behind differences. Argument for cultural uniqueness is a taboo, regarded as culpable for a perpetuation of cultural stereotypes and myths which stand in the way of intercultural communication. On the other hand, we are urged to be sensitized to cultural differences, ignorance of which would be detrimental to intercultural communication. Here the argument for sameness amounts to ethnocentrism in which one's own culture is imposed upon another as if there were no difference. I place myself somewhere between these two extreme messages, somewhere between universalism and relativism, for pragmatic reasons. Relativism in its extreme would be ridiculous if one means by uniqueness the absolute lack of similarity between cultures. With nothing in common, it would be futile to try to understand an alien culture at all, and I do not know of anybody's having argued the uniqueness of a culture in this sense. Also, universalism, unless relativized, would risk ethnocentric blindness and gross misunderstanding in cross-cultural communication.

In this chapter I focus on one salient cultural difference between

Japan and the United States as it interlocks with their respective communication modes. Far from arguing the immutable and insurmountable uniqueness of a culture, my goal is, instead, to suggest the possibility of widening the communicative repertoire of each culture, for decoding and encoding messages, through cross-cultural fertilization. This is because culture, while indispensable to make communication possible, also serves to block communication channels to an unreasonable degree, unreasonable in the sense of "unnatural": American and Japanese culture each imposes constraints upon its carriers in terms of what, when, and how they can or should communicate among themselves. Cross-cultural studies should lead us, I believe, toward an enrichment of our cultural storehouse to open up new channels of communication.

Communication, interpersonal communication in particular, may be viewed from the perspective of self-presentation in interaction with others. Styles of communication are likely to be affected by, and in turn, to affect cultural conceptions of the self. My discussion focuses upon cultural difference in the self to be presented, enacted, and further constructed through communication. Although attention is skewed toward the Japanese side, the two cultures are taken as open or hidden mirrors for one another.

American and Japanese individuals are alike in their deep involvement, to the point of obsession, with their selves, and in being anxious to present their selves in culturally appropriate or desirable ways, to give good impressions. In this sense, both are self-centered, perhaps as much as people in any other cultures. But when it comes to the conception of self itself, or to the "unreasonably" culturalized self, and to the modes of presenting and communicating the self, resemblances give way to contrasts. One observer after another, whether American, Japanese, or other, has reported cultural differences in this respect, and there is substantial coherence or overlap across these observations.

It is possible that one observer mimics another, new reporters repeating previous ones, which would result in an exaggerated consensus, namely, a stereotype. But I do not believe this is the case. Every researcher, to establish him/herself or simply out of self-respect, is eager to discover something new instead of just adding another voice in harmony with the mainstream chorus, and, if possible, to refute the previously established conclusions. Note that we live in an information-intensive world where novelty, not redundancy, is at a premium. The above coherence in characterization of the self, then, seems grounded in intersubjective "reality," not simply reflective of a biased opinion, as far as the Japanese self and American self are compared.

CULTURAL SHAPING OF THE SELF

Where the self ends and communication begins is a wrong question. Self and communication are interrelated in circularity in such a way that the culturally constructed self is defined and expressed in a certain communication style through certain channels which in turn backs up or reconstructs the self. (The same circularity holds for culture and language as will be noted throughout.) We can start at any point of this circle. To delineate the cultural self, I begin with a simple, obvious aspect of communication in the two cultures and turn around the circle. It will be noted that the self is the very process of communication itself.

Terminology

I start from the unquestionable, clear-cut, and familiar fact that there is no Japanese equivalent for the English "I" which is central to American conversational discourses. The Japanese "I" is either empty or multiple in that it is entirely muted in a discourse or worded differently according to different social, communicative situations, as well as the speaker's gender, age, and other social attributes, relative to the listener. A beginner in Japanese-language lesson may be taught that I is *watakushi* (or more informal *watashi*) in Japanese, but soon finds out that *watakushi* and I are totally alien to each other in that the usage of watakushi is quite limited unlike I, and must be replaced by other terms or "zero" term in a variety of circumstances. Between husband and wife, for example, *watakushi* may be used by the wife, but not by the husband because the term is associated with the female gender in this particular speech situation. He may call himself "*ore*." Nonetheless, *watakushi* can be used by the same man in speaking to his boss, in which case *watakushi* becomes degenderized and assumes a hierarchical implication of humility. (This may be another way of saying that femininity implies inferiority and humility and therefore that a man may express his humble posture by feminizing his self-reference.) The wife may call herself *watakushi* in conversing with her husband or other adults, but not with her child. There are dozens of self-references out of which the speaker must choose the most appropriate one in accordance to the listener, other persons in copresence, intimacy and distance, power and status hierarchy, situational variation such as formal versus informal occasions, social categories like gender and age. If unable to find a single appropriate term, the speaker opts to be mute about him/herself, letting the entire discourse signify the speaker as the referent, or implicitly loading the predicate with the speaker-subject.

Furthermore, in addressing a child, the adult speaker refers to him/herself by the term the child would use in addressing the adult: the mother replaces "I" with "mom," a middle-aged male stranger is likely to replace "I" with "uncle," a schoolteacher with "*sensei*" and so on. Through this teknonymic strategy, the speaker-I thus assimilates the listener-I into his/her self, or one might say the speaker-self is assimilated into the listener-self and vice versa. All this makes the Japanese "I" an oxymoron since the Japanese self and English "I" are inherently contradictory. Unlike the multiple or empty self, "I" is single, fixed, immutable, independent of the above factors which necessitate the Japanese speaker to switch from one self-term to another.

The same contradiction is noted in the Japanese equivalent for "you." Again many terms or zero term for you, unlike the English you, are available, and special cautions must be taken in choosing a proper one to achieve an optimal congruity between self and other in status and many other social variables. With a child in mind, two adults, in talking to each other, may replace "you" with the terms the child would use in addressing them, as when a woman calls her teen-age daughter "elder sister" as her younger child would. This is what Suzuki (1986) calls "empathetic identification." Such is not limited to adult-child conversations. I might call my friend's mother "Mother," taking over the friend's position. The same mode of "vicarious" addressing (Lebra 1976; p. 88) in adult conversations was observed in my study of the Japanese aristocracy: the aristocratic wife called her husband "your highness" as their servants would—a point that illuminates the indispensability of a servant in sustaining one's lordly status identity (Lebra, 1992). *Anata*, the most likely translation of you, is found very limited, more so than *watakushi*, in actual usage. As Japanese "I" is an oxymoron, so is Japanese "you." (For a great variety of terms, including "zero form," used in the family, see Fischer, 1964; Passin, 1965.)

The teknonymic usage of kin terms may be replaced by another strategy in a family which commands a live-in domestic work crew—a rare practice in today's Japan but once a very common phenomenon among upper- and middle-class families. My recent study of the prewar aristocracy (Lebra, 1992) shows how the wife addressed and referred to her husband, the head of the noble house, as "your (his) highness," appropriating the term that her servants would use in calling her husband. Such servant-centered terminology was so internalized that the wife might address her husband in this manner even when no servant was present, as much as an ordinary wife would call her husband "Father" regardless of a child's presence.

Situational fragility of terms for self and other is reflected in their historical evanescence, quick demise, and replacement by new terms. In every new conversational encounter, Japanese speakers must decide what to call themselves and their addressees. In contrast, the English you, like I, is transcendental to particular speech situations, doing away with such burdensome decisions—a point which makes many Japanese speakers envious of English speakers and which bilingual Japanese stress in explaining why they choose English whenever appropriate.

To this cultural contrast in terms for the first and second person, we might add terms for the third person, although the cultural contrast here is not as sharp. Both cultures use personal names as unambiguous identifiers noncontingent upon given speech situations, but Japanese speakers do so much less frequently. They use relational terms more than American speakers do: a Japanese woman talks about "my eldest son" when her American friend refers to her son as "John." But, of course, what term I use again depends upon who my listener happens to be. Imagine an embarrassing situation involving a new listener where a Japanese man has to choose an appropriate word for "my wife" from among several possible terms including frivolous ones.

Sociality

The terminological difference in self/other references strikes the very core contrast in selfhood between the two cultures. Long-term researchers on Japan tend to concur that the Japanese self, just like the Japanese self-reference, is socially contextualized, embedded, or situated. To the extent that the social construction of self is a universal fact, as theorized by Western social psychologists and symbolic interactionists, notably by Mead (1934), it may be better restated that the Japanese person not only acts in response to, but perceives his/herself as contingent upon, the social nexus. The result is the consciously socialized self. If viewed through the Western lens, the Japanese self indeed appears situationally circumscribed or on/giri-bound[1] (Benedict, 1946), dependency-prone (Doi, 1971), rank-conscious and group-oriented (Nakane, 1967), empathetic (Aida, 1970), mindful of sekentei[2] (Inoue, 1977), indeterminate (Smith, 1983), relativistic (Lebra, 1976), hanging "between" persons (Hamaguchi, 1977; Kimura, 1972), uncertain and multidimensional (Minami, 1983).

The content of social contingency is extremely variable and multiple, as multiple as the social boundaries and groupings in or between which an individual finds him/herself. Social "other" may be an individual person or a group of persons, small and large, which includes or excludes self; may be known or unknown to the self; in intimate contact with or at distance from self; friendly and empathetic or hostile and aloof; in structured relationship as in status hierarchy, authority, and super-subordination, or in personal, informal, equal relationship; a coactor, a rival, or audience. Some relations involve resonance between *kokoro* [the heart of things] in depth, while others only touch the surface of *kokoro*; some enhance or actualize the individual *kokoro*, but others inhibit or oppress it; a number of *kokoro* may be united around a collective symbol or may remain in separate bodies. Given such and more variations of social relations and boundaries, it makes sense that the terms for the socially contingent Japanese "I" are so variable.

The sociality of the Japanese self is observable from the way Japanese individuals change their behavior patterns and postures as interactive situations change in short periods of time or even within a matter of moments. Drawing upon the *uchi-soto* (inside/outside) and *omote-ura* (front/back) boundaries, I (1976, pp. 110-36) have proposed three situations, to simplify the infinitely variable situations, that call for three corresponding behavior patterns: intimate, ritual, and anomic. The main point here is that one pattern is displayed in distinction from another to acknowledge and mark a situational shift. Intimacy, characterized by acts of physical and emotional closeness and spontaneity to the point of "social nudity," is enacted to mark an occasion calling for such behavior, in contrast or opposition to a ritualistic, protocol-bound, nonspontaneous mode of behavior necessary for another social occasion. The consciously social self becomes strikingly apparent when a sudden shift takes place from the intimate to the ritual mode or vice versa, even while the self continues to interact with the same other. Such shifts, which may appear a sign of inconsistency or inscrutability to cultural outsiders, are indications of the social maturity of the Japanese self.

The anomic mode is differentiated from both the ritual and intimate modes in that the self here is out of communicative circuit and behaves in indifference to or even aggression against the people who happen to be nearby as if they do not exist. This behavior occurs toward strangers in certain situations of copresence, particularly in moving vehicles such as trains, elevators. Even when one sits or stands touching another passenger in a crowded train, bus, or elevator, mental distance is acted out. It may be questioned whether this behavior can be rightly called "anomic," a sort of social vacation away from the usual, socially overloaded situations, or it is a negative variety of ritual behavior show-ing one's consideration for another's wish to be left alone. Regardless of such different interpretations, however, the point holds that this mode of behavior is again displayed in clear opposition from the other two, reflecting the actor's [actress'] awareness of and behavioral respon-siveness to situational variability.

By contrast, Americans tend to perceive the self as socially inde-pendent and therefore internally consistent, if the authors of *Habits of the Heart* (Bellah, Madsen, Sullivan, Swidler, & Tipton, 1985) are right in describing them. If the self is likened to a container, the Amer-ican self is socially empty and subjectively filled up, while the Japanese self presents its opposite—socially filled, subjectively empty. The latter is socially loaded and encumbered, which necessitates its subjectivity to shift, decenter, to be multifaceted, malleable, relative, fuzzy, or empty.

This contrast does not necessarily reflect the experience and feel-ing of real persons in everyday life but shows the cultural constraint or construct whereby the personal experience is coded, represented, and thereby polarized. For Americans, gift-giving or hosting a dinner party, for instance, is made into an expression of the socially unencumbered, purely spontaneous self even when it is actually a repayment of an accumulated social debt. The idea of obligatory repayment may be dis-cussed, if at all, in a private discourse such as between husband and wife, but not in public or least of all with the repayee. For Japanese, such expressions of good will are the explicitly acknowledged repre-sentation of the socially indebted, encumbered self, even when the giver actually has no such feeling of being in debt.

Sociality should not be equated with sociability, solidarity, har-mony, consensus, or any other positive relationship which is often regarded, wrongly, as characteristically Japanese. Sociality includes all kinds of social relationships, positive and negative, friendly and hostile, fulfilling and frustrating, coordinated and conflicting, cooperative and competitive, warm and cold, intimate and distant, equal and hierarchi-cal, stable and transient, and so on. Indeed, as in most other societies, animosity is a common feature of Japanese social life, and often under-lies an admirable accomplishment. A person may be driven toward an extraordinary achievement by a revengeful passion against some people who in one way or another humiliated and left him/her with an unre-movable social scar (Lebra, 1984, p. 53). The point, however, is that the Japanese self is heavily encumbered and easily affected by varying social relationships, good and bad.

Cultural Modes of Subjectivity versus Objectivity

The above usage of "subjective" could be misleading. At the outset of this paper I stated that both Japanese and Americans are "self-centered," and in this sense subjective. But following the terminological discussion, I have characterized American speakers as more subjectively filled, and Japanese as socially loaded. Logically speaking, however, subjectivity should be differentiated from objectivity rather than sociality. The question is: Which of the two, the American or Japanese speaker, is more objective and which is more subjective, as far as terms for self are concerned?

To the extent that the English "I" transcends a given speech context, its user seems to maintain a higher level of objectivity (context-independence), whereas the Japanese speaker, because he/she must shift around in his/her self-terminology in relation to listeners and contexts, is compelled to be more consciously self-presentational. In this sense, one may see more subjectivity in the Japanese self. Indeed, because of the terminological uncertainty for the self, the entire Japanese discourse is geared to convey the identity and location of the speaker-self relative to the listener. Yamashita (1986) argues that Japanese speech is characteristically speaker-centered, with the speaker-self situated at the center of an everchanging concentric circle of speech context. The speaker's subjective perspective, the level and direction of his/her eyes, steers and dominates his/her discourse. How to get into the subjective focus of the Japanese speaker, says Yamashita, is the toughest point of mastery for foreigners learning Japanese. We shall come back to his thesis later. Suffice it here to say that his argument does not contradict my cultural comparison made in the first part of this section with regard to self and sociality.

The above contrast between the American and Japanese speaker in terms of objectivity and subjectivity can be reversed. To the extent that the American "I" is context-free, it asserts itself consistently, continuously, independently, and unyieldingly. In this sense the American self is more subjective. I am saying that what makes the American self more objective makes it more subjective, too. Likewise, the Japanese self is more subjective and more objective than the American self precisely because it is more socially embedded and encumbered. It is subjective because the self always enters into its assimilation of other, and objective because the self, far from being autonomous or assertive, perceives itself from other's point of view. Again, what makes Japanese subjective makes them objective. The cultural difference lies in the meaning of subjectivity and objectivity. We should rephrase the question, "Which is more subjective?" into "What criteria underlie the definitions of subjectivity/objectivity for the American and Japanese self?" The criterion for the former is the social transcendence of "I," while that for the latter is the social contextuality of the subject. This argument will become more clear as this paper unfolds.

Self in Rebirth

Self is thus culturally constructed so that its natural component, the body, is curtailed, distorted, or even overlooked. The best example is the American self constructed in uneasy denial of the biological bond and psychological interdependence between parent and child. Again to quote Bellah and colleagues (1985), there seems to be "a considerable amnesia about what one owes to one's parents," while "conversely, many Americans are uneasy about taking responsibility for children" (p. 82). It looks as if one gives birth to oneself as suggested by the same authors. Indeed, adolescence is the time for self-pregnancy leading to a second birth. Thomas Rohlen (1983) describes American high school students as being at that life stage for independent, exploratory self-creation.

The metaphor of second birth applies to the Japanese adolescent as well, as noted by Johan Galtung (1971), but in an entirely different context. It is preceded by a long period of strenuous preparation for ferociously competitive examinations, and rebirth coincides with a successful passage of the examination to enter a university, with a high risk of miscarriage. The high school stage, which is the blossoming period of second birth for American youth, is that of prolonged labor pain for Japanese adolescents. And it is during this period that the psychological umbilical cord is ever tightened up as implied by the "education-mama" or even the around-the-clock "education-maid," with the examination candidate as the center of not only his/her family but a wider social network of dependency and support. The candidate is reborn only with the help of many midwives and nurses around, which he/she acknowledges with gratitude or with an overwhelming sense of encumbrance. The second birth for the Japanese youth, far from marking a denial of the first birth, tends more or less to reinforce it. Furthermore, the successful rebirth, that is, admission to a desirable university, is believed to secure an eventual conveyance of the newly born into the established social structure, after a four-year "moratorium" of college life, with prospects of climbing up the organizational hierarchy. Rebirth is a crucial step into, not out of, society. Youth is a "stormy" phase of life for both cultures but with different forms of storminess.

I argue that this difference in the experience of adolescent rebirth has much to do with the cultural reproduction of the self, at least as much as early socialization does. In one culture, rebirth amounts to the maximum freedom and independence of the individual (particularly of a male) "I," whereas in the other it is a preparatory stage for the assimilation of the youth into the adult social structure, which is to be passed through with support and collaboration from parents, teachers, and other adults. It is as if the culturally constructed self is reproduced and reenacted in every rebirth.

Culturally different forms of rebirth in youth are replicated by therapeutic models. Naikan, literally meaning "looking inwards," is known as a Japanese psychotherapy or moral rehabilitation, founded by a Buddhist businessman, which is for self-transformation or "rebirth" through concentrated introspection. Under a counselor's guidance, a client or patient is supposed to recall a set of significant others serially and to relive the forgotten experiences he/she had with them. The most important is one's relationship with mother, and it is this bond that offers the basic Naikan model for self-reflection (see for the mother-child bonding, Lebra, 1984, 1991). In concentrated self-reflection, the client asks himself or herself a threefold question: what mother has done for him or her (in a certain period specified by the counselor, typically in childhood), what he or she has done for her in return, and what trouble he or she has caused her instead. If successful, the client, after several days of isolated, and often agonizing meditation, comes to a painfully vivid realization that he or she has accumulated an overwhelming debt to his or her mother (or another benefactor) and yet has been ingrate to her and a source of trouble and suffering for her. Naikan thus induces a rebirth through the insight that no person is what he or she is by his or her own strength and ability but owes everything to others (as represented by his or her mother). A new awareness of indebtedness and empathetic guilt is to result in one's determination to renounce one's selfish preoccupations and to devote oneself to others and society.

Naikan resembles the psychoanalytically oriented Western therapy in having the client recall and relive his forgotten past particularly of his childhood in relation to his parents. The similarity ends there, however. The whole purpose of such childhood recollection in the Western psychotherapy is to become emancipated from the unconscious bondage to which the client has been tied down, from the anomalous relationship he had with his/her parent(s) which is responsible for his/her psychic disturbance. The therapy is to restore or obtain the full autonomy and freedom of the self. Naikan reorients the client in a reverse direction in that he/she is to become sharply aware of being in debt to others and dependent upon their good will, and to bind himself/herself by the obligation to do his/her best to repay.

Morita therapy, another psychotherapy often juxtaposed with Naikan as the two major Japanese ethnotherapies, is quite different in method, purpose, and the professional status of the therapist (the Morita therapist is a psychiatrist with professional credentials while the Naikan therapist is a lay counselor), and addresses primarily neurotic patients. It finds its therapeutic leverage in the patient's realization of the futility of fighting his/her illness which should lead him/her to an acceptance of what is as is and thus rescues him/her out of the vicious circle of conflict between what he/she sees as real and what he/she aspires to. The ultimate purpose is to attain freedom, but freedom is to be attained, not by gaining autonomy from the existing constraint binding the patient, but by subordinating himself/herself to it and accepting it in its entirety. Ideally, the boundary between subject and object, self and nature, is to disappear, or to put it another way, the self is to attain the state of being no-self. Rebirth in Morita therapy is thus in sharp opposition to that in the Western therapy. Both Morita and Naikan, even though they are different from each other, radicalize Japanese selfhood, and thereby shed light upon its distinction from the therapeutically reborn Western self.[3]

Biological Metaphors

However culturally constructed one's self-image may be, and though one can undergo second birth, nobody is free from the biological conditions of first birth and genetic inheritance. Both Americans and Japanese are well aware of the biological self. Nevertheless, the ascribed, birth-determined self itself is, again, culturally conceived. For Americans, the ascribed self seems tied to the image of an inherently unique, nonduplicatable individual. Thus they are more susceptible than are Japanese to the idea of genius as inscribed in a unique constellation of genes of a particular individual. It is paradoxical that democratic Americans who believe in educational egalitarianism also have developed special-education programs for the gifted as well as handicapped children. Americans are opposed to the overly standardized and restrictive program of Japanese education because by ignoring individual uniqueness it is likely, they believe, to kill the genetically endowed potentials of individuals. Japanese, on the other hand, are more resistant to the idea of the specially gifted (Tobin, Wu, & Davidson, 1989), and more optimistic about "efforts" to improve themselves through training (White & LeVine, 1986). In this sense they are more egalitarian.

Japanese load birth-heritage with other symbols. First, birth is linked up with the ancestor cult in a broad sense, and with the symbol of overgenerational continuity from past through present to future, namely, the *ie*, stem-family household. The ascribed self for Japanese is, far from being unique, continuous with ancestors and descendants, reproducible and sharable through the *ie*. This is not all. Genes translate into fluid blood, capable of flowing into larger, and still larger kinship groups, which ultimately merges with the racial blood pool of the Japanese. Japanese culture is thus labeled the "culture of the blood" by Hayashida (1976, p. 85). The sense of having originated from the same racial stock lies at the core of the Japanese self. One is impressed with the cultural contrast: the birth-bound self for Americans sets a boundary between individuals as unique, irreproducible beings, while that for Japanese throws into relief the permeability of the individual with other individuals, generations before and after, family, collectivity, nation through blood flow. Again, the socially empty, unsituated American self is contrasted to the socially contingent and contextualized Japanese self. The blood metaphor goes with the externally visible body and supports the notion of racial commonality, whereas genes are hidden for good and thus become allied with the American mystique of optimism about the unlimited "potentials" of each individual.

The Mind and Body

The foregoing discussion leads to the cultural variation in the mind-body relationship, which takes us back to the Cartesian dualism as a still viable part of Western culture and epistemology despite the tides of postmodernism (in fact I believe that postmodernism is the latest, somewhat recalcitrant child of the Cartesian parent). The self in this Western tradition resides in the mind, apart from the body. It may be that the Western self can be socially empty because it is bodily empty, and that, so encapsulated in the invisible, transcendental mind, the self stands above social reality, as much as "I" stands aloof from social contingencies in discourses. One then realizes that there is no Japanese word corresponding with "mind" in the Cartesian sense of the word. It is as untranslatable as "I." Conversely, Japanese terms which come closest to the English "mind" are no more translatable into English.

The problem of translation reminds us of the Western logic of categorization based on exclusion, opposition, and differentiation: X is defined in exclusion of, opposition to, and differentiation from what X is not. Categorization based on this logical process of conceptual reductionism often makes it difficult or impossible to find an exact English equivalent for a Japanese word and vice versa. This is the more true, the more culture-loaded the word is. Take *on* for example. *On* refers to a debt or credit, which may be moral, social, or economic, and which arouses gratitude and humility in the debtor or drives him/her toward immediate repayment simply to unload the burden off the back, thus associated with either a positive or negative feeling of the debtor toward the creditor, the latter being painted either as an altruistic benefactor or as an egotistic manipulator. By the Western standard, this semantic overloading may well be taken as a sign of logical confusion, inconsistency, or conflation. For the Japanese, it only reflects the reality of human relationship in its depth and complexity which defies the analytical process of slicing the cake of reality in exclusion, opposition, and differentiation. The Japanese pay more attention to continuity, complementarity, and multiplicity.

At this juncture I should mention the recent work of Steven Cousins (1990). Cousins, in an attempt to explain the symptomatic differences between the Western and Japanese social phobia to which I will return later, proposes the Cartesian versus non-Cartesian epistemology in terms of impermeability versus permeability of mind and body. Unlike the Western, Cartesian notion of mind, the Japanese words which are often used in reference to the self suggest a non-Cartesian epistemology in that all these, while partially referring to the "spiritual" and "mental" functions, mean also feelings and emotions, and are not cut off from the body.

Let us consider some such words. *Kokoro*, like other words, is multivocal as illustrated by a string of various words given as its translation—heart, feeling, spirit, intention, will, mind—none of which, taken singly, is satisfactory. To delineate the above contrast between the Western logic of exclusion in favor of discreteness and the Japanese sensitivity to the continuity, complementarity, and multiplicity of reality, I propose that the *kokoro*, like other related terms to be mentioned below, is the embodied mind, contrary to the Cartesian dissociation of the mind from the body. Since even this definition, like all other definitions, is a simplification, too discrete to convey the fullness of the word, I should add that the *kokoro* spreads across the vast area which lies between the pure mind and the strictly physical body which includes sensation, feeling, emotion, psychic energy, desire, and so on. This is another important point of contrast because the Western mind differentiates itself not only from the body but also from these affective elements as demonstrated by the opposition of the (rational) mind and (irrational) emotion. While the *kokoro* can get excited through psychobiological combustion, the mind is supposed to remain cool. In other words, the *kokoro* as the embodied mind is fundamentally different from the Western mind.

The *kokoro*, when metaphorically associated with internal organs, is located in the chest, and more specifically in the "heart." There is a reason then why the *kokoro* is linked to the blood, which in Japanese discourse can translate into racial genes, as discussed above. In a weekly TV program (1990), showing several Peruvians of Japanese ancestry, the emcee, emotionally moved, commented, "Even though we, the two peoples (Japanese and Peruvians), do not understand each other's language, we share the same blood and therefore can get out our *kokoro* to reach one another." The connection between the *kokoro*, physical heart, blood, and racial genes is, needless to say, one of cultural assumptions which are taken as natural.

Hara is another word for the embodied mind which is physically located in the lower part of the belly. Like the *kokoro*, the *hara* refers to a person's inner state of mind, disposition, emotion, or intention, which is described as "big *hara*" (aloof from trivial matters), "*hara ga tatsu*" (upsetting the *hara*, that is, angry), and so on (Lebra, 1976, pp. 159-60). The *hara* in this symbolic sense is dissociated from the digestive system and instead regarded as the vital center of the body-mind. Further, as such, the *hara* is the focal point of concentration in controlled breathing for "abdominal respiration" and thus appropriates the function of lungs. It is interesting to see a close association of *kokoro* and *hara* as between blood and breath.

This respiratory function of the *hara* reminds us of another key term, *ki*. *Ki* (or its compound nouns like *kimochi*, *kibun* [both meaning mood or feeling], *kiryoku* [spiritual power]) also overlaps *kokoro*, for the two words are often used interchangeably. And yet, *ki* is even more multiple, amorphous, and less definable by the English system of categorization, as illustrated by Rohlen (1976, pp. 130-31). In *ki* the mind and body are even more permeable than the *kokoro* or *hara*. This characteristic of *ki* derives from the fact that it is not located in an internal organ but rather identified with *kitai* (gas) and air which, with all its kinetic property, circulates throughout a person's body-mind. Further, as air, *ki* moves into and out of the person as through inhalation and exhalation. Ideally, it is the *hara* as the center of abdominal respiration that is in charge of *ki* movement. This cultural trope of *hara-ki* complex so captivated McKim Marriott's (1992) imagination that he labeled the Japanese model of social science discourse "aerodynamic," distinct not only from the Western analytical model but from the Hindu "hydrodynamic" and the Moroccan "photodynamic" model (see Rosenberger 1989 for a kinetic analysis of *ki*).

Seishin, commonly translated as "spirit," is another term related to *kokoro*. If it is possible to line up these terms along the mind-body continuum, *seishin* may be placed at the mind pole, probably because *seishinryoku* (spiritual power) is evoked in order to transcend the bodily constraint or crisis. For the wartime generation, *seishin* is associated with the slogan, "*Seishin itto nanigoto ka narazaran*" (For the concentrated spirit nothing is impossible). For younger generations as well, it is common to attribute a hard-won success such as winning an athletic race despite a physical handicap to *seishinryoku* as the ultimate explanation. The English "mental" is usually translated as *seishin*, such as *seishinbyo* for mental illness. Nevertheless, even the *seishin* cannot be equated with the disembodied mind because it is driven by concentrated "energy." Among many meanings of the first character *sei* is virility, *seishi* being sperm.

If the mind is embodied, the body is minded. Here it is instructive to consider the word *mi*, which is at the body end of the above continuum. Cousins (1990) cites Ichikawa (1984), the author of *Mi no kozo* (The structure of *Mi*), to underscore his argument on the Japanese non-Cartesian epistemology. This term, as Ichikawa analyzes it, denotes the physical body at one level of usage but contains psychological, cultural, social meanings as well. While nutritional food, for example, enters and "sticks to *mi*" (*mi ni tsuku*) as a physiological body, learning, knowledge, or skill sticks to *mi* as a "cultural body" (Ichikawa, 1984, p. 45). *Mi* as an intricate, unbounded complex of self which combines spirit and body, mentation and sensation, the conscious and unconscious, and literal and metaphorical, is not a fixed entity but a "relational unity" which emerges out of involvement with other (persons or things). As such, *mi* is as multiple as these relations are, and forms a vulnerable unity open to constant reintegration including a dramatic self-transformation as when one cleanses one's body (*kessai*), just before engaging in a sacred ritual, in order to attain a supramundane status (1984, p. 47). Ichikawa thus illustrates how *mi* merges with the above terms like *seishin*, *kokoro*, and *ki*. In the *mi* concept, he finds a clue to going beyond the Cartesian metaphysics. Ichikawa takes a universalist viewpoint that his concept of *mi* holds not only for Japanese but across cultures, yet I think the striking novelty of his contribution is indebted to his native culture, to the extent that it reveals his own culture.

The spiritual status of the body (*mi*) is captured in a poem of a martial art school, quoted and translated by Dann (1978, p. 36):

> The body is a shrine
> Where the omniscient mind resides
> It's folly
> To worship elsewhere
> (*Mi wa yashiro, kokoro no kami no, aru mono wo, soto wo inoru wa, oroka nari keri*).

The translation of "*kokoro no kami*" (*kami* meaning a spirit or god) as the omniscient mind is problematical, but the poem as a whole conveys the body being sublimated to the sacred stature of a shrine. (The woman's body, or more specifically, *hara*, is identified as her womb, which is called *shikyu*, shrine for a child.)[4] But only a shrine, one might wonder, not a sacred being itself? Is the body nothing more than a place, vessel, or container of a *kami*, after all? It should be remembered that the *kami* remains hidden forever, and that all the worshiper can see is the physical structure of a shrine or an object symbolic of a *kami* (*shintai*, namely, the *kami* body) like a mirror, a piece of stone or paper. The result is a deification of the shrine itself or identification of a shrine as the *kami* enshrined, so that devotees find themselves affected by some mystic forces when they pass through the shrine gate, enter the shrine compound, and stand in front of the shrine structure.

In his discussion on *kendo*, swordsmanship, in the context of Japanese "martial culture," Dann mentions *koshi*, another untranslatable word, which together with the *hara* comprises "the physical map of the central torso region." While the *hara* "is located in the anterior lower torso," the "*koshi* is the posterior section comprising the lower back, buttocks and loins."[5] Obviously, the *koshi* is more physical, less spiritual, than the *hara*, and yet its "psychosomatic" potentials are illuminated by the way the word *koshi* is used. "Thus, to 'put *koshi* into . . .' (*koshi o ireru*) means to become earnest. To have a 'strong *koshi*' means one is strong willed while one with a '*weak koshi*' lacks determination. A Person with a '*pulled koshi*' (*koshinuke*) is 'gutless' or 'spineless'" (1978, pp. 140-41).

Unlike the heart (*kokoro*), belly (*hara*), body (*mi*), and even the posterior torso (*koshi*), the head (*atama*) does not take part in the Japanese spiritual anatomy. In fact, the head tends to connote something negative, Ichikawa (1984, p. 43) notes, as exemplified by *"atama de wakaru"* (understand through the head) implying the limited, superficial understanding. Again we should consider the Western anatomy where the head or brain is unquestioned as the primary focus of the Western mind, other parts of the body being either irrelevant to or disruptive of mentation. For the Japanese, sources of spiritual potency are located below the neck, in abdominal organs like *hara* or *kimo* (liver), or even around the buttocks. The insignificance of the head in the spiritual body may offer one of several possible explanations for the Japanese resistance to recognizing the brain death as a real death, and consequently to the idea of organ transplantation .

A certain inner state such as sincerity is said to manifest in externally visible signs such as eyes, and conversely, external forms like etiquette, posture, or attire are regarded as important aspects of discipline because they penetrate and shape up the inner state of self. It is no coincidence, then, that religious discipline, called *shugyo* or *gyo*, to improve one's spiritual condition consists primarily of bodily deprivation (fasting, cold bath in winter, fire walk, etc.), strenuous physical work and motion, and repetitive action, which appear to be mindless. We can also understand in the same light the primacy of *kata*, physically presentable forms or patterns, in Japanese esthetics, particularly in performing arts. *Kata* must be learned by stage actors through assiduous training in curbing and correcting the natural body state until the inner feelings can be directly expressed through particular *kata* forms of the body. Learning in general has body implications. The best way of learning something is, Japanese say, through the body, not with the brain. The traditionally ideal way of learning is *"mi ni tsukeru"* (to assimilate into the body).

Yuasa (1977) provides a philosophical background for the importance of the body in the Japanese selfhood. Japanese philosophical tradition, as represented by scholars like Watsuji Tetsuro and Nishida Kitaro, while strongly influenced by European intellectual traditions, has challenged the Cartesian dualism of mind and body. Watsuji, who characterized the human existence as *aidagara* (relationship between persons, or intersubjectivity), was bound to realize the priority of "space" in which *aidagara* is located. This spatial focus amounts to the rejection of the Cartesian emphasis upon "time," the flow of which is essential to the operation of the autonomous mind. The primacy of space over time, in Yuasa's interpretation, implies the recognized significance of the body, or the indivisibility of body and mind, of flesh and soul. While the mind itself can be conceptualized through time alone, the body-mind must be situated in space.

It may be summed up that all the points made here regarding the Japanese self, in contrast to the Western counterpart—terms for self, the socially encumbered self, rebirth, the blood, body and mind, and the spatial emphasis—are of a piece. It may be that Western individualism is a product of the disembodied mind free from the spatial and relational dimension. The disembodied mind is communicated best or even exclusively through digital signs, namely, words, whereas the embodied mind relies upon analogic and somatic signs as well. How often we hear Japanese refer to something "beyond words," something "indescribable with mere words"! For Japanese, words are not only inadequate in substituting for a rich reality of feeling and experience, but serve to mask and falsify the truth. Silence, then, emerges as a fully meaningful, communicative act, as will be shown below.

CONVERSATIONAL FEATURES

Turning around the self/communication circle, we ask how the above differences in selfhood influence communication styles. Or conversely, what communication styles presuppose or reinforce the above self-concepts? It is no coincidence that scholars in Japanese linguistics have paid much attention to what is called *taigu hyogen* because this category of speech patterns is most expressive of the socially loaded weight of the Japanese self as described above. *Taigu hyogen* refers to a wide category of linguistic devices to express a sense of psychological, social distance or closeness held by the speaker toward the listener and third persons referred to in conversation (Ide, 1982, p. 111). Involved here is linguistic variation along the degrees or levels from formal to informal, respectful to familiar, polite to intimate, humble to arrogant, indirect to blunt, etc. The same information takes different forms of *taigu hyogen* in accordance to variable conversational settings. A simple verb like "came" for example is worded variably as *kita, kimashita, irasshatta, irasshaimashita, oideninarimashita,* in an increasing order of politeness. In a sense, every conversational discourse may be said to be a mode of *taigu hyogen,* and if so the following selection of conversational features may well be taken as forms of *taigu hyogen.*

Fragmentation and Interruption

Based on a sample of taped audiovisual conversational discourses, Senko Maynard (1989) delineates major features of Japanese speech behavior. Fragmentation of a spoken discourse is one such characteristic. One discourse is fragmented into phrases and smaller units which are marked by certain tones or slowed-down speed which signal pauses (p. 24). The pauses are meant to elicit responses from the listener. The highly fragmented conversational discourse, then, entails the speaker's frequent insertion of pauses before a discourse-completion to invite the listener so many times to interrupt or participate. Along with fragmentation, the use of final particles (such as *ne, nee, na, yo, sa, saa*) and fillers—propositionally vacuous utterances "to fill a potential silence" (p. 30)—is to facilitate monitoring and appealing to the listener's feeling, and thus establishing and maintaining rapport, as well as to show the speaker's hesitancy or uncertainty in expressing him/herself. Fragmentation, together with fillers, allows the speaker to pay no attention to the word order. A conversational discourse, if transcribed out of context, therefore makes little sense to its reader.

How does the listener interrupt? If the conversation is carried on in a friendly or polite manner, then the listener will respond with supportive feedback called *aizuchi* (backchanneling), often accompanied by head movement. Maynard found that Japanese conversational partners backchannel more than twice as frequently as American partners. This difference reminds us of the familiar misunderstanding in American/Japanese conversation: the American speaker's annoyance at the noisy, untimely backchanneling by the Japanese listener (mis)taken as rude and insensitive, and the Japanese speaker's bewilderment and discomfort at the American listener's refusal to backchannel at expected moments, which is taken as a sign of indifference or hostility. The Japanese speaker welcomes such interruptions and invites them by means of frequent pause signals.

The literal translation of such a fragmented conversational discourse would then make no sense, but let me offer an example to convey Maynard's point. I want to say, "Professor Hayashi was talking intimately with Yuriko-san at that coffee shop around the corner." Yuriko's classmate, if talking to another classmate, might say, "*Nee, nee, hora* (Listen) *asoko ni* (over there) *aru-desho* (you know where?), *kado no tokoro ni* (around the corner) *sa, kissaten* (the coffee shop) *ne,* Hayashi *Sensei* (Professor Hayashi) *ttara nee, hanashiteta no* (was talking) *yo, Yurikosan to* (with Yuriko) *sa, ikanimo shinmitsusoo ni* (in a very intimate manner) *yo.*" Pause-signaling particles or attention-calling fillers are included to make the statement conversational. This line of utterances would sound ridiculous even to a Japanese listener if taken as one person's continuous speech. It sounds natural only if fragmented words or phrases are connected through the listener's interruptions into a jointly produced conversation.

This characterization of the Japanese conversation (to be distin-guished from formal speech-making which will be touched upon below) exactly matches the notion of self as socially loaded and situ-ated. The Japanese self is a communicative process itself in that without self-other communication there will be no self to be presented. Com-munication here refers to the mutual, reciprocal, empathetic process of "turn-giving" (rather than -taking) between conversational partners, involving not only propositional statements but, more importantly, responsive utterances and nonvocal signs. Self is expressed through the self-other "co-production" (Maynard, 1989) of conversation. When nonvocal signs are unavailable as in telephone conversation, vocal turn-taking such as interruption with *aizuchi* becomes that much more frequent and louder. This is for the listener to buttress the turn-giving speaker.

The Listener Role

It is difficult, then, to maintain conversational style without some lis-tener immediately interrupting vocally or at least visibly. Smith (1983, pp. 76-77) noted the key role of the listener. In television appearance, the speaker is accompanied by a *kikite*, listener-role player. Smith calls atten-tion to this Japanese practice in light of speech levels indicative of the speaker's higher, senior status supported by the inferior status of the *kikite*, usually a young woman. We can also see in this speaker-listener arrangement a social device to produce a conversational speaker while addressing the public viewers who are not in the immediate feedback circuit. Newscasters are also paired, usually male and female, so that the listening party backchannels the speaker to reduce the kind of stiff for-mality which would accompany a solo newscaster.

Is such a speaker-listener arrangement missing from American television programs? Certainly not. But the American listener, as far as I can judge, does not remain a listener making supportive and agreeable utterances only, but takes a more active role as an interviewer, ques-tioner, challenger, or debater. In other words, there tends to be turn-tak-ing between speaker and listener. (Television culture is constantly changing, and today's Japan has similar television programs, though of a milder version, which attract large audiences because of their nov-elty.)

The importance of the listener role is underscored by Patricia Clancy (1986) who rightly points out that "Japanese communication style places the main burden for successful communication upon the listener" (p. 220). The child is compulsively trained by his or her mother in playing the listener role well. If the child remains unresponsive to a question, request, or signal of friendly interaction from a speaker, Clancy observed, his or her mother is likely to insist on his or her making a proper response by repeating the speaker's demand until he or she responds. I have observed in a nursery school two-year-old children being taught to say, "Good morning," in response to the teacher's greeting. When one child was inattentive, an assistant teacher pushed down the child's head to the table to extract a bow out of the child while she was uttering "Good morning, good morning" on the child's behalf.

While the speaker is expected, particularly in making a request, declining a request, or saying no, to be so subtle, indirect, or cautious as to avoid overburdening or offending the listener, the latter is encouraged to be immediately responsive and articulate. In contrast to the heavy training in listener-responsiveness among Japanese, the American training, to my knowledge, is more focused on the speaker role, on smooth, articulate self-presentation.

PARADOXES IN COMMUNICATION

The foregoing characterization of self and communication in Japan has been more or less straightforward, and the Japanese-American contrast has seemed unproblematical. In this section, I look into a more problematical, seemingly contradictory aspect of Japanese communication style. This is my response to recent criticisms, which range from silly to noteworthy or from naive to sophisticated, targeted at Japanology in general, at allegedly stereotypic views of Japanese, and more specifically, at the chauvinistic, "fascist" claim of Japanese "uniqueness" attributed to Japanese authors. All these are lumped together under the ill-defined term, "*nihonjinron*," discourses on the Japanese (for a review of *nihonjinron* controversies, see Kelly, 1988). As characteristics of Japanese, the critics counterpose, for example, individualism to groupism, selfishness to altruism, egalitarianism to verticalism, confrontation and dissension to harmony and consensus, heterogeneity to homogeneity, universality to uniqueness, and so forth. Since these counterarguments cannot be dismissed entirely, I attempt to locate subtle paradoxes as a way of reconciling the oppositions. In final analysis I argue that exclusionary dichotomies, as implied in debates of *nihonjinron* versus counter-*nihonjinron*, are to be deconstructed.

Empathy: Other-Centered or Self-Centered?

The conversational features, as singled out in the previous section, whether of the speaker or listener, could be understood in light of conventional forms of empathy. Indeed, empathy underlies a diversity of modes of speech and behavior among Japanese including indirection, *enryo* (self-restraint out of considerateness toward others), evasiveness, circumspection, humility, apology, and probably *taigu hyogen* in general. The most direct expression for empathy is to "become another's *mi*," (*aite no mi ni naru*), and the most common idiom for empathy is *omoiyari*. These are so well known that I do not have to elaborate. I do want to point out, however, that empathy is a feature not of conversational attitude alone, but of linguistic structure as well, which is a source of trouble for translators.

According to Susumu Kuno (1986), Japanese is "a language which, in many cases, forces the speaker to make clear from whose point of view he or she is speaking" (p. 110). Taking such a point of view requires various forms of the speaker's empathy with other(s). This is best exemplified by verbs signifying transfers of objects between two persons, such as giving and lending. I paraphrase Kuno's insightful observation as follows. Let us take simple forms alone in disregard of various levels of politeness typical of *taigu hyogen* as discussed earlier. Still the speaker must choose either *yaru* or *kureru* for "give." The speaker S chooses *yaru* if S empathizes more with the giver G than with the receiver R of an object, but switches to *kureru* if S empathizes with R more. If S happens to be G or R, S is constrained in the choice of these verbs for the same reason: in this case, S naturally empathizes most with him/herself, S as G must describe his/her action as *yaru*, not as *kureru*, while *kureru* must be chosen in the case of S being R. In other words, it is difficult for a Japanese speaker to say "give" in an empathy-neutral, objective manner. The same empathy-bind accompanies the verb for "lend." Lend as a neutral form is *kasu*, and yet in speech it is combined with *yaru* or *kureru* to differentiate the focus of the speaker's empathy. If S empathizes more with the lender, then *kasu* becomes *kashite-yaru*; if the borrower is empathized with, the compound-form is *kashite-kureru*. Through this and many other differentiations in verbs, the speaker conveys his/her empathetic affect, which escapes translation.

Empathy can merge with interpersonal vulnerability or susceptibility. Here again I focus on speech. Japanese speakers often use passive forms of verbs in a way quite different from the English passive voice, which is no more than a grammatical transformation of the active voice.

The difference between the English and Japanese passivization can best be illustrated by the fact that, while English passivization is limited to transitive verbs, the Japanese counterpart is extended to intransitive verbs. This difference suggests that Japanese passivization involves much more than just a grammatical transposition of subject and object. "*Kodomo ni nakareta*," and "*Otto ni shinareta*" mean "My child cried," and "My husband died" respectively. Cry (*naku*) and die (*shinu*) are intransitive verbs which cannot be passivized in English but in the Japanese original they are both passivized as "*a-reta*."

Agnes Niyekawa (1968) calls this type of passive form the "adversative passive" in that it connotes the subject of the passivized verb being "adversely affected" (p. 6). Through passivization, the speaker is conveying, in other words, the mother's feeling perturbed by her child's cry, or the wife's suffering from her husband's death. Niyekawa adds another variety called the "passive causative" in which the subject feels "caused to" do something by someone else (who may or may not be identified). Thus *yomu* (read) and *kaku* (write), for instance, are reworded as *yom-a-sareru* (caused to read) and *kak-a-sareru* (caused to write), when an English speaker would say, "have to read," or "have to write." Very clearly, such causative passivization enables the actor (reader, writer here) to convey the feeling that his/her action is involuntary and is forced (by someone).

Niyekawa (1968) associates both types of passivization with "adversity," unpleasant, unwelcome experience. This association holds true in many cases, but not always. I can see in the examples of *nakareru/nakareta*, and *shinareru/shinareta* (cry/cried, die/died) a close bond of empathetic identification of mother with child, wife with husband, such that what happens to one affects the other in deep emotions. In other words, empathy entails psychological vulnerability and dependency. My reservation regarding adversity derives from examples which do not involve any unpleasant feelings but rather appreciations and gratefulness. When I say *ikasareru* rather than *ikiru* (live), I am expressing my appreciations to someone, human or supernatural, for letting me live, implying I alone would not be able to live.

Passivity expressive of empathetic vulnerability thus resonates with expressions of the self's incompleteness as a causal agent which necessitates help from, dependence upon, and indebtedness to, others. These feelings, culturally endorsed, crystallize into a polite causative form with *itadaku* (a polite form of "receive" from the receiver's point of view). For example, *manabu* (study) becomes *manabasete itadaku* (am caused to study [by benefactor X]); *tanoshimu* (enjoy) becomes *tanoshi-*

masete itadaku (am caused to enjoy [by X]). (For more extraordinary examples of causative-passives observed in a religious cult, see Lebra, 1986, p. 360.)

These features of speech maximize the impact of other as the focus of empathetic attention, as a source of emotional influence upon self, or as a causal agent to overcome self's incompleteness. They negate the autonomy of self and play up other-centeredness. But do they? Is it not true that these expressions can be reinterpreted as very indicative, instead, of the speaker's striking self-centeredness? Take another look at the empathy-bound differentiation of *kureru* and *yaru*, for instance. Empathy here implies the speaker's own point of view which alone determines the camera focus either on the giver or receiver, and without which one cannot describe the transaction, simply as an objective fact. Likewise, passivization and causation reflect an extraordinary degree of self-centered, subjective reading of situations. What is central here is the speaker's own feeling toward others. The passives in these examples signal the subject's or speaker's (in empathizing with the subject) "psychological unfolding" (Yamashita, 1986, p. 234) in a subtle manner which cannot be well captured by English translations.

I argue that the same speech structure can place self at the periphery or at the center of communicative context, because self and other are relative to each other so that other-centeredness translates into self-centeredness and vice versa. Self and other are, then, like two sides of a coin, and alternate in taking the front and back role. What is missing is the imaginary objective speaker who does not depend upon the listener and who does not have to adjust his/her speech to constantly changing communicative settings. Looked at this way, we can better understand why Yamashita (1986) insists upon self-centeredness or subjectivity as the main feature of Japanese. It is also understandable that Niyekawa (1968) stresses the selfish side of the Japanese use of "passive" or "passive-causative" in that these forms allow their users to attribute unpleasant outcomes or responsibility to others.

The issue extends beyond the linguistic field over to the social psychology of self and other or the conception of social environment. Yamashita correctly points out that, unlike *sekai* (world) and *shakai* (society) which are more or less objective, situation-free terms and thus easy to translate, a more culturally loaded and untranslatable word like *seken* refers to a psychological world defined by each self and around self from the self-centric point of view (1986, pp. 180-81). In self's view, *seken* consists of an unbounded group of people, visible and invisible, who surround and watch self's conduct. The self-centeredness of the *seken* concept may be underscored by substituting *mawari* or *shui* for it, both meaning "surrounding" and equivalent to *seken*. The point is that these terms, while indicative of each person's self-centered orientation, connote the oppressiveness, at the same time, of the surrounding social environment equipped with its eyes, ears, and mouth. The Japanese sensitivity to the *seken*'s sharp eyes and the *mawari*'s whisper entails both an egocentric concern for self-esteem and an allocentric readiness for conformity like two sides of a sheet of paper. The self-centeredness of *seken* or *mawari* is thus translatable into other-centeredness, but not into an autonomous, independent, or implacable individual. The latter is more likely to be a product of a culture where self-centeredness is rooted in the objective, unsituated, constant self like the English "I." We are back to the different modes of subjectivity and objectivity, which in turn relates to terminological difference in self-references with which this paper started.

Self-Presentation: Wrapped or Opened Up?

Closely linked to the empathy paradox is another one that centers around the question, which of the two speakers, American or Japanese, discloses his/herself more in communication? The answer seems obvious. Given the kind of self described above, the American speaker is likely to disclose him/herself more openly and explicitly than the Japanese speaker. We have already noted that the American speaker assumes a greater responsibility for communication than the Japanese speaker relative to the listener's responsibility. For Americans, communication is primarily for the speaker to make his/her message clearly understood and hopefully accepted by the listener or message-addressee, and for the latter to respond for the same purpose from his/her own point of view. As Dean Barnlund (1975) observed, the American self appears more ready for "self-disclosure" in communication with others, less defensive in holding itself in privacy, than the Japanese self.

To reinforce this observation, a brief return to Maynard (1989) is in order. She offers a cogent argument that the Japanese conversational features contribute toward "social packaging" which "is a socially motivated act to construct the content of the utterance in such a way as to achieve maximum agreeableness to the recipient. Just as packaging a product hides the content in visually pleasing form, frequent use of final particles and fillers help hide the message, delaying and softening its delivery" (p. 31).

The metaphor of "packaging" translates, in Joy Hendry's (1990) term, into "wrapping" as a principle of social ordering. Under this term, the author encompasses a wide range of communicative symbols and signs which have caught many observers' attention: elaborate gift-wrapping whether candy, tea, or any other gift-object; body wrapping as in the ancient court dress, *junihitoe*, literally meaning "twelve-layered" dress for court ladies; linguistic wrapping like *keigo* (honorifics), space wrapping by architectural design drawing boundaries between interior and exterior, etc. For the last item, I would like to call special attention to the shrine structure which locates the god's residence in the innermost space, and assigns human individuals according to their status or "purity" to the inner or outer space as a place for worshipping. That is, the higher the person, the more entitled to enter the interior section, to come closer to the god and thus to be wrapped up like the god. Sacred objects including symbols of gods are typically wrapped in many layers of cloth and preciously placed in wooden boxes.

I believe that like Maynard's (1989) social packaging, Hendry's (1990) wrapping throws light exactly upon self and communication. It is safe to say that the Japanese nonassertive, hesitant communication style is a device to wrap up the self which in turn demands such a communication style. The American self, by comparison, is "disclosed" through an open communication style of display. It is as if the selves in both cultures imitate the images of their respective gods: one being the wrapped-up, invisible, inaccessible symbol of a god residing behind the innermost screen of a shrine, and the other, the image of Christ on cross displayed on the church wall to be seen by all the worshippers in attendance, or God manifested in biblical words.

The only question that remains to be answered is why the communicationally sensitive, socially contextualized Japanese self, open to the listener's interruption, is less communicative than the American self. We then realize that communication or self-disclosure is usually understood as verbal/vocal, and that the above discussion has followed this convention in disregard of other ways of recognizing communication. It seems that communicational competence or mode means two different things for Americans and Japanese: the ability to speak in an articulate, coherent manner for Americans, and the ability to send, receive, or anticipate subtle, unstated messages for Japanese. Silence may be dismissed as uncommunicative by Americans, but is a significant mode of communication for Japanese. It is as communicative for Japanese as pauses and fillers are, or as signs and gestures are. In an earlier study (Lebra, 1987), I delineated a fourfold significance of silence: (a)

truthfulness or sincerity credited to the silent speaker or to the unex-
pressible inner state of the self, in contrast to deceptiveness attributed to
the spoken word or to the glib talker; (b) discretion or caution to gain
social approval or to avoid social penalty; (c) embarrassment inhibitive
of verbalizing true feelings in intimate relationship as in love; (d) defiance or outright expression of hostility through silence, which is
resorted to more by the status-inferior. Such multivocality of silence is
subject to misunderstanding even between Japanese, which accounts for
their ambivalence toward silence and reticence. The point here is that
silence is a semantically rich resource for communication.

The cultural significance of silence in Japanese communication
reflects the continuity of mind and body as analyzed above. If the body
is as much part of the self as the mind, "body language" should be integrated into the communicational repertoire. Indeed, Ichikawa's (1984)
concept of *mi* holds the spoken part of self only as the tiny tip of a huge,
unspoken iceberg. The opposite is true with the American self and
American mode of communication. Here, precisely because the self is
socially unsituated and unencumbered and because it is encapsulated in
the disembodied and invisible, verbal articulation is essential to communication.

Bodily communication is culturally perfected in *kata*, fixed forms
of aesthetic expression, best exemplified by performing arts such as the
noh drama, *kabuki*, Japanese dance. From Brandon's (1978) categorization of *kata* for the *kabuki* theater we can infer how minute and yet
encompassing *kata* can be: it ranges from performance styles to vocal
kata and sound effects to make-up, costumes, and staging. Whether or
not the word *kata* is used, the *kata* concept prevails in many other styl-
ized performances and representations such as the tea ceremony, flower
arrangement, music, poetry, calligraphy, painting, and the martial arts.
Further, Befu (1986) gives a sensitive analysis of dinner entertainment
which is conducted acording to the unwritten scenario involving the
implicit protocol for host-guest interaction. He is actually illustrating the
kata of etiquette. Spoken discourses under these circumstances tend to
be either informationally devoid, or to be understood as not really
meant, which may outrage a misled foreigner (Naotsuka et al., 1981).

The *kata*, like silence or other unspoken signs, thus provides a cultural means of communication. In this context, it may be noted that
Thomas Kasulis, characterizing the Japanese religious orientation in
terms of "intimacy," defines *kata* as "the somatic enactment of fixed
patterns or forms connected to intellectual, psychological, and affective states." Particularly notable is "the somatic enactment," which ties

in with Kasulis's notion of intimacy involving the somatic relationship (1990, pp. 438-39). It may be further noted that the best way of learning for Japanese is a somatic one. The somatic nature of *kata* is best manifested in its learning. In somatic pedagogy, *kata* is taught and learned through modeling and imitating in a teacher-pupil dyadic contact instead of verbal instructions and communication.

To sum up the foregoing, nonverbal/vocal modes of communication, whether silence, pause, fillers, signs, gestures, or *kata*, are indicative of the uncommunicative, wrapped-up self from the point of view of verbal/vocal cultures; whereas these are important vehicles of communication or self-disclosure in a culture where the spoken word is only a portion of communicative repertoire.

Is wrapping for self-defense? Barnlund (1975) does talk about the Japanese defensiveness, and perhaps many Americans see (or project) such defensiveness in the Japanese self-withholding. It is by questioning this preconception that we begin to unravel what is hidden behind the "wrapped-up" Japanese self. Here I draw upon Cousins' findings on social phobia in Japan and the West, the United States in particular. First it should be pointed out that social phobia had not been recognized as a mental disorder until the 1970s in Western psychiatry (Cousins, 1990, p. 113), whereas the Japanese counterpart, *taijinkyofusho*,[6] has long been identified, diagnosed, treated, and researched. As expected, symptoms also differ. One of the differences, perceived by Cousins, is interestingly demonstrative of the Cartesian versus non-Cartesian self or the unsituated versus situated self. *Taijinkyofusho*, unless it is a severe case, is situation-specific so that the fear of eye contact or blushing, for example, is aroused only in certain places (e.g., during a bus ride), in certain interaction settings such as in copresence with nonintimate peers but not with a superior or family. But the American social phobic is more context-free, and the symptom is carried across different situations. It is not particular situations but specific "activities" that are feared by the American patient (Cousins, 1990, p. 199). This leads to another difference which is more relevant to the present context.

Western social phobia is characterized by fear of the loss of control, of failure, of being seen as weak and incompetent, which is bound to arouse shame. Success or failure in performance, such as "meeting people in authority, public speaking, eating out, writing in public, urinating in a public lavatory" (Cousins, 1990, p. 205) are central to the Western phobic, but peripheral to Japanese patients. More central to the latter is the fear of eye contact, blushing, facial expressions—problems rare or practically nonexistent among Western patients. Put another way, one culture focuses on what the patient does voluntarily, the other on what he is or looks like involuntarily. Western social phobics, then, are likely to suffer from inhibition anxiety, and Japanese counterparts to suffer from the involuntary leakage of the self. The latter symptom was identified by Kasahara Yomishi (quoted in Cousins, 1990, p. 210) as that of "egorrhea," coined from diarrhea. Egorrhea or what I might call "social incontinence" may be contrasted to the Western "social constipation" (or egopation to follow Kasahara's example of neologism). Involuntary leakage must be counteracted by wrapping. The difference goes still further.

The Japanese *taijinkyofusho* patient, with a delusionary conviction of his/her bodily defect, fears causing discomfort to others by revealing (leaking) the defect such as sharp glancing or body odor. His/her symptom, in other words, is the delusion of victimizing others or being avoided by others because of his/her anomaly. It seems such delusions are not even mentioned in *Diagnostic Symptoms Manual-III*. If the Western social phobia is more shame-oriented, the Japanese *taijinkyofusho* is more guilt-oriented, contrary to the conventional understanding (see also Lebra, 1983).

Assuming this observation to be accurate, we can infer from it that social packaging or wrapping is not simply for self-defense to avoid shame or embarrassment, but more importantly, not to hurt others by an overdisclosure of self. I am not suggesting that we should rule out the self-defensive shame complex but rather that it should be balanced against the other-protective, empathy-motivated, guilt complex. Cautions not to violate a protocol may be motivated as much by concerns not to upset others as by a fear of being humiliated. Here we seem to be reconfirming the same paradox that was discussed in the previous subsection concerning the self-centered and other-centered poles of empathy.

I speculate that the fear of self-exposure, glossed as egorrhea, results from the Japanese self which is embodied and visible and therefore is more likely to risk involuntary exposure than the self encapsulated in an invisible, unsituated, disembodied mind. In other words, wrapping is more necessary for the Japanese self because it is more open and perceptible to others, *seken*, and *mawari*, while verbal disclosure is more necessary for the sealed American self. The paradox is: the American self is so closed that it can afford to open up in communication, whereas the Japanese self, so exposed and subject to involuntary leakage, must be wrapped up.

There is something else to consider regarding self-wrapping. For the socially contextualized and socially filled-up self, wrapping also is relative to situations. Some situations require tight wrapping, but some other situations may demand unwrapping. Familiar idioms characterizing Japanese social behavior should be recalled here: *uchi/soto* (inside/outside) or *ura/omote* (rear/front). The Japanese self, which is free from the dichotomy of mind and body, is bound for this very reason by a sharp sense of social-space divisions like *uchi/soto* and *ura/omote*. Wrapping can be reconstrued as a boundary separating a fully disclosed and socially undressed self on the one hand, and a well-concealed and fully clothed self on the other. Here, self-disclosure is not in the same sense as meant by Barnlund (1975), but more like the exposure of the entire self, body and soul altogether (*mi o sarakedasu*), in social nudity. In American culture, such self-exposure is likely to be confined to an exclusively intimate sexual dyad formed freely by two spontaneous, obligation-free selves. In Japan, not only a sexual pair but a larger group of intimate friends in specific situations can engage in such total communication, or to put it in a better term, in "communion" (Sekine, 1990).

The two sides of the boundary are dialectically interrelated. Since unwrapping can take place or social nudity be displayed inside only, that is, within an exclusive intimate group, such behavior signals the closure of the group to outsiders. In other words, the more unwrapping inside the boundary, the more wrapping vis-à-vis the world outside the boundary, and vice versa. This dialectic gives rise to more macrolevel communication barriers. Since the communion-type interaction, unless a sexual couple is involved, usually takes place within the same sex, it tends to constitute the last fortress for male dominance and other forms of gender discrimination in work places. Furthermore, to the extent that communion is based upon what is perceived as the shared "blood," it stands in the way of "internationalization," which, as pointed out by Sekine (1990), can result only from "communication" instead of communion.

CONFESSIONAL CONCLUSION

I have tried to delineate differences between Americans and Japanese in communicational styles from the standpoint of their cultural notions of self. The self was characterized in terms of: self-reference terminology; whether the self is stuffed socially or subjectively, which leads to different criteria for subjectivity and objectivity; the two different notions of rebirth in adolescence and psychotherapy; biological tropes of self in terms of genes associated with individual uniqueness in contrast to the blood which is collectively sharable; the status of mind and body in the two cultures. I then argued that these differences in the self give rise to, and in turn are reinforced by, differences in communication styles. I characterized Japanese conversational style in terms of: fragmentation to be accommodated by interruptions; the importance of the listener role. In the last section, I looked into a more problematical area: the seemingly paradoxical double-sidedness of communication modes for both Japanese and American cultures, in an attempt to respond to the current debates in Japanese studies. Regarding the question of self-centeredness versus other-centeredness, it was concluded that these are two sides of the same coin, far from being mutually exclusive oppositions. Likewise, the self can be viewed as wrapped up or disclosed depending upon the viewer's point of view. The main purpose of this paper was to present two different paradigms underlying the Japanese and American modes of communication so that the two cultural communities might be sensitized to one another's mode.

Throughout this chapter, I have set aside the methodological problem of cultural generalizations about "Japanese" and "Americans." My final comment is thus confessional. Particularly serious is the difficulty, if not impossibility, of generalizing Americans. I am aware that cultural insiders are resistant to generalizations about their own cultures. Americans, in particular (again, I am generalizing!), while they are quite ready to draw sweeping generalizations about outsiders including Japanese, are quick to rebut any generalization made by outsiders about themselves. Japanese react in a similar but less compulsive manner. The difference here stems partly from the "cultural" pride that Americans consciously draw from the ethnic diversity of their society. Resistance to generalizations is only natural because insiders characterize themselves by difference among themselves, between, for instance, the Jewish self and the Italian other. In Japan, too, a Tokyo Japanese may find an Osaka compatriot almost alien. To ethnic and regional variations, we might add a host of other variables for both cultures: urban-rural, gender, age, class, and so on.

If research focuses on the internal variation within American culture instead of difference between American and Japanese culture, a totally different picture will thus emerge. Deborah Tannen (1985) observed a Thanksgiving dinner gathering in which she herself participated, and came up with ethnic differences in conversational style.

New York Jews stood out in many ways, including: fast pace of talk, fast rate of turn-taking, persistence in turn-taking (note not turn-giving), preference for personal stories, tolerance of simultaneous speech. By comparison the other participants whom Tannen regards as mainstream American were slower talkers, less insistent on talking, more tolerant of silence. Here one is reminded that what I was characterizing as American is more like New York Jewish and what I attributed to Japanese is more like mainstream American. In short, what I emphasized in the United States-Japan comparison is the very point that divides Americans themselves into different ethnic subcultures. I do hope, however, that once the comparative reference is shifted from internal variation to the cross-cultural one involving Japan in particular, then my argument is not too far off the mark.

I should point out that Tannen (1985) reminds us of cultural variation in evaluating talkativeness and silence, fast-paced talk and slow talk. In one culture insistence on talking is appreciated positively as a sign of involvement and enthusiasm, and silence negatively, whereas in another culture silence is understood as a gesture of politeness, talkativeness as indiscreet. In other words, discomfort may be caused by fast-paced talk and turn-taking in one speech community, and by silence or slow speech in another.

Comparing Americans with Japanese, observers tend to concur that Americans are less tolerant of silence and hence more prone to talk compulsively and to interrupt one another to forestall silence. It should be remembered, however, that a culturally salient pattern of behavior is multivocal (otherwise it would not be salient). If silence is a salient pattern, it tends to send many different messages. So silence, as a salient mode of communication in Japan, conveys multiple meanings which can be sorted out by situational contexts. It could mean a sign of sincerity and trustworthiness in one situation, and a manifestation of deliberate impression management and the lack of frankness in another; likewise, silence may signal inhibitions from and therefore substitute for verbal expressions of positive feeling like love, while it also can be expressive of strong hostility and defiance. In other words, the same behavior is understood and evaluated differently not only from culture to culture, from one ethnic group to another, but also from one interactional situation to another.

Despite all these variations, there may be the same values lying behind them, which are universally shared but conveyed by different modes of communication. Both Japanese and Americans may attach special importance to the same value, be it politeness, sociability, or empathy, but they communicate it differently. Not only differently but often in opposite ways so that total misunderstanding, more dangerous than incomprehension, can ensue (Naotsuka et al., 1981). What is the very expression of empathy for Americans may be taken as an indication of aggressiveness by Japanese, or vice versa. I have shown in this paper how the cultural notions of selfhood serve as a variable to lead the same (universal?) value to different styles of communication. This is my way of handling the issue of universalism versus relativism. I hope that comparative studies will deepen our insight into the relationship between different or oppositional modes of communication on the one hand, and basic values shared in common by different cultural groups, on the other.

NOTES

Japanese names appear with the family name first except when the order is anglicized in English-language publications. At the editor's request, this paper refers to my earlier studies extensively. While preparing this paper I was financially assisted by a University of Hawaii Japan Studies Endowment Faculty Research Award.

1. *On* refers to a moral sense of being in debt to some others, which the debtor feels pressed by a sense of *giri* (obligation) to repay.

2. *Seken* refers to a group of others who surround the self as a sort of jury, and *sekentei* is the self's social standing in the eyes of the *seken*. There is brief discussion on *seken* below.

3. The question may arise whether these Japanese therapies are applicable to non-Japanese patients. For their application to American clients, see Reynolds (1989).

4. *Tensho kotai jingu kyo*, one of the postwar new religions, is said to have been born when its female founder, Kitamura Sayo, heard a voice of a male *kami* who had entered her womb as his shrine. She thus referred to him as *hara no kami*, or simply *hara*.

5. Despite this vagueness in its location and boundary, the *koshi* is often referred to as a locus of medical disorder to underline its physical nature: "the illness of *koshi*" (*koshi no yamai*), "the pain of *koshi*." For women, the *koshi* illness often refers to gynecological disorders.

6. *Morita* therapy, mentioned above, is said to be especially suited for the treatment of *taijinkyofusho*.

REFERENCES

Aida, Y. (1970). *Nihonjin no ishiki kozo*. Tokyo: Kodansha.

Bachnik, J. M. 1986. Time, space and person in Japanese relationships. In J. Hendry & J. Webber (Eds.), *Interpreting Japanese society: Anthropological approach*. Oxford: JASO Occasional Papers No. 5.

Barnlund, D. C. (1975). *Public and private self in Japan and the United States*. Tokyo: The Simul Press.

Befu, H. (1986). An ethnography of dinner entertainment in Japan. In T. S. Lebra & W. P. Lebra (Eds.), *Japanese culture and behavior: Selected readings*. Honolulu: University of Hawaii Press.

Bellah, R. N., Madsen, R., Sullivan, W., Swidler, A., & Tipton, S. (1985). *Habits of the heart: Individualism and commitment in American life*. New York: Harper & Row.

Benedict, R. (1946). *The chrysanthemum and the sword: Patterns of Japanese culture*. Boston: Houghton Mifflin.

Brandon, R. (1978). Forms in Kabuki acting. In J. R. Brandon, W. P. Malm, and D. H. Shively (Eds.), *Studies in kabuki*. Honolulu: University of Hawaii Press.

Clancy, P. M. (1986). The acquisition of communicative style in Japan. In B. Schieffelin & E. Ochs (Eds.), *Language socialization across cultures*. Cambridge: Cambridge University Press.

Cousins, S. D. (1990). *Culture and social phobia in Japan and the United States*. Ph.D dissertation, University of Michigan.

Dann, J. L. (1978). *"Kendo" in Japanese martial culture: Swordsmanship as self-cultivation*. Ph.D dissertation. University of Washington.

Doi, T. (1971). *Amae no kozo*. Tokyo: Kobundo.

Fischer, J. L. (1964). Words for self and others in some Japanese families. *American Anthropologist, 66*, 115-126.

Galtung, J. (1971). Social structure, education structure and lifelong education: The case of Japan. In *Reviews of national policy for education: Japan*. Paris: OECD.

Hamaguchi, E. (1977). *Nihon rashisa no saihakken*. Tokyo: Nihon Keizai Shinbunsha.

Hayashida, C. T. (1976). *Identity, race and the blood ideology of Japan*. Ph.D dissertation, University of Washington.

Hendry, J. (1990). Humidity, hygiene, or ritual care: Some thoughts on wrapping as a social phenomenon. In E. Ben-Ari, B. Moeran, & J. Valentine (Eds.), *Unwrapping Japan*. Honolulu: University of Hawaii Press.

Ichikawa, H. (1984). *"Mi" no kozo* (Structure of *mi*). Tokyo: Seidosha.

Ide, S. (1982). *Taigu hyogen to danjo-sa no hikaku*. (*Taigu hyogen* and gender difference). In T. Kunihiro (Ed.), *Nichi-eigo hikaku koza. Vol. 5, Bunka to shakai* (Culture and society, Comparative studies series on Japanese and English, Vol. 5). Tokyo: Taishukanshoten.

Inoue, T. (1977). *Sekentei no kozo*. Tokyo: Nippon Hoso Shuppankai.

Kasulis, T. P. (1990). Intimacy: a general orientation in Japanese religious values. *Philosophy East & West, 40*, 434-449.

Kelly, W. W. (1988). Japanology bashing. *American Ethnologist, 15*, 172-76.

Kimura, B. (1972). *Hito to hito to no aida*. Tokyo: Kobundo.

Kondo, D. K. (1990). *Crafting selves: Power, gender, and discourses of identity in a Japanese workplace*. Chicago: University of Chicago Press.

Kuno, S. (1986). The Japanese language. In H. Stevenson, H. Azuma, & K. Hakuta (Eds.), *Child development and education in Japan*. New York: W. H. Freeman and Company.

Lebra, T. S. (1976). *Japanese patterns of behavior*. Honolulu: University of Hawaii Press.

Lebra, T. S. (1983). Shame and guilt: A psychocultural view of the Japanese self. *Ethos, 11*, 192-209.

Lebra, T. S. (1984a). Nonconfrontational strategies for management of interpersonal conflicts. In E. S. Krauss, T. P. Rohlen, & P. G. Steinhoff (Eds.), *Conflict in Japan*. Honolulu: University of Hawaii Press.

Lebra, T. S. (1984b). *Japanese women: Constraint and fulfillment*. Honolulu: University of Hawaii Press.

Lebra, T. S. (1986). Self-reconstruction in Japanese religious psychotherapy. In T. S. Lebra & W. P. Lebra (Eds.), *Japanese culture and behavior: Selected readings*. Honolulu: University of Hawaii Press.

Lebra, T. S. (1987). The cultural significance of silence in Japanese communication. *Multilingua: Journal of Cross-Cultural and Interlanguage Communications, 6*, 343-57.

Lebra, T. S. (1991). *Mother and child in Japanese socialization*. Paper presented at workshop on "Continuities and Discontinuities in the Cognitive Socialization of Minority Children," Washington, D.C.

Lebra, T. S. (1992). *Above the clouds: Status culture of the modern Japanese nobility*. Berkeley: University of California Press. (forthcoming).

Marriott, M. (1992). Alternative social sciences. In J. MacAloon (Ed.), *General education in the social sciences: Centennial reflections*. Chicago: University of Chicago Press.

Maynard, S. K. (1989). *Japanese conversation: Self-contextualization through structure and interactional management*. Norwood, NJ: Ablex.

Mead, G. H. (1934). *Mind, self, and society*. Chicago: University of Chicago Press.

Minami, H. (1983). *Nihon-teki jiga*. Tokyo: Iwanamishoten.

Nakane, C. (1967). *Tate shakai no ningen kankei*. Tokyo: Kodansha.

Naotsuka, R., Sakamoto, N., et al. (1981). *Mutual understanding of different cultures*. Tokyo: Taishukan.

Niyekawa, A. (1968). *A study of second language learning (Influence of first language on perception, cognition and second language learning: A test of the Whorfian hypothesis)*. Final Report, Project No. 3260, Contract No. OE-6-10-308. U.S. Department of Health, Education, and Welfare. Office of Education, Bureau of Research.

Passin, H. (1965). Intrafamilial linguistic usage in Japan. *Monumenta Nipponica, 21*, 97-113.

Reynolds, D. K. (1989). *Flowing bridges, quiet waters: Japanese psychotherapies, Morita and Naikan*. Albany: State University of New York Press.

Rohlen, T. (1976). The promise of adulthood in Japanese spiritualism. *Daedalus*, Spring, 125-143.

Rohlen, T. (1983). *Japan's high schools*. Berkeley and Los Angeles: University of California Press.

Rosenberger, N. R. (1989). Dialectic balance in the polar model of self: The Japanese case. *Ethos, 17*, 88-113.

Sekine, T. T. (1990). *The internationalization of Japanese education, a speculative view on the concept*. Paper presented to the Conference: Continuity and change in Japanese education, Victoria, B.C.

Smith, R. J. (1983). *Japanese society: Tradition, self, and the social order*. Cambridge: Cambridge University Press.

Suzuki, T. (1986). Language and behavior in Japan: The conceptualization of personal relations. In T. S. Lebra & W. P. Lebra (Eds.), *Japanese culture and behavior: Selected readings*. Honolulu: University of Hawaii Press.

Tannen, D. (1985). Silence: Anything but. In D. Tannen & M. Saville-Troike (Eds.), *Perspectives on silence*. Norwood, NJ: Ablex.

Tobin, J. J., Wu, D., & Davidson, D. (1989). *Preschool in three cultures*. New Haven: Yale University Press.

White, M. & LeVine, R. (1986). What is an *ii ko*? In H. Stevenson, H. Azuma, & K. Hakuta (Eds.), *Child development and education in Japan*. New York: W. H. Freeman.

Yamashita, H. (1986). *Nihonno kotoba to kokoro* (Speech and the heart of Japan). Tokyo: Kodansha.

Yuasa, Y. (1977). *Shintai: Toyoteki shinshinron no kokoromi*. Tokyo: Sobunsha.

Chapter 4

SOCIOLINGUISTIC FACTORS INFLUENCING COMMUNICATION IN JAPAN AND THE UNITED STATES

Kaoru Akasu and Kojiro Asao

The aim of the present chapter is to compare and contrast English and Japanese cross-culturally and to examine sociolinguistic factors that influence everyday interaction. We will refer to intercultural matters where appropriate.

We will employ O. Mizutani's (1982) framework as a guide to show how English and Japanese are sociolinguistically similar and different. O. Mizutani (1982) isolates six dimensions that determine the choice of forms of expression in Japanese linguistic behavior: (1) properties of a speaker; (2) property of a dyad (i)—relations of belonging; (3) property of a dyad (ii)—relations of power or social standing, that is, superior-subordinate relations; (4) property of a dyad (iii)—kinds of roles that a speaker and a hearer have to play or, in other words, rules of turn-taking; (5) message—whether it is a fact or a feeling that is expressed; (6) ingress—the extent to which the speaker enters into the hearer's territory. He points out that the framework is not meant to be exhaustive, but it covers most of the differences in the two languages. In addition to these six dimensions, we include context-dependence and interdependence.

PROPERTIES OF A SPEAKER

In this section, we address how a speaker's identity affects his or her speech. To begin, let us examine the following conversation, which was taken from *Konjikiyasha*, a masterpiece by Koyo Ozaki, a well-known novelist in the Meiji period:

"Daiyamondo!"	(A diamond!)
"Umu, daiyamondoda."	(Hm, it's a diamond.)
"Naruhodo daiyamondo!"	(Sure, a diamond!)
"Maa, daiyamondoyo."	(My, a diamond.)
"Are ga daiyamondo?"	(Is that a diamond?)
"Mitamae, daiyamondo."	(Look, a diamond.)
"Ara, maa daiyamondo?"	(Oh my, a diamond?)

It is hard to tell from the English translation which speaker is a male and which a female, but, as Kindaichi (1982) points out, that is not the case in the original Japanese. We can tell, for example, that the second line "Umu, daiyamondoda" and the sixth line "Mitamae, daiyamondo" are uttered by male speakers because we know that the interjection *umu* is used by males and also that the verb *mitamae* is an imperative form used by males. A female speaker would say *mite* instead of *mitamae*. In the same vein, it can be said that the fourth line "Maa, daiyamondoyo" and the seventh line "Ara, maa daiyamondo?" are uttered by female speakers in view of the fact that the interjection *maa* is a form used by females and that the sentence-final particle *yo* after the noun is a form used by females. We cannot always identify the sex of a speaker by the overt form of an utterance. The fifth line, for instance, "Are ga daiyamondo?" is a question that can be used by either male or female speakers. Thus, lexical items, sentence-final particles, interjections and others, as the case may be, all combine to help determine which speaker is a male and which is a female.

Kindaichi (1982, p. 36) also mentions that written Japanese helps us envisage not just the sex of the speaker but also his/her age and/or social standing. He says, by referring to the following *senryu*,[1] that Mencius can be easily envisioned as an innocent child:

Okkasan	(Mommy,
mata kosunoka to	Moving again?
Moshi ii.	says Mencius.)

The address term *okkasan* suggests that the speaker is a naive child and his or her words *mata kosunoka*, with no honorifics involved, imply bluntness. Obviously, though, the male-female distinction in language is the most salient feature of Japanese as far as Mizutani's first dimension is concerned.

The focus here is not the so-called register or stylistic variation. People do change their manner of speaking according to the situation in which they find themselves, or depending on the kind of person with whom they are talking. This happens in English and Japanese alike. The distinction in question is not this kind of variation, rather it involves a variation that is predictable, to a certain degree at least, by the sex of the speaker and this variation is not dependent on the situation.

Male/female language has long attracted the attention of a large number of scholars (e.g., Lakoff, 1975; N. Mizutani, 1982; Shibamoto, 1987; Swacker, 1975). Ide (1982) isolates sex-exclusive[2] linguistic features in Japanese that involve intonation, sentence-final particles, interjections, adjectives, personal pronouns, greetings, and so on. Indeed, there are some, though definitely not as many, such features in English as well. Examples of intonation, interjections, and adjectives are referred to as such. This is shown in Table 4.1, which is a substantially simplified version of the list that Ide (1982) provides.

TABLE 4.1
Sex-Exclusive Features

	Japanese		English	
	Male	*Female*	*Male*	*Female*
Intonation		*		*
Personal pronouns	boku, ore	atakushi		
Particles	zo, ze	wa		
Interjections	ou, yaa	ara, maa	shit	Oh, dear
Adjectives	sugee	suteki	terrific	lovely
Greetings	osu	gokigenyo		
Others		*		

* Indicates omission of relevant material.

It must be noted that English, especially American English, is not a truly egalitarian language and contains distinctions of the sort mentioned here (Jorden, 1990). It is safe to say that sex differentiation in language is a matter of degree.

Still, it may be predicted that an American learner of Japanese will have more difficulty than a Japanese learner of English as far as the learning of female speech is concerned because the American has to learn many more distinctions of this sort in Japanese. Imagine a heavy-set American man saying, "Watashi mo nihongo ga dekiru wayo" (I, too, can speak Japanese). He would certainly make himself understood, but at the same time make a laughingstock of himself in front of Japanese because the combined particle *wayo* is definitely part of female speech.

Ide (1982) notes that previous studies on sex differences in language tended to be limited to the description of sex-exclusive phenomena in intralinguistic terms. Ide and McGloin (1990) go on to say that "studies of women's language in the United States and Europe over the last two decades initially emerged in the wake of the feminist movement. . . . Most of these studies reduce such differences to questions of social power" (p. i). They add that "social and psychological factors dependent on the variable of gender in Japanese are complex and cannot be reduced to questions of power and status only" (p. ii). We contend, however, that male/female differences in language also is a reflection of differences in the roles that men and women play in society and that there are a variety of values added on to them which people choose (not) to follow. We do not believe that the differences can be accounted for merely in some intralinguistic terms.

Ide (1983) provides two plausible reasons for the fact that women use female speech in Japan: one is their social position and the other is women's nature or psychology. In brief, the former is that women are inferior in social standing, which in turn makes an implicit demand on them to be tactful or polite in conversation. The latter comes from the traditional Japanese psychology of sex differences, which assumes that the existence of women presupposes dignity and this is related to the gracefulness of female speech. Be that as it may, research into this subject matter should be based on common ground.

Jorden (1990) observes that "only recently, American English, which had been assumed to be a language in which the language of men and women was without distinction, has begun to be described as indeed having some features and patterns that are gender-related" (p. 4). It would seem easy to see why it had been so assumed when you take into consideration the fact that in English you would have to keep adding such phrases as *he said* and *the girl exclaimed* on to each utterance made in a conversation like that from *Konjikiyasha* given earlier. The use of these phrases would not be necessitated to depict a conversation in Japanese. However, Ide and McGloin (1990) point out that "studies of women's language . . . have produced hundreds of examples of gender differences in language usage" (p. i).

Other properties of speakers also influence language usage. Koku-ritsu Kokugo Kenkyujo (1981), for example, reports the results of a fairly large-scale sociolinguistic survey made in 1974 and 1975 of the language usage of residents in two of the major cities in Japan, namely, Tokyo and Osaka. It sets up such attributes as sex, age, educational background, occupation, hometown, and so on. Some of the findings are as follows: (a) there is a correlation between age and the accent patterns of certain words; (b) the less school education one has, the less *keigo* or honorifics one uses; (c) managers and white-collar workers use a wider variety of first- and second-person pronouns than students and family business helpers, and housewives use less than students.

There are two alternative forms in Japanese meaning "to be able to get up": *okirareru* and *okireru*. Sanada (1990) reports that 45 percent of residents in Osaka in their seventies use *okireru*, while 87 percent of those in their twenties use this same form. Obviously, there is a gap between the two age groups. It would seem fair to say that age is another factor of considerable significance in the choice of forms in Japanese linguistic behavior.

It is reported by such scholars as Labov (1972), Trudgill (1974), and Wolfram and Fasold (1974) that there is a clear correlation between social class and certain linguistic forms in English. Labov (1972), for example, referring to the presence or absence of a final velar for unstressed *-ing* as one of the most general sociolinguistic markers in English, has shown that the higher on the socioeconomic scale one is, the more often one pronounces the velar. McDavid (1958) made a three-way distinction among informants in describing the pronunciation, vocabulary, and morphology and syntax of speakers in a number of regions of the United States and Canada. The three social classes were (a) old-fashioned, rustic, poorly educated speakers, (b) younger, more modern, better-educated speakers, (c) cultured, well-educated speakers.

BELONGING

A second dimension that influences Japanese communication is relations of "belonging." Unlike gender, which is an inherent feature that exists in a speaker, belonging is a feature that exists in the speaker-hearer dyad.

People accommodate their speech according to the psychological distance they feel vis-à-vis their listener (Brown & Gilman, 1960; Ikuta, 1983; Peng, 1974). In parting, for instance, saying "See you" would indicate a different kind of interpersonal relation from saying "Good-bye." In French people switch from *vous* to *tu* when they feel comfortable enough about their relations to the listener. Modifying speech according to the perceived interpersonal distance is a phenomenon that is seen in every language. Yet Japanese is distinguished clearly from most other languages in the extent that it incorporates in it the psychological distance the speaker projects upon the listener.

Most languages have at least two forms of speech level: formal, which is used in speaking to strangers or to people on ceremonial occasions, and informal, which is used with people familiar to the speaker. This means that, in terms of psychological distance between the speaker and the listener, most languages distinguish two kinds of interpersonal relations.

In addition to formal and informal distances, however, Japanese incorporates the distinction of *uchi* (ingroup) and *soto* (outgroup). These concepts have been used extensively by Nakane (1973) and Doi (1973), who investigated the structure of Japanese society and the Japanese mentality. A person we think is "one of us" is a member of the ingroup. If a person is considered to be "one of them," he or she belongs to an outgroup. An ingroup is characterized by a feeling of "oneness" and thus possesses a strong sense of exclusiveness.

The notion of ingroup and outgroup is crucial to understanding not only Japanese society but also Japanese communicative behavior. O. Mizutani (1979), observing the greeting behaviors of Japanese, has demonstrated that the notion of ingroup and outgroup governs the Japanese communicative behaviors. *Ohayo* (*gozaimasu*), *Konnichiwa*, and *Konbanwa* are Japanese greetings used respectively in the morning, the afternoon, and the evening. That is what language textbooks teach us. Yet, according to O. Mizutani (1979), the problem is not as simple as it appears. Mizutani classifies the interpersonal communicative distance into four categories: a member of the ingroup, a close friend or acquaintance, a person who is not close, and a stranger. The appropriate relations in which the three forms of greetings can be used are specified in table 4.2.

O. Mizutani (1979) illustrates this point by quoting a scene from a Yasujiro Ozu film in which a boy meets his father after many years. The boy's parents have been divorced and he is in his mother's custody. It is the first time he has seen his father since his parents separated.

TABLE 4.2
Forms of Greeting

Relation/Greeting	Ohayo	Konnichiwa	Konbanwa
"Ingroup" member	Yes	No	No
Person close to the speaker	Yes	Yes	Yes
Person who is not close	Yes	Yes	Yes
Stranger	No	Yes	Yes

The boy looks up at his father and says "Konnichiwa." This greeting is effective in indicating how the two people's relations have changed during the time they lived separately. As distinct from "Ohayo," which we can use with most people, "Konnichiwa" is a greeting that cannot be appropriately used with an ingroup person like a member of the family. The father was no longer a family member to the boy when they met after several years of separation. By having the boy say "Konnichiwa" to his father, Yasujiro Ozu tactfully used this scene to indicate the change that has taken place in the interpersonal relations between them.

The ingroup/outgroup feature is not inherent in the speaker or the hearer. It exists in the dyadic relation and is thus determined by the kind of person the speaker talks to. O. Mizutani (1979) demonstrates this point by an experiment he conducted. The sidewalk on the moat of the Imperial Palace in Tokyo is a favorite place for joggers. One morning, Mizutani, wearing a sweatshirt as most joggers do, ran along the side-walk and greeted everybody he passed on the way—joggers and non-joggers alike—and recorded their responses. Ninety-five percent of the joggers responded to him by replying "Ohayo gozaimasu" or by nod-ding to him, whereas the percentage of nonjoggers who responded in the same way was forty-two.

This behavioral difference is explained by the dyadic relation between Mizutani and the people he greeted. The researcher was dressed as a jogger. The joggers Mizutani greeted regarded him as an ingroup person even though he was a stranger to them. In contrast, the commuters regarded the researcher as a member of a different group. Many Japanese visiting the United States are shocked slightly when they are greeted with "Hello!" by a stranger in a hotel elevator. The shock comes from being greeted by an outgroup person from whom a greeting is not expected.

According to Kobayashi (1986), Americans' greeting behaviors are governed mainly by the private/public distinction. For example, when an office employee sees his or her boss in the morning, he or she has the following choices of greeting: *Good morning, Hello,* or *Hi.* Which form to choose is determined by where they meet. When they meet in the office, where formal interpersonal relations operate, *Good morning* would be the most probable choice. When they meet in the shopping mall on a Saturday morning, their interpersonal relations are no longer public. In a situation like this the employee would prefer to use *Hello* or *Hi.*

The ingroup/outgroup distinction influences not only greetings but most other communicative behaviors of Japanese. The use of honorific language also is governed by this distinction. Japanese has two noun forms that correspond to *father: chichi* and *otosan,* which is an honorific variant of the former. When children talk about their father in their family, they will use *otosan.* When they talk with somebody outside their family, they have to switch to *chichi* in referring to their father. Thus the English "I'll ask Father" can be rendered in two forms in Japanese according to whom we are talking. When family members talk with each other, they will use *otosan* because their father is to be treated with deference:

Otosan ni kiite miru.   (I'll ask Father.)

However, when they talk to somebody from another family, they should use the nonhonorific form in referring to their father.

Chichi ni kiite mimasu.   (I'll ask Father.)

The person to whom they are talking is an outgroup member and thus should be treated with deference. If the speaker used *otosan* in this context, it would indicate that he or she is slighting the group the listener represents. People who keep using *otosan* in a situation like this will be regarded as immature. In order to speak Japanese, in short, we have to learn, in addition to linguistic rules, interpersonal relations that operate between the speaker and the hearer.

In contrast to Japanese, there are a number of terms to be used for addressing one's father in English: *dad, daddy, father, papa,* and so on. Atwood (1962) states that "as a familiar and affectionate term for one's father, the most prevalent is *Papa*" (p. 66). Kunihiro (1990) observes, quoting the following conversation from *Airport* by Arthur Hailey, that a child's use of *father* in addressing his or her father usually indicates that the child does not have a tender feeling toward his or her father:

> If you say so, Father.
> And stop calling me Father!
> Very well, Father. (p. 7)

The above seems to suggest that familiarity, intimacy, or solidarity has a major role to play in the choice of the address terms. It might be concluded, again, that there is a different kind of factor at work in American communicative behavior. Incidentally, Suzuki (1982) observes that an analysis of the terms used by superiors to inferiors is a more fruitful study than an analysis of those used by inferiors to superiors. It is quite customary, for instance, for children to call their superiors like father or mother by the kinship term and they rarely address them by the first name. Hence there is a limited choice of address terms. Superiors addressing inferiors, however, have a choice between name and kinship term.

POWER

We will give consideration to those phenomena that involve *joge-kankei* in this section, a Japanese phrase that literally translates into top-down relation. What it is supposed to mean is vertical, as opposed to horizontal, human relations, such as that between parents and children. It is difficult, as observed by O. Mizutani (1982), to identify what this property of verticality or horizontality constitutes. Age, status, sex, and/or other attributes may be candidates, but it varies from culture to culture and it even varies from situation to situation in a single culture. This is what makes research into verticality/horizontality complicated as well as interesting. For instance, Americans, in most cases, will not look upon their brothers and sisters as being in a vertical relation with them, whereas Japanese will. It is interesting to note that this verticality even applies to twins born into a Japanese family. One of them has to be a big brother, and the other a little brother. This is not an ephemeral difference, for it will last throughout their lifetimes. We need to pay careful attention to what constitutes verticality/horizontality in each culture.

As noted by Nakane (1967, 1973), Japan is a vertically structured society. Japanese are very sensitive to the relative order of hierarchy and, as might be expected, this is usually expressed explicitly in words. This is where *keigo* or honorifics must be considered. *Keigo* typically is used to show deference to the listener, to some third party, or to some referent related to him/her. That means that the person to whom the *keigo* is directed must be someone worthy in some way of that deference. It follows that he or she is someone higher in status. So it is a matter of great concern that Japanese are always, consciously or unconsciously, trying to figure out whether the addressee is above them or not when they meet him or her for the first time. In other words, they feel quite uncomfortable until they are sure of their relative position to the addressee.

There also are cases reported where Americans make a point of following a hierarchy of social standing. Addressing comes under this heading. Brown and Ford (1964) investigated the selection of address terms used by Americans. They demonstrated that status plays a vital role in one of the three major patterns of address, namely, nonreciprocal exchange of TLN (title with last name) and FN (first name).[3] One such example is found between employer and employee, in which case the former calls the latter, say, John and the latter in return calls the former, say, Mr. Smith. The other two patterns are the reciprocal exchange of FN and of TLN. They found that "the vast majority of all dyads in the plays exchange FN [e.g., John-Tom]. . . . Mutual TLN is most commonly found between newly introduced adults [e.g., Mr. Jones, Mr. Smith]" (Brown & Ford 1964, p. 236). This is coincident with what Neustupny (1978) showed: the type of honorifics that Japanese and English have in common is titles.

While there are expressions such as "your esteemed letter" and "my humble opinion," they do not seem to be used much in English in ordinary life (Osugi, 1982). N. Mizutani (1985) gives expressions like "Here's a very small gift for you" as examples of humble expression, but again we have to wonder if it really is status difference awareness that directs people to use expressions like this. It is indeed hard to find other expressions that Americans use according to vertical relations. We may well conclude, therefore, that the vertical dimension is not as important to Americans as it is to Japanese, though it is not entirely right to say that they pay little or no attention to it.

Americans, on the other hand, very often use such expressions as "Could you please," "May I," and "Would you like to" so as to be polite to the addressee and it seems that these fulfill the kind of function that *keigo* is supposed to have in Japanese. Lakoff (1975) proposed the following rules of politeness in order to explain this phenomenon: (1) formality: keep aloof; (2) deference: give options; and (3) camaraderie: show sympathy. Some of the rule-related examples that she gives are: The use of *carcinoma* instead of *cancer*, academic passive, and the use of titles are instances of rule 1. Related to rule 2 are hesitancy in speech, tag questioning, and hedges like "sort of." Telling dirty jokes in certain situations, colloquial language, and the use of nicknames and first names are rule 3 linked examples. We see that the expressions given above have elements of both rule 1 and rule 2. What is remarkable about this is that she listed rule 3, saying, "the third rule is sometimes said not to be part of politeness; but in American society, gestures of friendliness are certainly considered in this category" (Lakoff, 1975, p. 67). The function of rule 3 is to reduce social/psychological distance between speaker and addressee, while the other two rules function to maintain the distance perceived, a role quite similar to that of *keigo*.

Distance is basically a horizontal concept. Accordingly, we have a contrast of horizontality/verticality between American and Japanese cultures. Again it must be emphasized that this is not an absolute dichotomy. As we have already seen, there are elements of both verticality and horizontality in American English though the latter are predominant there. For Japanese, *desu* and *masu* are typical forms of *teineigo* (literally, polite words), one of the major types of *keigo*, and these forms are generally used for superiors as are the other types of *keigo*. However, they are also used, say, when speaking to strangers. Strangers are placed on a scale of intimacy, rather than one of status. Intimacy, certainly, is a horizontal notion. So elements of the two dimensions are found in Japanese as well, but in this case there is more verticality and less horizontality.

Returning to Lakoff's (1975) rules of politeness, which she suggests are universal, it would not seem groundless to assume that a different rule is prioritized in different situations and in different cultures. Our assumption is that in Japan rule 1 is generally valued the most, whereas in the United States rule 3 generally is respected the most. It is true that there are status differences found in both cultures, but Japanese regard it, really or conventionally, as being polite to respect such differences. Hence their formality. They make so much of their human relations among themselves that they let status differences determine their levels or styles of speech. Once their speech level is established, it will, in most cases, be maintained and carried over. For instance, if a company employee met his/her boss on a Sunday by chance, they would speak to each other in the same way that they did at their office. The subordinate might well use *desu/masu*, but most likely the boss would not reciprocate with the same forms. Nonreciprocity of *keigo* is to be noted here.

By contrast, Americans make so much of equality or solidarity that they try, whether really or conventionally, to be friendly to their addressee to make him/her feel like their peer. However, attention must be drawn to the fact that it is not subordinates but superiors who take the initiative to do so. Notice the reciprocity of polite expressions in the following example. It is common for a mother to say to her child, "Peter, would you mind shutting the door, please?" (Leech & Thomas, 1987, p. F13). Akizawa (1989) observes that, in an American firm, it is rude of a boss to just say, "Copy this," in asking his or her secretary to do so. He comments that the boss is expected to add at least *please*. It is not necessarily the subordinates who are expected to be tactful and use polite forms, as is the case with Japanese. Americans tend to change their levels of speech according to the situation and/or the purpose of the utterance. They are expected to be "creative" in a sense in their verbal behavior.

Keigo is not the only way that Japanese can show that the speaker is being polite to the interlocutor. As N. Mizutani (1988a) notes, Japanese people look upon being hesitant and indirect as a sign of politeness, especially so when they talk to someone in higher position. Consider the following conversation between a student and a teacher taken from N. Mizutani (1988a, p. 98):

"Ano, sensei."	(Excuse me, teacher.)
"Hai."	(Yes?)
"Oisogashii tokoro osore irimasu ga.	(I'm so sorry to trouble you when you're very busy.)
"Iya."	(No.)
"Kono sakubun no koto nandesu kedo."	(This is about my composition.)
"Hai."	(Yes.)
"Chotto naoshite itadakemasendeshoka."	(Could you take a look at it and correct it?)

A Japanese reader would read the student's deference to or humbleness before the teacher from the way that the student spoke. N. Mizutani conducted a study where she took the role of the student and reproduced this conversation in English and asked an American respondent how he felt about the student's approach. She reports that "lack of skill" was his response. This seems understandable because it is not the case that Americans are supposed to say something in a hesitant and indirect manner if they want to be polite. Straightforwardness is what counts in American culture in general. What if the Japanese student above made the request in this way? "Oisogashii tokoro makotoni osore irimasuga, watashi no kono sakubun wo naoshite itadakemasendeshoka" (I'm very sorry to trouble you when you're so busy, but could you take a look at this composition of mine and correct it?). It is not necessarily considered polite by Japanese, says N. Mizutani, to utter this sentence fluently and without a break. She adds that it might create the erroneous impression that he was a bit too aggressive.

It is predictable from the discussion hitherto that a Japanese and an American, when they meet for the first time, are likely to have mis-understandings in trying to be polite. Lakoff (1975) adduces an inter-esting episode of what happens when an American, a German, and a Japanese meet. The American is described as overly brash, familiar, and prying. The epithet used for the Japanese is cloyingly deferential. Condon (1984) lists complaints that the two peoples often make about each other. Among them are the following: Americans are too direct in asking questions, giving opinions, and poking fun; the Japanese are so polite and so cautious that you never know what they are thinking; the Japanese are conformists; the Japanese are too formal. All these com-plaints may well be attributed to the different values that Japanese and Americans assign to the same norms of behavior.

It is interesting to note that in 1988 the National Language Research Institute (Kokuritsu Kokugo Kenkyujo) launched a three-year program to develop *Kanyaku Nihongo* (Simplified Japanese). There has recently been a great increase in the number of foreign learners of Japanese. Yet there also have been a large number of people who drop out before they attain any practical level of proficiency. Simplified Japanese is a language which is designed specifically for foreign learners. In order to make it easier for them to study Japanese, modifications have been applied to the gram-matical devices of contemporary Japanese. One major feature of the pro-posed simplified Japanese is the abolishing of sentence-final honorific devices. Unlike contemporary Japanese, which exhibits elaborate hon-orifics, simplified Japanese has one single grammatical device *desu/masu*, which will be used for all interpersonal relations.

ROLE

Role is another dimension that characterizes the dyadic relations in communication. In order for communication to take place we need a speaker and a listener. The speaker and the listener assume different roles in their verbal interaction. The listener, for instance, is expected to be silent until the speaker, by intonation or some other device, gives a signal that he/she has finished his/her utterance. If the listener fails to conform to this convention, it will be interpreted as a sign of impoliteness, arrogance, and impatience. In this sense, the speaker and the listener assume roles that are defined clearly.

The relation of the speaker to the listener, however, is different in Japan and the United States In Japanese communication the listener is expected to collaborate with the speaker to complement his or her function. This is observed most clearly in the use of *aizuchi*. It might be roughly translated as "response" or "reply," but the semantic content is different. The Japanese frequently intersperse *hai, ee, un,* and other short interjectional responses in their conversation while the speaker is doing the speaking. Thus when an office employee (E) talks to his or her boss (B), their conversation will look something like this:

B: Meiji Kaisha no ken dakedo.   (About Meiji Company.)
E: Hai.   (Yes.)
B: Kino denwa ga atte.   (I got a call yesterday.)
E: Hai.   (Yes.)
B: Murayama-san kara.   (From Mr. Murayama.)
E: Ee.   (Yes.)
B: Asu niji de dookatte.   (He said, "How about two o'clock?")
E: Hai.   (Yes.)

When the employee says *hai* or *ee*, he or she is not giving an affirmative answer, but is just signaling that he or she is being attentive. What he or she is trying to say is "OK. So far I understand what you mean. Go on." These small "replies" frequently given in the middle of the speech are what the Japanese call *aizuchi*.

The frequent use of *aizuchi* typically characterizes Japanese verbal communication. N. Mizutani (1988a) counted its occurrence in a radio talk show, with the average frequency of *aizuchi* by each participant being twenty times per minute. Japanese utterances tend to be short. They speak for a length of approximately twenty syllables and then wait for their interlocutor to give a signal to proceed. Maynard (1987) counted the instances of *aizuchi* in recorded conversations both in English and Japanese. In a sixty-minute conversation there were 614 instances of *aizuchi* in Japanese, while there were 215 for English.

Recall the conversation between the student and teacher discussed in the previous section. When the student wanted to have a composition corrected by the teacher, he or she did not directly make his or her request. The student first tried to create a rapport by initiating his or her conversation with "Ano, sensei" (Excuse me, Teacher) and "Oisogashii tokoro osore irimasu ga" (I'm so sorry to trouble you when you're very busy). Notice how the student tried to avoid going straight to the point. The student waited for the teacher's *aizuchi* before moving on to the next step in their conversation.

In intercultural communication context, *aizuchi* can be a source of misunderstanding. The Japanese *hai*, which is equivalent to *yes* in English, frequently is employed for *aizuchi*. When *hai* is used for *aizuchi*, it does not mean the affirmative response. It simply means that the listener is being attentive. Thus when an American talks to a Japanese, he or she might misinterpret the Japanese's *yes* as indicating an affirmative answer. The American might even feel that the listener is interrupting the speaker. The Japanese, on the other hand, when speaking to an American, would feel uncomfortable receiving no *aizuchi* from his interlocutor.

Aizuchi is so prevalent in Japanese speech acts that it has affected the language form they use. In Japanese speech, it is rare to make a complete utterance. Most utterances are constructed so they will look incomplete. The literal English translation of the dialogue above between a boss and his assistant might look something like this:

B: About Meiji Company, and . . .
E. Yes.
B: I got a call yesterday, and . . .
E: Yes.
B: From Mr. Murayama . . .
E: Yes.
B: He said, "How about two o'clock?" and . . .
E. Yes.

When the boss talks to his or her assistant, he or she does not make a complete utterance, but indicates that he or she has more to say. That's when the assistant is expected to chime in with an *aizuchi*. If the boss made the utterance in a complete form, it would appear blunt and cold. The employee would also be uncomfortable failing to find a space to chime in with an *aizuchi*.

Japanese utterances appear to be vague and incomplete on the surface, as if the last part of the utterance is left out. Yet this is to give the listener a chance to chime in. According to Maynard (1987), who counted *aizuchi* in English and Japanese, the two languages differed not only in the number of *aizuchi* and its equivalents but also in the position where *aizuchi* appeared. In English 82.8 percent of the *aizuchi* occurred at the end of a sentence, while in Japanese the *aizuchi* that occurred in the same place was 51.0 percent.

In Japanese communication *aizuchi* often is expanded to assume a semantic content. It often happens in Japanese communication that the speaker hesitates or stops in the middle of his or her sentence and lets the interlocutor complete the rest. When this happens, the distinction between the speaker and the listener disappears and it is hard to determine who is doing the speaking. It is as if two people were jointly creating a single utterance. N. Mizutani (1988b) calls this "*kyowa*" or concurrent speaking. The next dialogue is from Yoji Yamada's film *Otoko wa Tsuraiyo*. Sakura, a young housewife, is talking to Kyoko, her female acquaintance, about her family:

Kyoko:	Sakura-san no goryoshin wa?	(Your parents?)
Sakura:	Mo tokkuni inaino.	(Are dead. So I was
	Dakara, watashi, ima iru	raised by that aunt
	oba ni sodaterareta yona	of mine I am working
	monnanoyo.	with.)
Kyoko:	So. Ja, ano oniisan ga	(So your brother
	chichioya gawari?	helped you in place
		of your father?)
Sakura:	To iitai tokoro dakedo.	(I wish I could say that.)

Kyoko stops in the middle of her questions as if she was making her utterance intentionally open-ended. Each time this happens, Sakura takes over to complete it.

The next example will make this point clear. This also comes from the same series of the movie by Yoji Yamada, in which a young girl meets her lover at her father's funeral. She is in love with the young man but was having a hard time obtaining her father's approval of their marriage:

Man:	Kekkyoku, boku no	(After all, about me.)
	koto wa . . .	
Woman:	Ittawa. Mikka mae ni. . . .	(I told him. Three
	Soretonaku.	days ago. Casually.)
Man:	Soshitara?	(Then?)

Woman:	Omae ga eranda otoko	(He said, "If you love
	nara . . . nanimo	him, I have no
	iwante.	objection.")

When the young man arrives at the funeral, he thinks that his sweet-heart's father passed away without approving their marriage. When he says, "Kekkyoku, boku no koto wa . . .," he does not complete his utterance. He does not have to say all because he knows she knows how he feels. The direct translation above looks awkward in English. This would look more natural if rendered in the following manner:

Man:	After all, you . . .
Woman:	Told him three days ago . . . casually.
Man:	Then he . . .
Woman:	Said, "If you love him, I have no objection."

This example illustrates that in Japanese communication the roles of the speaker and the listener often merge. The function of the listener is not only to be attentive but to encourage the speaker and sometimes to join the speaker to help complete his or her utterance.

MESSAGE

In this section, we are concerned with a factor that is related to this problem of what is conveyed. To begin, let us examine the following conversation:

"Dochiramade?"	(Where are you going?)
"Chotto sokomade."	(Just around there.)
"Aa, sodesuka. Okiwo tsukete."	(Is that so? Take care.)

This is a typical dialogue between Japanese friends and acquaintances. When a Japanese happens to meet an acquaintance on the street, he or she may say, "Dochiramade?"[4] A Japanese addressee, who knows what the phrase is supposed to convey (i.e., "Hello. I'd like to interact with you and develop a friendship," but certainly not "I demand an answer from you") will just make a seemingly curt reply such as in the example. The inquirer may add something, but will in most cases not persist in asking the question and just let him or her go. Suppose that an American was addressed this way. What would be his or her reaction to this?

Nishida (1989) sent out questionnaires to 47 Japanese and 74 American students to find out how they would respond if they were Jane in the following conversation:

Jane: Morning.
Landlady: Good morning. How are you?
Jane: Fine, and you?
Landlady: I'm fine. You're going out? To work? To Ginza?
Jane: No, to Kichijoji to meet an old friend.
          (*Irritation in her voice*)
Landlady: Be careful and come back early.
Jane: Of course. Goodbye. (p. 39)

According to Nishida (1989), three-fourths of the Japanese subjects replied that they would take what the landlady said as a mere greeting. On the other hand, more than 40 percent of the Americans said that they would feel uncomfortable in the situation. As might be expected, more Americans than Japanese were displeased at being greeted that way because the former felt that their privacy was being invaded. It also is remarkable that nearly 60 percent of the American students said that they would respond favorably, thinking that the landlady was caring and thoughtful.

The point is that the question "Dochiramade?" is not really a query to inquire the addressee's destination. O. Mizutani (1982) points out that it is an expression of *kokoro* (heart or mind), rather than one of fact. What he means by that is that the speaker is trying to show his or her concern about or give attention to the addressee by directing that personal question to him or her. He or she is being polite in a way.

Let us turn our attention to what Americans would say. It is apparent that they would not use "Where are you going?" to greet someone in the situation in question, but the question is whether there are any expressions that they use in such a way that "Dochiramade?" is used. N. Mizutani (1988a) argues that "How are you?" is among those expressions. She herself felt some irritation, she says, every time people who met her asked her how she was while she was in the United States. She observes that "Ogenkidesuka?" or "Ikagadesuka?," equivalents in Japanese of "How are you?," are substantial questions and that Japanese do not say this to their colleagues or to someone whom they see every day. She points out that American speakers of Japanese tend to use "Ikagadesuka?" whenever they meet a Japanese friend. N. Mizutani (1988a) refers to some other examples like "Have a good weekend" and

"Have a nice time" as such. To the extent that this is true, it follows that there is a parallel drawn between certain expressions of Japanese and English. That is, "Dochiramade?" and similar expressions are quite analogous to expressions like "How are you?" in that, though they are questions in form, they do not really expect literal answers. It may well be concluded that their function is more or less phatic.

The expressions mentioned above form part of the greetings and their raison d'être is, as noted by Nomoto (1985), for the parties concerned to feel sympathy toward each other or develop a sense of unity through exchange of conventionalized or formalized expressions. Therefore, it is quite understandable that Japanese and Americans have a shared usage of certain expressions in this respect.

Yet it is possible to point out a few differences in greeting practices. According to Kobayashi (1981) and Okutsu and Numata (1985), Japanese express thanks or apology for whatever happened before, whereas Americans do not. If they ever do, they have to refer to something quite specific. Typically, Japanese say things like "Konomae wa domo" (Thank you for the other day) and "Senjitsu wa shitsurei shimashita" (I'm sorry for the other day). It is hard to tell from this what the person is being thanked for.

Expressions of good wishes are used by Americans and those of description by Japanese. To give just a few examples in English: (May you have a) "Good morning," "Have a nice evening," and (I wish you a) "Happy New Year." Japanese counterparts with literal translations: "Ohayo gozaimasu" (You are early), "Otsukaresan" (You must be tired), and "Shinnen omedeto" (It is a happy new year we're having). Probably most important, Japanese make use of a wider variety of, and depend more heavily on "formulas" than Americans do. Consequently, Americans are supposed to do much more "ad-libbing" in their give-and-take.

Higa (1985) notes two more differences. The first is that Japanese do not greet persons with whom they see no need of socializing, that is, someone too close or too distant (e.g., one's spouse on one hand and strangers on the other). By contrast, an American even greets a total stranger he or she happens to meet, say, in the elevator with a "Hi!" or perhaps nonverbally with a smile. The second is with reciprocity. American people who wait on customers, for instance, respond by saying, "Good morning. May I help you?" Reciprocity is maintained. Japanese counterparts usually say, "Irasshaimase" (literally, "Welcome," but equivalent to "What can I do for you?"). Customers do not respond. Nonreciprocity is occasionally found in Japanese greetings.

Finally, Kobayashi (1981) notes that Americans do use such expressions as "Where have you been?" and "What have you been up to?" when they meet close friends who they have not met for a long time. These questions are taken as expressing friendly concern. This shows that we cannot just compare between expressions and that we need to take into account the situations or context in which particular expressions are used.

DEGREE OF INGRESS

Another dimension that influences communicative behavior is the degree of ingress, or how far you penetrate into the "personal sphere" of the interlocutor. It is comparable to the concept of personal space discussed by Hall (1969). Hall classifies the use of proxemics into four categories: intimate, personal, social, and public. The distance we maintain vis-à-vis our interlocutor is determined by the kind of relationship we wish to have. The more intimate our relations get, the shorter will become the distance. This distance varies from culture to culture. Japanese, for instance, prefer to maintain greater interactional distance than most Latin Americans. It is as if we were carrying around us a bubble which defines our interactional distance. If people intrude beyond this bubble, it will make their interlocutor uncomfortable.

Just as we have a "bubble" that defines our personal space, we have our psychological sphere that defines our ego. People who meet for the first time usually begin their verbal interaction with small talk. Their interaction does not begin with topics that touch upon sensitive matters. People of closer relations like family members and friends, however, are more flexible in this regard. How far we allow our interlocutor to approach us is determined by the kind of relations we have with our interlocutor. How far are we allowed to intrude upon our interlocutor's personal sphere? O. Mizutani (1982) calls this distance of penetration *tachiirido*, or the degree of ingress.

How does the degree of ingress relate to our verbal behavior? In order to clarify this point, O. Mizutani (1982) classifies our speech acts into three categories in terms of the amount of burden placed upon the interlocutor by the speaker. The first category is when people talk to themselves. The speech act is directed toward the speaker himself or herself and thus it places the least burden on the interlocutor. The second category is when you try to activate your interlocutor's intellectual reception. It does involve the listener, but it is strictly a receptive activity. This ranges widely from listening to a casual talk to making a great deal of mental effort to understand a serious topic. The third category is when you have your interlocutor respond to you either verbally or physically. The interlocutor is expected to respond to the speaker and thus it imposes the greatest demand on the interlocutor.

When we ask a favor of other people, we accommodate our speech depending on the request we make. If the request is a simple one like passing the salt at the table, our speech will accordingly be simple and straightforward: "Will you pass me the salt?" When the request is more or less demanding, the expression will be more elaborate: "Would you mind speaking in our club?"In short, we vary politeness of expressions according to the kind of request we make. The more serious our request is, the more polite will become our expressions. Manipulating linguistic politeness according to the semantic content is observed in most languages.

What is characteristic about Japanese communication is, in addition to politeness, that they manipulate ingress to cope with a situation that demands tact. For instance, a boss asking his or her assistant to photocopy papers will say: "Kore, kopi shite kurenaikana" (Will you photocopy this?). This literally means "I just wondered if you could photocopy this." The boss is trying to avoid intruding upon his or her assistant's personal sphere by using a speech act that is directed to himself or herself. When the boss wants to point out a mistake in the work prepared by his or her assistant, he or she will say: "Korede iinokana" (Isn't this a mistake?). This is literally translated as "I am just wondering if this is all right." This utterance is directed toward the speaker rather than the listener. What the boss is doing here is taking care not to intrude upon his or her assistant's personal sphere, and thus to be tactful to achieve his or her purpose.

The notion of ingress is not a feature unique to Japanese. Most languages use it in some way or other. For instance, "Do you speak English?" is more polite than "Can you speak English?" in that the latter is directly asking the speaker's ability. Talking about the other person's ability represents a greater degree of ingress than talking about their life-styles and customs.

Just as different cultures have their own use of proxemics, the implication of personal sphere differs from culture to culture. O. Mizutani (1982) observes that American learners of Japanese sometimes embarrass their Japanese instructor by asking the following question: "Sensei, kono eigo ga wakarimasuka?" (Do you understand this English?). He points out that there are two problems involved in the use of *wakarimasuka* in this example. First, it is not appropriate in that the honorific form is not used. A student talking to a teacher is expected to use honorifics. Second, *wakaru* (to understand) is inappropriate because it directly refers to the interlocutor's ability. In other words, *wakaru* differs from, for example, *shiru* (to know) in the degree of ingress.

Likewise, Japanese students of English often embarrass their American instructors by asking questions like "How old are you?," "Are you married?," and "Do you have any children?" Two interpretations are possible about this Japanese tendency. We might interpret it as indicating that information about age and marital status does not constitute a prominent part of the personal sphere for Japanese. Or, alternatively, it is the type of information Japanese need to predict others' behavior.

Barnlund (1974) demonstrated that the degree of self-disclosure is greater in Americans than in Japanese. This might provide an answer to the frustration that both Japanese and Americans feel in their interaction with each other. What Barnlund's study indicates is that Japanese, in their interaction with Americans, would feel upset because Americans appear flippant, insensitive, and prying when Americans unknowingly invade their interlocutors' personal sphere. Likewise, Americans would feel uncomfortable because Japanese seem to them to be evasive when Japanese refrain from intruding upon their interlocutors' personal sphere. This, however, is an area that has not been fully explored and needs further investigation.

CONTEXT-DEPENDENCE AND INTERDEPENDENCE

Japanese often is considered ambiguous and vague. After World War II, Naoya Shiga, one of the leading novelists at the time, attributed the defeat of the war to the ambiguity of the language and went even further to present a proposal to make French the national language. The ambiguity of the Japanese language can be ascribed to context-dependence and interdependence. The former relates more directly to linguistic coding and the latter to human relations though we assume that they are connected to each other.

For instance, it is quite common in Japanese to use expressions like "Boku wa unagida" (literally, "I am an/the eel"). Taken out of context, the example sentence certainly sounds funny and seems illogical, but it has a variety of meanings depending on the situation in which it is used. It can mean "I'll have eel" if used at a restaurant, "I like eel" if favorite foods are discussed, "I will buy eel" if a shopping list is the topic, and so on. We should note, however, that no ambiguity arises in any of the situations described. Apart from grammatical descriptions of this type of sentence, the meaning is definite. The very same thing goes for English. Hoffer (1972) notes the following:

> Consider a situation in which a waitress approaches a table with several dishes on her tray. This conversation might take place.
>
> Waitress: "Now, who is the veal parmesan and who is the spaghetti?"
> Patron: "I'm the veal; he's the spaghetti."
>
> In different situations, . . . [He is the spaghetti.] could refer to the cooker of the spaghetti, an artist who drew a picture of spaghetti, a gourmet specializing in spaghetti, or any one of many other possibilities. (pp. 221-222)

Then it follows that English as well as Japanese has sentences that would be hard to interpret out of context. However, the type of sentence in question is more common in Japanese than in English. As communication does not take place in a vacuum, so language often loses its force without its context. We will see in what follows some more examples that will illustrate this point.

Imagine a situation where one brings a roll of film to a photo shop and places it on the counter to ask a clerk to have it developed and printed. Many Japanese would just say, "Onegai shimasu," which would be literally translated as "I have a favor to ask of you." This much is usually sufficient. The clerk would most likely reply, "Kashiko-marimashita" (a polite way of saying "OK"), and never ask the customer what it is. It would seem rather hard to imagine a thing like this happening at a shop of the same kind in the United States. When Americans say, "I have a favor to ask of you," the other person responds, "What is it?" or the like. Americans would say specific things like "I'd like to have this film developed, please," instead. Hinds (1986), referring to this expression in Japanese, observes that it commonly is used in other service counter situations of a similar kind, though it is possible say otherwise. As he points out, many Japanese would say "Onegai shimasu" rather than "Kono okane wo watashi no koza ni iretekudasai" (Please put this money into my account) when they hand money to the bank clerk, and again, "Onegai shimasu" rather than "Kono nimotsu wo azukattekudasai" (Please keep this bag for me) when they hand their luggage to the person in the luggage storage place.

Hinds (1986) also notes the following episode when he flew from Los Angeles to Tokyo on a Japanese airline with a Japanese friend, which clearly shows a contrast of the usage between the two languages under discussion: "When we were close to landing, the stewardess came around to see if we had filled the forms out yet. She said to me, 'Have you filled out the form yet?' To my friend she said, 'Yoroshi-idesuka?'" (p. 22). *Yoroshiidesuka* would be translated as "All right?" with no overt subject. The point is not the ellipsis of the subject here, but rather the fact that this way of saying things, including the ellipsis, is possible by virtue of the context provided. We see here that you are expected to specify what is being talked about in English while you are not in Japanese.

What would Japanese say to offer a friend some beer when they are drinking? "Biru wo nomimasenka?" (Won't you have some beer?) is a possibility, a fully grammatical sentence, but not very likely, as O. Mizutani (1979) points out. He says that "Nomimasenka?" (Won't you drink?) or "Ikagadesuka?" (How about it?) would be the most likely. The Japanese do not refer specifically to the beer in front of them. If they do ask "Biru wo nomukai?" (Want some beer?), argues Mizutani, it would presuppose the possibility that there are some other drinks and suggest that the offerer has dared to choose beer out of all the choices available. He indicates that it would not make sense to Americans to say, by analogy with the Japanese phrase, "Would you care for?" or "Do you want to have?"

All of these examples suggest that Japanese is heavily dependent on context whereas English is not as dependent. Hall (1976) identified two types of communication: high-context and low-context. In a high-context communication speakers do not have to encode every detail of meaning in the message because most of the relevant information is already stored in the context to which they are sensitive. In a low-context communication, however, people have to encode most of the meaning in the linguistic message. Given the distinction, it is obvious that Japanese is an example of the former type, whereas (American) English exemplifies the latter. Incidentally, this distinction parallels the notion of restricted and elaborated codes outlined by Bernstein (1966). Yet again it is to be borne in mind that Bernstein stated that "in any one case elaboration and restriction will be relative" (p. 441).

Examine further the following examples taken from O. Mizutani (1979): "Are wo motte kite kure" (Bring that to me) and "Are, do natta?" (What's happened to that?). *Are* is a deictic pronoun in Japanese, alongside of *kore* and *sore*, that is somewhat like *that* in English. Hence it is a highly context-dependent term. Kindaichi (1988) points out that it is favored by Japanese speakers and that it comes up in their conversation very frequently. Mizutani observes that *are* is used when the referent is distant from both speaker and listener and at the same time the two recognize what is referred to. To be more exact, it is used when there is a tacit assumption on the part of the speaker that his addressee knows what the referent is. It can be the case, therefore, that the addressee does not get it as in the following dialogue:

A:	Are wa doshita?	(What's happened to that?)
B:	Arette nani?	(What is that?)
A:	Are to ittara areda yo.	(That is that, I say.)

It should be noted, however, that *are* is used among ingroup people. Obviously, outgroup people would not know what is referred to by *are*. To put it differently, it seems that this way of communication serves the purposes of confirming and reinforcing group identity and solidarity.

A question might be raised as to how this is possible. Ishii (1984) attempts to account for the process of Japanese interpersonal communication by referring to the *enryo-sasshi* communication model. *Enryo* is reserve or modesty and *sasshi* is sharp guesswork or sensitivity or consideration. Ishii's model is roughly as follows: The sender's message is examined through the psychological filter of *enryo*. Then the parts of the message that have been judged to be safe and perhaps ambiguous are sent out to the receiver. The receiver makes the most of his or her *sasshi* to get the message through the limited information. He says that "it can be safely said that the Japanese communicator's 'exit' through which messages are sent out under the impact of his or her *enryo* is narrower and his or her 'entrance' to receive messages with *sasshi* are [*sic*] wider than those in low-context cultures respectively" (p. 50).

We will move on to a second factor of relational rather than contextual dependence, for which we will employ the term interdependence (see Lebra's chapter in this volume for a discussion of the Japanese self-concept). By that term is meant the communication form that is characteristic of interpersonal relationship among Japanese. We assume that it includes such concepts as Doi's (1971, 1974) *amae* (dependence), the well-known *wa* (harmony or conformity), and collectivism as opposed to individualism (see Gudykunst & San Antonio chapter).

Let us examine the following dialogue[6] between Japanese housewives taken from a study by Naotsuka and others (1981):

> Mrs. A: Your daughter has started taking piano lessons, hasn't
> she? I envy you, because you can be proud of her talent.
> You must be looking forward to her future as a pianist.
> I'm really impressed by her enthusiasm—every day, she
> practices so hard, for hours and hours, until late at night.
> Mrs. B: Oh, no, not at all. She is just a beginner. We don't know
> her future yet. We hadn't realized that you could hear
> her playing. I'm so sorry that you have been disturbed
> by her noise. (p. 70)

Naotsuka and colleagues asked 154 non-Japanese, including 47 Americans) the following question: Would you realize that Mrs. A was complaining (if you were Mrs. B)? They reported that 56 percent (87/154) of
the respondents said no to this question, and concluded that "Mrs. A's
expressing herself was too indirect for successful communication"
(p. 71). "Japanese . . . tend to identify directness with rudeness, and
politeness with indirectness, so that for them it seems impossible to be
both polite and direct" (p. 78).

Thus, we may well say that indirectness and politeness have a
role to play in Japanese ambiguity. However, it seems plausible to take
one more step forward and look at the issue here in another way. The
reason that Mrs. A expressed herself in the way she did was that she did
not want to embarrass her neighbor and aggravate or ruin her relationship with her. In other words, what she tried to do was put human
relations first and maintain *wa*, which led her to say apparently ambiguous things. This *wa* cannot be maintained by one person alone. Consequently, it definitely consists of interdependence. Okabe (1983) states
that "the cultural assumptions of interdependence and harmony require
that Japanese speakers limit themselves to implicit and even ambiguous
use of words" (p. 34). Doi (1974) also remarks that "Japanese hesitate or
say something ambiguous when they fear what they have in mind
might be disagreeable to others" (p. 22) as he discusses how *amae* and
Japanese reticence are related.

By contrast, it is a well-known fact that Americans are independent, individualistic, and straightforward in their expressions. Hence
there is less ambiguity. Okabe (1983) says of Americans that "reflecting
the cultural value of precision, Americans' tendency to use explicit
words is the most noteworthy characteristic of their communicative

style" (p. 34). To give a few examples, suppose you are invited to a dinner party in the United States. You will be sure to be asked what you would like to drink. You will most likely name a specific drink such as lemonade or beer without hesitation. What would a Japanese guest say in a situation like this? "Nandemo kekkodesu" (Any drink will do) would be his or her most likely response. An American host or hostess would probably feel an urge to insist on asking what he or she really wants. After dinner, you will make a personalized compliment like "The fish was great," or "The vegetables were so good. How did you make them?" The Japanese guest, on the other hand, would usually not refer to a specific item or items that were served, but just say "Gochisosama(deshita)" (Thank you for the dinner). Hinds (1986) confesses that he felt that he had not said enough when he followed suit by saying "Gochisosama" at a large dinner in Japan. Obviously, the American communicative style presents a striking contrast to the Japanese.

To return to the piano practice episode, Naotsuka and colleagues (1981) asked the respondents the following two questions: (a) How would you feel about Mrs. A's expressions? and (b) How would you make a complaint, if you faced a problem such as described above? To the first question, 35 responses were given by Americans and they were classified as follows: (a) positive acceptance 12 (34%), (b) conditional acceptance 17 (49%), and (c) emotional rejection 6 (17%). It should be noted that the percentage of category (c) was remarkably small. For the second question, only 26 concrete examples were obtained and they were classified into two categories: (a) using a special situation as an excuse 24 (92%), and (b) using flattery 2 (8%). By a special situation is meant such a situation as "My children are sleeping," or "I must study," or "My husband has to get up very early." It is not clear how many Americans were among the (a) respondents because Naotsuka and colleagues do not list all of the examples obtained, but they provide at least seven examples given by Americans. Incidentally, the (b) respondents were both from Hong Kong. What should be noticed here is that all of the seven Americans used a special situation as an excuse for complaining "to make the complaint more tactful by saving the other person's face and avoiding insulting or hurting her" (p. 76).

Let us examine another conversation between Japanese company employees taken again from Naotsuka and colleagues (1981):

Mr. A: How about going for a drink tonight?
Mr. B: Well . . . tonight? Let me see . . .
Mr. A: It's a long time since we had a drink together.

Mr. B: Yes, but my wife hasn't been well of late . . .

Mr. A: Really? I didn't know that.

Mr. B: She doesn't feel happy if I come home late. So I should go straight home. That's why . . . thought [sic] I'd like to go for a drink with you . . . you . . .

Mr. A: That's too bad . . . Well, all right . . . Let's leave it for another time. (p. 193)

They asked the non-Japanese respondents if they often used this sort of indirect expression of refusal in their country, and also asked them to write down some of the commonly used expressions if they did. The responses to the question were divided into two groups: often and seldom. The responses given by 39 Americans were as follows: often, 32 (82%); and seldom, 7 (18%). It should be noted that a large percentage of the Americans responded that they used some form of indirect refusal.

Based on the preceding analysis it might seem that Japanese and Americans share something in their style of refusing a social invitation. However, Naotsuka and colleagues (1981) point out several differences, one of which deserves special attention. They observe the following: "[As for Japanese], the excuse is explicit, but the refusal isn't actually stated in words. . . . In contrast, it would seem that among foreigners, the excuse is 'indirect,' often being either extremely vague or even nonexistent, . . . whereas the refusal is explicitly stated" (p. 99).

It follows from the preceding discussions that Americans do modulate their directness or explicitness according to the situation. It is true that they give preference to directness in general, but it would be wrong to assume that they always do so. In what situations and under what circumstances Americans vary their directness is the question that should be pursued further.

We mentioned earlier in this section that context-dependence and interdependence are related. We are dealing with the same issue of ambiguity whichever factor may be at work. Thus, it will be seen that Ishii's (1984) model that we referred to earlier works well for the phenomena centering around interdependence, too. To put it in different terms, human relations may be looked upon as context in the extended sense of the word.

CONCLUSION

An attempt has been made in the chapter to show how Japanese is sociolinguistically similar to or different from English. In so doing, we have selected seven factors, among others, that purport to be influential in the choice of linguistic forms.

It is apparent that we need a common or general framework that would enable us to effectively and efficiently compare and contrast Japanese and English and, for that matter, any other languages. To accomplish this, further research is needed. Although we have indicated in various places where further research is needed, the following suggestions also are made for future work. First, we have not dealt with regional differences concerning the properties of a speaker. It is true that, even in a small country like Japan, we do encounter a diversity of subcultural differences. It might be difficult to isolate only those factors of relevance, but it certainly would make an interesting study. Second, the claim should be challenged that the ingroup/outgroup distinction is peculiarly Japanese and that it is not applicable to Americans' interpersonal relationships. Americans do use informal language among their family members and close friends, as do Japanese. To what extent and in what way the idea of *uchi/soto* applies to Americans and their society, if it does at all, still remains to be seen. In the meantime, it should be studied whether or not the Japanese notion of *uchi/soto* has undergone any change among Japanese themselves over the years. Third, further studies into a variety of forms of politeness in Japanese and American cultures, including nonverbal ones, are to be conducted. As we mentioned before, *keigo* is not the only verbal means available to Japanese. By the same token, there should be many different ways available to Americans to convey interpersonal relationships whether they be vertical or horizontal.

Fourth, it seems that we have yet to provide social psychological reasons for the fact that the demarcation line between speaker and listener is not clear in Japanese conversation. Also, data containing conversations between Japanese and Americans are not sufficiently available as yet. Fifth, message has a great deal to do with what constitutes politeness. Therefore, messages should be studied from the wider perspective of the assumptions and values of a particular culture. Sixth, the degree of ingress is perhaps one of the fields where work is most lacking. For what kind of topics and in what type of interpersonal relationships the degree of ingress may differ between Japanese and Americans should be explored further. In addition, it is to be questioned why the public self is smaller in Japan than in the United States, as demonstrated by Barnlund (1974). Comparative studies of the development of ego in each culture should be of help. Seventh, it would seem that there are still some other possible sources of ambiguity that we have not referred to in the present chapter. One such candidate is logic.

Following the terminological distinction between *cross-cultural* and *intercultural* made by Gudykunst and Kim (1984), we might say that, in general, more cross-cultural work has been done than intercultural work so far. More intercultural research is needed. The accumulation of cross-cultural work enables predictions of what might happen in the intercultural setting. Data obtained by intercultural work and collected material on actual intercultural interactions would make it possible to verify or falsify the predictions and would give feedback to the cross-cultural work and vice versa. Our claim is that the two kinds of work should be seen as complementary to each other. It may also be added that cross-cultural work provides a static model of communication, while intercultural work helps build a dynamic model which, it is hoped, will account better for actual interaction.

Furthermore, it should be strongly suggested that more work be carried out on a variety of aspects of spoken language, along with its paralinguistic and perhaps kinesic elements. Linguists, it seems, have to be reminded at times that primacy of speech or spoken language has been a presupposition of modern linguistics for decades.

To conclude, although there are a variety of differences found between Japanese and English, they are relative rather than absolute. This cannot be emphasized too much.

NOTES

We would like to express heartfelt thanks to Professor William B. Gudykunst for his encouragement, assistance, and valuable comments and suggestions on earlier versions of this chapter. It goes without saying that whatever mistakes remain in the present chapter are our own.

1. *Senryu* is a form of poetry in Japan, which is the same in form as haiku. Its theme, however, consists in humor and insinuation.

2. There are two important notions of *sex-exclusive* and *sex-preferential*, which, to our knowledge, were introduced by Bodine (1975), that may deserve mention in this context. However, we will not draw a clear line between them in this chapter because these two notions are gradient and it is hard to draw the line between them in practice, though we certainly subscribe to the idea that they are theoretically distinct.

3. Brown and Ford (1964) give age as another factor that can generate this nonreciprocal pattern of address, of which we have made no mention here. We may point out, however, that a difference of age, which can be taken as

constituting *joge-kankei*, has to be fairly wide in American culture, whereas that is not the case in Japanese culture as the *twin* story that we referred to in the beginning paragraph of this section clearly shows.

4. It may possibly be the case that more and more people are taking this expression literally, that is, not as a mere greeting. O. Mizutani (1982), for instance, states that he was appalled when more than half of the fifty students attending his lecture told him that they would feel put off by the question and that they would not use it themselves. Further research is required to clarify this point.

5. We have used the term "degree of ingress" to refer to O. Mizutani's (1982) *tachiirido*. The literal translation of *tachiiri* is "stepping in." We considered using *intrusion*, but we decided against it because it has unnecessary negative connotations. The Japanese word is a neutral term, indeed. We hope that it is a happy translation.

6. The two conversations quoted here and below from Naotsuka et al. (1981) were presented English. The corresponding Japanese versions are found in Naotsuka (1980).

REFERENCES

Akizawa, K. (1989). *Nipponjin no eigo, aa dai-gokai!* (Japanese English—alas, great misunderstanding!). Tokyo: KK Bestsellers.

Atwood, E. B. (1962). *The regional vocabulary of Texas*. Austin, TX: University of Texas Press.

Barnlund, D. C. (1974). The public self and the private self in Japan and the United States. In J. C. Condon & M. Saito (Eds.), *Intercultural encounters with Japan: Communication—contact and conflict*. Tokyo: The Simul Press.

Bernstein, B. (1966). Elaborated and restricted codes: Their social origins and some consequences. In A. G. Smith (Ed.), *Communication and culture*. New York: Holt, Rinehart and Winston.

Bodine, A. (1975). Sex differentiation in language. In B. Thorne & N. Henley (Eds.), *Language and sex: Difference and dominance*. Rowley, MA: Newbury House.

Brown, R., & Ford, M. (1964). Address in American English. In D. Hymes (Ed.), *Language in culture and society*. New York: Harper & Row.

Brown, R., & Gilman, A. (1960). The pronoun of power and solidarity. In T. A. Sebeok (Ed.), *Style in language*. New York: John Wiley & Sons.

Condon, J. C. (1984). *With respect to the Japanese: A guide for Americans.* Yarmouth, ME: Intercultural Press.

Doi, T. (1971). *Amae no kozo* (The structure of dependence). Tokyo: Kobundo.

Doi. T. (1973). *The anatomy of dependence.* Tokyo: Kodansha International.

Doi, T. (1974). Some psychological themes in Japanese human relationships. In J. C. Condon & M. Saito (Eds.), *Intercultural encounters with Japan.* Tokyo: Simul Press.

Gudykunst, W. B., & Kim, Y. Y. (1984). *Communicating with strangers.* Reading, MA: Addison-Wesley.

Hall, E. T. (1969). *The hidden dimension.* New York: Doubleday.

Hall, E. T. (1976). *Beyond culture.* New York: Doubleday.

Higa, M. (1985). *Aisatsu to aisatsu kotoba* (Greeting and its expressions). *Nihongogaku, 4*(8), 15-22.

Hinds, J. (1986). *Situation vs. person focus.* Tokyo: Kurosio.

Hoffer, B. (1972). Contrastive analysis of basic sentence patterns in Japanese and English. In H. Miyauchi (Ed.), *Nichi-ei no kotoba to bunka.* Tokyo: Sanseido.

Ide, S. (1982). *Taigu-hyogen to danjo-sa no hikaku* (Comparison between expressions of treatment and between male and female language). In T. Kunihiro (Ed.), *Nichi-ei-go hikaku koza: Vol. 5. Bunka to shakai.* Tokyo: Taishukan.

Ide, S. (1983). *Onna-rashisa no gengogaku* (Linguistics of womanliness). In O. Mizutani (Ed.), *Koza nihongo no hyogen: Vol. 3. Hanashi-kotobo no hyogen.* Tokyo: Chikuma-shobo.

Ide, S., & McGloin, N. H. (1990). *Aspects of Japanese women's language.* Tokyo: Kurosio.

Ikuta, S. (1983). Speech level shift and conversational strategy in Japanese discourse. *Language Sciences, 6*(1), 37-53.

Ishii, S. (1984). *Enryo-sasshi* communication: A key to understanding Japanese interpersonal relations. *Cross-Currents, 11,* 49-58.

Jorden, E. H. (1990). Overview. In S. Ide & N. H. McGloin (Eds.), *Aspects of Japanese women's language.* Tokyo: Kurosio.

Kindaichi, H. (1982). *Nihongo semina: Vol. 1. Nihongo towa* (Seminar on Japanese: What is Japanese?). Tokyo: Chikuma-shobo.

Kindaichi, H. (1988). *Nihongo* (The Japanese language) (New ed., Vol. 2). Tokyo: Iwanami-Shoten.

Kobayashi, Y. (1981). *Eigo no aisatsu kodo* (Greeting behaviors in English). *Eigo Kyoiku, 30*(10), 9-11.

Kobayashi, Y. (1986). *Aisatsu kodo no nichi-bei hikaku kenkyu* (A comparative study of Japanese and American greeting behavior). *Nihongogaku, 5* (12), 65-75.

Kokuritsu Kokugo Kenkyujo. (1981). *Daitoshi no gengo seikatsu: bunseki-hen* (Sociolinguistic survey in Tokyo and Osaka). Tokyo: Sanseido.

Kunihiro, T. (1990). "*Kosho*" *no sho-mondai* (Problems of address terms). *Nihongogaku, 9*(9), 4-7.

Labov, W. (1972). *Sociolinguistic patterns*. Philadelphia, PA: University of Pennsylvania Press.

Lakoff, R. (1975). *Language and woman's place*. New York: Harper & Row.

Leech, G., & Thomas, J. (1987). Pragmatics and the dictionary. In D. Summers (Ed.), *Longman dictionary of contemporary English*. Harlow: Longman.

Maynard, K. S. (1987). *Nichi-bei kaiwa ni okeru aizuchi hyogen* (Back-channel expressions in Japanese and English conversation). *Gengo, 16*(12), 88-92.

McDavid, R. I., Jr. (1958). The dialects of American English. In W. N. Francis, *The structure of American English*. New York: Ronald Press.

Mizutani, N. (1982). *Eigo no seitai* (The facts about English). Tokyo: Japan Times.

Mizutani, N. (1985). *Nichi-ei hikaku: Hanashi-kotoba no bunpo* (Comparison of Japanese and English: Grammar of spoken language). Tokyo: Kurosio.

Mizutani, N. (1988a). *Hanashi-kotoba no hikaku taisho* (Comparison of spoken languages). In Kokuritsu Kokugo Kenkyujo (Ed.), *Hanashi-kotoba no komyunikeishon*. Tokyo: Bonjinsha.

Mizutani, N. (1988b). *Aizuchi-ron* (A view of *aizuchi*). *Nihongogaku, 7*(13), 4-11.

Mizutani, O. (1979). *Nihongo no seitai* (The facts about Japanese). Tokyo: Sotakusha.

Mizutani, O. (1982). *Gaikokugo toshite mita nihongo no gengo kodo* (Linguistic behavior of Japanese viewed as a foreign language). In K. Morioka, Y. Miyaji, H. Teramura, & Y. Kawabata (Eds.), *Koza Nihongogaku: Vol. 12. Gaikokugo tono taisho III*. Tokyo: Meiji-shoin.

Nakane, C. (1967). *Tate-shakai no ningen-kankei* (Human relations in vertical society). Tokyo: Kodansha.

Nakane, C. (1973). *Japanese society*. Harmondsworth: Penguin.

Naotsuka, R. (1980). *Obeijin ga chinmoku suru toki* (When Europeans and Americans become silent). Tokyo: Taishukan.

Naotsuka, R., Sakamoto, N., Hirose, T., Hagihara, H., Ohta, J., Maeda, S., Hara, T., & Iwasaki, K. (1981). *Mutual understanding of different cultures.* Tokyo: Taishukan.

Neustupny, J. V. (1978). *Post-structural approaches to language.* Tokyo: University of Tokyo Press.

Nishida, H. (1989). *Jitsurei de miru nichi-bei komyunikeishon gyappu* (Communication gaps between Japanese and Americans through examples). Tokyo: Taishukan.

Nomoto, K. (1985). *Aisatsu kotoba no genri* (Principles of greeting expressions). *Nihongogaku, 4*(8), 4-14.

Okabe, R. (1983). Cultural assumptions of East and West: Japan and the United States. In W. B. Gudykunst (Ed.), *Intercultural communication theory.* Beverly Hills, CA: Sage.

Okutsu, K., & Numata, Y. (1985). *Nichi-cho-chu-ei no aisatsu kotoba* (Greeting expressions in Japanese, Korean, Chinese, and English). *Nihongogaku, 4*(8), 53-69.

Osugi, K. (1982). *Eigo no keii-hyogen* (Deferential English). Tokyo: Taishukan.

Peng, F. C. C. (1974). Communicative distance. *Language Sciences, 31,* 32-40.

Sanada, S. (1990). *Sedai to kotoba* (Generations and speech). *Nihongogaku, 9*(4), 4-11.

Shibamoto, J. S. (1987). The womanly woman: manipulation of stereotypical and nonstereotypical features of Japanese female speech. In S. U. Philips, S. Steele, & C. Tanz (Eds.), *Language, gender & sex in comparative perspective.* Cambridge: Cambridge University Press.

Suzuki, T. (1982). *Jishoshi to taishoshi no hikaku* (A comparison between self-terms and other-terms). In T. Kunihiro (Ed.), *Nichi-ei-go hikaku koza: Vol. 5. Bunka to shakai.* Tokyo: Taishukan.

Swacker, M. (1975). The sex of the speaker as a sociolinguistic variable. In B. Thorne & N. Henley (Eds.), *Language and sex: Difference and dominance.* Rowley, MA: Newbury House.

Trudgill, P. (1974). *Sociolinguistics: An introduction.* Harmondsworth: Penguin.

Wolfram, W., & Fasold, R. W. (1974). *The study of social dialects in American English.* Englewood Cliffs, NJ: Prentice-Hall.

Chapter 5

JAPANESE AMERICAN VALUES AND COMMUNICATION PATTERNS

Harry H. L. Kitano

INTRODUCTION

One logical group to study when focusing on Japan and the United States are Japanese Americans. For they are products of both Japan and the United States; some, as the original Issei immigrants, are more Japanese than American, while subsequent generations are more American than Japanese. The central question concerns the ability of the group to live under, adjust to, and deal with these two powerful cultural influences. Specifically, have they found the Japanese and American systems incompatible? Have the values of one culture hindered their ability to deal with the other? Can we learn from their experiences?

There are a number of ways to look at the role of Japanese Americans in relation to Japan and the United States. One logical but very difficult role for Japanese Americans is to serve as a bridge between the two nations. The idealized image is that they have a common ancestry with Japan, and yet are Americans so that they have an understanding of both countries. The problem is that although they may be viewed as a bridge, they have little power to influence either of the two large powers. Instead, Japanese Americans are often victims of the conflicts between the two; the forced relocation during World War II remains as a tragic example. Further, many of the third and fourth generation know very little about Japan and do not wish to be identified with their ancestral homeland.

Another model is to view them as the "children" of an uneasy marriage between Japan and the United States. Both parents have relatively fixed ideas—the Japanese believe in the uniqueness of their culture, that no one can understand the Japanese unless they were born and raised in Japan. In contrast, Americans believe that everyone should try to be like them, that democracy and capitalism have been extremely successful and that they should serve as models for the rest of the world. Given such differences in expectations and behavior, can the marriage be successful (Booth, 1992)?

One possible approach to the question is to look at their "children," the Japanese Americans, as products of this interesting relationship. What have they learned from both "parents;" how have they managed to adapt to one culture, while bearing the influence of another? This model has the advantage of looking at change, continuity, generations, and acculturation.

The purpose of this chapter is to look at the Japanese Americans in order to ascertain the extent of the influence of these two cultures. The analysis will focus on the following questions:

1. What have been the influences of Japan? Is there a continuity in values and communication patterns between Japanese in Japan and Japanese Americans? If so, which values and communication patterns remain, which have been modified, and which have been discarded?
2. What have been the effects of the American system? What role has acculturation, generation, and minority status played?
3. What generalizations can we derive from an analysis of the Japanese American experience?

VICTIMIZATION

A constant concern among Japanese Americans is related to their victimization when conflicts arise between Japan and America, just as children are often the targets between fighting parents. To paraphrase an old saying, "When both Japan and America sneeze, the Japanese American catches a cold." For it is the inability of most Americans to differentiate between Japanese from Japan and Japanese Americans that leads to scapegoating and hostile actions.

For example, an erroneous remark that Prime Minister Kiichi Miyazawa was alleged to have made in 1992 concerning the lack of work ethic among American workers caused American tempers to flare. However, Charles Burress, a *San Francisco Chronicle* reporter, wrote to the *New York Times* that the furor was caused by a mistranslation. The disputed remark was in the context of the American shift from producing goods to that of money manipulation. A faithful translation of the prime minister's remark was, "In this area, I have long thought that something like a work ethic may be lacking." Although the phrase, "in this area," referred to nonproductive money manipulation, the phrase was left out so that it was construed that all Americans had lost their work ethic (Karatsu, 1992).

It is difficult to trace a direct cause-effect relationship between such remarks and prejudice against Japanese Americans, but it is conceivable that they provide a pretext for some Americans to vent their hostility and frustration. For example, the *Japan Times* led off one issue with an article titled, "Japanese Americans Pay Bashing Price" (Abramowitz, 1992). It indicated that a complex set of factors, including American insecurity stemming from the recession, the rising influx of Asian immigrants, and the changing position of the United States, led to a "Buy American" campaign. And the *Pacific Citizen* of 13 March 1992 reported that a sign in bold letters appeared on the campus of California State University, Pomona which read, "Asian Americans Die Now." So the background of misunderstanding, miscommunication, and hostility has created tensions with the Japanese Americans as victims.

The miscommunication works both ways. A Japanese television program from Hawaii on December 7, 1991 reported that President Bush, when asked about responsibility for the atomic bombing of Hiroshima and Nagasaki, was alleged to have said that no American president was responsible. What the president actually said was that "this president was not responsible," yet this translation was left out of the Japanese broadcast (Karatsu, 1992).

So, Japanese Americans, as children of this shaky relationship, suffer the ills of parental conflict. Their greatest tragedy occurred during World War II, when all persons of Japanese ancestry living along the Pacific coast, whether citizen or alien, were forced into wartime "relocation camps."

At the outbreak of World War II, Federal authorities rounded up a few thousand enemy aliens—Japanese, Germans, and Italians, and placed them in internment camps. Each internee was eventually given a hearing and, as a result of the hearing, some were released. Japanese Americans residing along the Pacific coast were not given a trial or a hearing; men, women, children, whether citizen or alien, were herded first into temporary assembly centers, then transferred to more permanent camps in the interior. As a result, over 110,000 Japanese Americans spent most or part of the war in these camps from 1942 to 1945. The assumption, based on racism, was that they would act more in accordance with their Japanese ancestry than with their American heritage. There is a wealth of material covering this period so that I will limit some of the effects of this period to a few generalizations.

1. The evacuation disrupted family life. The government took over such family responsibilities as housing, food, and clothing so that children were no longer dependent upon the family. Dining facilities were often arranged by peer group; there was no "home life." Individuals were encouraged to leave after a clearance procedure, so that many families began losing their most capable members.

2. There was an active attempt by the Federal authorities to limit the power and influence of the Issei and "Japanese ways." The American-born Nisei were given priority in terms of leadership. Japanese rituals and festivals were discouraged; celebrations such as the Fourth of July and the birthdays of the presidents were encouraged. The educational system emphasized American community life and democracy.

3. Although the governmental aim was on acculturation, acculturation meant adjusting to camp conditions, rather than to the American mainstream. Some of the following words reflected the evacuees' view of camp life:

a. "Inu," or dog, was used to identify individuals thought to be spies and informers.
b. "Bootchie" was used to identify the evacuees as Japanese Americans.
c. "Slop suey" was a reference to camp cuisine.
d. "Waste time" was a favorite phrase which included everything from going to school, to studying hard, to being placed in camp.

Perhaps the greatest change came in terms of work orientation; the work ethic of most Japanese Americans changed to a laissez-faire attitude; why work hard when the maximum pay was only $19 per month?

The evacuation also forced many Japanese Americans to move to the Midwest and East Coast; there were also Nisei who volunteered for the armed forces and served in Europe and Asia. As a result, Japanese Americans were exposed to a wider world, away from their prewar ethnic communities. The saving grace was that the evacuation was time limited, therefore, many of the values and life styles of living in camp were not internalized.

There are still many unresolved issues concerning the effects of this period on Japanese Americans. Survivors received a government apology and $20,000 beginning in 1990, but for many, such actions were felt to be too little, too late. It was difficult not to develop a cynical attitude towards governmental pronouncements.

CONTINUITY

The first question to be addressed focuses upon the continuity in values and communication between Japan and Japanese Americans. What did the immigrants bring with them and what changes have occurred?

It is important to recognize that the current generation of Japanese Americans is different from previous generations, just as the modern-day Japanese in Japan are different from past generations. The question of continuity is related to factors such as: (a) immigration, (b) reception by the host society, (c) isolation, and (d) the passage of time.

Immigration

There are several important factors to consider when dealing with continuity and immigration history. One deals with the motives for immigration: does the immigrant wish to forget his or her past and attempt to become a part of the host society? Another deals with the kind of immigrant: has he or she special skills and education which may lead to a closer interaction with the majority society? And finally, is there cultural compatibility, so that language, values, and life-styles will be congruent with the dominant society?

Although there is evidence that Japanese had arrived in the Americas prior to 1890, the significant Japanese immigration started in the 1890s. The majority of the first wave of immigrants were single males with a sojourner's orientation—the primary motive was to make money and return to Japan in triumph. As a consequence, there were few attempts to learn about the new country, the language, customs, and life-styles of the dominant society. There was minimal communication and interaction with the host society; the primary interaction was with other immigrants. They formed their own communities, with names such as Little Tokyo and Little Osaka, so that, like many other immigrant groups that came to the United States, they carried on their own customs and traditions (Kitano & Daniels, 1988). As a result, they maintained values and communication styles brought with them from Meiji Japan.

Reception by the Host Society

Although there was an initial welcome of the new immigrants, the hostility towards the massive Chinese influx was soon extended to the Japanese. The early history of the Issei was fraught with racism, discrimination, and attempts to keep them as second-class citizens. The most telling instances of the latter were a variety of discriminatory laws—they could not become citizens, but were "aliens ineligible for citizenship," and faced housing, marital, occupational, and social restrictions. As a result, their interaction with the dominant society was minimal; they were second-class aliens, with little power to effect change. One consequence was to turn inward to the ethnic community, and pin their hopes for an American future on their American-born children, the Nisei. But Issei parents also wished that their children should have a good knowledge of Japanese, so many Nisei in the pre-World War II years attended Japanese language schools with mixed results. Some studied Japanese diligently, others felt that the ethnic school was a bore and a waste of time.

The overall effects of the hostility they encountered and of their subsequent turning inwards were:

1. Most Issei were isolated from the mainstream.
2. Communication with the outside world was left to a few leaders.
3. Issei developed their own styles of communication, and maintained the values brought over from the old country.
4. Acculturation and becoming a part of the mainstream was left up to the Nisei.

So, continuing the parental analogy, the Issei, or the children of the marriage between Japan and the United States were influenced primarily by the Japanese parent. Rejection and hostility from the American parent reinforced their "Japaneseness." It was left to the grandchildren to become assimilated in American society.

Norms and Values

The Issei brought with them some of the norms and values of Meiji Japanese society. Norms are shared meanings in a culture that serve to provide the background for communication, while values refers to clusters of attitudes that give a sense of direction to behavior. Some of the norms included highly personalized modes of interaction, hierarchy of status positions, behavioral reserve, and discipline (Benedict, 1946). Other norms were obligation, loyalty to one's superiors, sensibility, and modesty. Indirect, rather than direct forms of communication were practiced, so that direct confrontations were discouraged. Speaking up and letting others know how one really felt were not high on the list of priorities.

In terms of communication styles, the Issei acknowledged status distinctions, preferred indirection, practiced modesty, praised conformity and humility, were service-oriented, and were highly sensitive to the needs of others, especially of those in superior positions. As Kitano (1976) writes: "Probably the one outstanding characteristic of Japanese norms is their adaptiveness to fixed positions and external realities. Rather than a stream making its own course, the stream follows the lines of least resistance—their norms emphasize duty and obligation; their values include conformity and obedience" (p. 123). Part of the Issei's ability to adapt to their lower status in the United States consisted in maintaining a low profile and practicing deference and humility so as not to directly challenge the more powerful, dominant society.

Iga (1967) hypothesizes a number of values and communication styles that were brought over from Japan by the Issei. They included a collective rather than individual orientation; particularism, loyalty to the house, family, employer, and nation; and conformism, obedience to rules and regulations, compromise, discipline, and obedience. Self-control, resignation, and gratitude were highly esteemed. There were also communication styles based on status distinctions, or "knowing one's place in society." Age, sex (masculine superiority), class, family lineage, and other variables of social status were important.

It is important to recognize that not all Japanese behaved according to the above norms and values, just as not all Americans embrace individualistic values. Nevertheless, Iga (1967) found that the Japanese in Japan adhered the most to these norms and values, followed by Japanese Americans, then Euro Americans. Significant differences were found between Japanese Americans and Euro Americans in conformity, compromise, success, ambition, sense of obligation, and dependency.

It is also important to emphasize that at the same time adaptations to the West were taking place in Japan, so there were changes in the home country as well. The Meiji Japan that immigrants remembered had continued to change, so that many of the values and images that they retained were of a bygone era. In the meantime, the Issei, or the first-generation, Japan-born immigrants were cut off from Japan, so that they retained much of their Meiji orientation. Their relative isolation suggests that if one wishes to study Meiji Japanese culture, one would find it more or less intact among the Issei, especially among those who have remained isolated from both Japanese and American influences.

The relative isolation of the Issei was enhanced by the 1924 United States Immigration Act which forbade immigration from Japan and other Asian countries. As a result, there was no further legal immigration from Japan until the passage of the McCarran-Walter Bill of 1952.

The Nisei, or the American-born second generation, were influenced by both Japan and the United States. Older Nisei held on to many of the Issei values and communication styles; younger ones were more apt to follow American models. The older Nisei felt the sting of discrimination more than their younger cohorts; there was even a book titled *The Second Generation Japanese Problem* (Strong, 1934), which focused upon the problem of discrimination and the lack of opportunities for the Nisei in the 1920s. There were some Nisei who emigrated to Japan, others thought of moving away from California; however, jobs were also scarce on the East Coast, so that the prevailing mood was one of frustration and despair. Some questioned the value of a college education—why try to do anything; perhaps the lot of the Nisei was to remain as second-class citizens. Strong's conclusion was that the Nisei were as capable as their American peers, but that discrimination had made life extremely difficult for them.

By the Sansei, or third generation, acculturation was almost complete so that Iga (1967) says:

> Their [the Sansei's] desire to be assimilated appears to be so complete and their knowledge of Japanese culture to be so marginal that we cannot anticipate their return to traditional Japanese cultural interests. The only factor which prevents them from complete assimilation seems to be the combination of their physical visibility, and racial prejudice on the part of dominant group members. (p. 1)

Early studies on the personality of the Issei and Nisei were conducted by Caudill (1952) and DeVos (1955). Caudill found a logical continuity between the values and adaptive mechanisms of the Issei and Nisei. Both pointed towards middle-class American life; another finding was the compatibility, not the sameness, of Japanese and American values.

DeVos (1955) found personality differences between Japanese and American norms. The Issei stressed the subordination of individual needs to family and group needs, and the use of rigid role definitions. They could function well in well-defined situations, but were relatively inflexible in the face of new experiences. Intrapsychic difficulties were more apt to show up in their personal and family lives, since their overt economic and social lives were much more amenable to ritualized behavior. The other generations showed acculturative changes toward American norms.

Personality research among Japanese Americans in Hawaii showed a number of differences between Japanese American and Euro American samples. Sansei males showed a high need for deference, abasement, nurturance, affiliation, order, and exuberance, and a correspondingly reduced need for dominance, aggression, autonomy, exhibition, and heterosexuality when compared to Euro American males. Sansei males also held a more "traditional Japanese" view of male dominance in marriage, which made them different from Sansei females and American college students. Sansei females expressed a need for deference, nurturance, and order, and less need for aggression, abasement, autonomy, exhibition, and heterosexuality than Euro American females (Arkoff, 1959; Fenz & Arkoff, 1962).

Meredith and Meredith (1966) studied the Sansei in Hawaii and found that Japanese American males were more reserved, more humble, more conscientious, and more regulated by external realities than Euro American males. Conversely, Euro American males were more outgoing, more assertive, more expedient, more venturesome, and more imaginative than Japanese American males. Japanese American females were more emotionally sensitive, more obedient, more suspicious and more apprehensive than Euro American females. Conversely, Euro American females were more emotionally stable, more independent, more trusting, and more self-assured than Japanese American females.

Contrasting Values

A study by Kawahara and Kitano (1992) compared a sample of Euro American and Asian American college students on a personal value survey. The Asian American sample consisted of Chinese, Japanese, and Korean Americans; a comparison of their mean scores showed no statistically significant differences, so their scores were combined. The value dimensions which showed a significant ethnic effect were: involved-casual, nonassertive-assertive, obligation-free will, group-individual, pessimism-optimism, and dependent-independent. A significant situation effect (work vs. party) was found on five dimensions: involved-casual, nonassertive-assertive, obligation-free will, cooperative-competitive, and happy-unhappy.

The overall generalization was that Asian Americans valued involvement and obligation more, and independence less than the Euro Americans. However, although there were many differences between the two samples, the groups were similar in both the work and party settings. The similarity of the factor structures indicates that both groups can at least understand each other, and are like each other some of the time. The conclusion was that the findings do not fit stereotypical patterns. The responses indicated an unexpected complexity; the interaction of ethnicity, values, experiences, and behavior has yet to be unraveled.

Child-Rearing Attitudes

Studies comparing the child-rearing attitudes of various Japanese groups also show the continuity from the Japanese to the American. A comparison of an Issei and a Nisei sample using the Parental Attitude Research Inventory (PARI) showed significant differences between Issei and Nisei mothers (Kitano, 1961). The Nisei mean score was 12.89, compared to the Issei mean score of 16.88, with the higher score representing a more restrictive and "old-fashioned" way of raising children. The Issei viewed children as dependent, quiet, unequal, and to be raised with strictness. The Nisei view was more "modern" and more American—children were viewed as comrades, with an emphasis on sharing experiences, asking questions, and with a more tolerant attitude towards sexual exploration.

Another study (Kitano, 1964), using the PARI, compared a younger and older Nisei sample in the United States with similar age cohorts in Japan. The findings were somewhat surprising in that the significant differences were between ages, rather than the national samples. Older Japanese, whether Nisei in America or Japanese in Japan, held similar attitudes towards child rearing, and so did the younger samples in the two countries. The findings suggest that age groups across national boundaries may have more attitudes and interests in common than older generations in the same country.

Other studies comparing the various Japanese American generations also show the continuity and change between generations. Connor (1977) studied three generations of Japanese Americans in the Sacramento area of California, and found that there was a move away from Japanese values towards American values.

Although there is a paucity of empirical studies on value changes among the present Japanese generations, it would appear safe to generalize that by the present fourth and fifth (Yonsei and Gosei) generations, acculturation is almost total. There is an interest on the part of some to reawaken parts of their ethnic heritage and identity by studying in Japan, taking language courses, and learning about the culture. Most of the Japanese are now quite American; however, they do not have the standard "American image," that is, tall, blond, and white. As one consequence, they are constantly mistaken for Japanese from Japan and remarks such as, "You speak English so well," or "We admire your cars," are reminders that one is not fully accepted by the American side of the family.

Most of the research indicates both continuity and change from the traditional Japanese culture toward American models. They indicate that the Issei, the original immigrant generation, is the most Japanese, followed by the Nisei, and that the Sansei and present younger generations are very close, if not identical to American norms. But, as we will see later, Japanese Americans, no matter what generation, also seem to have retained ways of perceiving and behaving that are Japanese.

ACCULTURATION AND LINEARITY

There are a variety of ways of analyzing acculturation. A linear model sees acculturation as a process of giving up the old while taking on the new. Therefore, as the Japanese becomes more American, he or she discards Japanese culture. It is a limited perspective and cannot answer questions concerning dual identities and people who are comfortable in several cultures. Hurh and Kim (1984) speak of an adhesive model; that the American culture is added onto the immigrant culture so that a person may be comfortable in both the ethnic and American life-styles. We, therefore, can consider acculturation or assimilation and ethnic identity as independent entities (see Figure 5.1).

FIGURE 5.1
Assimilation (Acculturation) and Ethnic Identity

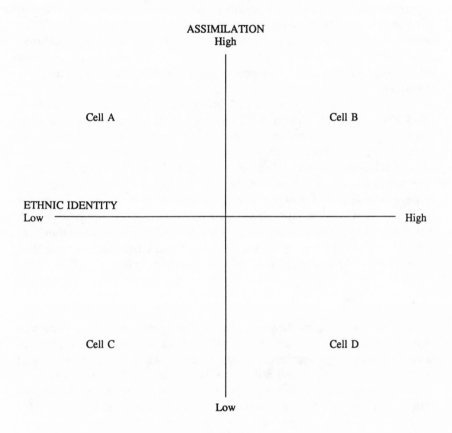

Figure 5.1 shows that assimilation and ethnic identity are independent dimensions whose intersection creates four types of adaptation. Cell A represents Japanese Americans high in assimilation and low in ethnic identity. The individual is more American than ethnic; many members of the third and subsequent generations fit into this category. Language, life-styles, values, and expectations will be American; the ethnic language and value systems will be all but forgotten. Japanese who desire to become totally American will fit into this cell. Friendship patterns, communication styles, food preferences, and the like will coincide with Japanese Americans with a similar orientation or with nonethnics.

Individuals who fit into cell B (high assimilation, high ethnic identity) are similar to those in cell A in terms of assimilation, but will retain a strong ethnic identity. Friendship patterns, communication styles, and values will be dependent on the situation; the individual will be able to move in and out of both the Japanese and American cultures. The individual is bicultural; the cell may include some academics and older individuals who have grown up in and are familiar with both cultures.

Cell C (low assimilation, low ethnic identity) describes the alienated, the disillusioned, and the disenchanted. The individual finds little meaning in the two cultures; he or she may opt for other means of achieving an identity.

Call D (low assimilation, high ethnic identity) describes most of the old Issei as well as newly arrived immigrants who are primarily Japanese in their value systems and communication styles. They prefer to interact with other Japanese; they read Japanese newspapers, watch Japanese television if available, and are more Japanese than American.

The model helps to explain some of the similarities and differences between various groups of Japanese Americans.

Interracial Marriage

One of the more interesting and unusual phenomena among Japanese Americans is that of marrying non-Japanese. At one time, especially among the Issei generation, the idea of marrying a non-Japanese must have been contemplated since the early male-female ratio was so unequal, but there were a variety of barriers to intimate interaction. There were language and cultural differences; there was little opportunity to meet other groups because of housing and occupational segregation; there were racist feelings of both the ethnic and nonethnic populations concerning the mixing of races, and, finally, there were antimiscegenation laws. Laws against interracial marriage were only overturned by the Supreme Court in 1967 (Kitano, 1976). But with each succeeding generation, Japanese Americans are marrying non-Japanese at increasingly high rates.

Figure 5.2 shows that the earliest figure for outmarriage of Japanese Americans in Los Angeles county was 2 percent. Subsequent studies show an increase, with a peak of 63 percent in 1979. Figures for 1989 indicate a 51.5 percent outmarriage rate; it is clear that for Los Angeles County, the trend of marrying non-Japanese continues. Early studies indicated that the preponderance of such marriages were by

FIGURE 5.2
Outmarriage Rates of Japanese Americans
in Los Angeles County, 1924-1984

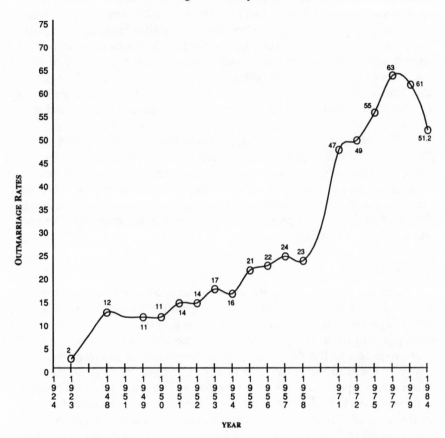

Source: Based on Burma (1963), Panurzio (1942), Risdon (1954), and Kikumura and Kitano (1973). For 1948 through 1959, total marriages with at least one Japanese partner include all interracial marriages recorded for those years; 1972 data are for January-June; 1975, 1977, 1979, and 1984 data are from the Los Angeles County Marriage License Bureau.

the women, though there has been a gradual increase in the number of male outmarriages (Kitano et al., 1992).

The strongest predictor of outmarriage is by generation; at the current time, the adult Japanese American population is primarily Sansei and Yonsei. Other variables related to outmarriage include the decreasing control over marriage by parents; a more tolerant racial atmosphere in both the dominant and ethnic community; demographic factors such as availability of fellow ethnics and the sex ratio; increased opportunities for social interaction due to mobility in occupation, education, and housing and to changes in the law. In terms of our model of assimilation and identity, those who outmarry are most likely to be in cell A (high assimilation, low ethnic identity). The majority of the Sansei and Yonsei fit into this category. We would expect even higher rates of outmarriage where the Japanese American population is small and scattered.

The phenomenon of native Japanese marrying foreigners, called "international marriages," has not been that widespread in Japan. The most common has been the Japanese "war bride." It may well be that, with increasing internationalization and the introduction of different cultures and different people into the country, there may be a change in Japan. However, it will probably never approach the marital patterns of the Japanese Americans.

Generation

An interesting group of Japanese Americans, born in the United States as Nisei but who spent part of their formative years in Japan, is the Kibei. The custom of sending children to live in Japan and acquire a Japanese education was prevalent in the late 1920s and 1930s. The Kibei were exposed to the nationalism and militarism of Japan of that era; many of them found it difficult to adjust to their more Americanized Nisei peers upon their return to America. The World War II evacuation was especially difficult for some Kibei since they sincerely believed in the invincibility of Japanese values and Japanese ways, and felt that the Nisei were "too soft" and "too American" in their orientation. Their experiences in Japan indicate a strong identity with their ancestral homeland, which places them in both cells B and D; some adopted an antiassimilationist perspective (cell D); others became bicultural (cell B). Very little empirical data is available on this group; their values and communication styles would be an interesting area for research.

In summary, there were a variety of influences shaping each generation of Japanese in the United States. Using the model developed in Figure 5.1, the following generalizations are appropriate.

The Issei. Most of the initial immigrant Issei are no longer alive, and the survivors are quite aged. They remained primarily Meiji

Japanese in their values and communication styles; those who were more isolated from the mainstream by residence and occupation remained the most "Japanese." Some who have made a relatively recent trip to Japan encounter culture shock. They find the dress, the talk, and the behavior of the new Japanese generation as difficult to understand as that of the Sansei and Yonsei in America. The noise, smoke, and bright lights of *pachinko* parlors; the flashiness and trendiness of big city life; and the materialistic orientation are especially difficult to fathom from the Issei perspective, especially since many of them lived quiet, frugal lives. The Issei were primarily in cell D of Figure 5.1, high ethnic identity, low assimilation.

The Kibei. The Kibei were influenced by the Japanese culture of the pre-World War II era. They were bilingual and bicultural, with varying degrees of identity with Japan and America. The practice of sending children to Japan during their formative years was a pre-World War II phenomenon; surviving Kibei are quite aged. As indicated previously, they fall primarily into cells D and B in Figure 5.1.

The Nisei. The Nisei were reared by the Japanese "parent," but were educated by the American "parent." Older Nisei were more "Japanese"—they could communicate better in Japanese than their younger cohorts. Acculturation meant that many opted for an American identity and felt that they were Americans, except for their visibility. However, discrimination, including the World War II evacuation, forced many to reevaluate who they were. The question was, "If we are Americans, why are we in the camps?"

As a result, some tried to become more American in order to escape from further discrimination, while others felt that their strength lay in their ethnic identity. The evacuation also introduced the Nisei to other parts of America, and a world that was different from their West Coast experience. Consequently, there were Nisei in the Midwest and on the East Coast who were exposed to mainstream values and communication styles.

Older Nisei could be found in cell B (high in assimilation and high in ethnic identity), while the younger Nisei were primarily in cell A (high in assimilation and lower in ethnic identity).

The Sansei and Succeeding Generations. Each succeeding generation has drifted away from traditional Japanese culture and become more American, so that the question of whether any Japanese values and communication styles remain is the focus of the final part of our paper.

The diversity of the Nisei experience has been felt in each succeeding generation; Japanese Americans born and raised in Massachusetts and New York will reflect the ambiance of those areas. Those who have grown up in Japanese American areas such as Honolulu and Los Angeles may continue to reflect the influences of the Issei and Nisei culture. Most of the newer generations can be placed in cell A (high in assimilation, low in ethnic identity).

Alcohol Consumption

A special issue when dealing with the Japanese in Japan and Japanese Americans is the consumption of alcoholic beverages. Befu (1986) provides a detailed analysis of the use of alcohol in Japan. Sake, the native alcoholic beverage, was initially a sacred drink, and was produced as an offering to the gods. The drinking was accompanied by conviviality and communality. But today drinking sake is totally secularized and the sacredness has disappeared. Nevertheless, there is a clear drinking etiquette in Japan. The pouring of the drink, who does the pouring, and how one shows that one has had enough, are social skills that indicate that one has acquired the first rudiments of drinking in Japan. Although a considerable amount of alcohol may be consumed during dinner, how drunk the participants appear to be is not related to alcohol intake. Socially defined rules of drunken behavior are situationally determined. Befu (1986) points out that at a party, "it takes very little alcohol to induce loud talking, shouting, loud laughter, singing and clapping hands in unison with a wild, off-tune chorus of school songs" (Befu, 1986, p. 118). But when it is time to go home, there is a sudden soberness, except for the few who have overimbibed.

Kitano and colleagues (1988) compared alcohol consumption between Japanese in Japan, Hawaii, and California. The Japanese in Japan drank the most, followed by an almost equal amount of alcohol consumption by the two Japanese American samples. Drinking seemed to follow local styles; wine was the favorite drink among northern Californians, while the Japanese in Hawaii preferred beer. Beer was also the favorite drink in Japan. A report by the National Tax Administration (*Japan Times*, 1992) also indicated that the Japanese imbibed a record 9.5 million kiloliters of alcoholic drinks in 1991.

A study comparing norms and actual drinking patterns of the Japanese in the same three areas provided some interesting findings (Kitano et al., 1992). There were statistically significant differences between areas in terms of age and drinking norms for males and females.

The question asked for attitudes towards drinking for 16-, 21-, 40-, and 60-year-olds. More permissive norms for male drinking were observed in Japan, followed by Hawaii and Japan, whereas a greater tolerance of female drinking was noted in Santa Clara (California), followed by Hawaii and Japan. All study areas were much more tolerant of male drinking than female drinking. Overall, there was a high degree of similarity in drinking norms between the Santa Clara and Hawaii samples, whereas the Japanese respondents often differed from their American counterparts. For example, Japanese Americans were more tolerant of female drinking than were the Japanese, whereas the Japanese were more tolerant of heavy drinking among adult males.

The results of this 1992 study were interpreted in terms of enculturation and acculturation. Most of the Japanese Americans were children and grandchildren of immigrants who left for Hawaii and California in the early part of the twentieth century, so that they missed what the Japanese in Japan have gone through (enculturation), and instead have adapted to life in the United States (acculturation). Since World War II, Japan has gone through a number of transformations, including a wartime occupation, heavy industrialization, and urbanization. Drinking has become a strong part of the cultural context of Japanese life, especially among businessmen.

Japanese Americans in Hawaii and California have developed their own styles of drinking. Since there was a long period of time when they were isolated from the white mainstream, their drinking was influenced by local conditions. Much of Japanese American drinking, whether in Hawaii or California, is done with other ethnic peers (somewhat similar to Japan), but the ambiance is different. There is no wide-ranging network of Japanese-owned and operated bars in the United States patronized by Japanese Americans, and most Japanese American wives would not tolerate their husbands going to drinking establishments regularly after work, as is common in Japan. It would appear that in terms of drinking, local life styles have been influential.

CULTURAL PRACTICES

Given this broad background and the similarities and dissimilarities among Japanese, are there values and communication styles among Japanese Americans that can be traced to Japan? On a trip to Japan in 1992, I found many behavioral and communication patterns which were familiar, but which had faded away through living among Americans.

But it all came back rather quickly, such as continually taking off one's shoes at the entrance of households, and the use of separate slippers for the bathroom. However, after a while it became a chore, especially if one was wearing laced shoes that could not be slipped off at a moment's notice. It is my observation that the Japanese in Hawaii have retained this custom more than their peers on the mainland.

Other typically Japanese patterns included the constant bowing, which was even done on television programs. There were the "Irrashais," and the "Arigatos," or the welcomes and thank yous upon entering and leaving business establishments that have all but disappeared in the United States. The politeness, and the pedestrians all waiting for the stop light to change, are reminders that there are some cultures where such signs are to be obeyed voluntarily. And it is a perplexing but welcome change to deal with a "no tipping" culture, for even taxi drivers are not tipped. But these are behaviors that can be easily changed; spending any time in Japan will shape all but the most rebellious into the local styles.

However, there are also practices that have remained, both among Japanese Americans and among Japanese in Japan. Some of these patterns include *enryo*, shame, indirect communication, and lack of verbal participation.

Enryo

Miyatake and Norton (1992), writing in the *Japan Times* discuss the problem of foreigners who ask for favors without realizing the importance of *enryo* for their hosts. "En" means far or distant, and "ryo" refers to consideration, so that *enryo* encourages Japanese to be reserved, to be modest, to show restraint, to hesitate, and to refrain from asking for favors too directly. They cite an example where a non-Japanese roommate continually asked for favors that were inappropriate from an *enryo* perspective. The authors indicate that when asking for a favor, one must show *enryo*, which includes a deferential attitude, a slight bowing posture, and a facial expression which communicates the idea of, "I'm sorry to bother you," as well as implying that the favor will be returned.

Japanese Americans also understand the meaning, if not all of the nuances of the term. *Enryo* helps to explain much of Japanese American behavior:

> It has both a positive and negative effect on Japanese (American) social interaction. For example, take observations of Japanese in

situations as diverse as their hesitancy to speak out at meetings; their refusal of any invitation, especially the first time; their refusal of second helping; their acceptance of a less desired object when given a free choice; their lack of verbal participation, especially in an integrated group; their refusal to ask questions; and their hesitancy in asking for a raise in salary—these may be all based on *enryo*. (Kitano, 1976, p. 125)

Feelings of shame are also connected with *enryo*. Parents may practice social control over their children through shame—of not bringing shame on the family, of not making a fool of oneself. It makes it difficult to take risks or to try something new, and contributes to shyness and a hesitancy in speaking out. It also means nonparticipation in activities where one has little talent and skill; therefore, it is surprising to see Japanese in Japan, also saddled with shame, participating so enthusiastically in *karaoke*, or public singing with the accompaniment of a recorded background. *Karaoke* does not seem to be that popular among Japanese Americans; some observers have inferred that Nisei and Sansei are "too uptight" about their image and self-esteem, and would only participate if they had an established talent. It is our observation that the Japanese individual in Japan practices before he sings publically, but that no matter how meager his or her talent, friends and peers enthusiastically applaud the effort. In contrast, the Japanese American will face a more critical audience in terms of the quality of the performance, which serves to inhibit participation.

Indirect Communication

Another communication style that is common both in Japan and among Japanese Americans is the preference for indirection, deflection, and cooperation over directness and confrontation. For example, instead of a parent saying, "Stop this very minute!" or "Do what I say!"; the Japanese style might be, "A good child does it this way," or "Let's do it together."

Family gatherings and the decision to hold an outing can be models of indecision. First, there is *enryo* and the fear of suggesting an unpopular place—then there is indirectness, so that a person might say that someone else thought one place was good, but he could not personally vouch for it. Another family member might make another suggestion, but indicate that it might not be too good if the weather happened to change. Then there are power and role relationships to consider so that several hours may pass before there is a final decision.

Lack of Verbal Participation

Teaching in Japan and teaching in a class made up of Japanese Americans, even of the third and fourth generations, is somewhat similar. Perhaps the only difference is that there is almost no participation in Japan—a fifty-minute lecture, leaving the last ten minutes for questions, generally ends up in total silence, while among Japanese Americans, there is an initial hesitancy, then a mild degree of verbal interaction.

A variety of reasons are used to explain this lack of verbal participation. In Japan, one answer is that, "It's the culture," with the inference that the professor is the expert so one shows respect by not raising questions. Family socialization may also discourage frank and open verbal interchanges; there are appropriate role expectations based on sex and age.

Japanese Americans indicate that unless their question is a gem, they are afraid to ask, so that by the time they have formulated one, the opportunity may have passed. They are also afraid of asking a stupid question, so *enryo* and shame are also involved.

Other values, such as an emphasis on hard work, on *gaman*, or "putting up with it," and "gritting one's teeth," are somewhat common among Japanese Americans, but other value-terms such as *on* and *giri*, obligation and honor, have little meaning for the present generation. Gift-giving has also died out, although it is still not uncommon to receive some form of gift when you have invited other Japanese Americans for a gathering. The *koden*, or the practice of giving a monetary gift at a funeral, continues, as well as the *orei*, or thank you, that follows.

The trend away from the Japanese culture is most pronounced among the younger generations. As Kitano (1976) writes:

> Although Japanese and Americans have differed in the past in their collective and individualistic orientations, the collectivity orientation has diminished among Sansei and at present is similar to that of Caucasian samples. Egoistic behavior and the importance of self over others has developed touch an extent that . . . on a question dealing with the family and the nation, the Sansei held a more individualistic position than did the non-Japanese American. (p. 141)

There also remain elements of the Japanese culture, some in almost stereotypical fashion. The tea ceremony, flower arranging, and other dances remain with select groups. Foods, such as sukiyaki, tofu and sushi have even become popular among non-Japanese Americans. It would be nice if values such as responsibility, concern for others, and quiet dignity would remain, while other aspects of Japanese culture, such as authoritative discipline, blind obedience to custom, and sexism, were discarded.

JAPAN, AMERICA, AND JAPANESE AMERICANS

The products of the relationship between Japan and the United States can be seen in their "children," "grandchildren," and succeeding generations. A few conclusions can be drawn from our study of this relationship:

1. A number of celebrations and rituals, such as New Year's (*o sho gatsu*) and the *koden* at funerals, are still observed by Japanese Americans. However, the Fourth of July, influences from the American side, have become just as important. Christmas is important in both cultures.

2. Values and communication styles are primarily functional— those that have been retained serve a useful purpose, those that have had less value tend to be discarded or modified. As Suzuki (1977) writes, cultural valves and social forces interact so that some cultural values are reinforced and strengthened, others punished or ignored and thus weakened, while some values are added from the dominant society.

3. Exchange theory (Homans, 1961) provides a useful explanation of the interchange between cultures, and the subsequent maintenance in succeeding generations. The theory posits that individuals and groups act rationally to maximize rewards and minimize costs to themselves. The rewards or profits may be in terms of time, energy, effort, and wealth, as well as psychological satisfaction such as a sense of self-worth and self-esteem.

4. The initial Japanese values and communication styles were embedded in a hierarchical structure. The Issei immigrants knew their place in Japanese society; entrance into the American system was not that different—their place was in the lower strata. Therefore, such an orientation was functional; it will be interesting to see if each succeeding generation changes as it becomes more American, more upwardly mobile, and more egalitarian. Their rate of marriage with non-Japanese is one indication that they are communicating intimately with the dominant population.

The question of whether the present generation will retain some semblance of the culture that has been passed down through the Issei and Nisei, especially with increased acculturation, assimilation, and outmarriage, would be an interesting area for further research. Will there be similar changes in Japan; does industrialization and urbanization and immigration forge new patterns?

As for the Japanese experience in America, their basic orientation was based on their powerlessness and an unequal relationship with the dominant society. Will they discard this orientation as they achieve a higher position in the hierarchy? The same may be true of the parent states, Japan and America—will a change in power alter previous relationships which were based on the dominance of the United States?

REFERENCES

Abramowitz, M. (1992, April 1). Japanese Americans pay bashing price. *The Japan Times*, p. 19.

Arkoff, A. (1959). Need patterns in two generations of Japanese Americans in Hawaii. *The Journal of Social Psychology, 50*, 75-79.

Befu, H. (1986). An ethnography of dinner and entertainment in Japan. In T. S. Lebra & W. P. Lebra (Eds.), *Japanese culture and behavior*. Honolulu: University of Hawaii Press.

Benedict, R. (1946). *The chrysanthemum and the sword*. Boston: Houghton Mifflin.

Booth, A. (1992, April 8). An accidental relationship. *Asahi Evening News*, p. 9.

Burma, J. H. (1963). Interracial marriage in Los Angeles. *Social Forces, 42*, 156-165.

Caudill, W. (1952). Japanese American personality and acculturation. *Genetic Psychology Monographs, 52*.

Connor, J. (1977). *Tradition and change in three generations of Japanese Americans*. Chicago: Nelson Hall.

DeVos, G. (1955). A quantitative Rorsarch assessment of maladjustment and rigidity in acculturating Japanese Americans. *Genetic Psychology Monographs, 52*, 51-87.

Fenz, W. D., & Arkoff, A. (1962). Comparative need patterns of five ancestry groups in Hawaii. *The Journal of Social Psychology, 58*, 67-89.

Homans, G. (1961). *Social behavior: Its elementary forms*. New York: Harcourt, Brace and World.

Hurh, W. M., & Kim, K. (1984). *Korean immigrants in America*. Cranbury, NJ: Farleigh Dickinson University Press.

Iga, M. (1967, June 21). Do most Japanese Americans living in the United States still retain traditional Japanese personality? *The Kashu Mainichi* (California Daily News), Los Angeles, California, p.1.

The Japan Times. (1992, April 26). Alcohol consumption soars to a new high, p. 2.

Karatsu, H. (1992, March 23). Never as easy as it sounds. *The Japan Times*, p. 24.

Kawahara, Y., & Kitano, H. H. L. (1992). Values study in progress.

Kikumura, A., & Kitano, H. H. L. (1973). Interracial marriage: A picture of Japanese Americans. *Journal of Social Issues, 29*(2), 67-81.

Kitano, H. H. L. (1961). Differential child rearing practices between first and second generation Japanese in the United States. *The Journal of Social Psychology, 53*, 13-19.

Kitano, H. H. L. (1964). Inter- and intragenerational differences in maternal attitudes toward child rearing. *The Journal of Social Psychology, 63*, 215-220.

Kitano, H. H. L. (1976). *Japanese Americans*. Englewood Cliffs, NJ: Prentice Hall.

Kitano, H. H. L., & Daniels, R. (1988). *Asian Americans*. Englewood Cliffs, NJ: Prentice Hall.

Kitano, H. H. L., Chi, I., Law, C. K., Lubben, J. E., & Rhee, S. (1988). Alcohol consumption in Japanese in Japan, Hawaii, and California. In L. H. Towle & T. Harford (Eds.), *Cultural influences and drinking patterns: A focus on Hispanic and Japanese Populations*. NIAA Research Monograph No. 19, DHHS Publication No. (ADM) 88—1563, Washington: Government Printing Office, 99-133.

Kitano, H. H. L., Chi, I., Rhee, S., Law, C. K., & Lubben, J. (1992). Norms and alcohol consumption: Japanese in Japan, Hawaii and California. *Journal of Alcohol Studies, 53*(1), 33-39.

Kitano, H. H. L., Fujino, D., & Tanaka, J. (1992). Interracial marriage among Japanese Americans (in process).

Meredith, G. M., & Meredith, C. (1966). Acculturation and personality among Japanese-American college students in Hawaii. *The Journal of Social Psychology, 68*, 175-182.

Miyatake, F., & Norton, J. (1992, April 2). Favor asking risks friendship. *The Japan Times*, p. 16.

Pacific Citizen. (1992, March 13). Racism hits California campus. Los Angeles, CA., p. 1.

Panunzio, C. (1942). Intermarriage in Los Angeles, 1924-33. *American Journal of Sociology, 47*, 690-701.

Risdon, R. (1954). A study of interracial marriages based on data for Los Angeles County. *Sociology and Social Research, 39*, 92-95.

Strong, E. K. Jr. (1934). *The second generation Japanese problem*. Palo Alto, CA: Stanford University Press.

Suzuki, B. (1977). Education and the socialization of Asian Americans: A revisionist analysis of the model minority thesis. *Amerasia Journal, 4*, 23-52.

PART III
COMPARING COMMUNICATION
IN SELECTED CONTEXTS

Chapter 6

INTERPERSONAL AND INTERGROUP COMMUNICATION IN JAPAN AND THE UNITED STATES[1]

William B. Gudykunst and Tsukasa Nishida

In recent years extensive cross-cultural research comparing patterns of interpersonal and intergroup communication in Japan and the United States, as well as research on Japanese-North American communication, has been conducted.[2] Space does not allow us to summarize results of each of the studies in detail. In presenting the results we, therefore, focus on major trends in the studies reviewed.

To begin, we examine cross-cultural similarities and differences in communication in interpersonal and intergroup relationships in Japan and the United States.[3] Following this, we summarize research on similarities and differences in the decoding and encoding of messages. Next, we review communication in Japanese-North American intercultural relationships. We conclude by discussing theoretical issues to be addressed in future research.

CROSS-CULTURAL SIMILARITIES AND DIFFERENCES
IN COMMUNICATION IN INTERPERSONAL AND
INTERGROUP RELATIONSHIPS

Initial Interactions

Individuals try to reduce uncertainty in initial interactions with strangers (Berger, 1979). Uncertainty in this context refers to two phenomena: the ability to accurately predict how others will behave and the ability to explain why others behave the way they do (Berger & Calabrese, 1975). Uncertainty reduction, therefore, involves the creation of proactive predictions and retroactive explanations about others' behavior. Uncertainty reduction theory (e.g., Berger & Calabrese, 1975) originally was formulated to explain communication in initial interactions. The desire to reduce uncertainty, however, does not stop with initial interactions. Rather, as Berger (1979) argues, "the communicative processes involved in knowledge generation and the development of understanding are central to the development and disintegration of most interpersonal relationships" (p. 123).

Gudykunst and Nishida (1986a) assume that reducing uncertainty is a major concern in Japanese interpersonal relationships. This assumption is based in part on the work of Japanese researchers (e.g., Nakane, 1974) and on Hofstede's (1980) dimensions of cultural variability (i.e., Japan has a high score on the uncertainty avoidance dimension). There are, however, different factors that are important in reducing uncertainty in Japan and the United States; that is, Japanese communication focuses more on nonverbal aspects of communication than communication in the United States (see Kunihiro [1976], Matsumoto [1988], Okabe [1983], Okabe [1987], and Tsujimura [1987] for discussions of this position).[4] Tsujimura (1987), for example, argues that much of Japanese communication is based on (1) ishin-denshin ("traditional mental telepathy"), (2) taciturnity, (3) kuuki (mood or atmosphere), and (4) respect for reverberation (indirect communication; see Tsujimura, 1968, for a complete discussion of these concepts).[5] Ito (1989b) argues that the need to be sensitive to others' true feelings is due to Japanese attitudes being "double structured" (i.e., Japanese draw a distinction between tatemae, diplomatic attitude or the attitude expressed to others, and honne, true attitude).

Because of the emphasis on indirect verbal communication and nonverbal communication, members of high-context cultures like Japan need to know whether others understand them when they do not verbally express their feelings in order to reduce uncertainty. It also is necessary for members of high-context cultures to know whether others will make allowances for them when they communicate for them to have confidence in predicting others' behavior (Note: attributional confidence is the inverse of uncertainty). The concept of *sasshi* illustrates this claim. Nishida (1977) defines *sasshi* as meaning conjecture, surmise, or guessing what someone means. In its verb form (*sassuru*), its meaning is expanded to include imagine, suppose, or empathize with, and make allowances for others. While nonverbal sensitivity to indirect forms of communication is necessary to reduce uncertainty in high-context cultures, it is information about others' attitudes, beliefs, values, etc. that is necessary to reduce uncertainty for direct communication used in low-context cultures.[6]

Gudykunst and Nishida (1986a) developed a two-dimensional measure of attributional confidence that is consistent with the descriptions of communication in low- and high-context cultures (see Gudykunst & San Antonio chapter in this volume for a description). In developing the measure, they assumed that members of low-context cultures focus on information specific to the individuals with whom they are communicating in order to increase the accuracy of their predictions in direct forms of communication. They also assumed that members of high-context cultures focus on nonverbal information to increase the accuracy of their predictions in indirect forms of communication. Confirmatory factor analysis supported the prediction that two factors exist in Japan and the United States. Results of Gudykunst and Nishida's study also indicated that both types of information are used in the United States and Japan. Members of high-context cultures like Japan use information on individuals' attitudes, beliefs, and feelings, but this information appears to be secondary to the information necessary to reduce uncertainty in indirect forms of communication. Similarly, people in low-context cultures like the United States use information on whether or not others understand their feelings or will make allowances for them, but this information is secondary to the others' attitudes, values, and beliefs.

The two dimensions of attributional confidence correlated differently with several variables in Japan and the United States in Gudykunst and Nishida's (1986a) study. Frequency of communication, for example, correlated more strongly with low- and high-context attributional confidence in the United States than Japan. Overlap in social networks, interaction with the partners' friends, and percent of free time spent with partners, in contrast, correlated more strongly with high-context (but not low-context) attributional confidence in Japan than the United States.[7] These results suggest that members of low-context cultures develop low- and high-context attributional confidence through communicating with others frequently (Note: it is not just frequency of communication; the greater the frequency the more the self-disclosure, interrogation, etc.). Members of high-context cultures, however, gain high-context attributional confidence through group-based communication activities.

In a study using uncertainty reduction theory, Gudykunst and Nishida (1984; Nishida & Gudykunst, 1986) found differences between respondents in Japan and the United States in terms of self-disclosure, interrogation, and attributional confidence. As predicted, respondents in the Japan sample displayed a higher degree of attributional confidence about strangers' behavior when provided background information (e.g., school attended) than the respondents in the United States sample. Background information provides a solid foundation on which to make predictions about others' behavior in collectivistic cultures like Japan, but not in individualistic cultures like the United States. Respondents in the United States sample also reported that they intended to self-disclose and interrogate strangers more than respondents in the Japanese sample. These results are consistent with research conducted by Barnlund (1975), Johnson and Johnson (1975), and Nakanishi (1986). Barnlund (1975), for example, found that North Americans self-disclose more to strangers than Japanese. The data from this study also are compatible with Barnlund's (1989) finding that North Americans communicate more frequently with strangers than Japanese.

Miyanaga (1991) provides the basis for an explanation for the differences in self-disclosure based on the Japanese conception of *tatemae* and *honne*. She argues that

> *honne* is what a person really wants to do, and *tatemae* is his [or her] submission to moral obligation. Interaction rituals begin with mutual expressions that are culturally prescribed when two parties meet; they develop from occasional (i.e., formal) to frequent (i.e., intimate) exposure of honest feelings. The particularites of the moral basis of interaction rituals is socially established and agreed upon. Honest feelings, however, are, by definition, personal. Premature expression of honest expectations can incite a strongly negative response from the other person in the relationship. (p. 89)

In collectivistic cultures like Japan, individuals do not expose their true feelings until they know another person well. In individualistic cultures, individuals are expected to express themselves to others, even if they do not know them well.

It is not only verbal aspects of communication which differ in initial interactions. The findings from Gudykunst and Nishida's (1984) study are compatible with nonverbal research on interaction distances. Sussman and Rosenfeld (1982), for example, found that when speaking their native language, Japanese sit further apart when communicating with strangers than North Americans. When speaking English, however, the distance that Japanese sit from each other approximates that used in the United States. Sussman and Rosenfeld's findings are consistent with Engebretson and Fullmer's (1970) earlier study. They found that Japanese prefer greater interaction distances with their friends, father, and professors than Euro Americans in the United States.[8]

There was one additional finding from Gudykunst and Nishida's (1984) study of initial interactions that was not expected; namely, Japanese respondents reported that they intended to display more nonverbal affiliative expressiveness to strangers than North American respondents. This finding, however, is consistent with Hofstede's (1980) uncertainty avoidance dimension; members of high uncertainty avoidance cultures (e.g., Japan) display emotions more than members of low uncertainty avoidance cultures (e.g., the United States). If the high uncertainty avoidance culture is also collectivistic, however, it would be expected that the emotions displayed would be limited to "positive" emotions since "negative" emotions are not conducive to maintaining group harmony. Friesen's (1972) research illustrates this point. He found that students in Japan and the United States display similar affect to a stressful film when viewing it alone, but when in the company of a peer, students from the United States show more negative affect than students from Japan. Similarly, Argyle and his associates (1986) found that the English and Italians (both individualistic cultures) display more anger and distress than Japanese.

Nakanishi and Johnson (1993) conducted a study of conversational logics in initial interactions in Japan and the United States. They discovered that Japanese felt a stronger obligation to respond to different levels of self-disclosure than North Americans. Japanese also perceived a stronger relationship-act connection than the North Americans. Further, Japanese reported that their responses to others have less influence on who they are as individuals than the North Americans. These findings are consistent with Hall's (1976) low- and high-context theory of cultural differences.

Barnlund (1975; his 1989 results are consistent with the 1975 data) found that tastes and opinions are viewed as the most appropriate topics for conversation in Japan and the United States, while physical attributes and personal traits are viewed as the least appropriate. He also discovered that the hierarchy of preferred target persons is the same in the two cultures: same-sex friend, opposite-sex friend, mother, father, stranger, and untrusted acquaintances. Overall, Barnlund's data indicate that North Americans engage in more self-disclosure than Japanese. This pattern was consistent across topics of conversation and target persons in Barnlund's studies

Asai and Barnlund (1991) argue that differences in self-disclosure between people in the United States and Japan are due to differing levels of self-knowledge. They found that students in the United States have greater self-knowledge and self-disclose more than students in Japan. They also discovered that level of self-knowledge correlates highly with amount of self-disclosure in both cultures.[9]

Nishida (1991) studied topics of self-disclosure in the first five minutes of initial interactions.[10] In the first five minutes, he found that North Americans would discuss (percentage indicating response in parentheses): the weather (80), names (79), immediate surroundings (47), time (45), academic majors (40), current courses (39), destinations (38), universities (38), mutual friends (36), surrounding activities (75), and hometowns (32). The corresponding topics for Japanese were: the weather (76), names (71), universities (61), ages (52), hometowns (48), academic majors (48), destinations (38), addresses (38), time (38), living arrangements (37), immediate surroundings (36), mutual friends (35), and commuting (31). Nine of the topics (out of eleven total for North Americans and thirteen total for Japanese) were common in the two samples. This study, therefore, is consistent with Barnlund's (1975, 1989) research.

Developing Relationships

Lu and Gudykunst (1988) demonstrated that uncertainty reduction and social penetration processes are related across relationships in Japan and the United States. Social penetration theory is used to explain relationship development process in the United States. This theory posits four stages of relationship development: orientation, exploratory affective exchange, affective exchange, and stable exchange. The orientation stage is characterized by responses that are stereotypical and reflect superficial aspects of the personalities of the individuals involved in a relationship. Exploratory affective exchange involves interaction at the periphery of the personality of the partners. This stage includes relationships that are friendly and relaxed, but commitments are limited or temporary. The third stage, full affective exchange, involves "loose" and "free-wheeling" interaction and an increase of self-disclosure in central areas of the partner's personalities. Stable exchange, the final stage, emerges when partners have fully described themselves to each other and involves few instances of miscommunication. While these stages were isolated in the United States, they appear to be applicable to interpersonal relationships in Japan.

Eight broad dimensions of communication behavior are hypothesized to vary with the stage of a relationship (Altman & Taylor, 1973; Knapp, 1978). As relationships become more intimate: (1) communication takes on a more "personalistic focus"; (2) depth of interaction increases; (3) breadth of interaction increases; (4) difficulty of interaction decreases; (5) flexibility of interaction increases; (6) spontaneity of interaction increases; (7) smoothness of interaction increases; and (8) evaluation of interaction increases. Knapp, Ellis, and Williams (1980) examined perceptions of communication along the eight dimensions. They found that the eight dimensions actually cluster into three distinct factors. The first factor, labeled "personalized communication," includes items that relate to the intimacy of communication (e.g., "We tell each other personal things about ourselves—things we don't tell most people"). The second factor, which involves items that relate to the coordination of communication between partners (e.g., "Due to mutual cooperation, our conversations are generally effortless and smooth flowing"), was labeled "synchronized communication." The final factor encompasses items that relate to communication "barriers" to communication (e.g., "It is difficult for us to know when the other person is being serious or sarcastic"); it was labeled "difficult communication." This study indicated that communication becomes more personalized and synchronized and less difficulty is experienced as relationships become more intimate.

Miyanaga (1991) provides a description of the stages of Japanese relationships that is similar to those posited in social penetration theory. She also points out, however, that there are differences in the communication that occurs within each stage. Miyanaga argues that Japanese strive for "perfect mutual understanding" in personal relationships and that this is possible because of the "interaction rituals" which take place in all stages of a personal relationship. A large part of the interaction rituals in Japanese personal relationships involve nonverbal cues. Miyanaga contends that communicators' body movements, tone of voice, degree of avoidance of eye contact, laughter, smiles, serious expressions, and even the degree of body tension are, to a certain extent, carefully controlled to constitute cues.

At the same time, a person tries as much as possible to catch the cues given by others. If a person keeps missing the given cues, he [or she] will be judged as "blunt" or "dull" (because he [or she] is unreceptive), "impolite" (when it is judged that he [or she] is deliberately choosing to miss cues), or *gaijin mitai* (like a foreigner). High receptivity is admired. The Japanese word generally used to indicate such receptivity is *sasshi*, which literally means "to guess." It implies that one guesses the real intention of others in spite of their surface disguise. . . .

Although a high *sasshi* ability in the recipient of cues is much appreciated, an expectation of *sasshi* effort from the other is discouraged. The word for this is *amae*. Although *amae* has been co-opted as a psychological concept by Takeo Doi (1973), in the interaction ritual it is simply used to indicate the restriction of excessive dependency on the *sasshi* of the other person. . . . *Amae*, when used in a conversation, signifies a passive aggression in which one depends on the manners of others. (pp. 85-86)

Miyanaga goes on to argue that in an "ideal" relationship where *sasshi* and *amae* are operating, Japanese communicate spontaneously. Each partner in a relationship understands when the other will follow behavior norms and when the other will abandon the behavioral norms. As relationships become more intimate, the interaction rituals used by the partners become more idiosyncratic. This idea is similar to Miller and Steinberg's (1975) argument that the rule structures guiding relationships become more idiosyncratic as relationships become more intimate.

Developmental theories such as social penetration theory suggest that as interpersonal relationships become more intimate, there should be fewer cultural differences in the nature of communication that takes place (see Gudykunst, 1989, for a summary of this argument). This assumption is supported, in part, by descriptions of communication in close friendships in Japan. Vogel (1963), for example, argues that in true friendships, "people are relaxed and do not worry about formalities. They can talk and joke about their innermost concerns. . . . With close friends, one can argue, criticize, and be stubborn without endangering the relationships. . . . These relationships are remarkably intimate" (p. 136). Atsumi (1980) also points out that the number of friendship relationships is small in Japan (less than half dozen), that they usually are with members of the same sex, and that they also generally are with former classmates. Some friendship relationships are *shin-yu* (intimate friends). In these relationships, Japanese feel "completely open and relaxed" (p. 70).

Gudykunst and Nishida (1983) examined perceptions of social penetration in close same-sex friendships across ten topics of conversation. Social penetration was operationalized by combining the frequency respondents discussed the topics and the intimacy ratings they assigned to the topics. Significant differences emerged on only three of the ten topics: own marriage and family, love and dating, and emotions and feelings (the seven topics on which significant differences were not observed are: parental family, physical condition, money/property, interests/hobbies, relationships, attitudes/values, and school/work). The means for the United States sample were higher than the means for the Japanese sample on each of the topics on which significant differences emerged.

The differences that emerged in Gudykunst and Nishida's (1983) study can be interpreted using Hofstede's masculinity dimension. Specifically, it would be expected that members of highly masculine cultures (e.g., Japan) discuss topics dealing with opposite-sex relationships less than people in cultures lower on the masculinity index (e.g., the United States). The topics on which there were not significant differences appear to be compatible with Barnlund's (1989) research. As indicated earlier, he found that Japanese and North Americans agree on the ordering of the first four topics they prefer to discuss in conversations: tastes, general background information, work/school, and feelings.

There were cultural differences for three of the topics of conversation in Gudykunst and Nishida's (1983) study, but there were no significant differences in social penetration between the Japanese and North American respondents for seven of the topics. While this is not unambiguous evidence, these data do support the assumption that there are few differences in communication in close friendships attributable to culture. Takahara's (1974) data also suggest that friendships in Japan and the United States share many common characteristics. The four most frequently mentioned characteristics in Japan were togetherness, trust, warmth, and understanding. The corresponding characteristics in the United States were understanding, respect/sincerity, trust, and helping. These studies are compatible with several writers' contentions that close friendships are voluntary relationships in which communication has a personalistic focus (e.g., Bell, 1981; Suttles, 1970; Wright, 1978).

Gudykunst and Nishida (1986b) extended Knapp, Ellis, and Williams' (1980) earlier work. This study involved two separate surveys. The first survey involved intimacy ratings of relationship terms in Japan and the United States.[11] Consistent with Triandis' (1988) conceptualization of individualism, Japanese respondents rated relationship terms associated with two of their ingroups (university classmates and coworkers) as more intimate than respondents from the United States. The Japanese respondents also perceived six of the nine family relationship terms as less intimate than the North American respondents. These results also appear to be consistent with an extension of Triandis' argument; namely, that collectivistic cultures which do not rank the family ingroup first, do not perceive family relationships as highly intimate (Nakane [1970, 1974] argues that Japanese rate the company ingroup first). The data for ratings of opposite-sex relationship terms were consistent with Hofstede's (1980) masculinity dimension. Specifically, six of the seven opposite-sex terms were rated less intimate by the Japanese respondents than the respondents from the United States (the only term Japanese respondents rated as more intimate than North Americans was "date"). Since highly masculine cultures like Japan have strong sex-role differentiation, there is little informal contact between males and females.

While there were differences in the mean ratings of relationship terms in Gudykunst and Nishida's (1986b) study, there also was a similar pattern of increasing intimacy for several terms across the two cultures. If the five "interpersonal" terms are examined, the same pattern of intimacy emerges in the two cultures (from least to most intimate): stranger, acquaintance, friend, close friend, and best friend. These data support the generalizability of the stages of social penetration theory (Altman & Taylor, 1973) across cultures.

The second survey in Gudykunst and Nishida's (1986b) study focused on the eight dimensions of communication hypothesized to vary as relationships increase in intimacy. Respondents were assigned randomly to answer questions about two of six relationships which varied in intimacy (stranger, acquaintance, classmate, friend, close friend, lover). Confirmatory factor analysis revealed that the eight dimensions cluster around the same three factors (i.e., personalization, synchronization, and difficulty) as Knapp, Ellis, and Williams (1980) found in the United States. This study also revealed that the more intimate the relationship, the greater the personalization and synchronization, and the less the difficulty of communication in both cultures. Similar patterns emerged for low- and high-context uncertainty reduction on the survey instrument (Gudykunst & Nishida, 1986a). The increases in social penetration and attributional confidence as relationships become more intimate are consistent with Knapp and colleagues' (1980) intracultural research and with social penetration theory (Altman & Taylor, 1973) in general. These findings also are compatible with developmental trends (e.g., the closer the relationship, the greater the self-disclosure) in Barnlund's (1975, 1989) data.

Many scholars (e.g., Altman, Vinsel, & Brown, 1981) argue that self-disclosure should be studied as one component of privacy regulation. Privacy regulation is a process through which individuals make themselves accessible or inaccessible to others (Altman, 1977). People in all cultures regulate privacy, but the specific mechanisms people use varies across cultures (Altman, 1977).

Baker and Gudykunst (1990) developed a measure to study privacy regulation strategies in Japan and the United States. The measure was developed in two phases. In the first phase, North American and Japanese students studying in the United States were interviewed regarding the way they regulate their privacy. The results of these interviews were incorporated in a questionnaire that was administered in the two cultures.

Five factors emerged in Baker and Gudykunst's (1990) study. The first factor, attentiveness, contained six items (the response category for each item was 1 = not likely to use, 7 = very likely to use): I would give direct eye contact, My response to questions would be smooth, I would move closer to the person, I would answer fully, I would be attentive to the verbal exchange, and I would talk a lot. The second factor, avoidance, contained three items: I would stand in the corner, I would turn my back, and I would ignore the person. Four items loaded on the third factor, direct verbal strategies: I would say, "I don't want to"; I would say, "Don't ask that sort of thing"; I would say, "I want to be alone"; and I would ask that person why they are asking the question. The fourth factor, indirect verbal strategies, included four items: I would use short words, I would be evasive, I would start talking with someone else, and I would answer in a roundabout way. The final factor, retreat strategies, included three items: I would go for a drive, I would go to my room and close the door, and I would sleep.

Cultural differences emerged on two of the five factors in Baker and Gudykunst's (1990) study: attentiveness and indirect strategies.

The mean for the United States sample was higher than the mean for the Japanese sample on attentiveness. This indicates that Japanese are more likely to use lack of attentiveness as a privacy control mechanism than North Americans. The mean for indirect strategies was higher in the Japan sample than the United States sample, indicating that Japanese are more likely to indirectly tell others they want privacy than are North Americans.

The cultural differences in Baker and Gudykunst's (1990) study are consistent with individualism-collectivism and previous research.[12] Barnlund (1975), for example, found that Japanese prefer "passive-with-drawal" strategies when confronted with a threat to the self. North Americans, in contrast, preferred "active-aggressive" strategies. Naotsuka, Sakamoto and colleagues (1981) found similar results. They discovered that Japanese avoid direct confrontation and use indirect strategies when their privacy is threatened by others.

Baker (1990) examined cultural differences in individuals' responses to Altman's (1977) conceptualization of privacy (a description of Altman's conceptualization [i.e., privacy is a process where people make themselves open and closed] was provided and respondents were asked to agree or disagree and explain why). Based on the responses to open-ended questions, Baker found that Japanese disagree with the notion that openness is an aspect of privacy, while North Americans do not disagree. She also discovered that people in Japan and the United States report using all four boundary control mechanisms (verbal, par-averbal, nonverbal, and territorial). Baker's study further suggests that North Americans see privacy regulation as a self-orientation process, while Japanese incorporate an other-orientation in regulating their privacy. Finally, she discovered that Japanese and North Americans see privacy as extending to the dyad or group (e.g., family privacy must be maintained).[13]

The preceding studies generally have examined communication in same-sex relationships. There are few studies comparing communication in romantic relationships in Japan and the United States. Cushman and Nishida (1983), for example, examined desired characteristics of mates. They found that North Americans look for intelligence, physical attraction, sex appeal, affection, trust, and psychological support in mates. Japanese, in comparison, looked for intelligence, health, honesty, affection, common values, the ease with which they could talk to the partner, the how good the partner was with money.[14]

Gudykunst and Nishida (1992) designed a study to extend Berscheid, Snyder, and Omoto's (1989) research by comparing scores on the Relationship Closeness Inventory (RCI) in Japan and the United States. Their data indicated that students in the United States are more likely to select a romantic relationship than a friend or family relationship as their closest relationship. Students in Japan, in contrast, are more likely to select a friend relationship than a romantic or family relationship. Students in the United States also report greater frequency and diversity, but not strength, of interdependence in their closest relationships than students in Japan. Consistent with Berscheid, Snyder, and Omoto's research, scores on the RCI do not appear to be associated with the length of the relationships.

The sex of the person with whom an individual is communicating (i.e., a male or a female) should influence the nature of communication that takes place. In a recent study, Gudykunst, Nishida, and Schmidt (1989) examined the influence of dyadic composition on uncertainty reduction processes. Following Hofstede (1980), they argued that there should be large differences in communication in same-sex and opposite-sex relationships in highly masculine cultures like Japan, but there should only be small differences in cultures lower on the masculinity index like the United States. The data indicated that there was more self-disclosure, attraction, and high-context attributional confidence in opposite-sex relationships than in same-sex relationships in the Japan sample. No significant differences emerged between same- and opposite-sex relationships in the United States sample. Gudykunst, Nishida, and Schmidt argued that the specific patterns that emerged in this study were due to the Japanese respondents selecting "dates" as the opposite-sex relationships and a less intimate same-sex acquaintances about whom to answer the questions (Japanese perceive dates as more intimate than North Americans; Gudykunst & Nishida, 1986b). If same- and opposite-sex relationships at the same level of intimacy were studied, there should be greater self-disclosure, for example, in same-sex relationships than in the opposite-sex relationships in Japan.

Unreported data from Gudykunst, Yang, and Nishida's (1985) study support the argument outlined here. These data indicate that Japanese engage in more intimate communication with same-sex close friends than with dates. The data reveal few differences in the intimacy of communication in the two relationships in the United States sample. These data, therefore, clearly support predictions that would be derived from Hofstede's (1980) masculinity dimension. The overall patterns for the two cultures also were consistent with Barnlund's (1975, 1989) research. Specifically, the North American sample had significantly higher means on all variables than the Japanese sample for both relationships.

Ingroup and Outgroup Relationships

Triandis (1988) argues that members of collectivistic cultures draw a sharper distinction between ingroup and outgroup communication than members of individualistic cultures.[15] Consistent with Triandis' conceptualization, Gudykunst and Nishida (1986a) found that Japanese students have more attributional confidence regarding classmates (members of an ingroup in Japan) than students in the United States, while the reverse pattern exists for strangers (potential members of an outgroup in Japan). Gudykunst and Nishida's (1986b) data also are consistent with Triandis' description of the focus on ingroup relationships in collectivistic cultures. The Japanese respondents in this study reported greater differences in personalization, synchronization, and difficulty of communication between ingroup (classmate) and outgroup (stranger) relationships than the North American respondents.

Gudykunst, Yoon, and Nishida (1987) also examined the influence of individualism on social penetration in ingroup and outgroup relationships in Japan, Korea, and the United States. The findings of this study indicated that the greater the degree of collectivism present in a culture, the greater the differences in ingroup (i.e., classmate) and outgroup (i.e., stranger) communication in terms of amount of personalization (e.g., intimacy of communication), synchronization (e.g., coordination of communication), and difficulty in communication (see also Triandis', 1990, reanalysis of these data). These results clearly supported predictions derived from Triandis' (1988) conceptualization of individualism-collectivism.

Research on uncertainty reduction processes is consistent with the conclusions from the social penetration studies. Gudykunst, Nishida, and Schmidt (1989), for example, found differences in uncertainty reduction processes between ingroup and outgroup relationships in the Japan sample, but not in the United States sample. In a recent study, Gudykunst, Gao, Nishida, Bond, Leung, Wang, and Barraclough (1992) extended the earlier study of uncertainty reduction processes in ingroup and outgroup relationships to include Australia, Japan, Hong Kong, and the United States. The results for ingroup-outgroup communication clearly support the predictions. There was a main effect for group membership (ingroup vs. outgroup) in the Japan and Hong Kong samples, but there was not a main effect for group membership in the United States and Australia samples. The specific patterns that emerged in the mean scores for the six dependent measures in Japan and Hong Kong were generally all consistent. As expected, the scores on the variables were higher for communication with members of ingroups than for communication with members of outgroups.

There is further support for the findings outlined here in two studies replicating Asch's (1956) classic study of conformity in Japan. Frager (1970) found that levels of conformity are low in Japan (in fact, the conformity was lower than in Asch's study in the United States) when the confederates in the study are strangers (i.e., not members of an ingroup). More recently, Williams and Sogon (1984) discovered than when confederates are members of the respondents' ingroup, conformity is much higher than in Asch's original study.[16]

Additional support is presented by Gudykunst, Nishida, and Morisaki (1992). They designed a study to extend Hoyle, Pinkley, and Insko's (1989) research by examining the influence of personal and social identity on perceptions of interpersonal and intergroup encounters in Japan and the United States. The results supported Hoyle and colleagues' findings; that is, interpersonal encounters are perceived to be more agreeable and less abrasive than intergroup encounters. In addition, Gudykunst, Nishida, and Morisaki's data indicated that respondents in the United States also expected encounters to be more abrasive than respondents in Japan. This finding is consistent with the United States being a low uncertainty-avoidance culture and Japan being a high uncertainty-avoidance culture. Since high uncertainty-avoidance cultures have clear rules for social interaction in different contexts, they would not necessarily expect intergroup encounters to be abrasive. Gudykunst and colleagues' study also indicated that social identity influences expected agreeableness and abrasiveness of encounters, but personal identity does not.

CULTURAL SIMILARITIES AND DIFFERENCES IN THE ENCODING AND DECODING OF MESSAGES

Communicator Style

People perceive not only the content of verbal and nonverbal cues, but also the way the cues are communicated. The latter provides information concerning how the former is to be interpreted. Norton (1978, 1983) refers to the way the content is communicated as communicator style. More specifically, he defines this construct as "the way one verbally and paraverbally interacts to signal how literal meaning should be taken, interpreted, or understood (1978, p. 99).

The communicator style construct includes ten styles that are used to used to predict an individuals communicator image (the overall assessment of a person's style of communication). The predictor styles involve ways of dealing with people during interaction: (1) dominant—strategies that lessen the roles of others during communication, (2) dramatic—the exaggeration and/or coloring of communication content, (3) contentious—negative aspects associated with being aggressive or argumentative, (4) relaxed— a calm, collected, not anxious strategy, (5) impression leaving—the affect communicators have on those with whom they interact, (6) animated—the frequent and intense use of behaviors such as eye contact, body movement, etc., (7) precise—a concern for proof and accuracy in discourse, (8) attentive—social sensitivity as illustrated by listening and showing interest in what others are saying, (9) friendly—the tendency to encourage others to acknowledge their contributions to actions, and (10) open—the tendency to express opinions, feelings, and emotions.

To the best of our knowledge, there has been only one study of Norton's communicator style construct in Japan and the United States. Klopf and Cambra (1981) found differences on eight of the ten styles. In comparison to Japanese, North Americans in their study were more attentive, contentious, animated, impression leaving, and had stronger communicator images than the Japanese. The Japanese, in contrast, scored higher than North Americans on the dramatic, open, and relaxed dimensions than the North Americans. These findings appear to be consistent with Hofstede's (1980) dimensions of cultural variability. Specifically, it would be expected that members of high uncertainty avoidance cultures (Japan) would be more open and dramatic than members of low uncertainty avoidance cultures (United States). It also would be predicted that members of individualistic cultures would be more attentive to verbal communication, more contentious, leave stronger impressions based on verbal communication, and present a stronger communicator image than members of collectivistic cultures.[17]

Communicative Style

Barnlund and his students (Barnlund & Araki, 1985; Barnlund & Yoshioka, 1990; Nomura & Barnlund, 1983) have conducted a series of studies designed to examine "communicative style" differences in Japan in the United States. Nomura and Barnlund examined patterns of interpersonal criticism. They discovered that individuals in both cultures preferred to express dissatisfaction in a direct way. The North Americans in their study preferred "active" forms of criticism (e.g., express dissatisfaction by making "constructive suggestions"), while Japanese preferred "passive" forms of criticism (e.g., express dissatisfaction nonverbally, ambiguously). Nomura and Barnlund also discovered that the relationship individuals have with others influences the type of criticism used in Japan (i.e., the closer the relationship, the more "active" the criticism), but not in the United States.

In a related study, Barnlund and Araki (1985) examined the management of compliments in Japan and the United States. They discovered that Japanese prefer to express admiration nonverbally, by commenting on their own limitations, or by keeping their opinions to themselves. North American respondents preferred to direct their admiration to a third person, keep it to themselves, or express it nonverbally.[18]

Barnlund and Yoshioka (1990) studied apologies in situations where individuals had consciously or unconsciously harmed another person. They found that individuals in both cultures prefer to apologize directly, but Japanese tend not to explain their behavior while North Americans tend to offer explanations. Barnlund and Yoshioka also discovered that Japanese use a wider range of apology strategies and adapted their strategies more to their partner's status than North Americans.

In addition to Barnlund and his colleagues' studies of communicative style, there are two recent studies of responses to embarrassing situations. Sueda and Wiseman (1992) examined responses to embarrassing situations in work settings.[19] They found that respondents in the United States use justification, statements of fact, humor, and aggression more than Japanese respondents. Sueda and Wiseman interpreted their findings as indicating that members of individualistic cultures use autonomy-preserving strategies more than members of collectivistic cultures.

Imahori and Cupach (1991) studied embarrassing predicaments, responses to these predicaments, and coping mechanisms used to deal with the predicaments.[20] They found that North American respondents mentioned "accident" type predicaments, while Japanese respondents mentioned "mistakes." North Americans also use humor as a coping strategy more than the Japanese, while Japanese use remediation more than North Americans. Finally, Imahori and Cupach found that North Americans experience embarrassment and "stupidity" in predicaments, while Japanese experience shame.

Predispositions toward Verbal Behavior

Uncertainty avoidance should influence the degree of social anxiety individuals experience. Specifically, the greater the uncertainty avoidance in a culture, the more individuals within the culture should experience anxiety when communicating. Consistent with this prediction, Gudykunst and colleagues' (1987) Japanese and Korean respondents report higher levels of social anxiety than their North American respondents. Ting-Toomey and colleagues' (1992) results are similar. The results for social anxiety in these studies are consistent with cross-cultural studies of communication apprehension. Klopf and Cambra (1979), for example, found that Japanese and Koreans have higher levels of communication apprehension than North Americans (see Klopf, 1984, for a summary of other research comparing communication apprehension in Japan and the United States). Nishida (1988), however, found that communication apprehension in Japanese adults is not different from that of adults in the United States.

The finding that Japanese and Koreans students report higher levels of communication apprehension than North Americans should not be interpreted to as implying that communication apprehension is a problem in Japan or Korea. In fact, probably the opposite is true—it is valued. Elliot, Scott, Jensen, and McDonald (1982), for example, found that Koreans are attracted more to individuals who do not engage in a lot of verbal activity than they are to those who engage in high levels of verbal activity. A similar argument can be made for Japan. To illustrate, Okabe (1983) contends that Japanese see verbal communication as a means of communication, not the only means of communication. Further, several other writers argue that Japanese do not value verbal communication and avoid it whenever possible (e.g., Nakane, 1970; Naruke, 1974; Nishiyama, 1973). The Japanese concept of *enryo* (feelings of constraint or reserve) explains these patterns.[21] Lebra's (1987) argument that silence is a significant aspect of communication in Japan must also be considered.[22]

Several other studies have investigated similarities and differences in various aspects of verbal behavior in Japan and the United States.[23] Mortensen, Arnston, and Lustig (1977) argued that individuals speaking styles involve five factors: domination of conversations, frequency and duration of speaking, the ability to initiate and maintain conversations, a general inclination to talk, and fluency of delivery. Cambra, Ishii, and Klopf (1978) found that students in the United States are more dominant, speak more frequently and longer, initiate conversations and maintain them more, are more inclined to talk and are more fluent than Japanese students. More recently, Geatz, Klopf, and Ishii (1990) found differences on only two of the dimensions (domination of conversations and general inclination to talk), with North Americans scoring higher than Japanese on both dimensions.

Richmond and McCroskey (1989) argue that individuals' social styles involve two primary dimensions: assertiveness and responsiveness. Assertiveness concerns individuals' abilities to state their opinions with conviction and defend themselves against verbal attacks from others. Responsiveness involves individuals' sensitivity to others' verbalized feelings. Ishii, Thompson, and Klopf (1990) found that Japanese are less assertive and responsive than North Americans using Richmond and McCroskey's measures. Patridge and Shibano (1991), nevertheless, argue that Japanese do behave assertively. Japanese assertiveness, however, takes place within the situational contexts in which they embed their behavior. Research that does not take the context into consideration would not tap this form of assertiveness.

A concept closely related to assertiveness is verbal aggressiveness. Infante and Wigley (1986) see verbal aggressiveness as involving individuals' tendencies to attach others' self-concepts verbally. Harman, Klopf, and Ishii (1990) compared Japanese and North American students' verbal aggressiveness, finding no significant differences between the two groups.

Infante and Rancer (1982) isolated argumentiveness as a personality trait involving individuals' tendencies to approach or avoid arguments with others. Prunty, Klopf, and Ishii (1990) found that Japanese are less argumentative than North Americans.

Booth-Butterfield and Booth-Butterfield (1990) argue that affect orientation involves individuals' tendencies to use feelings and emotions that are expressed in conversations as information in verbal exchanges. Frymier, Klopf, and Ishii (1990) found that North Americans rely on affect orientation in oral exchanges more than Japanese.

Another closely related construct is immediacy. Richmond, McCroskey, and Payne (1987) suggest that immediacy behaviors are the way individuals express approval of others and indicate that they want to continue communicating. Boyer, Thompson, Klopf, and Ishii (1990) used Richmond and colleagues' Self-Assessment of Immediacy Scale to examine differences in Japan and the United States. Their research revealed that North Americans report that they are more immediate than Japanese.

The results of the studies of predisposition toward verbal behaviors summarized here appear to be consistent with cultural differences in individualism-collectivism.[24] Okabe (1983), for example, argues that in individualistic cultures like the United States people use an *erabi* (selective) worldview. With respect to verbal communication, they believe that "the speaker consciously constructs his or her message for the purpose of persuading and producing attitude change" (p. 36). People in collectivistic cultures like Japan, in contrast, hold an *awase* (adjustive) worldview. With respect to verbal messages, they believe that a speaker should attempt "to adjust himself or herself to the feelings of his or her listener" (pp. 36-37).[25] Miyanaga (1991) makes an important point when she argues that "to the Japanese, to be quiet and to listen is active, not passive" (p. 96). This explanation is linked clearly to self-conception and face-negotiation in individualistic and collectivistic cultures.

In individualistic cultures self-esteem comes from the individual being a dynamic agent and mastering his or her environment. In collectivistic cultures self-esteem emerges from the individual adjusting herself or himself to the members or her or his ingroup.[26] Given the Japanese (collectivistic) concern for adjusting to others when communicating, it would be expected that they would engage in less domination of conversations, argumentativeness, aggression, or assertiveness than North Americans (individualistic), who are concerned with influencing others. The results for responsiveness, immediacy, and affect orientation also are compatible since each of these constructs involves aspects of verbal communication (at least as conceptualized in the United States studies on which they were based).

Topic Management and Turn Taking in Conversations

Yamada (1990) argues that the individual-group dimension influences topic management and turn distribution in Japanese and North American conversations.[27] She found that Japanese "take short turns, distribute their turns relatively evenly, and continue to distribute their turns evenly regardless of who initiates a topic" (p. 291). North Americans, in contrast, "take long monologic turns, distribute their turns unevenly, and the participant who initiates a topic characteristically takes the highest proportion of turns in that topic" (p. 291). Yamada concludes that Japanese organize topics interdependently, while North Americans organize their topics independently. These patterns can be linked directly to cultural differences in individualism and collectivism.

Recent research also indicates that Japanese send backchannel signals to the person with whom they are communicating more than North

American English speakers (LoCastro, 1987; Mizutani, 1984; Maynard, 1986; White, 1989). Backchanneling also performs different functions in Japanese and English. Hayashi (1990), for example, argues that backchanneling is used to display understanding of content in English, while it is used mostly as an emphatic response and to indicate agreement in Japanese.[28]

In her study of floor management, Hayashi (1990) found that Japanese use verbal and nonverbal complementary expressions and repetition in floor support and maintenance negotiations. North Americans, in contrast, use less synchronizing behaviors and repetition than Japanese. According to Hayashi, North Americans tend to use feedback devices (e.g., questions, comments) to indicate they are attentive, while Japanese tend to use backchanneling (e.g., brief utterances such as *soo*) to accomplish this purpose. Hayashi also found that when North American "speakers orient attention, they focus on the specific topical content. Japanese speakers only value the emphatic interactional behavior and tend to consider the message exchange secondary" (p. 188).

Persuasive Strategy Selection

Hirokawa and Miyahara (1986) studied the persuasive strategies used by North American and Japanese managers to persuade their subordinates in two situations.[29] The first situation involved how the manager would try to persuade consistently tardy employees to change their behavior. Japanese managers indicated that they would appeal to the employees' "duty" (e.g., "It is your duty as a responsible employee of this company to begin work on time"). The North American managers preferred to "threaten" the employees (e.g., "If you don't start reporting to work on time, I will have no choice but to dock your pay") or to give an "ultimatum" (e.g., "If you can't come to work on time, go find yourself another job"). The second situation in this study involved how the managers would persuade employees to give their ideas and suggestions to managers. Japanese managers tended to prefer to use "altruistic" strategies (e.g., "For the sake of the company, please share your ideas and suggestions with us") or appeal to "duty" (e.g., ""Remember that it is your duty as a good company employee to suggest how we can improve the overall performance of the company"). The North American managers preferred to make "direct requests" (e.g., "I want you to feel free to come to me with any ideas you have for improving the company"), to make "promises" (e.g., "Don't hesitate to offer ideas and suggestions because we always reward good suggestions"), or to "ingratiate" themselves to the employees (e.g., "You are one of our best people and I really value your judgment, so please feel free to come to me with ideas you have").

Burgoon, Dillard, Doran, and Miller (1982) examined preferences for persuasive strategies among Asian Americans and Caucasian Americans in Hawaii. They discovered that in comparison to Caucasian Americans, Asian Americans preferred to use the strategies of "promise" (e.g., "If you comply, I will reward you"), "positive expertise" (e.g., "If you comply, you will be rewarded by the nature of things"), "pregiving" (e.g., rewarding the person before request), "liking" (e.g., person is friendly to get the other in good frame of mind), "positive altercasting" (e.g., "A person with 'good' qualities would comply"), "negative altercasting" (e.g., "Only a person with 'bad' qualities would not comply"), "positive self-feeling" (e.g., "You will feel better about yourself if you comply"), and "positive self-esteem" (e.g., "People you value will think better of you if you comply"). All of these strategies tend to involve high degrees of social acceptability.

While the research on persuasive strategy selection has not been theoretically grounded, the results appear compatible with cultural differences in individualism-collectivism. It would be expected, for example, that members of collectivistic cultures would use strategies that are altruistic and those based in "duty" more than members of individualistic cultures.

Recognition and Expression of Emotions

Darwin's (1872) evolutionary-genetic theory predicts that the expression of emotions is innate and universal. Extensive research has been conducted to test this hypothesis (see Gudykunst & Ting-Toomey, 1988, for a summary). Our focus here involves only comparisons including Japan and the United States.

Izard (1968; summarized in Izard, 1980) found that there is high agreement when individuals classify photographs of facial expressions into one of eight categories of emotions (interest-excitement, enjoyment-joy, surprise-startle, distress-anguish, disgust-contempt, anger-rage, shame-humiliation, and fear-terror). Overall, in the United States sample there was 83.4 percent agreement across the eight emotions, while there was 65.4 percent agreement in the Japan sample. Ekman and Friesen (1971) found higher levels of agreement on six of these eight emotions in their Japanese sample (interest-excitement and shame-humiliation were not included). Izard (a study summarized in Izard,

1971) also presents data indicating that disgust and contempt are recognized differently and correctly identified in Japan and the United States. In the same study, Izard also found that Japanese understand the emotion joy the best, shame the least, and dreaded disgust-contempt the most.

Recent research by Ekman and his associates (1987) indicates that agreement on labeling fundamental emotions is not limited to conditions in which observers are required to select only one emotion for each facial expression. They found that there is agreement in the United States and Japan on which emotion is strongest and which emotion is second strongest. Beier and Zautra (1972) also found that Japanese are as accurate at decoding vocal emotional expressions as students in the United States when they are provided a sufficiently long sample of vocal communication.[30]

There is preliminary evidence that accuracy in judgments of emotions are a function of developmental characteristics of children across cultures. Matsumoto and Kishimoto (1983), for example, played audio tapes for children (from four to nine years old) in Japan and the United States and asked them to select a photograph depicting the emotion of the person talking. They found that four- and five-year-old North Americans could correctly identify only surprise, while Japanese children of the same age could identify surprise and sadness. The 6-year-old and older North Americans could identify all four emotions (surprise, sadness, happiness, and anger), while 6-year-old Japanese could not identify anger, but 7-year-old and older Japanese could. Matsumoto and Kishimoto, however, point out that the overall recognition of anger in the Japanese sample was low. They argue that this is due to Japanese children being socialized to avoid the expression of negative emotions.

Watson, Clark, and Tellegen (1984) found that there is a large number of mood categories with equivalent Japanese and English markers and that Japanese and North Americans tend to agree on the "positive" and "negative" affect associated with mood categories. One exception involved the category "sleepy." Sleepy had a negative connotation in the United States, but not in Japan. There also were several mood terms in English that were not well-represented in Japanese (i.e., contempt, shyness, fear, blameworthiness, rage, pride, torment) and several Japanese terms not well-represented in English (i.e., nostalgia, irritability, reluctance, general unpleasantness, pain).[31]

Matsumoto, Kudoh, Scherer, and Wallbott (1988) examined the antecedents of and reactions to emotions in Japan and the United States.[32] Matsumoto and his colleagues discovered numerous similarities in their Japanese and North American samples. The ordering of the most recent emotion experienced by the respondents was the same in the two cultures: disgust > joy = anger = shame = guilt > fear = sad. The North Americans, however, reported experiencing the emotions longer and with more intensity than the Japanese. The emotions respondents expected to experience also was the same: joy = guilt > fear = anger = sad = disgust = shame. Further, the relative pleasantness of the emotions was the same: joy > fear = shame = guilt > anger = disgust = sad. Emotion-eliciting events had a more positive effect on the self-esteem and self-confidence of the North Americans than the Japanese. North Americans also reported more bodily symptoms than Japanese when experiencing emotions than Japanese. Japanese, in contrast, reported that no action was necessary to cope with emotional experiences more than North Americans. Matsumoto and his associates concluded that "evaluation and reactions to emotion antecedents are universal" (p. 281), while "cultural differences appear to be concerned primarily with experiential and reactive aspects of emotions" (p. 283).

Matsumoto and Ekman (1989) examined differences in intensity ratings of photographs of individuals expressing the emotions of anger, disgust, fear, happiness, sadness, and surprise. They found that North American means are higher for all emotions except disgust (regardless of the gender or culture of the person in the photograph). North Americans rated the happy and angry photographs as the most intense, while the Japanese rated the disgust photograph as most intense.

Face-Negotiation and Conflict Resolution

"Face" involves the projected image of one's self in a relational situation. More specifically, face is conceptualized as the interaction between the degree of threats or considerations a member offers to another party, and the degree of claim for a sense of self-respect (or the demand of respect) by the other party in a given situation (Ting-Toomey, 1985, 1988a).[33]

Cole (1989) found similarities and differences in the way Japanese and North Americans define face, based on interviews conducted in English. Japanese definitions included honor, pride, claimed self-image, trustworthiness, individual standing or rank, politeness, respect extended by others, considerateness, and dignity. North American definitions included credibility, individual reputation, self-respect, ego, claimed position in interaction, appearance of strength, recognized positive worth, pride, status, lack of embarrassment, and self-defense.

Japanese perceived they lost face when they were not able to maintain ingroup harmony (e.g., when they shamed or disgraced a friend or coworker). North Americans, in contrast, perceived they lost face when they personally failed (e.g., lost an argument). Japanese perceived insults/criticisms and rude/inconsiderate behavior from others as face threats, while North Americans threats to their credibility and/or self-image as face threats. Both groups, however, agreed that a face threat requires some self-protective action. Japanese saw allowing others to look good or take a prestigious position as giving face. The North Americans interviewed, in comparison, did not associate any particular behaviors with giving face. There also were differences in the situations individuals thought maintaining self-face was important. Japanese wanted to preserve self-face in private, informal, and intimate situations. North Americans, in contrast, wanted to maintain self-face in public, formal, and nonintimate settings.

Ting-Toomey (1988a) presented a face-negotiation theory designed to explain how people in individualistic and collectivistic cultures deal with conflict. She assumes that: (1) people in all cultures try to maintain and negotiate face in all communication situations; (2) the concept of face is especially problematic in uncertainty situations when the situated identities of the interactants are called into question; (3) conflict, as a class of uncertainty situations, demands active facework management by both conflict parties; (4) conflict parties, in a conflict situation, will engage in two types of facework management: self-face concern and mutual-face concern, and negative-face maintenance (control need) and positive-face maintenance (affiliative-inclusion need); and (5) the cultural variability dimension of individualism-collectivism will influence members' selection of one set of conflict styles (e.g., avoidance and obliging styles) over others (e.g., confrontational and solution-oriented styles).

Based on the dimensions of self-face concern and mutual-face concern, and negative-face maintenance and positive-face maintenance, Ting-Toomey (1988a) developed theoretical propositions to account for the relationship among individualism-collectivism, face-management, and conflict styles. With respect to face-maintenance, Ting-Toomey contends that members of individualistic cultures like the United States express more self-face maintenance than members of collectivistic cultures like Japan. Members of collectivistic cultures, in comparison, express greater mutual-face and other-face maintenance than members of individualistic cultures. With respect to conflict resolution styles, she argued that members of individualistic cultures like the United States use dominating, integrating, and compromising styles more than members of collectivistic cultures like Japan. Members of collectivistic cultures, in contrast, use avoiding and obliging conflict resolution styles more than members of individualistic cultures.

Ting-Toomey, Trubisky, and Nishida (1989) tested the conflict style portion of Ting-Toomey's (1988a) theory in Japan and the United States. They found that North Americans report using dominating, integrating, and compromising conflict resolution styles more than Japanese. Their data also revealed that Japanese report avoiding conflict more than North Americans. The prediction for obliging (i.e., that Japanese would be more obliging than North Americans) was not supported.

Ting-Toomey, Trubisky, and Nishida's (1989) findings are compatible with previous research on conflict in Japan and the United States. Cushman and King (1985), for example, argue that Japanese value public face in conflict situations and prefer a collaborative style. North Americans, in contrast, prefer a compromising style. Nomura and Barnlund (1983) found that Japanese use "passive" accommodating styles when criticized, while North Americans prefer "active" confrontational styles. Kumagai and Strauss (1983) discovered similar patterns.[34] The results of Ting-Toomey and colleagues' study also are compatible with discussions of conflict in Japan contained in Krauss, Rohlen, and Steinhoff (1984). Further, their data are consistent with studies of privacy regulation (e.g., Baker & Gudykunst, 1990; Naotsuka & Sakamoto et al., 1981) and the expression of emotion (Matsumoto et al., 1988).

Ting-Toomey, Gao, and colleagues (1991) tested the face-maintenance portion of her theory and extensions of the theory that link face to conflict resolution styles. Their results for Japan and the United States are not consistent with the theoretical predictions. They found that students in the United States are concerned more with other-face than students in Japan, while students in Japan are concerned more with self-face than students in the United States. Morisaki and Gudykunst (in press) argue that these findings are due to the measurement of face-work used in the study (i.e., it was a measure developed in the United States and not modified for use in Japan).[35]

Given that individualism-collectivism affects ingroup and outgroup communication, it also is necessary to examine differences in face-negotiation and conflict resolution styles used with members of an ingroup and members of an outgroup in individualistic and collectivistic cultures. Cole (1990) found that Anglo students in the United

States tend to use integrating and obliging styles more with members of ingroups than with members of outgroups. He also found that Japanese students studying in the United States tend to use an obliging style more with members of ingroups than with members of outgroups, and they tend to use a dominating style more with members of outgroups than with members of ingroups.[36]

Morisaki and Gudykunst (in press) summarized work on face in Japan and the United States. They argue that the conceptualization of face is different in Japan and the United States. In the United States individuals focus on meeting their need for autonomy and establishing boundaries by maintaining their independent self- and other-face, as well as mutual-face when they communicate. In Japan individuals focus on meeting their need for inclusion and approval by maintaining their interdependent mutual self- and other-face when they communicate. Face is more of a concern in uncertain situations in Japan than in the United States. In the United States individuals are concerned with maintaining face in the immediate situation more than over the course of a relationship. In Japan individuals are concerned with maintaining face over the course of a relationship more than in the immediate situation.

Morisaki and Gudykunst's (in press) propositions are compatible with Ting-Toomey's (1988a) theory. Morisaki and Gudykunst's propositions, however, differ in several respects. First, the propositions involve drawing a distinction between independent and interdependent face in individualistic and collectivistic cultures. Second, Morisaki and Gudykunst's propositions are based on the assumption that there is not conceptual equivalence between independent face in individualistic cultures and interdependent face in collectivistic cultures. Third, given the lack of conceptual equivalence, the propositions Morisaki and Gudykunst suggest that researchers must make comparisons within cultures rather than cross-cultural comparisons in studying face.

COMMUNICATION IN JAPANESE-NORTH AMERICAN INTERCULTURAL RELATIONSHIPS

Initial Interactions

One of the cross-cultural studies summarized earlier (Gudykunst & Nishida, 1984; Nishida & Gudykunst, 1986) also was designed to examine initial Japanese-North American interactions. In this study, Gudykunst and Nishida assigned Japanese and North Americans randomly to conditions of cultural similarity (i.e., answering questions about communication with someone from their own culture; cross-cultural comparisons of these responses were reported earlier) and cultural dissimilarity (i.e., answering questions about someone from the other culture). Culture did not interact with cultural similarity/dissimilarity, suggesting that Japanese and North Americans use similar uncertainty reduction strategies when communicating with someone from the other culture. The data from this study suggest that both groups intend to ask questions, self-disclose, and display nonverbal affiliative expressiveness more in initial interactions with strangers from the other culture than with strangers from their own culture.[37]

Gudykunst and Nishida (1984) did not take language spoken into consideration. They assumed that the results are applicable when the respondents are speaking English. In a follow-up study, Gudykunst, Nishida, Koike, and Shiino (1986) manipulated language spoken with Japanese respondents. They conducted regression analyses to determine the degree to which the variables in uncertainty reduction theory (i.e., self-disclosure, interrogation, attitude similarity, attraction, nonverbal affiliative expressiveness, reciprocity, and amount of communication) contributed to predicting low-context attributional confidence (the measure of high-context attributional confidence had not been developed when this study was conducted). The data revealed that the variables in uncertainty reduction theory explain the same amount of variance when Japanese are speaking English and when they are speaking Japanese. The specific variables that explained the variance, however, were different. In the speaking English with a North American condition, amount of communication, nonverbal affiliative expressiveness, and attitude similarity were the main predictors. In the speaking Japanese with a North American condition, attitude similarity, reciprocity, and self-disclosure were the main predictors.[38] The results of this study do not appear to be due to differences in levels of communication apprehension when Japanese are speaking English and Japanese. McCroskey, Gudykunst, and Nishida (1985) found that there is not a significant difference in the level of communication apprehension Japanese report when speaking Japanese and when speaking English.

Intimacy of Relationships

Gudykunst, Nishida, and Chua (1986, 1987) conducted two studies of uncertainty reduction and social penetration processes in Japanese-North American relationships. Both studies examined communication in low intimacy (e.g., strangers, acquaintances), high intimacy (e.g., close friendships, romantic relationships), and "mixed" dyads (e.g., relationships that are in transition from low to high, or where the partners disagree on the intimacy of the relationship). Since both partners in the relationships were studied, Gudykunst, Nishida, and Chua analyzed the data using summation scores (adding the scores for the two respondents and dividing by two) and dispersion scores (subtracting the score of one partner from the other).

Results of Gudykunst, Nishida, and Chua's (1986; Nishida, Gudykunst, & Chua, 1987) study are consistent with predictions derived from previous research on uncertainty reduction theory. The summation scores indicate that high-intimacy dyads engage in greater self-disclosure, interrogation, shared networks, amount of communication, and low-context attributional confidence than low-intimacy dyads based on the summation analyses. These findings are consistent with Gudykunst's (1985) research on intercultural communication in general and Gudykunst, Sodetani, and Sonoda's (1987) study of Japanese American-Caucasian interethnic communication in Hawaii.

The results from the analysis of the dispersion scores revealed that high-intimacy dyads are more consistent in the amount they self-disclose and the degree of high-context attributional confidence they have about each other. While no previous uncertainty reduction research has examined dispersion scores, the present findings are consistent with the theory. The findings for mixed dyads do not follow a set pattern. Mixed dyads have more agreement on self-disclosure than either of the other types of dyads, but fall in between the high- and low-intimacy dyads on high-context attributional confidence.

Several noteworthy patterns emerged in a post hoc correlation analysis in Gudykunst, Nishida, and Chua's (1986) study. The data indicate that self-disclosure, interrogation, amount of communication, length of relationship, and shared networks are correlated with low-context, but not high-context attributional confidence. Perceived second language competence is correlated with self-disclosure, interrogation, low-context attributional confidence, and length of relationship.

Results of Gudykunst, Nishida, and Chua's (1987) study are consistent with predictions derived from Altman and Taylor's (1973) social penetration theory, as well as with Knapp, Ellis, and Williams' (1980) intracultural research in the United States. Summation scores for high-intimacy dyads revealed that they involved more personalized and synchronized communication, but less difficulty in communication than low-intimacy dyads. Mixed dyads, however, are between the low- and high-intimacy dyads with respect to personalized communication and higher than both groups for synchronized communication and difficulty of communication.

The results from the analysis of the dispersion scores in Gudykunst, Nishida, and Chua's (1987) study reveal that mixed dyads have significantly less agreement than high-intimacy dyads on the amount of personalized communication and less, but not significantly less, agreement than low-intimacy dyads. On the remaining two factors, high intimacy dyads have lower dispersion scores than low-intimacy dyads, but the low-intimacy dyads' scores are higher than the mixed dyads' scores. These findings suggest that there is greater agreement in high-intimacy dyads than low-intimacy dyads, but mixed dyads do not fit a specific pattern. In contrast to personalized communication, no significant differences in synchronized or difficulty of communication emerged.

Several noteworthy patterns also emerged in Gudykunst, Nishida, and Chua's (1987) correlation analysis. Synchrony and difficulty of communication, for example, have a high negative correlation suggesting that as difficulty is reduced synchronization occurs, or vice versa. Further, while personalized and synchronized communication have a moderate correlation, personalized and difficulty of communication are uncorrelated. These patterns imply that personalization and synchrony covary in intercultural dyads, but personalization and difficulty do not, a finding consistent with Knapp, Ellis, and Williams' (1980) intracultural research. The length of relationship and frequency of communication also are correlated moderately with personalized communication, but neither correlates with synchronization or difficulty of communication. These findings, in combination with the analysis by relationship type, suggest that relationship type, not length or frequency, influences synchronization and difficulty, consistent with Altman and Taylor (1973). Only the synchronization findings, however, are consistent with Knapp, Ellis, and Williams' research. This may suggest that relationship type has more of an influence on difficulty of communication in intercultural relationships than in intracultural relationships.

Perceived second language competence also is correlated moderately with each of the three social penetration variables. It, therefore, appears that the ability to use the partners' native language facilitates social penetration in intercultural dyads. It should be noted, however, that these results may be due primarily to the Japanese partners' ability to use English rather than the North American partners' ability to use

Japanese or a combination of the two because the ethnolinguistic vitality (cf. Giles, Bourhis, & Taylor, 1977) of Japanese probably was low.

Effectiveness and Satisfaction

Effectiveness refers to minimizing misunderstandings or making isomorphic attributions (see Gudykunst, 1988, for a discussion of this conceptualization). Satisfaction refers to the degree to which the participants liked the communication they have with the other person (see Hecht, 1978, for a discussion of communication satisfaction).

Research on Japanese-North American dyads (Gudykunst, Nishida, & Chua, 1986, 1987; Nishida, Gudykunst, & Chua, 1987) indicates that uncertainty reduction processes and social penetration are correlated with perceived intercultural effectiveness and satisfaction. In the uncertainty reduction study, Gudykunst, Nishida, and Chua (1986) found that perceived effectiveness is related to self-disclosure, interrogation, attraction, and similarity, as well as both low- and high-context attributional confidence. Further, communication satisfaction correlates with self-disclosure, interrogation, attraction, similarity, effectiveness, and low- and high-context attributional confidence. The data further revealed a high correlation between satisfaction and effectiveness. In the social penetration study (Gudykunst, Nishida, & Chua, 1987), perceived effectiveness was related moderately to highly to each of the three social penetration dimensions. Further, communication satisfaction is correlated with each of the dimensions of social penetration, with the weakest correlation occurring with personalization.

The correlation between the summation scores for perceived second-language competence and perceived intercultural effectiveness were not significant in Gudykunst, Nishida, and Chua's (1986, 1987) studies. The findings for the two studies, however, may be due to combining the scores for both members of the dyad (i.e., the lack of North American competence in Japanese canceled out the effect for Japanese competence in English). Support for this interpretation emerges from Nishida's (1985) study. She found that speaking and listening skills in English are the only good predictors of perceived intercultural effectiveness for a group of Japanese students studying in the United States.[39]

There are several related studies that have examined effectiveness or satisfaction in Japanese-North American relationships.[40] Wiseman and Abe (1986) examined the effectiveness of Japanese students involved in home-stays in the United States and the host mothers of the families with which they stayed. They found that cognitively simple dyads (i.e., dyads where both individuals use a small number of constructs to understand others) perceive themselves to be more effective than cognitively complex dyads (i.e., dyads where both individuals used a large number of constructs to understand others). This finding is the opposite of what they predicted based on research on cognitively complexity in the United States (e.g., Applegate & Delia, 1980). Wiseman and Abe argue, however, that their findings are consistent with Detweiler's (1980) research on category width. Specifically, they contend that people who are wide categorizers (whom they equated with being cognitively simple) are better able to integrate disparate information about others than are narrow categorizers (whom they equated with being cognitively complex). An alternative interpretation is that cognitively simple individuals construct systems are not complex enough to recognize problems when they occur. Cognitively simple people, therefore, perceive that they are effective, when they are not. Differentiating between these interpretations requires additional research where perceived and actual effectiveness are measured.

An earlier study by Gudykunst, Wiseman, and Hammer (1977) focused on United States Navy personnel's satisfaction with living in Japan. This study revealed that variables associated with intercultural competence such as behavioral skills (e.g., language, ability to use local transportation), positive stereotyping, and third-culture perspective (e.g., open-minded, low ethnocentrism) are related to the amount of interaction Navy personnel have with Japanese. The third-culture perspective, amount of social interaction, and the degree to which these interactions are evaluated positively are related to satisfaction with living in Japan.[41]

More recently, Wiseman, Hammer, and Nishida (1989) examined indicators of perceived intercultural communication competence (while they use the term "competence" their outcome measures appear to be indicators of "effectiveness").[42] They found, for example, that understanding the other culture (e.g., Japanese understanding of the United States), understanding of foreign cultures in general, and impressions of the other culture (e.g., North Americans' impression of Japan) are related to perceived social distance (an indicator of effectiveness).

Ting-Toomey and Gao (1988) examined the relationships among perceived similarity, self-consciousness, language competence, and perceived effectiveness of sojourners in Japan. They found that language competence, perceived similarity, and private self-consciousness are related to perceived effectiveness.

There is one other line of research on Japanese-North American communication that has examined intercultural "effectiveness" (a more appropriate label, however, would be "perceived competence"). Hammer, Gudykunst, and Wiseman (1978) isolated three behavioral dimensions of perceived intercultural competence using North Americans who had lived in many diverse cultures: ability to deal with psychological stress, ability to communicate effectively, and ability to establish interpersonal relationships. Abe and Wiseman (1983) attempted to replicate these three factors in a study of Japanese tourists in the United States. Their data revealed five factors: ability to communicate interpersonally, ability to adjust, ability to cope with different societal systems, ability to establish interpersonal relationships, and the ability to understand another. Gudykunst and Hammer (1984) argued that the five factor structure was compatible with the three factor structure obtained in the earlier study and that the differences are due to the small number of respondents and the nature of the sojourn of the Japanese in Abe and Wiseman's study (i.e., they were on a short tourist type trip rather than residing in the culture).

Miyahira (1991) interviewed ten Japanese and ten North American students. He asked the Japanese students to describe their prototype of the "ideal" North American with whom they would like to communicate. This prototype involved a person who is tolerant of silence, listens to others, is not too direct, keeps one's word, and does not dominate the conversation. The North Americans' prototype of an "ideal" Japanese with who they would like to communicate is a person who has a good sense of humor, favors confrontations, is not overly polite, is expressive, and is not unduly self-conscious.

Themes in Relationships

Recently, themes in Japanese-North American relationships have been examined by studying participants "accounts" of their communication. Accounts are individuals' stories about their patterns of interactions (Harvey et al., 1986). Themes are issues or concerns around which interaction is focused (Owen, 1984). Spradley (1979) argues that while some themes are explicit, most are tacit and taken for granted. In addition, as themes connect different domains of meaning, they are interrelated and overlap.

In the first study of themes in intercultural relationships, Sudweeks, Gudykunst, Ting-Toomey, and Nishida (1990; Nishida, Sudweeks, Gudykunst, Ting-Toomey, & Yoshizawa, 1989) examined female-female Japanese-North American relationships. The respon-

dents' accounts suggest that subthemes under communication competence (language/cultural knowledge, empathy, and accommodation)
are rare in low-intimacy dyads, present in some moderate-intimacy
dyads, and prominent in high-intimacy dyads. A parallel pattern
emerged for the similarity theme. Background/life-style or
attitude/value similarity is not reported in the accounts of partners in
low-intimacy dyads, some are observed in moderate-intimacy dyads,
and many similarities are noted in the high-intimacy dyads. Further,
lack of cultural similarity is reported as a problem in low-intimacy
dyads, it is noted only minimally in moderate-intimacy dyads, and it is
a positive factor in high-intimacy dyads.

The participants in the low-intimacy dyads in Sudweeks and colleagues' (1990) study report little involvement (amount and intimacy of
interaction, and shared networks), while partners in high-intimacy
dyads characterize their relationships as having high levels of involvement (the moderate-intimacy dyads fell in between the two extremes).
All participants in low-intimacy dyads report using relational tests,
while only some of the partners in moderate-intimacy dyads and none
in the high-intimacy dyads test their relationships. In addition, mutual
responsiveness is not reported in low-intimacy dyads, only a little
mutual responsiveness appears in moderate-intimacy dyads, while both
partners in high-intimacy dyads mention mutual responsiveness in
their accounts. Finally, episodes which increase understanding of the
partner do not change the intimacy of the relationship in low intimacy
dyads, but do in high-intimacy dyads.

In the second study of themes, Gudykunst, Gao, Sudweeks, Ting-
Toomey, and Nishida (1991; Nishida, Gudykunst, Gao, Sudweeks, &
Ting-Toomey, 1989) looked at communication in opposite-sex relationships. For the typicality theme, no subthemes were observed. Partners
in acquaintance relationships are viewed as relatively typical of their
culture, while partners in friend and romantic relationships are seen as
somewhat atypical members of their culture. Two subthemes emerged
under communication competence: cultural/linguistic knowledge and
ability to understand. In the acquaintance relationships, the partners
have an interest in each other's culture, but linguistic knowledge
inhibits them from getting to know each other. In the friend and romantic relationships, the partners have an interest in and knowledge of each
other's culture and there are few linguistic barriers to communication.
There is only minimal understanding of the partner in the acquaintance
relationships, while there is moderate understanding at the verbal level
in the friend relationships. Only the romantic partners report deep

understanding at both the verbal and nonverbal levels.

There also were two subthemes for similarity in Gudykunst and colleagues' (1991) opposite-sex study: cultural similarity and attitude/interest similarity. There is a relatively low level of awareness of cultural differences in the acquaintances, some awareness of general cultural differences in the friendships, and cultural differences are noticed and evaluated positively in the romantic relationships. No attitude/interest similarity is recognized in the acquaintance relationships, but many similarities are recognized in the friend and romantic relationship. Two subthemes also emerged for involvement: amount and intimacy of communication. The small amount of time spent together limits the development of the acquaintance relationships. There is, in contrast, sufficient time spent together for relationships to develop in the friendships and romantic relationships. Finally, there is little self-disclosure of intimate information in the acquaintance relationships, but there is some in the friendships, and there are high levels in the romantic relationships.

Four themes were isolated in the Kertamus, Gudykunst, and Nishida (1991) study of male-male, Japanese-North American relationships: communication competence (with subthemes of linguistic/cultural knowledge and nonverbal knowledge), similarity (with subthemes of cultural similarity and attitude/interest similarity), involvement (with subthemes of amount of communication, intimacy of communication, and obligation), and relational tests. Overall, the themes which emerged in the male-male study were similar to those in the Sudweeks and colleagues (1990) study of female-female dyads.

The differences in the subthemes in participants' accounts of low- and high-intimacy relationships appear to be related to their cultural identities. Partners' cultural identities are a salient factor influencing how they present themselves and how they interpret each other's behavior in low-intimacy relationships. More specifically, when participants first get to know their partner from another culture, there is a need for them to express their cultural identities (Ting-Toomey, 1989a). The accounts suggest that in low-intimacy relationships, cultural identity is managed as a problematic issue or not recognized as a factor influencing their communication. This is expressed through not knowing or using the other person's language, seeing cultural differences as problems, and not accommodating the other's style of communication. In high-intimacy relationships, in contrast, cultural identity is recognized, but not seen as problematic. Partners involved in intimate relationships know the other person as an individual and accommodate to the partner's personal and cultural communication style.

CONCLUSION

Generally, the results of the cross-cultural research conducted on communication in interpersonal relationships in Japan and the United States indicate that uncertainty reduction theory (Berger & Calabrese, 1975; Berger & Gudykunst, 1991) and social penetration theory (Altman & Taylor, 1973; Taylor & Altman, 1987) generalize to Japan. The similarities and differences in communication in Japan and the United States isolated are consistent with Triandis' (1988) conceptualization of individualism-collectivism, Hofstede's (1980) dimensions of cultural variability, and Hall's (1976) low-/high-context continuum. Some specific findings in particular studies have been inconsistent with predictions made from these theories, but the inconsistencies are "exceptions to the rule."

The ultimate objective of cross-cultural research is to develop a broad theoretical perspective to explain communication in Japan and the United States. Work to date is a modest beginning. Some "individualistic" theories of communication appear to generalize to communication in Japan. Given the potential cultural bias of these theories (i.e., they were developed in the United States), Japanese concepts have been integrated into research conducted to date. More work in this area, however, is still needed. Work of Japanese scholars (e.g., Befu, 1980a, 1980b; Doi, 1973, 1975, 1986; Haga, 1979; Minami, 1971; Nakane, 1974; Tsujimura, 1987) needs to be integrated more thoroughly with the theories used to guide research. The role of Doi's (1973) concept of *amae* (feeling of dependence), and Fujihara and Kurokawa's (1981) measure of the concept, in uncertainty reduction, for example, need to be determined and integrated with current theorizing. To illustrate, it could be predicted that feeling *amae* reduces high-context uncertainty in Japan, but not in the United States.[43] Other important Japanese concepts that must be incorporated into theories include, but are not limited to, *tatemae* and *honne*, *sasshi*, *enryo*, *ishin-denshin*, and *kuuki*.

In addition to developed "derived etic" theories, the dialectical aspects of individualism-collectivism (and the other dimensions of cultural variability) must be incorporated into theories. Recent research (e.g., Gudykunst et al., 1992) clearly indicates that Japanese and North Americans hold both individualistic and collectivistic values. Miyanaga (1991) argues that the individualism-collectivism dialectic in Japan is a result of modernization. She also points out that although it is "rarely mentioned in the literature about Japan, 'dropping out' of established groups for the purpose of self-realization, a form of 'passive individualism,' has been a long standing tradition" (p. 4). Similarly, Triandis and colleagues (1988) contend that Japanese students are only collectivistic in selected spheres of their lives. Recently, several writers (e.g., Wuthnow, 1991) also have drawn attention to collectivistic aspects of the culture in the United States.

Recognizing that individualism-collectivism is a dialect requires that predictions based on this dimension of cultural variability become more specific than the general predictions in past research. To illustrate, if researchers are interested in differences between how individuals in a culture communicate with members of their ingroups and their outgroups, they must isolate the specific individualistic value or collectivistic value influencing the behavior. It might be argued, for example, that "being independent" is the appropriate value. The prediction, therefore, would have to take the form of the more people in a culture value being independent, the less the difference in their communication with members of their ingroups and outgroups.

An alternative approach would be to focus on personality equivalents of individualism-collectivism: idiocentrism-allocentrism, respectively (e.g., Triandis et al., 1985).[44] Using the same topic of research, it might be predicted that the more idiocentric individuals are, the less the difference in how they communicate with members of their ingroups and outgroups. It is probable, however, that idiocentrics and allocentrics in individualistic and collectivistic cultures may respond differently to the same situation. Sinha (cited in Triandis et al., 1988), for example, argues that allocentrics in individualistic cultures yield to the ingroup more than idiocentrics in collectivistic cultures. Given this position, future research ideally will take into consideration both the specific individualistic and collectivistic values, and idiocentrism-allocentrism in predicting cultural differences and similarities in communication.[45]

There are several other issues that also need to be addressed in future research on communication in Japan and the United States. To illustrate, recent work on developing a measure of self-monitoring that is appropriate in Japan and the United States opens a new line of research that should be pursued. Do the two general factors (self-monitoring and concern for social appropriateness) and the seven specific factors, for example, influence communication differently in Japan and the United States? How do the various factors affect communication in Japanese-North American relationships? Extensive research is needed to answer these questions and incorporate the derived etic conceptualization of self-monitoring that Gudykunst, Gao, Nishida, Nadamitsu, and Sakai (1992) proposed into the theories used to explain Japanese-North American communication.

Future research regarding uncertainty reduction processes in Japan and the United States also is needed. Gudykunst (1988, 1989), for example, argues that uncertainty does not decrease linearly in relationships (see also Baxter [1990] and Ting-Toomey [1989a] for discussions of this issue). Rather, he suggests that uncertainty decreases and increases over the life of a relationship (and possibly even in the same conversation; i.e., it is a dialectic). To date, there is no research on the "dialectical" nature of uncertainty in relationships across cultures (there is one study [Sodetani & Gudykunst, 1987] of increases in uncertainty in Japanese American-Caucasian relationships). Further, there is a need for longitudinal research using the dyad as the level of analysis when comparing Japanese and North American patterns of communication.

Ting-Toomey (1989a) suggests three other issues that should be considered in future research. She argues that research needs to focus on factors that contribute to relational changes. Are the factors that contribute to relationships changing from acquaintances to friends the same in Japan and the United States? Relationships in Japan and the United States need to be compared with Japanese-North American intercultural relationships. Ting-Toomey also contends that the effect of communication reciprocity in the dyad needs to be examined. This issue is critical given that her earlier research (Ting-Toomey, 1986) revealed that Japanese see an "obligatory" reciprocity system operating in interpersonal relationships, while North Americans see a "voluntary" reciprocity system operating (see also Atsumi, 1980). Finally, Ting-Toomey suggests that the context in which communication occurs must be examined. The role of context is critical given that Japan is a high-context culture and the United States is a low-context culture.

In the future, work on social penetration and uncertainty reduction processes needs to be extended to "social" relationships; for example, superior-subordinate communication in organizations. Uncertainty reduction theory has been used to explain selected aspects of communication in organizations in the United States (e.g., socialization of new employees; see Berger & Gudykunst, 1991, for a summary of this work), but it has not been applied to Japanese organizations. This extension is critical given Atsumi's (1979, 1980) contention that communication in obligatory (e.g., tsukiai relationships with fellow employees) and nonobligatory (e.g., friendships) relationships is different in Japan. Extensions such as this are necessary to generate a broad theory of communication and culture that is not limited to interpersonal relationships. Such a theory must transcend individual cultures and, at the same time, be sensitive to communication in specific cultures.

NOTES

1. We want to thank Youichi Ito, Stella Ting-Toomey, Harry Triandis, Richard Wiseman for comments on an earlier version of the chapter. We also want to thank Seiichi Morisaki and Hiroshi Ota for reading a draft of the chapter. This chapter is an extensive revision of an earlier summary of our cross-cultural research program in Japan and the United States (Gudykunst & Nishida, 1990). We have integrated research conducted by other scholars and extended the chapter to include intercultural research as well.

2. Our review is limited to cross-cultural and intercultural research on interpersonal and intergroup communication involving Japanese and North Americans. We do not include research on language per se (e.g., Hildebrandt & Giles, 1980; Hinds, 1983) since this is the topic of another chapter in the volume (Akasu & Asao). See Wierzbica (1991) for a recent discussion of key words in understanding Japanese society. We also omit research that deals with psychological differences not directly linked to communication (for example, research on self-conceptions in Japan and the United States [e.g., Bond & Cheung, 1983; Cousins, 1989], person perception [e.g., Bond, Nakazato, Shiraishi, 1975], individual coping mechanisms [e.g., Kashima & Triandis, 1986], distributive justice [e.g., Berman, Berman, & Singh, 1985; Hamilton & Saunders, 1992], to name only a few of the possibilities that could be included). For a recent review of psychological research in Japan, see Misumi and Peterson (1990).

3. For a discussion of the dimensions of cultural variability we use in drawing conclusions about cultural similarities and differences, see Gudykunst and San Antonio's chapter in this volume.

4. Lebra (1976) points out that there is a general stranger anxiety (*hitomishiri*) in Japan. Maeda's (1969) research suggests that this anxiety exists in "normal" adults.

5. It should be noted that there is at least one study that suggests that North Americans prefer an indirect rhetorical style more than Japanese (Ting-Toomey, 1988b). The results of Ting-Toomey's study, however, may be due to cultural bias in Hart, Carlson, and Eadie's (1980) measure of rhetorical sensitivity used. The instrument does not include items that would tap indirect forms of communication used in Japan.

6. See also the discussion of *erabi* and *awase* world views (Okabe, 1983) in the section on predispositions toward verbal behavior below.

7. This finding is consistent with Minami and Yamaguchi's (1990) finding that social networks in the United States tend to be heterogeneous, while social networks in Japan tend to be homogeneous.

8. There is other research on nonverbal communication in Japan which does not make direct comparisons with nonverbal communication in the United States which we do not include here. For general discussions see Morsbach (1973, 1980, 1988a, 1988b); for examples of specific research see Bond and Iwata (1976); Bond and Komai (1976); Kudoh and Matsumoto (1985).

9. The correlations observed in this study may be the result of common methods used to measure the two constructs.

10. Nishida (1991) also looked at topics that would be discussed in the periods six-15 minutes and 16-30 minutes, but only the first five minutes are reported here.

11. Renshaw, Tudman, Aoki, and Kumagai (1991) conducted a similar study. The results are compatible with those presented below.

12. For a general discussion of privacy regulation issues across cultures see Gudykunst and Ting-Toomey (1988) and Burgoon (1992).

13. See also Weisz, Rothbaum, and Blackburn (1984) for an alternative view of privacy in Japan and the United States.

14. See also Simmons, Vom Kolke, and Shimuzu (1986) for a discussion of differences in the way romantic relationships are experienced in Japan and the United States. Thakerar and Iwawaki (1979) also found that females in Japan and the United States perceive the same male faces to be attractive.

15. See Wetzel (1985) for a discussion of how language is used as an ingroup marker in Japan.

16. It should be noted that recent studies (e.g., Larsen, 1974) have failed to replicate Asch's (1956) findings. It might be argued that Asch's findings in the United States are a function of the historical period (i.e., McCarthyism).

17. No specific generalization is made based on this study. It, however, contributes to the generalization offered in the section on predispositions toward verbal behavior.

18. See Daikuhara (1986) for another study of compliments in Japan and the United States.

19. Interpretation of the data from this study must be made with care since the samples are not equivalent. The United States sample consisted of college students (all of whom had some work experience) while the Japanese sample consisted of employees in organizations.

20. In a pretest of their questionnaire, Imahori and Cupach found that there is no conceptual equivalence for the English term embarrassment and the Japanese translation of the term.

21. Hiroshi Ota (personal communication) argues that *enryo* is an "active" process in Japan, not a "passive" process like reticence (the nearest equivalent concept) in the United States.

22. Lebra isolates four salient and contradictory aspects of silence in Japanese communication: truthfulness, social discretion, embarrassment, and defiance.

23. Many of the studies discussed in this section are summarized in Klopf (1991).

24. While we attempt to explain these findings conceptually, we believe it is important to recognize that these studies all involve the administration of translated instruments used in the United States in Japan. Few, if any, of the studies address the issue of conceptual equivalence of meaning in interpreting the results or conceptually explain why the differences exist.

25. Reynolds (1976) makes a similar point with respect to how individuals attempt to change in therapy. He argues that people in the United States (individualists) engage in "activity directed toward changing objective reality," while people in Japan (collectivists) engage in "activity directed toward changing one's inner attitudes or attention to objective reality" (p. 110).

26. See Okabe (1983) and Tezuka (1992) for a more extensive discussion of *awase*. Tezuka points out that the adjustment that takes place is reciprocal—both communicators adjust to each other. She also suggests that *sunao* ("being upright, obedient and docile without a negative connotation" [p. 41]) is important to understanding Japanese communication. See Murase (1982) for a discussion of the concept.

27. This section overlaps issues discussed in Akasu and Asao's chapter in this volume. The focus here, therefore, is on aspects of discourse related directly to encoding and decoding of messages. For an extensive discussion of topic management in business meetings, see Yamada (in press).

28. See Hayashi (1988) for a discussion of differences in use of simultaneous talk in English and Japanese.

29. There are other studies of persuasive strategy selection in Japan and the United States. There are, however, methodological problems with these studies that make their findings difficult to interpret. Neulip and Hazelton (1985), for example, studied Japanese and North Americans, but the research instrument administered in Japan was in English. Shatzer, Funkhouser, and Hesse (1984) and Shatzer, Burgoon, Burgoon, Korzenny, and Miller (1988) compared North Americans and Japanese students studying in the United States. Shatzer et al. (1988) found a significant effect for language of questionnaire administration for the Japanese students.

30. Ujitani (1991), however, found that North Americans were significantly better at identifying vocal expressions of emotions (surprise, love, happiness, anger) by English speakers than Japanese.

31. Sato, Mauro, and Tucker (1990) found that there are four cognitive dimensions used for the appraisal of emotions in Japan and the United States: pleasantness, certainty, attentional activity, and coping ability.

32. This data set is part of a larger study of emotions in 27 countries on five continents which is summarized in Wallbott and Scherer (1986).

33. See Tada (1958) and Pharr (1990) for discussions of face in Japan. Seiichi Morisaki (personal communication) argues that scholars in the United States use the concept of face differently that Chinese and Japanese scholars. He argues that in Japan and China face is related to social identity, not personal identity. As scholars in the United States use the concept, in contrast, face is based in personal identity. This distinction has important implications for studying face in Japan and the United States and needs to be pursued in future research.

34. Other studies (e.g., Henderson, 1975; Kawashima, 1963; Peterson & Shimada, 1979) indicate that mediation is the preferred method for resolving disputes in Japan.

35. Ting-Toomey, Trubisky et al. (1991) inductively derived a taxonomy of facework strategies using data from Japan and the United States.

36. See Pharr (1989) for case studies of intra- and intergroup conflict in Japan.

37. As indicated in the next note, Imahori (1987a, 1987b) also examined initial Japanese- North American relationships in a laboratory setting. The language level of his Japanese confederates and statistical problems with the analysis make his results equivocal.

38. Imahori's (1987a, 1987b) research also did not support uncertainty reduction predictions in Japanese-North American interactions in a laboratory setting. He argues that his results are due to language problems (e.g., Japanese were not fluent in English). There also were statistical problems with the analysis in this study (e.g., the confederate X interaction type effect was not examined and there were major differences in behavior across confederates) that make Imahori's data equivocal.

39. Powell (1986) found that a Japanese speaker's English ability does not contribute to satisfaction with conversations with other Japanese speaking English. Rather, the partner's perceived contribution to the conversation was the best predictor of satisfaction. Given that Japanese speaking to other Japanese in English is not a "natural" occurrence, it is questionable if this finding will generalize to Japanese-North American conversations in English.

40. There also is a study of turn-taking in Japanese-North American small groups conducted in Japanese and English (Clarke & Kanatani, 1980), but this study does not relate turn-taking to outcomes. This study is based on data collected at the Japan-United States Intercultural Communication Workshop held in Nihonmatsu, Japan in July 1974. Small discussion groups were held over five days and video recorded. This is an excellent source of "live" Japanese-North American communication data that has not been sufficiently studied. Minimally, we encourage the individuals holding the tapes to make audio recordings of the meetings available to other researchers.

41. There are several other studies of North Americans adjustment to living in Japan and Japanese adjustment to living in the United States. Most of these studies, however, are not communication based. See Diggs and Murphy (1991); Kawabata, Kume, and Uehara (1989); Obazaki-Luff (1991); Patridge (1988); Uehara (1988); Uehara and Hicks (1988) for recent discussions.

42. There is much confusion in the literature over the use of the terms effectiveness and competence. As we use the terms effectiveness is an outcome of communication (i.e., minimizing misunderstandings or making isomorphic attributions) and competence is a characteristic of the communicator (or perceived characteristic of the communicator).

43. Miyanaga (1991) points out that Doi has co-opted the definition of amae and this has to kept in mind.

44. Hamaguchi (1980b) developed a Japanese measure of contexualism-individualism which is similar to Triandis et al.'s conceptualization (see Appendix 2 in Befu, 1990a, for an English translation of the scale).

45. Gudykunst et al.'s (1992) research also indicates that individuals' strength of cultural identity interacts with their cultural background (e.g., the individualism-collectivism of their native culture) to influence the values members of a culture hold. Researchers, therefore, would be advised to assess strength of cultural identity as well.

References

Abe, H., & Wiseman, R. L. (1983). A cross-cultural confirmation of the dimensions of intercultural effectiveness. *International Journal of Intercultural Relations, 7,* 53-67.

Altman, I. (1977). Privacy: Culturally universal or culturally specific. *Journal of Social Issues, 33,* 66-84.

Altman, I., & Taylor, D. (1973). *Social penetration processes.* New York: Holt, Reinhart, and Winston.

Altman, I., Vinsel, A., & Brown, B. (1981). Dialectical conceptions in social psychology. In L. Berkowitz (Ed.), *Advances in experimental social psychology* (Vol. 14). New York: Academic Press.

Applegate, J., & Delia, J. (1980). Person-centered speech, psychological development and the contexts of language usage. In R. St. Clair & H. Giles (Eds.), *The social and psychological contexts of language.* Hillsdale, NJ: Erlbaum.

Argyle, M., Henderson, M., Bond, M., Iizuka, Y., & Contarelo, A. (1986). Cross-cultural variations in relationship rules. *International Journal of Psychology, 21,* 287-315.

Asai, A., & Barnlund, D. (1991). *Boundaries of the unconscious, private and public self in Japanese and Americans: A cross-cultural comparison.* Paper presented at the Speech Communication Association convention, Atlanta.

Asch, S. E. (1956). Studies of independence and conformity. *Psychological Monographs, 70,* No. 9 (whole No. 416).

Atsumi, R. (1979). *Tsukiai*—Obligatory personnel relationships of Japanese white collar employees. *Human Organization, 38,* 63-70.

Atsumi, R. (1980). Patterns of personal relationships: A key to understanding Japanese thought and behavior. *Social Analysis, 5/6,* 63-78.

Atsumi, R. (1989). Friendship in cross-cultural perspective. In Y. Sugimoto & R. Mouer (Eds.), *Constructs for understanding Japan.* London: Kegan Paul.

Baker, J. (1990). *Conceptions of privacy in Japan and the United States.* Paper presented at the Intercultural and International Communication Conference, California State University, Fullerton.

Baker, J., & Gudykunst, W. B. (1990). *Privacy regulation in Japan and the United States.* Paper presented at the International Communication Association convention, Dublin.

Barnlund, D. (1975). *The public and private self in Japan and the United States.* Tokyo: Simul Press (Japanese version: *Nihon-jin no hyogen kozo.* Tokyo: Simul, 1973).

Barnlund, D. (1989). *Communicative styles of Japanese and Americans.* Belmont, CA: Wadsworth.

Barnlund, D., & Araki, S. (1985). Intercultural encounters: The management of compliments by Japanese and Americans. *Journal of Cross-Cultural Psychology, 16,* 9-27.

Barnlund, D., & Yoshioka, M. (1990). Apologies: Japanese and American styles. *International Journal of Intercultural Relations, 14,* 193-205.

Baxter, L. (1990). Dialectical contradictions in relationship development. *Journal of Social and Personal Relationships, 7*, 69-88.

Befu, H. (1966). Gift giving and social reciprocity in Japan. *France-Asia, 188*, 161-177.

Befu, H. (1977a). Power in the great white tower. In R. Fogelson & R. Adams (Eds.), *The anthropology of power*. New York: Academic Press.

Befu, H. (1977b). Social exchange. *Annual Review of Anthropology, 6*, 255-281.

Befu, H. (1980a). A critique of the group model of Japanese society. *Social Analysis, 5/6*, 29-43.

Befu, H. (1980b). The group model of Japanese society and an alternative. *Rice University Studies, 66*, 169-187.

Befu, H. (1987). *Ideorigi to shite no Nihon bunkaron* (Cultural theories of Japanese ideology). Tokyo: Shiso no Kagokusha.

Befu, H. (1989a). A theory of social exchange as applied to Japan. In Y. Sugimoto & R. Mouer (Eds.), *Constructs for understanding Japan*. London: Kegan Paul.

Befu, H. (1989b). The emic-etic distinction and its significance for Japanese studies. In Y. Sugimoto & R. Mouer (Eds.), *Constructs for understanding Japan*. London: Kegan Paul.

Befu, H. (1990a). Conflict and non-Weberian bureaucracy in Japan. In S. Eisenstadt & E. Ben-Ari (Eds.), *Japanese models of conflict resolution*. London: Kegan Paul.

Befu, H. (1990b). Four models of Japanese society and their relevance to conflict. In S. Eisenstadt & E. Ben-Ari (Eds.), *Japanese models of conflict resolution*. London: Kegan Paul.

Beier, E., & Zautra, A. (1972). Identification of vocal components of emotions across cultures. *Journal of Consulting and Clinical Psychology, 34*, 166-175.

Bell, R. (1981). *Worlds of friendship*. Beverly Hills, CA: Sage.

Bellah, R., Madsen, R., Sullivan, W., Swidler, A., & Tipton, S. (1985). *Habits of the heart: Individualism and commitment in American life*. New York: Harper and Row.

Bellah, R., Madsen, R., Sullivan, W., Swidler, A., & Tipton, S. (1991). *The good society*. New York: Knopf.

Bem, S. (1981). Gender scheme theory. *Psychological Review, 88*, 354-364.

Berger, C. R. (1979). Beyond initial interaction. In H. Giles & R. St. Clair (Eds.). *Language and social psychology*. Oxford: Basil Blackwell.

Berger, C. R., & Bradac, J. (1982). *Language and social knowledge*. London: Edward Arnold.

Berger, C. R., & Calabrese, R. (1975). Some explorations in initial interactions and beyond: Toward a developmental theory of interpersonal communication. *Human Communication Research, 1*, 99-112.

Berger, C. R., & Gudykunst, W. B. (1991). Uncertainty and communication. In B. Dervin & M. Voigt (Eds.), *Progress in communication sciences* (Vol. 10). Norwood, NJ: Ablex.

Berman, J., Berman, V., & Singh, P. (1985). Cross-cultural similarities and differences in perceptions of fairness. *Journal of Cross-Cultural Psychology, 16*, 55-67.

Berscheid, E., Snyder, M., & Omoto, A. (1989). The relationship closeness inventory. *Journal of Personality and Social Psychology, 57*, 792-807.

Bond, M. H., & Cheung, T. (1983). College students spontaneous self-concept: The effects of culture among respondents in Hong Kong, Japan, and the United States. *Journal of Cross-Cultural Psychology, 14*, 153-171.

Bond, M. H., & Iwata, Y. (1976). Proxemics and observation anxiety in Japan. *Psychologie, 19*, 119-126.

Bond, M. H., & Komai, H. (1976). Targets of gazing and eye contact during interviews: Effect of Japanese nonverbal behavior. *Journal of Personality and Social Psychology, 34*, 1276-1284.

Bond, M. H., Nakazato, H., & Shiraishi, D. (1975). Universality and distinctiveness of Japanese person perception. *Journal of Cross-Cultural Psychology, 6*, 346-357.

Booth-Butterfield, M., & Booth-Butterfield, S. (1990). Conceptualizing affect as information in communication production. *Human Communication Research, 16*, 451-476.

Boyer, L., Thompson, C., Klopf, D., & Ishii, S. (1990). An intercultural comparison of immediacy among Japanese and Americans. *Perceptual and Motor Skills, 71*, 65-66.

Burgoon, J. (1992). Applying a comparative approach to nonverbal expectancy violations theory. In J. Blumler, J. McCleod, & K. Rosengren (Eds.), *Communication and culture across time and space*. Newbury Park, CA: Sage.

Burgoon, M., Dillard, J., Doran, N., & Miller, M. (1982). Cultural and situational influences on the process of persuasive strategy selection. *International Journal of Intercultural Relations, 6*, 85-99.

Byrne, D., Gouolax, C., Griffitt, W., Lamberth, J., Murakawa, N., Prosad, M., Prosad, A., & Ramirez, M. (1971). The ubiquitous relationship: Attitude similarity and attraction. *Human Relations, 24*, 201-207.

Cambra, R., Ishii, S., & Klopf, D. (1978). *Four studies of Japanese speech characteristics.* Paper presented at the Communication Association of the Pacific Convention, Tokyo.

Caudill, W., & Scarr, H. (1961). Japanese value orientations and culture change. *Ethnology, 1*, 53-91.

Chinese Culture Connection. (1987). Chinese values and the search for culture-free dimensions of culture. *Journal of Cross-Cultural Psychology, 18*, 143-164.

Christie, R., & Geis, F. (1970). *Studies in machiavellianism.* New York: Academic Press.

Clarke, C., & Kanatani, K. (1970). Turn-taking *no shikumi* (Turn-taking in small group communication: A cross-cultural study). *Daiikkai Gaikokugo Kyoiku Kindaika Sekaitaikai Annai* (Language Laboratory), *17*, 12-24.

Clatterbuck, G. (1979). Attributional confidence and uncertainty in initial interactions. *Human Communication Research, 5*, 147-157.

Cole, M. (1989). *A cross-cultural inquiry into the meaning of face in the Japanese and United States cultures.* Paper presented at the Speech Communication Association convention, San Francisco.

Cole, M. (1990). *Relational distance and personality influence on conflict communication styles.* Paper presented at the Speech Communication Association convention, Chicago.

Cousins, S. (1989). Culture and self-perception in Japan and the United States. *Journal of Personality and Social Psychology, 56*, 124-131.

Cushman, D., & King, S. (1985). National and organizational cultures in conflict resolution. In W. B. Gudykunst, L. P. Stewart, & S. Ting-Toomey (Eds.), *Communication, culture, and organizational processes.* Beverly Hills, CA: Sage.

Cushman, D., & Nishida, T. (1983). *Mate selection in Japan and the United States.* Unpublished paper, State University of New York, Albany.

Daikuhara, M. (1986). A study of compliments from a cross-cultural perspective: Japanese and American English. *Working Papers in Educational Linguistics, 2*(2), 103-135.

Darwin, C. (1872). *The expression of emotions in man and animals*. London: John Murray.

DeGooyer, M., & Williams, J. (1990). *Self-concepts in Japan and the United States*. Paper presented at the Congress of the International Association for Cross-Cultural Psychology, Nara, Japan.

Detweiler, R. (1980). Intercultural interactions and the categorization process. *International Journal of Intercultural Relations, 4*, 275-293.

Diggs, N., & Murphy, B. (1991). Japanese adjustment to American communities. *International Journal of Intercultural Relations, 15*, 103-116.

Doi, T. (1973). *The anatomy of dependence* (J. Bester trans.). Tokyo: Kodansha (Japanese version: *Amae no kozo*. Tokyo: Kobundo, 1971).

Doi, T. (1975). *Amae zakko* (Collected essays on *amae*). Tokyo: Kobundo.

Doi, T. (1986). *The anatomy of self* (M. Harbison trans.). Tokyo: Kodansha (Japanese version: *Omote to ura*. Tokyo: Kobundo, 1985).

Edelstein, A., Ito, Y., & Kepplinger, H. (1989). *Communication and culture: A comparative approach*. New York: Longman.

Edgerton, R. B. (1985). *Rules, exceptions, and social order*. Berkeley: University of California Press.

Ekman, P., & Friesen, W. (1971). Constants across cultures in the face and emotion. *Journal of Personality and Social Psychology, 17*, 124-129.

Ekman, P., Friesen, W., O'Sullivan, M., Diacoyanni-Tarlatzis, I., Krause, R., Pitcairn, T., Scherer, K., Chan, A., Heider, K., Compte, W., Ricci-Bitti, P., Komita, M., & Tzavaras, A. (1987). Personality processes and individual differences: Universals and cultural differences in the judgments of facial expressions. *Journal of Personality and Social Psychology, 53*, 712-717.

Elliot, S., Scott, M., Jensen, A., & McDonald, M. (1982). Perceptions of reticence: A cross-cultural investigation. In M. Burgoon (Ed.), *Communication yearbook 5*. New Brunswick, NJ: Transaction Books.

Engebretson, D., & Fullmer, D. (1970). Cross-cultural differences in territorality: Interaction differences of native Japanese, Hawaii Japanese, and American caucasians. *Journal of Cross-Cultural Psychology, 1*, 261-269.

Fenigstein, A., Scheier, M., & Buss, A. (1975). Public and private self-consciousness: Assessment and theory. *Journal of Consulting and Clinical Psychology, 43*, 522-527.

Field, N. (1991). *In the realm of a dying emperor*. New York: Pantheon.

Frager, R. (1970). Conformity and anticonformity in Japan. *Journal of Personality and Social Psychology, 15,* 203-210.

Fredrick, J., Sorrentino, R., & Hewitt, E. (1985). *Need for uncertainty scoring manual.* Department of Psychology, University of Western Ontario, Research Bulletin #618.

Friesen, W. (1972). *Cultural differences in facial expression in a social situation: An experimental test of the concept of display rules.* Unpublished Ph.D. dissertation, University of California, San Francisco.

Frymier, A., Klopf, D., & Ishii, S. (1990). Japanese and Americans compared on the affect orientation construct. *Psychological Reports, 66,* 985-986 (also published in *Communication Research Reports,* 1990, *7,* 63-66).

Fujihara, T., & Kurokawa, M. (1981). *Taijinkankei ni okeru "amae" ni tsuiteno jisyoteki kenkyu* (An empirical study of *amae* [dependence] in interpersonal relations). *Jikkenshakaishinrigigaku Kenkyu* (The Japanese Journal of Experimental Social Psychology), *21,* 53-62.

Gao, G., & Gudykunst, W. B. (1990). Uncertainty, anxiety, and adaptation. *International Journal of Intercultural Relations, 14,* 301-317.

Geatz, L., Klopf, D., & Ishii, S. (1990). *Predispositions toward verbal behavior of Japanese and Americans.* Paper presented at the Communication Association of Japan Convention, Tokyo.

Giles, H., Bourhis, R., & Taylor, D. (1977). Towards a theory of language in ethnic group relations. In H. Giles (Ed.), *Language, ethnicity, and intergroup relations.* London: Academic Press.

Gouldner, A. (1960). The norm of reciprocity. *American Sociological Review, 25,* 161-179.

Gudykunst, W. B. (1985). The influence of cultural similarity, type of relationship, and self-monitoring on uncertainty reduction processes. *Communication Monographs, 52,* 203-217.

Gudykunst, W. B. (1988). Uncertainty and anxiety. In Y. Y. Kim & W. B. Gudykunst (Eds.), *Theories in intercultural communication.* Newbury Park, CA: Sage.

Gudykunst, W. B. (1989). Culture and communication in interpersonal relationships. In J. Anderson (Ed.), *Communication yearbook 12.* Newbury Park, CA: Sage.

Gudykunst, W. B. (forthcoming). *Interpersonal and intergroup communication: Bridging theory and application.* Newbury Park, CA: Sage.

Gudykunst, W. B., Gao, G., Nishida, T., Bond, M. H., Leung, K., Wang, G., & Barraclough, R. A. (1989). A cross-cultural comparison of self-monitoring. *Communication Research Reports, 6*(1), 7-12.

Gudykunst, W. B., Gao, G., Schmidt, K., Nishida, T., Bond, M. H., Leung, K., Wang, G., & Barraclough, R. A. (1992). The influence of individualism-collectivism on communication in ingroup and outgroup relationships. *Journal of Cross-Cultural Psychology, 23*, 196-213.

Gudykunst, W. B., Gao, G., Nishida, T., Nadamitsu, Y., & Sakai, J. (1992). Self-monitoring in Japan and the United States. In S. Iwaki, Y. Kashima, & K. Leung (Eds.), *Innovations in cross-cultural psychology.* The Hague, The Netherlands: Swets and Zeitlinger.

Gudykunst, W. B., Gao, G., Sudweeks, S., Ting-Toomey, S., & Nishida, T. (1991). Themes in opposite-sex Japanese-North American relationships. In S. Ting-Toomey & F. Korzenny (Eds.), *Cross-cultural interpersonal communication.* Newbury Park, CA; Sage.

Gudykunst, W. B., & Hammer, M. R. (1984). Dimensions of intercultural effectiveness: Culture specific or culture general. *International Journal of Intercultural Relations, 8*, 1-10.

Gudykunst, W. B., & Hammer, M. R. (1988). The influence of social identity and intimacy of interethnic relationships on uncertainty reduction processes. *Human Communication Research, 14*, 569-601.

Gudykunst, W. B., & Kim, Y. Y. (1984). *Communicating with strangers.* Reading, MA: Addison-Wesley.

Gudykunst, W. B., & Nishida, T. (1983). Social penetration in Japanese and American close friendships. In R. Bostrom (Ed.), *Communication yearbook 7.* Beverly Hills, CA: Sage.

Gudykunst, W. B., & Nishida, T. (1984). Individual and cultural influences on uncertainty reduction. *Communication Monographs, 51*, 23-36.

Gudykunst, W. B., & Nishida, T. (1986a). Attributional confidence in low- and high-context cultures. *Human Communication Research, 12*, 525-549.

Gudykunst, W. B., & Nishida, T. (1986b). The influence of cultural variability on perceptions of communication behavior associated with relationship terms. *Human Communication Research, 13*, 147-166.

Gudykunst, W. B., & Nishida, T. (1989). Perspectives for studying intercultural communication. In M. Asante & W. B. Gudykunst (Eds.), *Handbook of international and intercultural communication.* Newbury Park, CA: Sage.

Gudykunst, W. B., & Nishida, T. (1990). Communication in interpersonal relationships in Japan and the United States: Overview of a research program. *The Bulletin of the Institute for Communications Research, Keio University, 35,* 1-48.

Gudykunst, W. B., & Nishida, T. (1992). *Relationship closeness in Japan and the United States.* Paper presented at the Speech Communication Association convention, Chicago.

Gudykunst, W. B., Nishida, T., & Chua, E. (1986). Uncertainty reduction in Japanese-North American dyads. *Communication Research Reports, 3,* 39-46.

Gudykunst, W. B., Nishida, T., & Chua, E. (1987). Perceptions of social penetration in Japanese-North American dyads. *International Journal of Intercultural Relations, 11,* 171-189.

Gudykunst, W. B., Nishida, T., Chung, L., & Sudweeks, S. (1992). *The influence of strength of cultural identity and perceived typicality on individualistic and collectivistic values in Japan and the United States.* Paper presented at the Asian Regional Congress of the International Association for Cross-Cultural Psychology, Kathmandu, Nepal.

Gudykunst, W. B., Nishida, T., Koike, H., & Shiino, N. (1986). The influence of language on uncertainty reduction: An exploratory study of Japanese-Japanese and Japanese-North American interactions. In M. McLaughlin (Ed.), *Communication Yearbook 9.* Beverly Hills, CA: Sage.

Gudykunst, W. B., Nishida, T., & Morisaki, S. (1992). *The influence of cultural and social identity on the evaluation of interpersonal and intergroup encounters in the United States.* Paper presented at the International Communication Association convention, Miami.

Gudykunst, W. B., Nishida, T., & Schmidt, K. L. (1989). Cultural, relational, and personality influences on uncertainty reduction processes. *Western Speech Communication Journal, 53,* 13-29.

Gudykunst, W. B., Sodetani, L., & Sonoda, K. (1987). Uncertainty reduction in Japanese-American/Caucasian relationships in Hawaii. *Western Journal of Speech Communication, 51,* 256-278.

Gudykunst, W. B., & Ting-Toomey, S., with Chua, E. (1988). *Culture and interpersonal communication.* Newbury Park, CA: Sage.

Gudykunst, W. B., Wiseman, R. L., & Hammer, M. R. (1977). Determinants of a sojourner's attitudinal satisfaction. In B. Ruben (Ed.), *Communication yearbook 1.* New Brunswick, NJ: Transaction.

Gudykunst, W. B., Yang, S. M., & Nishida, T. (1985). A cross-cultural test of uncertainty reduction theory: Comparison of acquaintances, friends, and dating relationships in Japan, Korea, and the United States. *Human Communication Research, 11,* 407-454.

Gudykunst, W. B., Yang, S. M., & Nishida, T. (1987). Cultural differences in self-consciousness and self-monitoring. *Communication Research, 14,* 7-36.

Gudykunst, W. B., Yoon, Y. C., & Nishida, T. (1987). The influence of individualism-collectivism on perceptions of communication in ingroup and outgroup relationships. *Communication Monographs, 54,* 295-306.

Haga, Y. (1979). *Nihonjin no hyogen shinri* (Psychology of Japanese expression). Tokyo: Chuhko Sohsho.

Hall, E. T. (1976). *Beyond culture.* New York: Doubleday.

Hamaguchi, E. (1977). *"Nihon rashisa" no saihakken* (The rediscovery of "Japaneseness"). Tokyo: Nihon Keizai Simbunsha.

Hamaguchi, E. (1982a). *Nihonjin no ningen moderu to "aidagara"* (Human model of Japanese and their relationships). *Osaka Daigaku, Ningen Kagaku, 8,* 207-240.

Hamaguchi, E. (1982b). *Nihonteki shuhdanshugi towa nanika* (What is the Japanese groupism). In E. Hamaguchi & S. Kumon (Ed.), *Nihonteki shudanshugi* (Japanese groupism). Tokyo: Yuhikaku (Sensho).

Hamaguchi, E. (1983). *Kanjin-shugi no shakai Nihon* (Japan, society of contextual men). Tokyo: Touyou Keizai.

Hamaguchi, E. (1985). A contextual model of the Japanese. *Journal of Japanese Studies, 11*(2), 289-321.

Hamilton, V., Blumenfeld, P., Akoh, H., & Miura, K. (1991). Group and gender in Japanese and American elementary classrooms. *Journal of Cross-Cultural Psychology, 22,* 317-346.

Hamilton, V., & Saunders, J. (1992). *Everyday justice: Responsibility and the individual in Japan and the United States.* New Haven, CT: Yale University Press.

Hammer, M. R., Gudykunst, W. B., & Wiseman, R. L. (1978). Dimensions of intercultural effectiveness. *International Journal of Intercultural Relations, 2,* 382-393.

Harman, C., Klopf, D., & Ishii, S. (1990). Verbal aggression among Japanese and American students. *Perceptual and Motor Skills, 70,* 1130.

Hart, R., Carlson, R., & Eadie, W. (1980). Attitudes toward communication and the assessment of rhetorical sensitivity. *Communication Monographs, 47,* 1-20.

Harvey, J. H., Weber, A. L., Galvin, K. S., Huszti, H. C., & Garnick, N. N. (1986). Attribution and the termination of close relationships: A special focus on the account. In R. Gilmour & S. Duck (Eds.), *The emerging field of personal relationships*. Hillsdale, NJ: Erlbaum.

Hayashi, R. (1988). Simultaneous talk from the perspective of floor management of English and Japanese speakers. *World Englishes, 7*, 269-288.

Hayashi, R. (1990). Rhythmicity, sequence and synchrony of English and Japanese face-to-face conversations. *Language Sciences, 12*, 155-195.

Hecht, M. (1978). The conceptualization and measurement of communication satisfaction. *Human Communication Research, 4*, 253-264.

Henderson, D. (1975). *Foreign enterprise in Japan*. Chappel Hill: University of North Carolina Press.

Hildebrandt, N., & Giles, H. (1980). The English language in Japan: A social psychological perspective. *JALT Journal, 2*, 63-87.

Hinds, J. (1982). Japanese conversational structures. *Lingua, 57*, 301-326.

Hinds, J. (1983). Contrastive rhetoric: Japanese and English. *Text, 3*, 183-195.

Hirokawa, R., & Miyahara, A. (1986). A comparison of influence strategies utilized by managers in American and Japanese organizations. *Communication Quarterly, 34*, 250-265.

Hofstede, G. (1980). *Culture's consequences*. Beverly Hills, CA: Sage.

Hoyle, R., Pinkley, R., & Insko, C. (1989). Perceptions of social behavior: Evidence of differing expectations for interpersonal and intergroup encounters. *Personality and Social Psychology Bulletin, 15*, 365-376.

Imahori, T. (1987a). *An exploratory comparison of initial intracultural and intercultural interactions*. Paper presented at the Western Speech Communication Association convention, Salt Lake City.

Imahori, T. (1987b). *Intercultural interpersonal epistemology*. Paper presented at the Speech Communication Association convention, Boston.

Imahori, T., & Cupach, W. (1991). *A cross-cultural comparison of the interpretation and management of face: American and Japanese responses to embarrassing predicaments*. Paper presented at the Conference on Communication in Japan and the United States, California State University, Fullerton.

Infante, D., & Rancer, A. (1982). A conceptualization and measurement of argumenentativeness. *Journal of Personality Assessment, 46*, 72-80.

Infante, D., & Wigley, C. (1986). Verbal aggressiveness. *Communication Monographs, 53*, 62-69.

Ishii, S. (1984). *Enryo-sasshi* communication: A key to understanding Japanese interpersonal relations. *Cross Currents, 11,* 49-58.

Ishii, S., Thompson, C., & Klopf, D. (1990). A comparison of the assertiveness/responsiveness construct between Japanese and Americans. *Otsuma Review, 23,* 63-71.

Ito, Y. (1989a). A nonwestern view of the paradigm dialogues. In B. Dervin, L. Grossberg, & E. Wartella (Eds.), *Rethinking communication.* Newbury Park, CA: Sage.

Ito, Y. (1989b). Socio-cultural backgrounds of Japanese interpersonal communication style. *Civilisations, 39,* 101-137.

Ito, Y. (1992). Theories of interpersonal communication style from a Japanese perspective. In J. Blumler, J. McCleod, & K. Rosengren (Eds.), *Communication and culture across space and time.* Newbury Park, CA: Sage.

Iwata, O. (1987). *Nihonjin daigakuseiniokeru puraibashi shikosei to jinkakutokusei no kankei* (The relationship between orientation toward privacy and personality traits in Japanese undergraduates). *Shakaishinrigaku Kenkyu* (Research in Social Psychology), *3,* 11-16.

Izard, C. (1968). *The emotions as a culture-common framework of motivational experiences and communication.* Technical Report No. 30, Vanderbilt University Contract No. 2149(03)-NR 171-6090, Office of Naval Research.

Izard, C. (1971). *The face of emotion.* New York: Appleton-Century-Crofts.

Izard, C. (1980). Cross-cultural perspectives on emotion and emotion communication. In H. Triandis & W. Lonner (Eds.), *Handbook of cross-cultural psychology* (Vol. 3). Boston: Allyn & Bacon.

Johnson, C., & Johnson, F. (1975). Interaction rules and ethnicity. *Social Forces, 54,* 452-466.

Joreskog, K., & Sorbom, D. (1981). *LISREL V: Users guide.* Chicago: National Educational Resources.

Jung, C. (1933). *Psychological types.* New York: Harcourt, Brace.

Kashima, Y., & Triandis, H. C. (1986). The self-serving bias in attributions as a coping strategy. *Journal of Cross-Cultural Psychology, 17,* 83-97.

Kawabata, M., Kume, T., & Uehara, A. (1989). *Nihonjin ni okeru kokusaishishitsu ni kansuru kenkyujosetsu* (An exploratory study of intercultural qualities, abilities, and attitudes for Japanese). *Tokyo Gagugei Daigaku Kaigaishijo Kyoiku Senta Kenkyuyoki* (Journal of Education Center for Returnees, Tokyo Gakugei University), *5,* 63-91.

Kawashima, T. (1963). Dispute resolution in contemporary Japan. In A. von Mehren (Ed.), *Law in Japan*. Cambridge, MA: Harvard University Press.

Kertamus, L., Gudykunst, W. B., & Nishida, T. (1991). *Relational themes in male-male, Japanese-North American relationships*. Paper presented at the Conference on Communication in Japan and the United States, California State University, Fullerton.

Kimura, B. (1988). *Aida* (Inbetweenness). Tokyo: Kobunsha.

Kimura, B. (1989). *Hito to hito no aida* (Between people). Tokyo: Kobunsha.

King, S., Minami, Y., & Samovar, L. (1985). A comparison of Japanese and American perceptions of source credibility. *Communication Research Reports, 2*, 76-79.

Klopf, D. (1984). Cross-cultural communication apprehension research. In J. Daly & J. McCroskey (Eds.), *Avoiding communication*. Beverly Hills, CA: Sage.

Klopf, D. (1991). Japanese communication practices: Recent comparative research. *Communication Quarterly, 39*, 130-143.

Klopf, D., & Cambra, R. (1979). Communication apprehension among college students in America, Australia, Japan, and Korea. *Journal of Psychology, 102*, 27-31.

Klopf, D., & Cambra, R. (1981). A comparison of communication styles of Japanese and American college students. *Current English Studies, 20*, 66-71.

Kluckhohn, F., & Strodtbeck, F. (1961). *Variations in value orientations*. New York: Row, Peterson.

Knapp, M. (1978). *Social intercourse: From greeting to goodbye*. Boston: Allyn and Bacon.

Knapp, M., Ellis, D., & Williams, B. (1980). Perceptions of communication behavior associated with relationship terms. *Communication Monographs, 47*, 262-278.

Koike, H., Gudykunst, W. B., Stewart, L., Ting-Toomey, S., & Nishida, T. (1988). Communication openness, satisfaction, and length of employment in Japanese organizations. *Communication Research Reports, 5*(2), 97-102.

Kondo, D. K. (1990). *Crafting selves: Power, gender, and discourses of identity in a Japanese workplace*. Chicago: University of Chicago Press.

Krauss, E., Rohlen, T., & Steinhoff, G. (Eds.). (1984). *Conflict in Japan*. Honolulu: University of Hawaii Press.

Kudoh, T., & Matsumoto, D. (1985). Cross-cultural examination of the semantic dimensions of body posture. *Journal of Personality and Social Psychology, 48,* 1440-1446.

Kumagai, F., & Strauss, M. (1983). Conflict resolution tactics in Japan, India, and the United States. *Journal of Comparative Family Studies, 14,* 337-387.

Kumon, S. (1982). *Soshiki no Nihongata moderu to obeigata moderu* (Japanese and American models of organizations). In E. Hamaguchi & S. Kumon (Eds.), *Nihonteki shuhdanshugi* (Japanese groupism). Tokyo: Yuhikaku (Sensho).

Kunihiro, M. (1976). Indigenous barriers to communication. *Japan Interpreter,* Winter, 96-108.

Larsen, K. (1974). Conformity in the Asch experiment. *Journal of Social Psychology, 74,* 303-304.

Lebra, T. S. (1976). *Japanese patterns of behavior.* Honolulu: University of Hawaii Press.

Lebra, T. S. (1987). The cultural significance of silence in Japanese communication. *Multilingua, 6,* 343-357.

Lebra, T. S. (1984). *Japanese women.* Honolulu: University of Hawaii Press.

LoCastro, V. (1987). *Aizuchi:* A Japanese conversational routine. In L. Smith (Ed.), *Discourse across cultures.* New York: Prentice Hall.

Lu, H. N., & Gudykunst, W. B. (1988). *The relationship between social penetration and uncertainty reduction across relationships and cultures.* Paper presented at the Western Speech Communication Association convention, San Diego, CA.

Maeda, S. (1969). *Hitomishiri* (Stranger anxiety). *Seshin Bunseki Kenkyu* (The Japanese Journal of Psychoanalysis), *15*(2), 16-19.

Markus, H., & Kitayama, S. (1991). Culture and the self: Implications for cognition, emotion, and motivation. *Psychological Review, 98,* 224-253.

Marsella, A. J., DeVos, G., & Hsu, F. L. K. (Eds.). (1985). *Culture and self: Asian and Western perspectives.* New York: Tavistock Publications.

Matsumoto, D., & Ekman, P. (1989). American-Japanese cultural differences in the intensity ratings of facial expressions of emotions. *Motivation and Emotion, 13,* 143-157.

Matsumoto, D., & Kishimoto, H. (1983). Developmental characteristics in judgments of emotion from nonverbal cues. *International Journal of Intercultural Relations, 7,* 415-424.

Matsumoto, D., Kudoh, T., Scherer, K., & Wallbott, H. (1988). Antecedents of and reactions to emotions in Japan and the United States. *Journal of Cross-Cultural Psychology, 19*, 267-286.

Matsumoto, M. (1988). *The unspoken way* (W. Ross trans.). Tokyo: Kodansha (Japanese version: *Haragei*. Tokyo: Kodansha, 1984).

Maynard, S. (1986). On back-channel behavior in Japanese and English casual conversations. *Linguistics, 24*, 85-114.

McCroskey, J. M., & Daly, J. (Eds). (1987). *Personality and interpersonal communication*. Beverly Hills, CA: Sage.

McCroskey, J. M., Gudykunst, W. B., & Nishida, T. (1985). Communication apprehension among Japanese college students in native and second language. *Communication Research Reports, 2*, 85-94.

Mead, G. H. (1934). *Mind, self, and society*. Chicago: University of Chicago Press.

Miller, G., & Steinberg, M. (1975). *Between people*. Chicago: Science Research Associates.

Midooka, K. (1990). Characteristics of Japanese-style communication. *Media, Culture, and Society, 12*, 477-489.

Minami, H. (1971). *Psychology of the Japanese people* (A. Ikoma trans.). Tokyo: University of Tokyo Press (Japanese version: *Nihonjin no shinri*. Tokyo: Iwanami Shoten, 1953).

Minami, H., & Yamaguchi, S. (1990). *A multivariate comparison of social support structures of college freshmen in the U.S.A. and Japan*. Paper presented at the Congress of the International Association for Cross-Cultural Psychology, Nara, Japan.

Minami, Y. (1985). *A cross-cultural study of source credibility: A case of the United States and Japan*. Paper presented at the International Communication Association convention, Honolulu.

Misumi, J., & Peterson, M. (1990). Psychology in Japan. In M. Rosenzweig & L. Porter (Eds.), *Annual review of psychology* (Vol. 41). Palo Alto, CA: Annual Reviews, Inc.

Minamoto, R. (1969). *Giri to ninjo* (Obligation and human feeling). Tokyo: Chuo Koronsha.

Mito, T. (1991). *Ie no ronri* (The theory of *ie*) (two vols.). Tokyo: Bunshindo.

Miyahira, K. (1991). *Need profiles of intercultural communication competence in Japanese-American student dyads*. Paper presented at the Conference on Communication in Japan and the United States, California State University, Fullerton.

Miyanaga, K. (1991). *The creative edge: Individualism in Japan*. New Brunswick, NJ: Transaction.

Mizutani, N. (1984). *Aizuchi to ootoo* (Back channel and response). In O. Mizutani (Ed.), *Hanahi kotoba no hyoogen* (Expression of spoken language). Tokyo: Chikumashobo.

Mizutani, O. (1981). *Japanese: The spoken language in Japanese life* (J. Ashby trans.). Tokyo: Japan Times (Japanese version: *Nihongo-no seitai*. Tokyo: Sotakusha, 1979).

Morisaki, S., & Gudykunst, W. B. (in press). Face in Japan and the United States. In S. Ting-Toomey (ed.), *The challenge of facework*. Albany: State University of New York Press.

Morsbach, H. (1973). Aspects of nonverbal communication in Japan. *Journal of Nervous and Mental Disease, 157*, 262-277.

Morsbach, H. (1980). Major psychological factors influencing Japanese interpersonal relations. In N. Warren (Ed.), *Studies in cross-cultural psychology* (Vol. 2). London: Academic Press.

Morsbach, H. (1988a). Nonverbal communication and hierarchical relationships. In F. Payatos (Ed.), *Cross-cultural perspectives in nonverbal communication*. Toronto: C. J. Hogrefe.

Morsbach, H. (1988b). The importance of silence and stillness in Japanese nonverbal communication. In F. Payatos (Ed.), *Cross-cultural perspectives on nonverbal communication*. Toronto: C. J. Hogrefe.

Mortensen, C., Arnston, P., & Lustig, M. (1977). The measurement of verbal predisposition. *Human Communication Research, 3*, 146-158.

Murakami, Y. (1983). *Shin-chukantaishu no jidai* (The age of the new middle masses). Tokyo: Chuokoronsha.

Murakami, M., Kumon, S., & Sato, S. (1979). *Bunmei toshiteno ie-shakai* (*Ie* society as culture). Tokyo: Chiukoronsha.

Murase, T. (1982). *Sunao*: A central concept in Japanese psychotherapy. In A. Marsella & G. White (Eds.), *Cultural conceptions of mental health and therapy*. New York: Reidel.

Murayama, S., Nojima, K., & Abe, T. (1988). Person-centered groups in Japan. *Person-Centered Review, 3*, 479-492.

Nakamura, H. (1967). Consciousness of the individual and the universal among the Japanese. In C. Moore (Ed.), *The Japanese mind*. Honolulu: East West Center Press.

Nakamura, M. (1990). *Daigakusei no yujinkankei no hattenkatei ni kansuru kenkyu-Kankeikanyosei o yosokusuru shakai kokanmoderu no hikankukento* (A study of the developmental processes of friendship in college students: A comparative examination of social exchange models predicting relationship commitment). *Syakaishinrigaku Kenkyu* (Research in Social Psychology), *5*, 29-41.

Nakane, C. (1970). *Japanese society*. Berkeley: University of California Press (Japanese version: *Tate shakai no Ningen kankei* [Interpersonal relations in a vertical society]. Tokyo: Kohdansha, 1967).

Nakane, C. (1974). The social system reflected in interpersonal communication. In J. Condon & M. Saito (Eds.), *Intercultural encounters with Japan*. Tokyo: Simul Press.

Nakanishi, M. (1986). Perceptions of self-disclosure in initial interactions: A Japanese sample. *Human Communication Research, 13*, 167-190.

Nakanishi, M., & Johnson, K. (1993). Implications of self-disclosure on conversational logics, perceived communication competence, and social attraction: A comparison of Japanese and American cultures. In R. Wiseman & J. Koester (Eds.), *Intercultural communication competence*. Newbury Park, CA: Sage.

Naotsuka, R., Sakamoto, N., et al. (1981). *Mutual understanding of different cultures*. Osaka, Japan: Science Education Institute.

Naruke, N. (1974). Selected characteristics of Japanese communication. *Speech Education, II*, 12-20.

Neulip, J., & Hazelton, V. (1985). A cross-cultural comparison of Japanese and American persuasive strategy selection. *International Journal of Intercultural Relations, 9*, 389-404.

Nishida, H. (1981). Value orientations and value changes in Japan and the U.S.A. In T. Nishida & W. Gudykunst (Eds.), *Readings in intercultural communication*. Tokyo: Geirinshobo.

Nishida, H. (1985). Japanese intercultural communication competence and cross-cultural adjustment. *International Journal of Intercultural Relations, 9*, 247-270.

Nishida, H., & Nishida, T. (1978). *Giri and its influence on Japanese interpersonal communication*. Paper presented at the Speech Communication Association Summer Conference on International and Intercultural Communication, Tampa, FL.

Nishida, T. (1977). An analysis of a cultural concept affecting Japanese interpersonal communication. *Communication, 6*, 69-80.

Nishida, T. (1988). *Daigakusei no komyunikeishon fuan* (Communication apprehension among Japanese college students). *"Kokusaikankei Kenkyu" Nihon Daigaku* (Nihon University Studies on International Relations), *8* (3), 171-183.

Nishida, T. (1991). *Sequence patterns of self-disclosure among Japanese and North American students.* Paper presented at the Conference on Communication in Japan and the United States, California State University, Fullerton.

Nishida, T., & Gudykunst, W. B. (1986). *Uncertainty reduction riron no bunseki hani kojinteki oyobi bunkateki eikyo* (Individual and cultural influences on uncertainty reduction). *"Kokusaikankei Kenkyu" Nihon Daigaku* (Nihon University Studies on International Relations), *7* (1), 295-308.

Nishida, T., Gudykunst, W. B., & Chua, E. (1987). *Beikokujin to Nihonjin no daiado ni okeru fukakujitsusei no gensyo* (Uncertainty reduction in Japanese American dyads). *"Kokusaikankei Kenkyu" Nihon Daigaku* (Nihon University Studies on International Relations), *8* (2), 159-171.

Nishida, T., Gudykunst, W. B., Gao, G., Sudweeks, S., & Ting-Toomey, S. (1989). *Isei-ibunka no taijinkankeini arawareru wadai* (Themes in opposite-sex Japanese-North American relationships). *"Kokusaikankei Kenkyu" Nihon Daigaku* (Nihon University Studies on International Relations), *10* (2), 81-98.

Nishida, T., Sudweeks, S., Gudykunst, W. B., Ting-Toomey, S., & Yoshizawa, T. (1989). *Nihonjin to Beikokujin no taijinkakankei ni okeru tema to shinmitsudo* (Developmental themes and intimacy in Japanese-American dyads). *"Kokusaikankei Kenkyu" Nihon Daigaku* (Nihon University Studies on International Relations), *9* (3), 135-153.

Nishiyama, K. (1973). English training for Japanese executives. *Communication, II*, 91-92.

Nomura, N., & Barnlund, D. (1983). Patterns of interpersonal criticism in Japan and the United States. *International Journal of Intercultural Relations, 7*, 1-8.

Norton, R. (1978). Foundations of a communicator style construct. *Human Communication Research, 4*, 99-112.

Norton, R. (1983). *Communicator style.* Beverly Hills, CA: Sage.

Okabe, K. (1987). Indirect speech acts of the Japanese. In D. L. Kincaid (Ed.), *Communication theory from eastern and western perspectives.* New York: Academic Press.

Okabe, R. (1983). Cultural assumptions from eastern and western perspectives. In W. B. Gudykunst (Ed.), *Intercultural communication theory.* Beverly Hills, CA: Sage.

Obazaki-Luff, K. (1991). On the adjustment of Japanese sojourners. *International Journal of Intercultural Relations, 15*, 85-102.

Ohtsuka, H., Kawashima, T., & Doi, T. (1976). *Amae to shakaikagaku (Amae* and social science). Tokyo: Kobundo.

Owen, W. F. (1984). Interpretive themes in relational communication. *Quarterly Journal of Speech, 70*, 274-287.

Parks, M., & Adelman, M. (1983). Communication networks and the development of romantic relationships : An expansion of uncertainty reduction theory. *Human Communication Research, 10*, 55-80.

Parlee, M. (1979, October). The friendship bond. *Psychology Today*, pp. 42-54.

Patridge, K. (1988). Acculturation attitudes and stress of westerners living in Japan. In J. Berry & R. Annis (Eds.), *Ethnic psychology*. Amsterdam: Swets & Zeitlinger.

Patridge, K., & Shibano, M. (1990). *Assertiveness in Japan: Individualism in a collectivistic culture*. Paper presented at the Conference on Individualism-Collectivism, Seoul, Korea.

Peterson, R., & Shimada, J. (1978). Sources of management problems in Japanese-American joint ventures. *Academy of Management Review, 3*, 796-804.

Pharr, S. J. (1989). Resolving social conflicts: A comparative view of interpersonal and intergroup relations in Japan. In Y. Sugimoto & R. Mouer (Eds.), *Constructs for understanding Japan*. London: Kegan Paul.

Pharr, S. J. (1990). *Losing face: Status politics in Japan*. Berkeley: University of California Press.

Powell, R. (1986). Participant satisfaction in second language conversations. *Communication Research Reports, 3*, 135-139.

Prunty, A., Klopf, D., & Ishii, S. (1990). Japanese and American tendencies to argue. *Psychological Reports, 66*, 802 (also published in *Communication Research Reports*, 1990, 7, 75-79).

Renshaw, S., Tudman, C., Aoki, E., & Kumagai, M. (1991). *Terms for friendship: Similarities and differences in Japanese and American perspectives*. Paper presented at the Conference on Communication in Japan and the United States, California State University, Fullerton.

Reynolds, D. (1976). *Morita psychotherapy*. Berkeley: University of California Press.

Richmond, V., & McCroskey, J. (1989). *Communication: Apprehension, avoidance, and effectiveness* (sec. ed.). Scottsdale, AZ: Gorsuch.

Richmond, V., McCroskey, J., & Payne, S. (1987). *Nonverbal behavior in interpersonal relationships.* Englewood Cliffs, NJ: Prentice-Hall.

Rogers, C. (1970). *Carl Rogers on encounter groups.* New York: Harper and Row.

Rohlen, T. (1973). Spiritual education in a Japanese bank. *American Anthropologist, 75,* 1542-1562.

Sato, K., Mauro, R., & Tucker, J. (1990). *A cross-cultural examination of the cognitive dimension of human emotions.* Paper presented at the Congress of the International Association for Cross-Cultural Psychology, Nara, Japan.

Schrag, R., & Seichi, C. (1991). *Peter Rabbit meets Gon-Fox together with mother on Seasame Street: An intercultural analysis of first stories told to American and Japanese children through books and television.* Paper presented at the Speech Communication Association convention, Atlanta.

Shatzer, M., Funkhouser, A., & Hesse, M. (1984). *Selection of compliance-gaining strategies among four culturally diverse groups.* Paper presented at the International Communication Association convention, San Francisco.

Shatzer, M., Burgoon, J., Burgoon, M., Korzenny, F., & Miller, M. (1988). *A cross-cultural comparison of compliance-gaining styles between Japanese and North Americans.* Paper presented at the International Communication Association convention, New Orleans.

Simmons, D., Vom Kolke, A., & Shimuzu, H. (1986). Attitudes toward romantic love among Americans, Germans, and Japanese. *Journal of Social Psychology, 126,* 327-336.

Singer, K. (1973). *Mirror, sword, and jewel.* Tokyo: Kodansha.

Sodetani, L. L., & Gudykunst, W. B. (1987). The effects of surprising events on intercultural relationships. *Communication Research Reports, 4* (2), 1-6.

Spradley, J. P. (1979). *The ethnographic interview.* New York: Holt, Reinhart and Winston

Stewart, L. P., Gudykunst, W. B., Ting-Toomey, S., & Nishida., T. (1986). The effects of decision-making style on openness and satisfaction in Japanese organizations. *Communication Monographs, 53,* 236-251.

Sudweeks, S., Gudykunst, W. B., Ting-Toomey, S., & Nishida, T. (1990). Developmental themes in Japanese-North American interpersonal relationships. *International Journal of Intercultural Relations, 14,* 207-233.

Sueda, K., & Wiseman, R. (1992). A cross-cultural study of embarrassment: The United States and Japanese cultures. *International Journal of Intercultural Relations, 16,* 159-174.

Sussman, N., & Rosenfeld, H. (1982). Influence of culture, language, and sex on conversational distance. *Journal of Personality and Social Psychology, 42*, 66-74.

Suttles, G. (1970). Friendship as a social institution. In G. McNall (Ed.), *Social relationships*. Chicago: Aldine.

Tada, M. (1958). *Haji to taimen* (Shame and face). In *Gendai rinri* (Contemporary ethics) (Vol. 6). Tokyo: Chikuna Shoboo.

Takahara, N. (1974). Semantic concepts of marriage, work, friendship, and foreigner in three cultures. In J. Condon & M. Saito (Eds.), *Intercultural encounters with Japan*. Tokyo: Simul Press.

Taylor, D., & Altman, I. (1987). Communication in interpersonal relationships: Social penetration processes. In M. Roloff & G. Miller (Eds.), *Interpersonal processes*. Beverly Hills, CA: Sage.

Tezuka, C. (1992). *Awase* and *sunao* and their implications for Japanese and American cross-cultural communication. *Keio Communication Review, 14*, 37-50.

Thakerar, J., & Iwawaki, S. (1979). Cross-cultural comparisons in interpersonal attraction of females toward males. *Journal of Social Psychology, 108*, 121-122.

Ting-Toomey, S. (1985). Toward a theory of conflict and culture. In W. Gudykunst, L. Stewart, & S. Ting-Toomey (Eds.), *Communication, culture, and organizational processes*. Beverly Hills, CA: Sage.

Ting-Toomey, S. (1986). Japanese communication patterns: Insider versus the outsider. *World Communication, 15*, 113-126.

Ting-Toomey, S. (1988a). Intercultural conflict styles: A face-negotiation theory. In Y. Y. Kim & W. B. Gudykunst (Eds.), *Theories in intercultural communication*. Newbury Park, CA: Sage.

Ting-Toomey, S. (1988b). Rhetorical sensitivity style in three cultures: France, Japan, and the United States. *Central States Speech Journal, 39*, 28-36.

Ting-Toomey, S. (1989a). Culture and interpersonal relationship development: Some conceptual issues. In J. Anderson (Ed.), *Communication yearbook 12*. Newbury Park, CA: Sage.

Ting-Toomey, S. (1989b). Identity and interpersonal bonding. In M. Asante & W. Gudykunst (Eds.), *Handbook of international and intercultural communication*. Newbury Park, CA: Sage.

Ting-Toomey, S. (1991). Intimacy expressions in three cultures: France, Japan, and the United States. *International Journal of Intercultural Relations, 15,* 29-46.

Ting-Toomey, S., & Gao, G. (1988). Intercultural adaptation process in Japan: Perceived similarity, self-consciousness, and language competence. *World Communication, 17,* 193-206.

Ting-Toomey, S., Gao, G., Trubisky, P., Nishida, T., Lin, S., & Kim, H. (1992). *Self-consciousness dimensions and conflict styles in five cultures.* Paper presented at the Asian Regional Congress of the International Association for Cross-Cultural Psychology, Kathmandu, Nepal.

Ting-Toomey, S., Gao, G., Trubisky, P., Yang, Z., Kim, H., Lin, S., & Nishida, T. (1991). Face maintenance and styles of handling interpersonal conflict: A study in five cultures. *International Journal of Conflict Management, 2,* 275-296.

Ting-Toomey, S., Trubisky, P., Bruschke, J., Nadamitsu, Y., Sakai, J., Nishida, T., & Baker, J. (1991). *Face and culture: Toward the development of a face-work taxonomy.* Paper presented at the Western Speech Communication Association convention, Phoenix, AZ.

Ting-Toomey, S., Trubisky, P., & Nishida, T. (1989). *Conflict resolution styles in Japan and the United States.* Paper presented at the Speech Communication Association convention, San Francisco.

Triafimow, D., Triandis, H. C., & Goto, S. (1991). Some tests of the distinction between the private self and the collective self. *Journal of Personality and Social Psychology, 60,* 649-655.

Triandis, H. C. (1988). Collectivism vs. individualism: A reconceptualization of a basic concept in cross-cultural psychology. In G. Verma & C. Bagley (Eds.), *Cross-cultural studies of personality, attitudes and cognition.* London: MacMillan.

Triandis, H. C. (1989). The self and social behavior in differing cultural contexts. *Psychological Review, 96,* 506-517.

Triandis, H. C. (1990). Cross-cultural studies of individualism-collectivism. In J. Berman (Ed.), *Nebraska symposium on motivation* (Vol. 37). Lincoln: University of Nebraska Press.

Triandis, H. C., Bontempo, R., Villareal, M., Asai, M., & Lucca, N. (1988). Individualism-collectivism: Cross-cultural perspectives on self-ingroup relationships. *Journal of Personality and Social Psychology, 54,* 323-338.

Triandis, H. C., Davis, E., & Takezawa, S. (1965). Some determinants of social distance among American, German, and Japanese students. *Journal of Personality and Social Psychology, 2,* 540-551.

Triandis, H. C., Leung, K., Villareal, M., & Clack, F. (1985). Allocentric vs. idio-centric tendencies. *Journal of Research in Personality, 19,* 395-415.

Triandis, H. C., Malpass, R. S., & Davidson, A. R. (1973). Psychology and cultures. *Annual Review of Psychology, 24,* 355-378.

Tsujimura, A. (1968). *Nihon bunka to komyunikeishon* (Japanese culture and communication). Tokyo: NHK Bukkusa.

Tsujimura, A. (1987). Some characteristics of the Japanese way of communication. In D. L. Kincaid (Ed.), *Communication theory from eastern and western perspectives.* New York: Academic Press.

Uehara, A. (1988). *Ryugakusei no ibunka tekio* (Foreign students cultural adjustment). *Gengo shutoku oyobi ibunka tekio no rironteki, jissenteki kenkyu* (Theoretical and practical studies on language acquisition and cultural adjustment). Hiroshima: Faculty of Education, Hiroshima University.

Uehara, A. (1991). *The Japanese self and shintoism.* Paper presented at the Conference on Communication in Japan and the United States, California State University, Fullerton.

Uehara, A., & Hicks, J. (1989). Institutional responses to sociocultural adjustment: Problems of foreign students in Japan. In E. Ebuchi (Ed.), *Foreign students and internationalization of higher education.* Hiroshima: Hiroshima University Institute for Higher Education.

Ujitani, E. (1991). *Emotion recognition from voice across American and Japanese cultures.* Paper presented at the Conference on Communication in Japan and the United States, California State University, Fullerton.

Vogel, E. (1963). *Japan's new middle class.* Berkeley: University of California Press.

Wallbott, H., & Scherer, K. (1986). How universal and specific is emotional experience: Evidence from 27 counties on five continents. *Social Science Information, 25,* 763-795.

Watson, D., Clark, L., & Tellegen, A. (1984). Cross-cultural convergence in the structure of mood: A Japanese replication and a comparison with U.S. findings. *Journal of Personality and Cross-Cultural Psychology, 47,* 127-144.

Weisz, J., Rothbaum, F., & Blackburn, T. (1984). Standing out and standing in: The psychology of control in America and Japan. *American Psychologist, 39,* 955-969.

Wetzel, P. (1985). In-group/out-group deixis: Situation variation in the verbs of giving and receiving. In J. Forgas (Ed.), *Language and social situations.* New York: Springer-Verlag.

White, M. (1988). *The Japanese overseas: Can they go home again?* New York: Free Press.

White, S. (1989). Back channels across cultures: A study of Americans and Japanese. *Language in Society, 18,* 59-76.

Wierzbica, A. (1991). Japanese key words and cultural values. *Language in Society, 20,* 333-385.

Williams, T., & Sogon, S. (1984). *Nihonjin daigakusei niokeru shudankeisei to tekio kodo* (Group composition and conforming behavior in Japanese students). *Nihon Shinrigaku Kenkyu* (Japanese Psychological Research), *126,* 231-234.

Wiseman, R. L., & Abe, H. (1986). Cognitive complexity and intercultural effectiveness: Perceptions in American-Japanese dyads. In M. McLaughlin (Ed.), *Communication yearbook 10.* Beverly Hills, CA: Sage.

Wiseman, R. L., Hammer, M. R., & Nishida, H. (1989). Predictors of intercultural communication competence. *International Journal of Intercultural Relations, 13,* 349-370.

Wright, P. (1978). Toward a theory of friendship based on a conception of self. *Human Communication Research, 4,* 196-207.

Wuthnow, R. (1991). *Acts of compassion: Caring for others and helping ourselves.* Princeton: Princeton University Press.

Yamada, H. (1990). Topic management and turn distributions in business meetings: American versus Japanese strategies. *Text, 10,* 271-295.

Yamada, H. (in press). *Topic management strategies in American and Japanese business meetings.* Norwood, NJ: Ablex.

Yamaguchi, S. (1990). *Empirical evidence on collectivism among the Japanese.* Paper presented at the Conference on Individualism-Collectivism, Seoul, Korea.

Yamaguchi, S. (1991). *"Jiko" no shitenkara no shudan oyobi bunkasa eno apurochi* (An approach to group processes and cultural differences from the perspective of the self). *Syakaishinrigaku Kenkyu* (Research in Social Psychology), *6,* 138-147.

Yamazaki, M. (1985). *Yawarakai kojinshugi no tanjo* (The birth of modern individualism). Tokyo: Chukoronsha.

Yamazaki, M. (1990). *Nihonbunnka to kojinshugi* (Japanese culture and individualism). Tokyo: Chukoronsha.

Yoneyama, T. (1973). Basic notions in Japanese social relations. In J. Bailey (Ed.), *Listening to Japan.* New York: Praeger.

Zander, A. (1983). The value of belonging to a group in Japan. *Small Group Behavior, 14,* 3-14.

Chapter 7

ORGANIZATIONAL COMMUNICATION IN JAPAN AND THE UNITED STATES

Lea P. Stewart

Organizational communication theorists and researchers examine the communication process within the context of complex organizations. The study of organizational communication began in the United States in the 1940s and continues today. As interest in international trade and cultural diversity grows, scholars are beginning to examine communication within organizations in other nations and to compare it with communication processes in U.S. organizations. Given the importance of Japan in the world economy and the apparent success of so-called Japanese management, researchers are now studying organizational communication in Japan. Although much of this work is more impressionistic and anecdotal than theoretical, the amount of serious scholarly research on organizational communication in Japan is increasing.

Although research on organizational communication in Japan is increasing, most of this research is cross-cultural (that is, comparing organizational communication in Japan and the United States). Adler (1983c) identifies five approaches to research examining organizations in different countries: (1) ethnocentric—studies that attempt to replicate North American management research in other countries; (2) polycentric—studies that focus on describing, explaining, and interpreting the patterns of management and organizations in countries other than the United States; (3) comparative management studies—studies that attempt to identify those aspects of organizations that are similar and those aspects that are different in countries/cultures around the world; (4) geocentric—studies of organizations that operate in more than one country/culture (often conducted so that multinational corporations can have unified policies); and (5) culturally synergistic studies—studies that emphasize creating universality and that attempt to create transcultural structures and processes that can be used throughout the world while maintaining an appropriate level of cultural specificity. According to this conceptualization, research on organizational communication in Japan and the United States is primarily polycentric or comparative.

Cross-cultural studies, in general, have been criticized for their lack of focus on culture. Van Fleet and Al-Tuhaih (1979) argue that studies that use national boundaries as the differentiating factor among groups should be called cross-national rather than cross-cultural. Murray, Jain, and Adams (1976) list four characteristics that should be considered in determining whether groups can be differentiated by culture: (1) educational factors—literacy level, types of specialized training available, general attitude toward education; (2) sociological factors— attitudes toward work, authority, money, achievement, planning; (3) political and legal factors—organizational policies (collective bargaining, unions, etc.), work legislation, political organization, judicial system; and (4) economic—economic stability, industry, labor force characteristics, market size, and amount of interorganizational cooperation. The last three of these factors are particularly important when determining whether organizational communication research is cross-cultural. Given the differences in these factors between the United States and Japan, studies examining differences in organizational communication in the United States and Japan can be meaningfully characterized as cross-cultural research. (An extensive discussion of the differences between U.S. and Japanese culture is beyond the scope of this chapter. For more extensive overviews of Japanese versus U.S. culture, see Ben-Ari, Moeran, & Valentine, 1990; Lebra, 1976; Okabe, 1983; van Wolferen, 1990.)

Support for the cross-cultural nature of research comparing organizational communication in the United States and Japan can also be found in Hofstede's (1984) classic study in which he surveyed the cultural values of employees of a multinational company in forty different nations. He found highly significant differences in the behavior of employees working for the same organization in different countries. Results of the survey were analyzed along four dimensions: (1) power distance—the difference between the extent to which an organizational superior can determine the behavior of a subordinate and the extent to which a subordinate can determine the behavior of a superior; (2) uncertainty avoidance—the extent to which individuals are able to tolerate ambiguity; (3) individualism—the degree of individualism versus collectivism expected of individuals; and (4) masculinity—the degree to which individuals adhere to a collection of aggressive, object-centered traits. Hofstede found that culture (country) explained more of the variance in individual attitudes than other variables such as level within the hierarchy, specific job, age, or gender. In this conceptualization, U.S. employees are characterized by relatively high tolerance for uncertainty, extremely high individualism, and moderate levels of masculinity (general assertiveness). Workers in Japan exhibit high power distance, very high uncertainty avoidance, collectivistic behavior, and extremely high on the masculinity dimension.

Given the above constraints, this chapter focuses on cross-cultural research on organizational communication in Japan and the United States. Most of the research reviewed in this chapter examines communication and related phenomena in organizations in Japan and the United States. Some of these studies examine data collected in both the United States and Japan, while other studies examine communication phenomena in Japan and draw conclusions based on current knowledge of communication practices in U.S. organizations. There is very little empirical research on *intercultural* organizational communication (that is, on interactions among individuals from different cultures). For example, Adler (1983b) found that between 1971 and 1980 only .8 percent of the articles published in twenty-four leading management journals examined intercultural issues. As a consequence, this chapter takes a primarily cross-cultural perspective (that is, comparing organizational communication and related management issues in Japan and the United States).

COMPARATIVE FRAMEWORK: JAPAN VERSUS THE UNITED STATES

As a multitude of writers and researchers have noted, organizational management in Japan is different in several distinct ways from its counterpart in the United States. (For a general discussion of organiza-

tions and management issues in Japan, see Aoki, 1988; Lee & Schwendiman, 1982; Odaka, Ono, & Adachi, 1988; Richardson & Ueda, 1981. For
a Japanese perspective on management issues, see Hazama, 1971; Mito,
1981; and Urabe, 1978.)

Lincoln (1989) conducted an extensive study of Japanese organizations in Japan and concluded that these organizations can be differentiated from organizations in the United States by the proliferation of
four major management practices: (1) cohesive work groups; (2) quality
circles; (3) participatory (but not delegated) decision making; and
(4) company-sponsored services.[1] These differences are graphically outlined in Table 7.1 (McMillan, 1980).

TABLE 7.1
Contrasts in North American and Japanese Organizations

	North American	Japanese
Employment	Short term, market oriented	Lifetime, career oriented
Management values	Openness and accountability	Harmony and consensus
Management style	Action oriented, short-term horizons	Perfectionism in long term, delay in short term
Work values	Individual responsibility	Collective responsibility
Control processes	Formalized and explicit	Not formalized and implicit
Learning systems	External consultants and universities	Internal consultants and company training

Source: Adapted from McMillan (1980), p. 29.

Pascale and Athos (1981) compared two large corporations in the
United States (ITT) and Japan (Matsushita Electric Company) along
seven dimensions: staff, superordinate goals, style, systems, strategy,
structure, and skills. Their findings are summarized in Table 7.2. (Other
discussions of differences between United States and Japanese organizational communication and management can be found in Itami, 1982,
and Kagono et al., 1983.)

According to McMillan (1980), the Japanese organization is "essen-

TABLE 7.2
Summary of Pascale and Athos' (1981) Comparison of
Management in Japan and the United States

Japan	*United States*
Caters to whole of human needs	Caters to limited needs of workers
Attempts to develop extraordinary qualities in ordinary workers	Attempts to standardize the workers in various skill categories
Manages through internalized motivation	Manages through reward and control
Rotates all new employees through a variety of organizational roles	Assigns new employees to a specialized task role
Attempts to learn about subordinates' potential from multiple dimensions	Attempts to evaluate subordinates against standardized performance criteria
Attempts to elicit large number of suggestions from employees	Subjects employees to tiers of authority
Encourages interdependency and mutual support	Encourages internal competition
Accepts ambiguity, uncertainty, and imperfection	Demands certainty and precision

Source: Adapted from Shani and Basuray (1983), p. 6.

tially a community, a partnership among three basic groups: managers, shareholders, and workers" (p. 30). The typical U.S. organization is viewed from a more individualistic perspective in which each group sees itself as distinct from the others and often sees its interests in opposition to the interests of the other two groups. The studies reviewed in this chapter reflect this distinction.

Smith and Misumi (1989) reviewed studies of human resources management in Japan and concluded that there are four distinctive aspects of management in Japanese organizations. The first aspect is a *time perspective* emphasizing planning as a long term strategy to insure survival of the organization. This strategy is characterized by the recruitment of a loyal and skilled work force, investment in long-term research, identification of distinctive markets, and lifetime employment (for male workers within larger corporations). The second aspect is a *collective orientation* reflecting the nature of Japanese society. In

Japan, the "work organization provides the principal locus of adult male Japanese identity, and identification with one's immediate work group of peers and superior is frequently very intense" (p. 333). This strong organizational identification is in contrast to the basic individualistic assumption of employees in U.S. organizations. The third aspect is a *seniority system* based on a hierarchical status system. For example, workers refer to organizational superiors by their job titles not by their names. Japanese organizations have two types of hierarchy—a seniority system for individuals and hierarchy of organizational ranks. These hierarchies do not necessarily overlap. The fourth aspect concerns *influence processes*. Most discussions of management in Japanese organizations focus on the *ringi* system of decision making and the use of quality control circles. (The *ringi* system will be discussed in more detail later in this chapter. Lincoln [1989] sees these techniques as particular instances of a more fundamental attribute, however. He contends that in Japan the senior manager is not threatened by suggestions from below since the seniority system makes his power invulnerable. This situation is different in a U.S. organization, in which a junior person can be promoted into a senior person's job, and, thus, the senior person may be motivated by the need to protect his or her position within the organization.) Quality control (QC) techniques may be losing favor in Japan, however. For example, Cole (1980) reports that workers perceive QC participation as one more chore demanded by management. Lincoln and McBride (1987) found that attendance at QC meetings in one automotive plant had fallen to roughly 50 percent and that the state of the program was of serious concern to the company. (For a more extensive discussion of quality control circles in Japanese organizations, see Munchus, 1983.)

In Japan, superior-subordinate relationships are represented by the *sempai-kohai* or senior-junior system. This system is an intense relationship of mutual obligation (Befu, 1990; Herschman, 1983). A senior employee is expected to protect a junior employee's interests, develop a junior employee's skills through training and feedback, and advance a junior employee's position in the organization. In return, a junior employee shows deference to a senior employee, makes suggestions, works unpaid hours, gives gifts to a senior employee, and demonstrates loyalty and commitment to an organization. Perhaps because of this system of mutual obligation, Japanese employees appear to have more respect for formal authority than U.S. employees (Kelley, Whatley, & Worthley, 1987). In fact, as Hayashi (1988) notes, when business associates meet in Japan the junior person is often introduced first. This custom is in direct contrast to the U.S. practice of introducing the senior person first.

Although many aspects of organizational communication and management practice in Japan are viewed positively, there is some research to suggest the more negative aspects of this system. For example, Mroczkowski and Hanaoka (1989) discuss a phenomenon they label the "romantic myth of Japanese management." They contend that the system of manpower management developed in the 1960s and 1970s is gradually being transformed. They list several inherent weaknesses of the traditional approach to management in Japan:

1. The system of lifetime commitment and groupism encourages employee dependency and suppresses individual creativity.
2. The employment system discriminates against non-lifelong employees (temporary employees, women, part-timers, seasonal laborers, and employees hired midway through their careers) and prevents the formation of a free horizontal labor market.
3. The seniority-based system of rewards creates a promotion gridlock for middle management and especially for the younger outstanding employee. (p. 40)

In addition, despite social reforms since World War II, Japanese society is still largely based on separate roles for men and women in both public and private life (Lebra, 1984; Taylor, 1983). Women workers are more likely than men to be part-time and ineligible for the benefits offered to full-time male workers by the Japanese system. (See, for example, Cook & Hayashi, 1980, Kondo, 1990, and Saso, 1990, for discussions of the roles of women workers in large and small Japanese workplaces.)

In the 1980s, Japanese organizations began to be concerned with motivating employees who have changing attitudes and expectations (Miyanaga, 1991; Schwind & Peterson, 1985; Weisman, 1992). One of the current challenges for management in Japan, according to Mroczkowski and Hanaoka (1989), is "how to redesign employment relationships in a way that would blend the advantages of the older system of dependence on the company with the necessity to promote employee self-reliance, initiative, and creativity" (p. 43). (See Okubayashi, 1986, for a more extensive discussion of these issues.) Some authors argue, however, that Japanese and U.S. attitudes are not converging as fast as some people anticipate (see, for example, Maguire & Kroliczak, 1983).

Cultural versus Structural Influences

Although most writers agree that the differences in Japanese and U.S. management practices described above exist, there is a theoretical debate concerning the antecedents of these practices. Jain (1990) examines the culturist versus structural view of management practices in Japan. Culturist writers argue that the Japanese have combined up-to-date Western management techniques with traditional Japanese attitudes and behavior to create a flexible yet productive work environment. Supporters of this view contend that members of the Japanese culture value harmony and order and, as a consequence, management practices in Japan emphasize harmonious and consensual employer-employee relations. Critics of this approach (structural advocates) argue that the paternalistic system in modern, large Japanese corporations is based on an economically rational response of employers to a severe shortage of desired types of employees. In this view, contemporary management strategies in Japan are seen as a pragmatic response to prevailing economic conditions rather than as decisions based on cultural values. For example, Kagono and colleagues (1985) examine management practices in several Japanese firms and conclude that the management strategies described previously emerge from organizational structure and processes, not from essential differences between Japanese and Western cultures.

Smith and Misumi (1989) note the "wide divergence of views as to whether the essence of Japanese management lies in its structures or within the processes or styles with which those structures are operated" (p. 329). They view structure and process as "yin and yang." In other words, scholars can "understand little about organizational behaviour if we do not take account of both structures and processes" (p. 329).

In a similar manner, according to Jain (1990), the cultural and structural schools of thought reinforce each other for large companies. Strategies developed by large Japanese firms are designed to achieve both harmonious relations and economic efficiency. Jain studied eight Japanese-owned firms in Canada (four in manufacturing, four in services) and their parent companies in Japan. In Canada, he found that the companies successfully transfer Japanese practices of internal promotion, layoff policies, extensive benefits, and genuine concern for the well-being of employees. Japanese managers adapt to the Canadian industrial environment in decision-making style, group work, and labor-management relations. For example, managers in the Japanese parent companies consult their peers and subordinates in making decisions more frequently than do their counterparts in Canadian subsidiaries. Yet the *ringi* system is almost nonexistent in Canadian companies and quality control circles exist in very few of the subsidiaries in Canada even though all of the Japanese parent companies use them extensively. Jain explains these differences by noting that the North American work ethic is different from the Japanese work ethic and that North American employees usually do not strongly identify themselves with the company. Because of this lack of identification, employees are not willing to meet and discuss office problems after working hours without pay. In Canada, when managers try to employ the quality circle technique, they meet with resistance from employees and unions. Employees contend that it is management's job to look after quality and productivity and that they are not responsible for finding solutions to management problems. Thus, Jain argues that cultural factors and structural constraints play important roles in determining organizational communication and management strategy.

Whitehill's (1991) examination of management practices in Japan also balances cultural and structural factors and their influence on organizational communication. He notes, for example, that in most Japanese organizations only the senior managing directors and above have private offices. Working together in one big room results in discussion of suggestions and an exchange of ideas among levels of workers. Nevertheless, he notes that this situation reflects the "Japanese manager's strong preference for open, oral communication" (p. 119).

Effects on Job Satisfaction

In addition to describing the differences in typical management practices in the U.S. and Japan, researchers have examined the level of job satisfaction that results from participation in these organizational systems.

Lincoln (1989) surveyed 106 factories in the United States and Japan (8,302 employees) and found that Japanese employees are more highly committed to their organizations, but report lower job satisfaction than U.S. workers. Lincoln speculates that the lower level of job satisfaction on the part of Japanese workers may be a reflection of dissatisfaction with working conditions, such as working extremely long hours for inadequate pay (with especially low wages among younger workers), or may be due to Japanese workers' higher aspirations for their jobs which lead to expectations that their organizations cannot fulfill. Ito and Kohei (1990) suggest that the fact that Japanese workers are less satisfied than U.S. workers may be due to a general level of "Japanese pessimism."

Kumara and Koichi (1989) surveyed 150 employees of two mid-sized Japanese manufacturing companies, including supervisors and production workers. They measured employee satisfaction with job climate and supportive supervision (personal commitment to employees, approachability of supervisor, and feedback receptiveness), coworker social support (trust, cooperation, mutual respect, and friendliness), and job awareness (image of workload and severity of job). They found a highly significant effect for supportive supervisor on employee satisfaction with job climate and a significant effect for coworker social support on employee satisfaction with job climate. There was also an interaction between supportive supervisor and job awareness. Thus, Kumara and Koichi conclude that Japanese employees in stressful jobs need a supportive supervisor in order to be satisfied with their jobs. In such a situation, the supervisor appears to mitigate the negative effects of the stressful job.

Thus, Japanese and U.S. organizations differ in a number of significant ways including employment/seniority systems, work values, and control processes. These differences are supported by differences in time perspective (emphasis on long-term versus short-time goals), collective orientation (importance of the group versus importance of the individual), and influence processes (respect for seniority versus respect for accomplishments). These differences are brought about and influenced by both cultural factors and structural constraints. Workers participating within these contrasting organizational systems exhibit different levels of job satisfaction. With this framework as a background, this chapter will now turn to a review of research focusing on organizational communication and related management issues.

CROSS-CULTURAL COMMUNICATION RESEARCH

According to Smith and Misumi (1989), "research methods [for studying cross-cultural communication and management issues in general] have . . . evolved over time with the early preponderance of case studies giving way to more systematic surveys and studies using comparative measures collected in several countries" (p. 330). This pattern has been followed in the cross-cultural research on U.S. and Japanese organizational communication and related management issues.

Although Venkatesh and Wilemon (1980) list eight basic themes of cross-cultural management research (superior-subordinate relationship, managerial needs or motivation, interpersonal processes, organizational goals, perceptions of equity, decision making under uncertainty, values, and relationship between managerial attitudes and other organizational and environmental variables) the preponderance of research on organizational communication in Japan and the United States relevant for consideration in this chapter focuses on the first category, superior-subordinate relationships with special emphasis on direction of communication within the hierarchy. This literature is reviewed below. Because of its relevance to organizational communication research, a review of research on decision-making styles also is included.

Superior-Subordinate Relationships

Leadership. Smith and Misumi (1989) cite evidence suggesting that the effects of leadership and group processes differ between U.S. and Japanese organizations. They argue, however, that the distinctive qualities of management practices in Japan have evolved over the past few decades and are not a fixed and static entity. As Mroczkowski and Hanaoka (1989) note, Japanese organizational leadership is responding to a changing work force. Thus, it is important to remember that the differences in leadership processes in U.S. and Japanese organizations may be changing. Nevertheless, specific distinctions in leadership have been found in cross-cultural research focusing on U.S. and Japanese organizations. These differences often focus on perceptions of leadership style.

Kagono and colleagues (1985) surveyed Japanese organizations and found that Japanese leaders score more highly than U.S. managers on measures of strictness in applying rewards and punishments, clarifying and gathering information, adherence to the values of the current chief executive officer or founder, conflict resolution through the use of authority, exchange of information prior to meetings, sharing of information down the line, use of a control system based upon employee self-discipline and commitment to work, long-term performance evaluation, consensus decision making, frequent informal and social exchange, commitment to change, and reliance on policies of promotion from within.

Misumi and Peterson (1985) report the results of thirty years of studying leadership in Japanese organizations based on the research of Kurt Lewin. When compared with leadership in U.S. organizations, leadership at lower and middle management levels in Japan may be a more important determiner of subordinates' performance. The use of performance-maintenance (PM) leadership is consistent with the Japanese norm of valuing individual and group outcomes. Misumi and Peterson found that in Japanese organizations M-type leadership (emphasizing maintenance functions or consideration for subordinates) may be preferred in situations with highly anxious subordinates, while P-type leadership (concern for task or initiating structure) may be desired in situations with a temporary group used to accomplish a task that requires quick work but little quality or involving members who have low levels of achievement orientation.

Furakawa (1981) studied 1,576 male first-line supervisors engaged in railway traffic at the Japanese National Railway. Each person had fifteen subordinates on the average and took a central role in the daily job performance of his subordinates. The supervisors rated their own behavior on initiating structure and consideration as well as their own most important management objective. Initiating structure was measured by items such as: "I let subordinates know the work procedures in detail"; "I blame subordinates who upset the discipline of the work unit." Consideration was measured by items such as: "I praise subordinates when they have done an excellent job"; "I ask for opinions of subordinates before making my decisions." Management objectives were listed as: to develop a steady and dependable relationship with subordinates; to accomplish the goals of the work unit; to establish order in the work unit; to create a peaceful work unit; to increase subordinates' work motivation. Furakawa found a clear tendency for supervisors to relate their primary management objective to perceptions of favorableness of the conditions in the work unit. Scores on the initiating structure dimension were significantly higher for supervisors with task-oriented management objectives than for supervisors with a human relations orientation. Scores on consideration were significantly higher for supervisors with human relations management objectives. Supervisors believed that initiating structure was more instrumental in accomplishing task-oriented objectives and that consideration behavior was more influential in accomplishing human relations-oriented objectives.

Misumi and Peterson (1985) note that "personal leadership by a supervisor is more consistently important in Japan than in the U.S." (p. 218). They argue that, in comparison with North American supervisors, Japanese supervisors have greater legitimate power, as well as reward power and coercive power based on recognition and symbolic exchanges. Perhaps because of this emphasis on legitimate power,

Japanese employees prefer a more passive mode of decision-making, from their perspective, in which they can be consulted by their supervisors before a decision is made or persuaded to accept a decision that has already been made by a supervisor (Stewart, Gudykunst, Ting-Toomey, & Nishida, 1985).

Yokochi-Bryce (1989) contends that leaders in major Japanese corporations practice a "transformational leadership style" (as opposed to transactional and laissez-faire styles) because they possess both high humanistic values and high corporate goals. Yokochi-Bryce found that leaders in major Japanese corporations are more likely to emulate upper-management leadership behavior because of strong company management philosophies.

Hayashi (1988) notes that the role of the traditional Japanese leader is inconspicuous. This position is in contrast to the classic position of the Western leader such as an orchestra conductor, who directs from in front of the orchestra. Hayashi contends that the communal nature of Japanese employees ensures that they will create harmony by paying close attention to the movements of those nearby. Thus, the leader can assume a position "behind" the group to see if it is functioning well together. To achieve success in this manner, Hayashi believes that the leader must be "skillfully unassertive" (p. 117).

Downward Communication. Communication between individuals in Japanese and U.S. organizations will be discussed in this chapter in terms of downward, upward, and horizontal communication. Obviously, communication does not occur in such a restricted manner within organizations, but it has become conventional to talk about communication flow in U.S. organizations in this way (Jablin, 1979). Some researchers have adopted these directional terms when studying communication in Japanese organizations, even though the communication process is much more circular.

Downward communication in Japanese organizations may also be more informal and intimate than in U.S. organizations. Jain (1990) describes the Japanese holistic approach to management in which managers spend a great deal of time talking informally to employees about non-job-related matters. In addition, workers and supervisors are expected to socialize together after office hours to maintain a steady flow of ideas (Hayashi, 1988). Johnson (1990) contends that the goal of downward communication in Japanese organizations is "to create a sense of harmony through collective understanding and collective agreement (p. 20), while in U.S. firms, the goal of downward communication is to cause specific actions to be taken (orders to be carried out). Conflict is encouraged in U.S. organizations, while collective agreement is sought in Japanese organizations.

Hirokawa and Miyahara (1986) conducted a comparative study of U.S. and Japanese managers' communication style. They surveyed managers from U.S. and Japanese companies who were given two problematic situations and asked to indicate in writing how they would respond. In one situation, managers were asked to persuade a subordinate to perform an obligatory work-related action (report to work on time). In the other situation, they were asked to persuade a subordinate to perform a nonobligatory work-related action (communicate ideas and suggestions to management).

For the obligatory actions, Hirokawa and Miyahara (1986) found that U.S. and Japanese managers rely on different communicative strategies. The U.S. managers use punishment-based strategies such as threat ("If you don't start reporting on time for work, I will have no choice but to start docking your pay"), warning ("Unless you stop being late for work, your future with this company will be in serious jeopardy"), or ultimatum ("If you can't come to work on time, go find yourself another job"). Japanese managers rely on employee identification with the organization to influence them. Japanese managers rely on duty ("It is your duty as a responsible employee of this company to begin work on time") or counsel ("Is there anything I can do to help you overcome the problems that are preventing you from coming to work on time?").

For nonobligatory actions in Hirokawa and Miyahara's (1986) study, U.S. and Japanese managers also rely on different communicative strategies. U.S. managers use rationale-based or reward-based strategies such as direct request ("I want you to feel free to come to me with any ideas that you have for improving our company"), promise ("Don't hesitate to offer ideas and suggestions because we always reward good suggestions"), and ingratiation ("You are one of our best people and I really value your judgment, so please feel free to come to me with any ideas you have"). Japanese managers use altruism-based strategies ("For the sake of the company, please share your ideas and suggestions with us") or duty ("Remember that it is your duty as a good company employee to suggest how we can improve the overall performance of the company"). Thus, U.S. managers rely more on reward power, coercive power, or legitimate power than their Japanese counterparts.

Sullivan, Suzuki, and Kondo (1986) surveyed Japanese and U.S. managers and asked them to respond to an organizational scenario which varied on group influence (high/low), manager's expectation (expected performance/unexpected performance), and performance (successful performance/unsuccessful performance). They found that both Japanese and U.S. managers see responsibility for individual and group performance as influenced by the amount of interacting a person does with the group. Nevertheless, U.S. managers give greater rewards to a subordinate for successful performance when the group influence is low rather than high. Japanese managers give the same rewards regardless of performance outcome, but they give a greater reward to the subordinate who has been influenced by the group than to the isolated performer. Thus, Japanese managers seem to see rewards as an incentive to encourage employees to interact with their work groups, not as a reward for successful performance. U.S. managers view work groups as a method to reduce unexpected outcomes. Japanese managers, conversely, see groups as a way to facilitate unexpected performance by individual members and believe that work groups are productivity enhancers that bring out more from workers. Sullivan, Suzuki, and Kondo speculate that this desire to bring about exceptional performance is the reason that Japanese managers reward individuals for taking part in group functioning.

Upward Communication. Upward communication is an important concept in Japanese organizations. Upward communication in Japanese organizations includes personal contact, meetings, *ringi*, suggestion system, joint council, and quality circles (Ruch, 1984). In terms of amount of communication, Pascale (1978) found that three times as much communication is initiated at lower levels of management in Japanese companies than in comparable U.S. companies. McMillan (1980) maintains that open communication between worker and manager characterizes a climate of shared responsibility in Japanese organizations. He notes that the average worker is given information on trends in prices, productivity, technical procedures, competition, and costs. The use of company seminars and training programs to present this information is evidence that "information and knowledge diffusion are major company goals" (McMillan, 1980, p. 30).

The principle organizationally structured mode of upward communication in Japanese organizations is the *ringi* system. According to Kagono and colleagues (1985), proposals for new policies, procedures or expenditures are circulated through the firm for comment, at least in theory. The initial proposal is written by a junior member of the organization. The paper is then sent to all who might be affected if it were implemented. Each person writes comments or indicates approval with a personal seal. The document is circulated in ascending order of senior-ity. In actual practice, however, an organization may use ringi only for important decisions. In U.S. organizations, in contrast, circulated docu-ments are criticized, negotiated over, and amended. Employees in Japanese organizations, however, engage in consultations before a *ringi* proposal is circulated. This process is referred to as *nemawashi*, literally translated as trimming of a tree's roots prior to its being transplanted. A written *ringi* proposal is put forward only when it is clear from *nemawashi* that a proposal is likely to succeed. Since the Japanese nego-tiate orally before a written proposal is made, *ringi* is more a method of recording and reporting decisions rather than a method of decision-making.

Horizontal Communication. Bowers (1988) interviewed manage-ment-level employees in four large Japanese organizations. He found that communication networks tend to use a one-to-many communica-tion format that focuses on information sharing and coordination of tasks. Information is disseminated rapidly and in detail to colleagues and subordinates in each division. Informal networks are consciously formed, cultivated, and maintained. They are in constant use and are essential for making decisions, solving problems, and resolving con-flicts. These networks are formed through interpersonal contacts and spread across division boundaries through routine rotation of junior employees. In this way, the structure of a typical Japanese company affects the communication process. In these information networks, com-munication is face-to-face in dyadic or small group contexts, usually after working hours in eating or drinking establishments.

Table 7.3 presents a summary of communication-related behaviors in U.S. versus Japanese organizations.

Decision Making

In a general sense, management in Japanese organizations is character-ized by a bottom-up approach to decision-making, while U.S. organi-zations are characterized by a top-down decision-making approach (Johnson, 1990). More specifically, decision-making, at least in the ideal Japanese firm, tends to flow upward from middle-level management rather than downward from top management as is typical in U.S. orga-nizations (Richardson & Ueda, 1981). In U.S. organizations, authority and responsibility are delegated through a relatively clear chain of com-mand. In contrast, in the typical Japanese organization, information is more likely to circulate throughout the organization before a policy is

TABLE 7.3
Communication Behavior in Japanese versus U.S. Organizations

Japan	*United States*
Organizational integration and information processing are achieved by frequent interaction within and between groups. Effort is expended to build and maintain a strong interpersonal network	Organizational integration and information processing are achieved by means of hierarchy, vertical information channels, plans, and result-oriented performance appraisals
Frequency of interactions facilitates sharing of information and values	Knowledge and information are systematically accumulated by, and tend to be concentrated among, one "elite" group at the top
Decision-making power is diffused throughout the organization that resembles loosely coupled linking-pin forms	Firms are characterized by self-containment, divisional organization
Learning activities are encouraged throughout the organization, and knowledge is shared through interaction	Learning is supported and fostered only in certain segments of the organizational hierarchy
Principle value orientation is one of building and maintaining harmony and cohesiveness within the organization	Principal value orientation is one of assessing environmental opportunities and risks through analytical forecasting and strategy formulation through deductive logic, and maintaining operations congruent with derived strategies

Source: Adapted from Kagono, Nonaka, Sakakibara, and Okumura (1983), cited in Shani and Basuray (1988).

adopted. This does not mean, however, that individuals at upper levels in Japanese organizations do not take an active role in setting and communicating corporate policy (Jensen, 1984).

The actual decision-making process is quite different in Japanese organizations than in U.S. organizations. Hayashi (1988) notes that in a typical decision-making situation in Japan decisions are usually made by unanimous agreement not by majority vote. In a typical decision-making situation, the official decision-making meeting (*tatemae*) is followed by a party when individuals can express candid opinions (*honne*). The concept of *tatemae* implies a "facade of what one should do or say because of one's position or current situation" (Whitehill, 1991). Because this type of discussion is based on perceived obligation, there may be individuals who do not agree during the official decision-making meeting, but who are unable to express their dissent. To ameliorate their concerns, a group leader may address issues of conflict during a post-meeting gathering or social event where individuals feel freer to express dissenting opinions. Hayashi (1988) notes that this gathering often is followed by a second party (*nijikai*) that is more informal in nature; fewer people are present and official rank is not a concern. Individuals feel free to express opinions that they believe are not acceptable to express in earlier, more formal sessions. In this way, candor is encouraged during informal sessions and more information is shared than could be obtained in other settings. Thus, the typical decision-making structure involves consulting all interested individuals in advance, holding an official meeting, having a party to celebrate the decision, and finally meeting in an informal gathering. Communication progresses from consultation (*nemawashi*) to expressing opinions appropriate to one's organizational position (*tatemae*) to saying what one really intends (*honne*) to informally expressing possibly more controversial opinions (*nijikai*).

The decision-making system in Japanese organizations is characterized by the extensive involvement of mid-levels of the organization. For example, Richardson and Ueda (1981) note the extensive involvement of mid-level managers (section chiefs up to department heads) in strategic decision-making. They observe that Japanese mid-level managers act as planning aides and advisors to upper-level management in addition to their supervisory duties of implementing company policy.

Shenkar (1988) contends that the benefits of this type of consensual decision making and mid-level managerial involvement in Japanese organizations include increased commitment and support from employees when decisions are implemented. In addition, more knowledge is accumulated during the decision-making process, more information is circulated throughout the organization, initiative is encouraged in lower levels of the hierarchy, and younger managers are provided with important experiences while relieving some of the burden from more senior managers. Leonard and Thanopoulos (1982) observe that the consensual decision-making process allows for a greater number of reasonable alternatives to be considered. In addition, although the decision-making time may be slower, because of the process of extensive information sharing, the implementation time to sell/explain a decision is faster than in the United States.

Shenkar (1988) believes that some negative outcomes of consensual decision-making, such as groupthink (accepting a poor decision merely to maintain cohesiveness within a group) and blurring of authority lines, are avoided by other factors within the Japanese organization. For example, Japanese mid-level managers are highly competitive and constantly debate alternative solutions, which minimizes the tendency toward groupthink. As discussed previously, the strongly hierarchical nature of the Japanese organization prevents any blurring of organizational lines of authority.

As stated earlier, because of the differences in seniority system versus hierarchy of organizational ranks, to Western eyes, Japanese organizations may appear both autocratic and participative. To support this perception, Kelley, Whatley, and Worthley (1987) report that Japanese employees have more positive attitudes than U.S. employees to both centralized decision-making and participation in decision-making. Centralized decision-making, however, does not mean autocratic decision-making. For example, the majority of Japanese workers surveyed by Takezawa and Whitehill (1983) in 1960 and again in 1976 preferred supervisors who used either a persuasive style (decide on changes in work methods and then ask for the cooperation of workers) or a consultative style (first ask workers for their suggestions regarding proposed changes in work methods and then decide what to do). Only 3 percent of respondents preferred supervisors who used an autocratic style of decision-making in which a supervisor decides what work methods should be changed and puts the changes into effect without seeking any information from the employees affected by the change. Stewart, Gudykunst, Ting-Toomey, and Nishida (1985) found that Japanese employees prefer a supervisor who uses a persuasive rather than a consultative style of decision-making. Japanese employees prefer managers who effectively persuade them of the soundness of their decisions rather than those who engage in a participative style in which employees actually make management decisions.

Pascale (1978) examined the similarities and differences in decision-making styles between U.S. and Japanese managers in an extensive study of communication practices in U.S. and Japanese corporations. He found that managers in Japanese firms engage in over 30 percent more face-to-face contacts each day than do managers in U.S. firms. In addition, Japanese managers rate themselves higher on decision quality and substantially higher on implementation quality than U.S. managers.

Pascale argues that face-to-face communication is encouraged by the crowded Japanese work setting in which many levels of the hierarchy are located in the same open work space. Thus, the work setting (structural factor), as opposed to solely cultural variables, may be a major determinant of Japanese managers' communication styles. This view is opposed by Shenkar (1988) who argues that the seemingly consensual decision-making process in Japan is rooted in the homogeneous nature of Japanese culture, which emphasizes the collective. No matter what the ultimate source, however, the use of face-to-face communication style in Japanese organizations leads to higher perceived decision quality and higher perceived implementation quality.

Yet according to Pascale (1978) there is no significant difference in the style of decision-making used by Japanese and U.S. managers. For example, Japanese managers do not use a consultative decision-making process more often than U.S. managers. The predominance of face-to-face communication in the Japanese workplace, however, may account for the perception that there is more openness about major decisions in Japanese firms and "more desire to explore and learn together" (McMillan, 1980). While Japanese managers are not actually using a consultative decision-making style more than U.S. managers, they are talking directly to their workers a great deal. This increased face-to-face contact is interpreted by observers of the system as openness.

Lincoln and McBride (1987) contend that there is disagreement about how truly "bottom-up" decision-making is within Japanese organizations. Clark (1979) maintains that a more senior executive can encourage loyal subordinates to initiate proposals supporting his ideas. In addition, founding entrepreneurs often still control their organizations and maintain considerable control over the company. Nevertheless, no matter what the level of upper-managerial control, information sharing throughout the organization is facilitated through the decision-making process (Nonaka & Johansson, 1985). As Wood (1989) observes: "The Japanese system of labor management attempts to create conditions under which workers will be encouraged to cooperate and develop their awareness and diagnostic skills, and to create a climate in which workers will not withhold information because they see knowledge as power" (p. 452).

INTERCULTURAL RESEARCH

The studies reviewed in this chapter focus on cross-cultural differences in organizational communication between Japan and the

United States. A growing body of research, however, deals with the behavior of people from different cultures working together within organizational settings. These studies have examined traditional organizational issues such as motivation, leadership, decision-making, and group dynamics. The central questions of these studies include: (1) What is the impact of culture on the behavior of people within organizations?; (2) To what extent must managerial styles be altered when working with people from different cultures?; and (3) To what extent is the managing of cross-cultural interaction different from managing interaction within culturally homogeneous groups? (Adler, 1983a). As the number of Japanese corporations in the United States increases and as more U.S. organizations begin to operate in Japan, more sophisticated studies in this area need to be conducted.

Communication in Japanese Organizations in the United States

The growth in the number of Japanese organizations that are operating in the United States has met with mixed responses. Some authors see this situation as an economic threat and warn of a day when Japanese companies will dominate the U.S. market in industries such as computer technology, steel, and automobile manufacturing (Kearns, 1992). Others welcome the opportunity to learn new management techniques from their Japanese counterparts. As a reflection of this trend, there are many descriptive or anecdotal accounts of communication between U.S. workers and Japanese managers in Japanese-owned companies in the United States, especially in the automobile industry (see, for example, Fucini & Fucini, 1990; Levin, 1992).

Nakanishi, Schwartz, and Awa (1992) attempt to distinguish between culture-universal and culture-specific dimensions of leadership in organizations that combine leaders from one culture with subordinates from another culture. They examined Japanese and U.S. nonmanagerial employees who are supervised by Japanese managers in nine Japanese-owned companies in the United States. Japanese and U.S. subordinates express the highest satisfaction with Japanese managers who use a PM (balance of performance and maintenance functions) style of leadership. U.S. subordinates cite several effective leadership behaviors used by Japanese managers, including consulting with subordinates about new work procedures, discussing subordinates' personal problems sympathetically, seeing subordinates constantly at the workplace, socializing with subordinates outside work, and talking with subordinates about their careers and future plans.

Although Nakanishi, Schwartz, and Awa (1992) expected Japanese and U.S. subordinates to perceive leadership behaviors differently, both identify six effective leader behaviors that balance concern for task and concern for maintenance functions: (1) listening to subordinate's personal difficulties; (2) instructing subordinates about how to increase their job skills; (3) talking about immediate work problems with subordinates; (4) arranging for subordinates to help others with personal problems; (5) encouraging subordinates to help coworkers with work problems; and (6) talking to subordinates about progress in the work schedule. The authors note that U.S. subordinates may share similar perceptions with Japanese subordinates, in part, due to the strict screening criteria used by Japanese managers when hiring U.S. workers. In addition, in response to their U.S. subordinates, Japanese managers in the United States may be adopting a hybrid management style incorporating some aspects of typical U.S. leadership behavior.

Stage (1992) examined the compliance-gaining behavior of Japanese managers in Japanese companies in the United States and Japanese managers in Japan using Hirokawa and Miyahara's (1986) coding scheme, discussed previously. Japanese managers prefer non-sanction strategies (e.g., "I would tell the employee how much each person can contribute to benefit the entire company by bringing up ideas") when supervising both Japanese and American employees. Japanese managers use more rationale-based strategies with Japanese subordinates (for example, "I would explain and let him understand that his behavior was causing difficulty in our task accomplishment") and more altruism-based strategies with U.S. employees (for example, "I would stress the importance of cooperation in work"). Stage explains her results in terms of the necessity to foster a cooperative/teamwork atmosphere with U.S. workers.

Problems in Japanese-U.S. organizational communication may be at an even more fundamental level than those situations examined previously. Yamada (1990) examined interactions in three business meetings—one Japanese intracultural meeting conducted in Japanese, one American intracultural meeting conducted in English, and one American-Japanese cross-cultural meeting conducted in English. After analyzing the conversations at these meetings, she found that Japanese and Americans use different turn-distribution patterns in conversations. For example: "Japanese take short turns, distribute their turns relatively evenly, and continue to distribute their turns evenly regardless of who initiates a topic. Americans take long monologic turns, distribute their turns unevenly, and the participant who initiates a topic characteristically takes the highest proportion of turns in that topic" (p. 291). Yamada believes these differences occur because Japanese and Americans organize their topics differently. Japanese organize topics interdependently, while Americans organize topics more autonomously. Yamada contends that this organization pattern is another reflection of the Japanese respect for the group and the American reliance on individualism.

Communication in U.S. Organizations in Japan

There are few theoretically based, empirical studies of Japanese and Americans working together in Japan (e.g., Hamada, 1991; San Antonio, 1991). Hamada (1991), for example, examined a U.S.-Japan joint-venture company operating in Japan. She views corporate culture as "an 'unfinished' process of dialogue between different social groups" (p. 8). In the joint-venture company, she examined competing managerial ideologies, values, and norms. Hamada notes the importance of "personal communication" to Japanese managers. In assessing the difficulties involved in the joint venture, the Japanese managers believed that they had to develop formal and informal communication channels with joint-venture management at the beginning. Hamada notes that "the Japanese used more personal and informal channels and preferred indirect influence on their decision-making policy. [The U.S. partner] tended to consider control in terms of legal contracts, equity ownership, and representation on the board" (p. 212). Hamada claims that these narratives portray two opposing management doctrines. She contrasts the U.S. managers' "aggressive individualism" with Japanese insularity and ethnocentrism.

San Antonio (1991) studied Japanese and Americans working together in a U.S. electronics firm in Japan. She highlighted the importance of middle managers as mediators between Japanese and American employees. San Antonio (1991) notes:

> The difference between American cultural and management style was confusing to traditional Japanese employees who were disappointed by their lack of input and access to the Americans. Americans were confused by the Japanese expectations of frequent interaction and open communication at meetings. . . . In American companies, middle managers are used to ease the interaction between organizational levels. In order to successfully mesh management styles, non-traditional Japanese employees with

good cross-cultural knowledge were necessary as facilitators. When Japanese and Americans tried to combine the two styles without the aid of such an employee, both Japanese and Americans were dissatisfied with the interaction. (pp. 221-22)

A similar process was observed with respect to decision-making. More effective decision-making occurred when a nontraditional Japanese manager mediated between the American tendency to avoid disagreement with supervisors and the Japanese managers' willingness to accept unlimited facts and opinions from subordinates during decision-making processes. San Antonio felt a middleman was necessary in this situation because "Americans misunderstood the openness of the Japanese decision-making style as indecision and often acted to assert their control in the process" (p. 223).

Whitehill (1991) provides an extensive discussion of the problems faced by U.S. managers who work in Japan and suggestions for improving relations between American managers and their Japanese counterparts. He contends that U.S. managers in Japan often fail in their business dealings due to several factors including self-reference tendencies. Whitehill notes that U.S. managers are sometimes uncomfortable with the long periods of silence that are characteristic of Japanese business meetings, but that Japanese managers are often adverse to asking for information and treat written documents in a relatively casual manner compared to U.S. managers. These behaviors are the basis for potential conflict in intercultural interactions.

LIMITATIONS OF THE RESEARCH

Negandhi (1983) cites several problems with research on cross-cultural management that can be applied to comparative research on organizational communication in Japan and the United States. He acknowledges that attitudes, beliefs, values, and need hierarchies are different in different societies (and subgroups within societies), but notes that it is difficult to draw a conceptual link between culture and attitudes, attitudes and behavior, and behavior and effectiveness. He believes that most of these concepts are ill-defined and that operational measures are poorly conceived. He cites increasing evidence that management behavior (and communication) is a function of contextual and environmental variables such as size, technology, location, and economic, market, and political conditions. Cross-cultural scholars continue to use cultural variables as residual elements without explicitly defining and operationalizing them. There is a need to define and operationalize cultural variables as well as a need to look at patterns of relationships (multivariate models). In addition, there is a need to look at how results of studies done in other countries can be transferred to the United States.

Metaphors that are convenient to describe communication within U.S. organizations have been adapted for studying communication within Japanese organizations without critical examination. For example, some researchers study "downward communication" in Japan. These studies are based on the assumption that information travels "up" and "down" the organizational hierarchy in Japan in the same manner as it does in U.S. organizations. As can be seen in previous discussions in this chapter, this assumption is not appropriate in the typical Japanese decision-making situation and should be replaced by a more circular model of information sharing.

Unfortunately, U.S. scholars often tend to assume that knowledge only transfers from the United States to the rest of the world and not vice versa, but it should occur in both directions. Accordingly, research in cross-cultural organizational communication requires four types of models: (1) descriptive models to map out the components of the communication process; (2) analytic models that ask why certain practices are followed and establish priorities of importance for systems and processes (critical theory); (3) evaluative models that measure results; and (4) prescriptive models that provide direction for managers (Negandhi, 1983). Studies of organizational communication in Japan tend to focus on descriptive models, in large part. Often suggestions are made for practitioners without critically examining analytic or evaluative models.

Movement beyond the descriptive stage is difficult, however, for numerous reasons. For example, Ito and Kohei (1990) note the difficulties of doing field research in Japan since most of the basic assumptions of field research are based on Western views of societies and individuals. Nevertheless, it may be more possible to obtain longitudinal data in Japan than in the United States. Ito and Kohei have discussed the availability of longitudinal data in Japan due to the lifetime employment of researchers with one organization. Few U.S. researchers continue their studies over a period of years and build up a database of studies. This type of work is a more common practice in Japan.

Sekaran (1983) examines the methodological and theoretical issues in cross-cultural organizational management research. She notes five major methodological concerns: ensuring functional equivalence, problems of instrumentation, data-collection methods, sampling design issues, and data analysis. Functional equivalence focuses on issues of relevance to responding to surveys such as equivalence in vocabulary, idioms, grammar and syntax, and inferences drawn by the respondent. Problems of instrumentation include different responses to scaling (for example, 4-point scales versus 7-point scales) and other biases in measurement such as asking respondents about culturally sensitive topics. Data collection problems include timing of data collection in different cultures, status and other psychological issues, and cross-sectional versus longitudinal data collection. Each of these problems is evident in organizational communication research in Japan and the United States.

Data collection in Japan is complicated by the very nature of the Japanese organization. As noted previously, Japanese organizations have two types of hierarchy—a seniority system for individuals and a hierarchy of organizational ranks. These hierarchies do not necessarily overlap. Western measures may not capture this complexity (Smith & Misumi, 1989). In addition to potential confusion resulting from an inadequate understanding of Japanese organizational structure, Lincoln (1989) notes that it is generally problematic when U.S. questionnaires are translated into Japanese. For example, Japanese respondents may show lower scores on any self-descriptive measure because of the cultural norm of modest presentation of self.

Sekaran (1983) suggests selecting matched samples in countries of investigation due to the difficulty of obtaining participants who are representative of the central tendencies of their nations. Obviously this is not possible in the great majority of cross-cultural organizational research studies in Japan and the United States. Sekaran notes that to overcome this problem qualitative researchers are beginning to move away from impressionistic studies to more rigorous quantitative data and sophisticated analysis. Sophisticated qualitative studies have been conducted in Japan (see, for example, Kondo, 1990), but more are needed.

ISSUES FOR FUTURE RESEARCH

Dunphy (1987) suggests that Japanese and Western management practices are converging. This observation highlights the continuing debate among researchers concerning the issues of organizational convergence and divergence (see, for example, Maguire & Kroliczak,

1983). Child (1981), a British management theorist, reviewed a large number of cross-cultural organizational studies. One subset of these studies concludes that the tendency is toward *convergence* among organizations in different national cultures. In other words, organizations are becoming more and more similar across cultures. The implication of these studies is that scholars should look for universal theories of management. The other subset of these studies concludes that the tendency is toward *divergence*—that is, organizational issues across cultures will remain different. Child reconciles these conflicting views by noting that most convergence studies focus on macrolevel issues (the structure and technology used by organizations), while divergence studies focus on microlevel issues (the behavior of people within organizations). Thus, Child concludes that organizations around the world are becoming more alike, but that the behavior of people within organizations is maintaining its cultural specificity. Yet Ito (1989) predicts that "if the horizontal mobility of American managers and workers decrease and team work and human relations in factories become emphasized, the American communication style may come closer to the Japanese style" (p. 122). Further research is necessary to resolve this issue.

The role of women in Japanese organizations is particularly problematic. As noted previously, Japanese women and men tend to occupy relatively distinct roles. Researchers tend to assume, however, that organizational processes apply equally to men and women. Consequently, more research needs to be done focusing on the organizational communication processes that have a significant impact on women. Researchers need to move beyond large Japanese companies to study smaller, family-owned enterprises that are more likely to employ women in higher level positions (see Kondo, 1990, for an example of this type of research).

In examining a more specific line of inquiry (in studying leadership in a cross-cultural context, for example) researchers should be careful to differentiate between normativism and positivism (Van Fleet & Al-Tuhaih, 1979). It is necessary to differentiate between perceptions of how Japanese and U.S. organizational leaders *should act* and how they *do act*. Additionally, one could also examine how subordinates *want them to act* (Stewart, Gudykunst, Ting-Toomey, & Nishida, 1985).

Thus, studies comparing Japanese and U.S. organizational communication have many positive qualities, but as can be seen from our review in this chapter, further research is needed to improve our understanding of these phenomena.

NOTE

1. Any statement about "Japanese organizations" in this chapter refers to Japanese organizations in Japan unless otherwise noted. Similarly, the term "U.S. organizations" refers to U.S. organizations in the United States unless otherwise noted.

REFERENCES

Adler, N. J. (1983a). Cross-cultural management research: Issues to be faced. *International Studies of Man and Organization, 8*(1-2), 7-45.

Adler, N. J. (1983b). Cross-cultural management research: The ostrich and the trend. *Academy of Management Review, 8,* 226-232.

Adler, N. J. (1983c, Fall). A typology of management studies involving culture. *Journal of International Business Studies,* pp. 29-47.

Aoki, M. (1988). *Information, incentives, and bargaining in the Japanese economy.* New York: Cambridge University Press.

Befu, H. (1990). Conflict and non-Weberian bureaucracy in Japan. In S. N. Eisenstadt & E. Ben-Ari (Eds.), *Japanese models of conflict resolution.* London: Kegan Paul.

Ben-Ari, E., Moeran, B., & Valentine, J. (Eds.). (1990). *Unwrapping Japan.* Manchester: Manchester University Press.

Black, J. S. (1988, Summer). Work role transitions: A study of American expatriate managers in Japan. *Journal of International Business Studies,* pp. 277-294.

Bowers, J. R. (1988). *Formal and informal horizontal communication networks in large Japanese organizations.* Paper presented at the International Communication Association conference, New Orleans, LA.

Child, J. D. (1981). Culture, contingency and capitalism in cross-national study of organizations. In L. L. Cummings & B. M. Staw (Eds.), *Research in organizational behavior.* Greenwich, CT: JAI Publishers.

Clark, R. (1979). *The Japanese company.* New Haven, CT: Yale University Press.

Cole, R. E. (1980, September). Learning from the Japanese: Prospects and pitfalls. *Management Review,* pp. 22-42.

Cook, A. H., & Hayashi, H. (1980). *Working women in Japan: Discrimination resistance and reform.* Ithaca, NY: New York State School of Industrial and Labor Relations.

Dunphy, D. (1987). Convergence/divergence: A temporal review of the Japanese enterprise and its management. *Academy of Management Review, 12*, 445-459.

Fucini, J. J., & Fucini, S. (1990). *Working for the Japanese: Inside Mazda's American auto plant.* New York: Free Press.

Furukawa, H. (1981). Management objectives, conditions in workunit, and leadership behavior. *Psychologia, 24,* 176-184.

Hamada, T. (1991). *American enterprise in Japan.* Albany, NY: State University of New York Press.

Hayashi, S. (1988). *Culture and management in Japan* (F. Baldwin, Trans.). Tokyo: University of Tokyo Press.

Hazama, H. (1971). *Nihonteki keiei* [Japanese management]. Tokyo: Nihon Keizai Shimbunsha.

Herschman, C. (1983). *Communication and decision making as reflected by the Japanese culture.* A paper presented at the International Communication Association conference, Dallas, TX.

Hirokawa, R. Y., & Miyahara, A. (1986) . A comparison of influence strategies utilized by managers in American and Japanese organizations. *Communication Quarterly, 34,* 250-65 .

Hofstede, G. H. (1984). *Culture's consequences: International differences in work-related values.* Beverly Hills, CA: Sage.

Ishikure, K. (1988). Achieving Japanese productivity and quality levels at a U.S. plant. *Long Range Planning, 21*(5), 10-17.

Itami, H. (1982). *Nihonteki keiei o koete—kigyo keieiyoku no nichi-bei hikaku* (Beyond Japanese management: A comparison of Japanese and American practices). Tokyo: Toyo Keizai Shimposha.

Ito, Y. (1989). Socio-cultural backgrounds of Japanese interpersonal communication style. *Civilisations, 39,* 101-127.

Ito, Y., & Kohei, (1990). Practical problems in field research in Japan. In U. Narula & W. B. Pearce (Eds.), *Cultures, politics, and research programs: An international assessment of practical problems in field research.* Hillsdale, NJ: Lawrence Erlbaum.

Jablin, F. (1979). Superior-subordinate communication: The state of the art. *Psychological Bulletin, 86,* 1201-1222.

Jain, H. C. (1990). Human resource management in selected Japanese firms, their foreign subsidiaries and locally owned counterparts. *International Labour Review, 129,* 73-84 .

Jensen, S. A. (1984). Decision making in Japanese organizations: A proposed template of understanding. Unpublished master's thesis, Purdue University, West Lafayette, IN.

Johnson, S. G. (1990, Summer). Not cut from the same bolt: Underneath the management fabric of Japan and the United States. *Baylor Business Review*, pp. 18-21.

Kagono, T., Nonaka, I., Sakakibara, K., & Okumura, A. (1983). *An evolutionary view of organizational adaptation: United States vs. Japanese firms.* Paper presented at the Second U.S.-Japan Business Conference, Tokyo.

Kagono, T., Nonaka, I., Sakakibara, K., & Okumura, A., with Sakamoto, S., & Johansson, J. K. (1985). *Strategic vs. evolutionary management: A U.S.-Japan comparison of strategy and organization.* New York: North-Holland.

Kagono, T., et al. (1983). *Nichi-bei kigyo no keiei hikaku, senryakuteki kankyo tekio no genri* (A comparison of Japanese and American management methods). Tokyo: Nihon Keizai Shimbunsha.

Kearns, R. L. (1992). *Zaibatsu America: How Japanese firms are colonizing vital U.S. industries.* New York: Free Press.

Kelley, L., Whatley, A., & Worthley, R. (1987, Summer). Assessing the effects of culture on managerial attitudes. *Journal of International Business Studies*, pp. 17-31.

Kondo, D. K. (1990). *Crafting selves: Power, gender, and discourses of identity in a Japanese workplace.* Chicago: University of Chicago Press.

Kumara, U. A., & Koichi, F. (1989) . Employee satisfaction and job climate: An empirical study of Japanese manufacturing employees. *Journal of Business and Psychology, 3*, 315-329 .

Lane, H. W. (1980). Systems, values and action: An analytic framework for intercultural management research. *Management International Review, 20* (3), 61-70.

Lebra, T. S. (1976). *Japanese patterns of behavior.* Honolulu, HI: University Press of Hawaii.

Lebra, T. S. (1984). *Japanese women: Constraint and fulfillment.* Honolulu: University of Hawaii Press.

Lee, S. M., & Schwendiman, G. (1982). *Japanese management: Cultural and environmental considerations.* New York: Praeger.

Leonard, J. W., & Thanopoulos, J. (1982). Japanese management: Reasons for success. In S. M. Lee & G. Schwendiman (Eds.), *Japanese management: Cultural and environmental considerations.* New York: Praeger.

Levin, D. P. (1992, May 5). Toyota plant in Kentucky is font of ideas for U. S. *New York Times*, pp. A1, D8 .

Lincoln, J. R. (1989, Fall). Employee work attitudes and management practice in the U.S. and Japan: Evidence from a large comparative survey. *California Management Review*, pp. 89-106.

Lincoln, J. R., & McBride, K. (1987). Japanese industrial organization in comparative perspective. *Annual Review of Sociology, 13*, 289-312.

Maguire, M. A., & Kroliczak, A. (1983). Attitudes of Japanese and Americans workers: Convergence or diversity. *Sociological Quarterly, 24*, 107-122.

Maguire, M. A., & Pascale, R. T. (1978). Communication, decision making and implementation among managers in Japanese and American managed companies in the United States. *Sociology and Social Research, 63*, 1-23.

McMillan, C. (1980). Is Japanese management really so different? *Business Quarterly, 45*(3), 26-31.

Misumi, J., & Peterson, M. F. (1985). The performance-maintenance (PM) theory of leadership: Review of a Japanese research program. *Administrative Science Quarterly, 30*, 198-223.

Mito, T. (1981). *Nihonjin to kaisha* [Corporations and individuals]. Tokyo: Chuo Koronsha.

Miyanaga, K. (1991). *The creative edge: Emerging individualism in Japan*. New Brunswick, NJ: Transaction.

Mroczkowski, T., & Hanaoka, M. (1989, Winter). Continuity and change in Japanese management. *California Management Review*, pp. 39-53.

Munchus, G. (1983). Employer-employee based quality circles in Japan: Human resource policy implications for American firms. *Academy of Management Review, 8*, 255-261.

Murray, V. V., Jain, H. C., & Adams, R. J. (1976, July). A framework for the comparative analysis of personnel administration. *Academy of Management Review*, pp. 47-57.

Nakanishi, M., Schwartz, D. F., & Awa, J. (1992). *Communicating for effective leadership: A study of Japanese managers in the United States*. Paper presented at the International Communication Association conference, Miami, FL.

Negandhi, A. R. (1983, Fall). Cross-cultural management research: Trend and future directions. *Journal of International Business Studies*, pp. 17-28.

Nonaka, I., & Johansson, J. K. (1985). Japanese management: What about the "hard" skills? *Academy of Management Review, 10*, 181-191.

Okabe, R. (1983). Cultural assumptions of communication theory from eastern and western perspectives: The cases of Japan and the United States. In W. B. Gudykunst (Ed.), *Intercultural communication theory*. Beverly Hills, CA: Sage.

Odaka, K., Ono, K., & Adachi, F. (1988). *The automobile industry in Japan: A study of ancillary firm development*. Tokyo, Japan: Kinokuniya Company and Oxford University Press.

Okubayashi, K. (1986). Recent problems of Japanese personnel management. *Labour and Society, 11,* 17-37.

Pascale, R. T. (1978). Communication and decision making across cultures: Japanese and American comparisons. *Administrative Science Quarterly, 23,* 91-110.

Pascale, R. T., & Athos, A. G. (1981). *The art of Japanese management: Applications for American executives*. New York: Warner Books.

Richardson, B. M., & Ueda, T. (1981). *Business and society in Japan: Fundamentals for businessmen*. New York: Praeger.

Ruch, W. V. (1984). *Corporate communications: A comparison of Japanese and American practices*. Westport, CT: Quorum Books.

San Antonio, P. M. (1991). *The cultural interface: The Japanese manager in an American company in Japan*. Unpublished doctoral dissertation, Arizona State University, Tempe.

Saso, M. (1990). *Women in the Japanese workplace*. London: Hilary Shipman.

Schwind, H. F., & Peterson, R. B. (1985). Shifting personal values in the Japanese management system. *International Studies of Management and Organization, 15*(2), 60-74.

Sekaran, U. (1983, Fall). Methodological and theoretical issues and advancements in cross-cultural research. *Journal of International Business Studies,* pp. 61-73.

Shani, A. B., & Basuray, T. (1983). *Towards a conceptual synthesis of United States and Japanese management systems: An action research perspective*. A paper presented at the Academy of Management conference, Dallas, TX.

Shani, A. B., & Basuray, M. T. (1988). Organization development and comparative management: Action research as an interpretive framework. *Leadership & Organization Development Journal, 9*(2), 3-10.

Shenkar, O. (1988). Uncovering some paths in the Japanese management theory jungle. *Human Systems Management, 7,* 221-230.

Smith, P. B., & Misumi, J. (1989). Japanese management—A sun rising in the West? In C. L. Cooper & I. Robertson (Eds.), *International review of industrial and organizational psychology*. New York: John Wiley.

Stage, C. W. (1992). *Compliance-gaining among Japanese managers supervising in Ohio and Japan*. Paper presented at the International Communication Association conference, Miami, FL.

Stewart, L. P., Gudykunst, W. B., Ting-Toomey, S., & Nishida, T. (1985). The effects of decision-making style on openness and satisfaction within Japanese organizations. *Communication Monographs, 53*, 236-251.

Sullivan, J. J., Suzuki, T., & Kondo, Y. (1986). Managerial perceptions of performance: A comparison of Japanese and American work groups. *Journal of Cross-Cultural Psychology, 17*, 379-398 .

Takezawa, S-I., & Whitehill, A. M. (1983). *Work ways: Japan and America*. Tokyo: Japan Institute of Labour.

Tanaka, K., Isaka, H., & Toshima, Y. (1991). A study on the residents' opinions toward Japanese-owned companies in the U.S.A.: Determinants of unfavorable opinions toward Japanese-owned companies. *Research in Social Psychology* (Japanese Society of Social Psychology), *6*, 112-118.

Taylor, J. (1983). *Shadows of the rising sun: A critical view of the "Japanese miracle."* New York: Quill.

Tsurumi, Y. (1978). The best of times and the worst of times: Japanese management in America. *Columbia Journal of World Business, 13*(2), 56-61.

Urabe, K. (1978). *Nihonteki keiei o kangaeru* [On Japanese management]. Tokyo: Chuo Koronsha.

Van Fleet, D., & Al-Tuhaih, S. (1979). A cross-cultural analysis of perceived leader behaviors. *Management International Review* (Germany), *19*(4), 81-87.

van Wolferen, K. (1990). *The enigma of Japanese power*. New York: Vintage Books.

Venkatesh, A., & Wilemon, D. (1980, Fall). American and European product managers: A comparison. *Columbia Journal of World Business*, pp. 67-74.

Weisman, S. R. (1992, March 3). More Japanese workers demanding shorter hours and less hectic work. *New York Times*, p. A8.

Whitehill, A. M. (1991). *Japanese management: Tradition and transition*. London: Routledge.

Wood, S. (1989). The Japanese management model: Tacit skills in shop floor participation. *Work and Occupations, 16*, 446-460.

Yamada, H. (1990). Topic management and turn distribution in business meetings: American versus Japanese strategies. *Text, 10*, 271-295.

Yokochi-Bryce, N. (1989). Leadership styles of Japanese business executives and managers: Transformational and transactional. *Dissertation Abstracts International, 50*(6), 2655-B. (University Microfilms No. DA8921303)

Chapter 8

MASS COMMUNICATION THEORIES IN
JAPAN AND THE UNITED STATES

Youichi Ito

Books and articles on journalism and mass communications began
to be published in Japan in the late nineteenth century (Ito, 1987). The
subjects dealt with in the books and articles published in those days
were limited to normative and descriptive ones such as the ethics and
morals of journalists, the structure and practices of the newspaper
industry, the history of newspapers and journalism, as well as policies
and legal frameworks for journalism and newspaper companies in
Japan and the West. Theoretical or empirical studies on the roles and
influences of the mass media did not exist before the 1930s.

One of the early theoretical attempts made in Japan was the study
of propaganda supported by the military and other government agen-
cies beginning immediately after the Manchurian Incident of 1931.
Japanese propaganda experts translated many books on propaganda
published in the West soon after the First World War,[1] carefully analyzed many actual cases described in those books and articles, and
reached surprisingly similar conclusions or findings as those obtained
by American experimental psychologists in the 1950s (see Ito, 1990, for
details).

Marxist theories of journalism imported in the middle of the 1920s
had a strong influence on Japanese journalists and intellectuals. Accord-

ing to this theory (e.g., Aono, 1926; Fukumoto, 1926; Hayasaka, 1926; Koadoya, 1929), Japanese "bourgeois newspapers" serving the capitalist class and the capitalist-dominated state helped suppress and exploit Japanese workers and farmers. Marxist scholars, however, were oppressed by the militaristic government in the late 1930s and were silenced until the end of the Second World War.

After the Second World War, many theoretical models for mass-media influence were imported from the United States. Since then, many Japanese scholars have treated American and European theories with an assumption that what is applicable to Western society is automatically applicable to Japanese society. Only a few scholars have seriously considered whether these theories are really applicable to Japanese society.

There are several views in Japan regarding the extent a social theory developed in one culture can be applied in another culture. There are scholars and teachers who just translate and teach social theories developed in the West without thinking about whether it can shed light on Japanese society. This is an extreme attitude. On the other hand, there are extremists who claim that no social theory developed in the West can be applied to Japanese society because our basic values and assumptions are different. The intellectual movement called *nihon shugi* (Japanism) in the 1930s is an example of this.

The present author does not agree with either of the two extreme views. There are many social theories, including widely accepted theories, that do not explain the Japanese experience at all. Yet there *are* other social theories developed outside Japan that explain the Japanese experience quite well. Furthermore, there are social theories that explain Western *and* Japanese experiences very well but do not explain the experiences of Third World countries.

In this sense, social theories, unlike natural science theories, are culturally bound. Many social theories reflect cultural norms, biases, and other characteristics. Theoretical models on mass media influence that were developed in the West and are applicable to the Japanese situation and the alternative models Japanese experts have developed are discussed in this chapter.

It is recognized widely that the mass media are not the *sole* source of influence on social decision-making or individual attitudes and behavior. However, in order to make theories simpler, most models of mass-media influence consider only two components, that is, the receiving individual or society and the mass media including the sender and messages.

From a macroscopic viewpoint, however, these are all "bipolar" models in the sense that there are only two "poles" in the theories, the mass media in a broad sense (including the sender and messages) on the one hand and the receiving individual or society on the other hand. The "third factors" such as the third person, ingroups, "reference groups," direct experiences, and information through non-mass media channels can be included in the receiver side together with receivers' predispositions, personality, and so on, since they function only as intermediate variables. In some theories, the "feedback" loop is considered (e.g., DeFleur & Ball-Rokeach, 1966; Schramm, 1965). It is, however, incorporated only as a channel for small modifications on the mass media side and the direction of flows of information, and influence in "bipolar models" is predominantly one way, that is, from the mass media to receiving individuals or society.

After overviewing major bipolar models developed in the United States and Europe, we will discuss a tripolar model consisting of the mass media, government policies, and public attitudes. This is also a kind of multipolar model in which more than three components of social consensus formation, including the mass media, influenced each other. In this model, the mass media are treated only as one of three components which can be influenced by the other two. After elaborating on the mechanisms of mutual influence among these three factors, two case studies on tax increase and the Japanese government's unsuccessful plan to dispatch noncombat troops to the Gulf War are discussed.

BIPOLAR MODELS OF MASS MEDIA INFLUENCE

As mentioned earlier, the "bipolar" models of mass media influence refer to the models in which only two components, the receiving individual or society and the mass media including the sender and messages are considered. These models are further divided into the following two categories: (1) theories which do not assume homogeneity of mass media contents, and (2) theories which assume homogeneity of mass media contents.

Do mass media contents on the whole tend to be homogeneous or heterogeneous? Of course, it depends upon the subject, time, situation, and other factors. However, major theories and models of mass media effects can be classified by which characteristics the theorists assume, homogeneity or heterogeneity of mass media contents.

Generally speaking, the models whose major concern is influence on the whole society tend to assume homogeneity of media contents and the models whose major concern is influence on individual psychology and behavior tend to assume heterogeneity of media contents. Furthermore, the models whose major concern is the influence or roles of the whole mass media naturally tend to assume homogeneity of media contents and the models whose major concern is the influence of specific messages, programs, or articles tend to assume heterogeneity of contents. American scholars tend to assume heterogeneity of contents and European and Japanese scholars tend to assume homogeneity of contents.

Models Which Do Not Assume
Homogeneity of Mass Media Content

The Classical Model of Democracy and Public Opinion Formation. According to this model, individuals' unsystematic impressions, needs, hopes, reactions, and so forth are rationalized, justified, and systematized by the mass media. Thus, unsystematic impressions and reactions are transformed into systematic opinions and those opinions are further refined and systematized through public debates and "public opinions" are formed. These conscious and rational public opinions determine the direction for the society (e.g., Bryce, 1923; Cooley, 1956; Hume, [1741] 1963; Ross, [1908] 1969; Tarde, 1901). This model has been criticized for being too optimistic regarding the nature of human being as well as that of mass media (e.g., Lippman, 1922; Wallas, 1948).

The Mass Persuasion Model. This model has been called the "hypodermic model" or "atomic bomb model." As these names imply, this model assumes the mass media's powerful effects on individual attitudes and behavior. According to this model, mass media contents are not unstructured or fragmented. They are well structured for the purpose of leading individuals to a certain goal. It is assumed in this model that, through rhetoric and various other persuasion techniques, the mass media have an overwhelming influence on individual attitudes and behavior. Most studies of propaganda belong to this category (e.g., Doob, 1935; Lasswell, 1927; Lerner, 1951; Merton, 1946). The only difference in this model is that mass media contents are not unstructured or fragmented.

What is not clear in this model is what will happen if individuals are exposed to competing or contradictory media contents. The term "hypodermic" implies that a person receives overwhelming influence from the mass media that he or she is usually exposed to or happens to be exposed to ("*de facto* selectivity").

The Uses and Gratification Model. While the receiver of information in the propaganda or persuasion model is considered to be passive, this model emphasizes active aspect of the receiver. The receiver is considered to *use* mass media to satisfy his or her various needs. If mass media contents are not useful or incapable of satisfying the receiver's needs, he or she will not pay attention. The mass media, therefore, influence individuals only when they provide them with information that satisfies their needs (e.g., Edelstein, 1973; Katz, Gurevitch & Hass, 1973; Rosengren, 1974). Like the classical model of democracy and public opinion formation, this model also assumes independent and autonomous individuals.

The Joho Kohdo (Information Behavior) Model. This model emerged as a part of Japanese *johoka shakai* (information society) studies (Ito, 1981, 1987). It resembles the uses and gratification model. The difference, however, is that while individuals in the uses and gratification model seek the information they need only in mass media, individuals in this model are thought to *extract* the information they need from their environment including the mass media, other individuals, letters from foreign friends, foreign visitors, imported commodities, and so forth.

Ito (1991) asked why many socialist regimes collapsed despite the fact that the government had almost a complete monopoly of the domestic mass media. If the mass media influence was as powerful in maintaining the status quo and the existing political regime, as assumed in the mass persuasion, Marxist, or "environmentalist" models (to be discussed below), how could the collapse of socialist regimes be explained? The mass media cannot be influential under all conditions. They can be influential under only certain conditions. Then what are the conditions?

One answer to this question is that once credibility is lost, even monopolistic mass media cannot maintain influence any longer. Then how is credibility lost? It is when mass media information does not explain the reality that receivers know, or when mass media information is always incongruent with the information that receivers extract from their direct environment or other non-mass media channels.

Individuals not only passively receive information from the mass media, but also actively gather, collect, and extract information from their environment. Individuals do this through imported goods, letters from foreign friends, conversations with foreign visitors, pictures in foreign magazines, and direct experiences and observations during overseas travels, and they use this information in their opinion formation. If mass media contents are congruent with the "extracted information," the mass media have some influence. However, if mass media contents contradict or are not congruent with "extracted information," people come to disbelieve the mass media because even if mass media information overwhelms "extracted information" in quantity, the credibility of extracted information is always higher than that of mass media information.

Once people come to discredit the mass media, the mass media no longer have any influence on them. As a Croatian mass communication scholar Novosel (1991) states based on Yugoslavian experiences, people came to "interpret" mass media contents in their own way and often reach conclusions opposite from the intention of the state-controlled mass media.

Ito (1991) argues that the information behavior model is especially important in considering mass media influence in information societies. One of the characteristics of current "informization" is the rapid expansion of non-mass media channels including sophisticated libraries, electronic data bases, and computer communication. In pre-information societies, people do not have many non-mass media channels to use to gather information about reality. Therefore, they have to depend on mass media information. In information societies, however, people's dependence on the traditional mass media tends to decline and the mass media have an influence only when their contents are congruent with the information that people obtain through non-mass media channels.

The Personal Influence or "Two-Step Flow" Model. In this model, individuals are considered to be less independent and less individualistic. They are group members of some kind and parts of human networks. They receive "personal influence" from other people, especially "opinion leaders" around them. Opinion leaders expose themselves to the mass media more than ordinary people and receive mass media influence first, which is gradually transmitted to their "followers." In other words, mass media influence on the general masses is considered to be indirect.

Although Katz and Lazarsfeld (1955) did not mention it in their original work, this model was later interpreted by other scholars like Merton (1957) to suggest that receivers can check what they receive from the mass media with their opinion leaders. This implies that receivers are influenced only when what they receive from the mass media is endorsed by their opinion leaders.

Models Which Assume Homogeneity of Mass Media Content

Many scholars have claimed or assumed that mass media contents are by and large homogeneous. The reasons for homogeneity are varied. Marxists and neo-Marxists assume the existence of a power elite *class* (apart from to what extent it is rigid) which controls and manipulates mass media contents (Gitlin, 1980; Hall, 1982; Mills, 1956; Schiller, 1973; Yamamoto, 1980). Some other critical scholars who may be called "political economists" are less concerned with the "manipulation by the power elite *class*" but believe that the (capitalist) nature of the mass media industry itself inevitably makes mass media contents homogeneous (Garnham, 1990; Gerbner & Gross, 1976). Furthermore, mass media contents can be homogeneous because of the news gathering system in which journalists work and the deterioration of journalists' morals (Lippmann, 1927; Uemae, 1977), the antigovernment mass media culture (Noelle-Neumann, 1973, 1984, 1989; Tsujimura, 1976b), or simply the critical importance of the event (Fujitake, 1967; Katz, 1980). If the mass media are homogeneous and other sources of information are not counted, mass media influence naturally becomes powerful because they become the only source of information regarding the reality beyond people's direct environment.

The (Neo-)Marxist Model. A characteristic of this model is that mass media contents are considered to be controlled by the power elite or the establishment. If mass media contents are really controlled by or destined to serve the power elite or the establishment, they naturally become homogeneous as far as basic values and ideologies are concerned. Proponents of this model (e.g., Garnham, 1990; Gitlin, 1980; Hall, 1982; Inaba, 1987; Mills, 1956; Schiller, 1973; Yamamoto, 1980) admit the existence of "superficial" or temporary differences among different mass media in capitalist democracies. They claim, however, that these superficial differences are not important. An important point is that members of the mass media share the same basic values and ideologies with the status quo and the present establishment. Therefore, the mass media are an "ideological apparatus" for the power elite to maintain social integration and secure their "class interests" (Gitlin, 1980, p. 252; Hall, 1982, p. 87). They also claim that the tastes, values, and ideologies of the masses, which are seemingly independent, are not at all independent. They are manipulated by the power elite and their conscious and unconscious servants including the mass media.

The Marxist model explains the situation in countries where the mass media are operated directly or controlled strictly by the government rather than in countries where mass media are operated by free commercial enterprises. In countries where the mass media have to compete with each other for more readers or viewers, they cannot help respecting readers' or viewers' tastes, values, and ideologies. Otherwise, the media would decline in the long run, and be replaced by other media whose contents are congruent with mass tastes, values, and ideologies. As Mr. Hata, a former chief editorial writer of *Asahi Shimbun*, states, the mass media influence the general public, but the general public also influences the mass media.

According to the (neo-)Marxists, independent mass tastes and values are an illusion. They are fabricated through subtle and complicated mechanisms by capitalist power elites and their servants. To what extent this assumption is realistic is questionable.

The Cultivation Model. All critical scholars are not necessarily (neo)Marxists. It is not easy to draw a distinction between (neo-)Marxist and non-Marxist critical scholars. There are a number of possible criteria used to distinguish them, but the criterion used here is the extent that *class* is considered to be rigid or the extent that mobility among different social classes, statuses, and positions is considered to be high in the society. If social classes, statuses, professions, and positions can be easily changed by individual effort through fair interindividual competition, the class or even the "manipulation by the ruling class" is not a serious social problem.

Class, however, is not the only problem in capitalist societies. Capitalism can cause various other socially undesirable problems. One can, therefore, be critical of the existing socio economic system and its underlying assumptions without being (neo-)Marxist.

The cultivation model of Gerbner and his colleagues is an example. According to this model, mass media companies in capitalist economies are operated based on profit-making motives. As a result, the mass media tend to distort reality in their efforts to entertain and please their "customers." Each distortion may be trivial, but in the long run, it has influence on people's recognition of reality.

Research by Gerbner and Gross (1976), Gerbner, Gross, Jackson-Beeck, Jeffries-Fox, and Signorielli (1978), and Gerbner, Gross, Morgan, and Signorielli (1980) suggests that the "reality" in television programs affects heavy television viewers recognitions of reality. For example, it was found that heavy television viewers tend to overestimate the American population and the crime rate in the United States (Gerbner, Gross, Morgan, & Signorielli, 1980). This model is similar to the "environmentalist model" to be discussed next in the sense that they focus on long-term comprehensive influence rather than short-term influence on specific issues. This model, however, is more critical (of television in capitalist economies) and more empirical than the environmentalist model.

There are other similar models which emphasize the long-term socialization effects of the mass media. The foci of these socialization models tend to be social and cultural norms, basic principles and ideologies, behavioral inclinations like violence and sexual behavior attitudes to the opposite sex, and so on, rather than opinions regarding specific issues. However, since the focus of this chapter is social consensus formation, models on long-term cultural impacts are not discussed.

The Environmentalist Model. This model was created by Lippmann (1922) but was accepted widely and developed in Japan more than in any other country for cultural reasons (see Ito, 1987, for the reasons). According to this model (Fujitake, 1968; Lang & Lang, 1960; Lippmann, 1922; Shimizu, 1951), individuals judge, decide, and behave reacting to and trying to adapt to their environment. However, the range of environment that they can directly perceive and recognize through their sensory organs is limited to a very small space. This small range of environment perceived through the sensory organs is called the "direct environment" or "real environment." In modern society, individuals cannot live depending solely on the "direct environment." They have to understand the world beyond their direct experience and try to adapt to it. This world beyond individuals' direct experiences is called the "indirect environment" or "pseudo-environment," which is created and maintained by mass media activities.

According to this model, people's reactions and adaptation to the pseudo-environment create, maintain, and change the real environment. Through this mechanism the pseudo-environment created and maintained by the mass media becomes the real environment. Therefore, according to this model, the mass media's ability to determine our social environment is overwhelming. Elihu Katz's ideas on "media events" may be included in this category (Katz, 1980; Katz, Dayan, & Motyl, 1981).

Although proponents of this approach have never stated that mass media contents are always homogeneous, they always use unusual major events as examples in which media contents cannot help becoming homogeneous because of their critical importance. The Olympics (Fujitake, 1967; Fujitake & Akiyama, 1967), General MacArthur's parade

(Lang & Lang, 1960), the landing on the moon (Katz, 1980; Katz, Dayan, & Motyl, 1981), and Sadat's visit to Jerusalem (Katz, 1980) are such examples.

What will happen to this model if we do not assume the homogeneity of mass media contents? Then mass media provide receivers with many different kinds of pseudo-environments, which means that receivers can have a variety of images about their environment. Also, if an individual is exposed to many kinds of pseudo-environments provided by different mass media, he or she may synthesize them and have an image of the real environment different from any of those provided by the mass media. If these phenomena occur, mass media influence on individuals cannot be overwhelming, therefore mass media influence on the real environment becomes limited.

The Agenda-Setting Model. In this model, the mass media are considered to influence people's issue salience, or which issues they think are important, rather than their attitudes per se (McCombs, 1976; McCombs & Shaw, 1972; Weaver, Graber, McCombs, & Eyal, 1981). In other words, mass media influence which issue people should think about now (e.g., issue salience) rather than what their attitudes regarding that issue should be (e.g., persuasion).

Unlike the previous two models, this model does not necessarily assume homogeneity in terms of political or ideological inclinations. However, it emphasizes commonality in agenda or the issues that the mass media report at a specific time. Because the mass media emphasize the same issue at a certain time, people, even if their opinions differ, come to think about a particular issue at the same time. Although this is a different kind of influence than those considered in previous two models, it certainly has important social and political implications. Whether the mass media emphasize defense issues, domestic economic issues, or sex scandals before an important election certainly affects the result of the election.

The "Spiral of Silence" Model. Katz (1983, p. 89) summarizes this theory proposed by Noelle-Neumann (1973, 1984, 1989) as follows:

(a) Individuals have opinions;
(b) Fearing isolation, individuals will not express their opinions if they perceive themselves unsupported by others;
(c) A "quasi-statistical sense" is employed by individuals to scan the environment for signs of support;
(d) Mass media constitute the major source of reference for infor-

mation about the distribution of opinion and thus for the climate of support/nonsupport;

(e) So do other reference groups;

(f) The media tend to speak in one voice, almost monopolisti-
cally;

(g) The media tend to distort the distribution of opinion in society,
biased as they are by the (leftist) views of journalists;

(h) Perceiving themselves unsupported, groups of individuals—
who may, at times, even constitute a majority—will lose confidence and withdraw from public debate, thus speeding the
demise of their position through the self-fulfilling spiral of
silence. They may not change their own minds, but they stop
recruitment of others and abandon the fight;

(i) Society is manipulated and impoverished thereby (for the
absence of dialogue and/or the repression of truth—these
inferences are not spelled out by Noelle-Neumann).

While political or ideological similarity among different mass
media is not assumed in the agenda-setting model, it is assumed in this
model as indicated in (f) and (g). The similarity appears not so conspic-
uously, but in a more subtle way. It appears in the way that the position
supported by the mass media looks like the majority opinion (even if it
is actually a minority opinion). The situational background of this theory is easy for Japanese to understand, and it may be one of the reasons
why this theory is popular in Japan.

The postwar German and postwar Japanese political situations
and intellectual atmospheres were very similar to each other until the
early 1970s. The experiences before and during the Second World War
were a trauma for both nations, especially for intellectuals and journalists. German and Japanese intellectuals had strong guilt complexes, and
they were against everything that reminded them of the prewar experience, such as the military, military alliances, suppressive police activities, restrictions on demonstrations, and capital punishment. Moreover, they had strong sympathy for and guilt complexes regarding
neighboring nations which became socialist countries, that is, Russia
for Germany and China for Japan.

On the other hand, the masses were more pragmatic and were
concerned with the economy and security, therefore they needed the
United States, which provided them with markets and security. As a
result, leftist-oriented intellectuals and mass media coexisted with conservative pro-American governments in postwar Germany and post-

war Japan. Before *shimbun hihan* (criticism of newspapers) occurred in Japan in the mid-1970s, the disagreement between the mass media and the government was very clear in Japan. This was reflected in then Prime Minister Kishi's statement during the political turmoil in the early 1960s regarding the U.S.-Japan Security Treaty: "[Although the mass media are all against me], I am supported by *koe naki koe* (silent voices)."

This kind of situation can be well explained by this "spiral of silence" theory. A question, however, remains: If the German and Japanese public have kept voting for conservative pro-American parties, have mass media had any influence on public attitudes and (voting) behavior?

A TRIPOLAR MODEL OF SOCIAL CONSENSUS FORMATION

As mentioned earlier, all bipolar models basically consider only two components, the mass media including the sender and messages and the receiver including other people and ingroups. Other people and ingroups are considered only as intermediate variables. The direction for information flow and influence is always from the mass media to the receiver, although feedback loops are incorporated in some models. In other words, in bipolar models the receiver is always a dependent variable and the mass media are always independent variables.

This section deals with multipolar models in which more than three components of social consensus formation, including the mass media, influence each other. In other words, mass media and the receiver are interchangeable and can become an independent or a dependent variable. The number of components for social consensus formation may be four or five, but in order to make the model as simple as possible, let us limit the number of components to three. The three most important components of social consensus formation are the mass media, government policies, and public attitudes.

In this chapter, the influence of the mass media on public attitudes and government policies are discussed as a part of the tripolar model of social consensus formation. The tripolar model of social consensus formation proposed is based on three kinds of previous studies: (1) social scientific analyses of the tripolar relationship between government, the mass media, and public opinion by Tsujimura (1976a, 1976b, 1981) and Nakano (1977), (2) Shichihei Yamamoto's study of *kuuki* (Yamamoto, 1977), and (3) historical analyses of the roles of Japanese newspapers in the 1930s and 1940s (Ikei, 1981, 1988; Kakegawa, 1972; Toriumi, 1973).

Sociological Analyses of the Tripolar Relationship between Government, the Mass Media, and Public Opinion

Many experts on press freedom have pointed out that the significance of press freedom in the classical theory of democracy of the eighteenth and nineteenth centuries has changed in the twentieth century. The mass media and the public in classical theories of democracy could be identified as one unit resisting a government dominated by a feudalistic or capitalistic elite class. Mass media companies in those days were small and ordinary citizens could start publishing newspapers relatively easily. In the twentieth century, however, mass media companies have grown quite large, giving them monopolistic or oligopolistic control of the market. Employees of large, modern mass media companies are elite intellectual and professional specialists; they are no longer "ordinary citizens." Thus, it is no longer appropriate to regard the mass media and the public as one unit.

In some cases, the mass media as profit-making companies serve particular individual, group, or class interests and no longer represent the public interest. Press freedom in such cases becomes freedom for monopolistic corporations and their shareholders, not for the general public. If "press freedom" is not used for the general public but is abused for special interest groups, such freedom may be restricted by the government. Thus, the tripolar relationship between government, the mass media, and the public was proposed to consider "press freedom for whom?" (see, for example, Brucker, 1949; Peterson, 1956; Schramm, 1957). These studies, however, focused on normative, ethical, and legal discussions and did not discuss influence relationships among the three entities.

Tsujimura (1976a, 1976b, 1981) persistently pursued the relationship between newspaper editorials and public opinion polls over a long period of time and collected many interesting case studies. According to his surveys, all major newspapers were against the government drafts for the San Francisco Peace Treaty in 1952 and the Japan-Korea Normalization Treaty in 1964, but public opinion polls supported the government in both cases. Japanese newspapers persistently have been critical of the Self-Defense Forces, but public opinion polls have always endorsed them. Major Japanese newspapers have always been sympathetic to workers' strikes, whereas opinion polls have always been negative.

Tsujimura (1976a) demonstrated that many antigovernment editorials of Japanese newspapers did not represent public opinion. He also found that the influence of public opinion could not be determined in general terms because it "depends on the issue and its interactive patterns with the government and newspapers" (Tsujimura, 1976a, p. 238).

Nakano (1977) also discussed the tripolar relationship between politics, newspapers, and public opinion. According to Nakano (1977), newspapers before this century could be identified with public opinions. Newspapers in this century, however, became "separated from the public" (p. 268) due to the reasons mentioned earlier as well as the "emergence of professional writers and reporters" (p. 267). If newspapers are really separated from the public, the influence of newspapers on the political process declines, which Nakano (1977) considered dangerous. Nakano argues:

> If newspapers are not well supported by public opinion, their influence on the political process becomes limited. Those in power will take advantage of it and claim that they are the ones supported by the public. If this state lasts for a long period of time, the public will become apathetic, inactive, and powerless, and only a handful of self-righteous journalists' noisy voices will remain. (p. 265)

Although Nakano (1977) provided insights into mass media influence on the political process, he did not provide any empirical data except several examples. His study would be better accepted if he backed up his theory with empirical studies.

Tsujimura (1976a, 1987b, 1981), however, conducted many empirical surveys to study the patterns of relationships between the government, the mass media, and public opinion, using expressions like "tripolar relationship" and "tripolar structure." Tsujimura, though, did not discuss these relationships as a dynamic process for social consensus formation or as a theoretical model to explain mass media influence. Tsujimura, therefore, did not fully discuss why disagreements occur between those three components and why and how those disagreements are resolved. The reason may be that a major purpose of his studies was to demonstrate that Japanese "leftist-oriented" newspapers were not supported by public opinion in many cases.

Another weakness in Nakano's and Tujimura's studies is that they treated the government, newspapers, and public opinion as homogeneous entities and ignored disagreements *within* each of the three. In many of Tsujimura's studies, only the *Asahi Shimbun* was analyzed and opinions of other more conservative newspapers were ignored. Disagreements among government leaders or ruling party Diet members or minority opinions in public-opinion survey data were also practically ignored.

Shichihei Yamamoto's "Study of Kuuki"

Kuuki usually refers to the dominant "air" or "atmosphere" in a group or society and has a high level of intensity. It is also a powerful and stubborn "standard of judgment," resistance to which might "result in the person's social destruction as heresy" (Yamamoto, 1977, p. 19). *Kuuki* is not just "air," "atmosphere," or "standard of judgment." It requires each individual, group, or organization to accept and comply with it, making those who do not agree with it silent or reluctant to speak up. If you cannot simply say "I don't agree with it" and instead need to give many long reasons to explain why you don't agree, or if you need strong courage to say in public that you do not agree with it, that is *kuuki* (Yamamoto, 1977, pp. 7-19). Yamamoto suggests that the process of creating *kuuki* is usually "unconscious, unintentional, and spontaneous, but this does not preclude the possibility of creating artificial *kuuki*" (Yamamoto, 1977, p. 21).

When the group is dominated by irrational, crazy, or desperate *kuuki*, it can cause serious results. Yamamoto (1977) provided many examples of this phenomenon. Upon being asked why they allowed many suicidal military operations, ex-admirals and ex-commander-in-chiefs were embarrassed and answered, "Now you can talk like that, but you don't know [the] *kuuki* at that time." Or, some said, "You were not there, so you don't know [the] *kuuki* at that meeting" (Yamamoto, 1977, pp. 7-19). Yamamoto (1977) claimed that it was the *kuuki* at that time more than anything else that dragged Japan into the war.

Historical Analyses on the Roles of Japanese
Newspapers in the 1930s and 1940s

Kakegawa (1972) and Ikei (1981, 1988) both analyzed prewar Japanese newspapers and severely criticized Japanese journalism before the war. Ikei (1981, 1988) emphasized that it was only after 1937, or 1934 at the earliest, that the government control of journalism became tight. Before

1937 the government control of journalism was loose. Despite that, major Japanese newspapers not only supported the military in the Manchurian Incident in 1931 but also criticized "weak" government leaders, and invented chauvinistic and sentimental stories to make the Japanese public more psychologically involved in the war.

According to Ikei (1981, p. 142) Japanese newspapers at that time were following the line established by Ruiko Kuroiwa, a famous journalist and manager of a major newspaper in the late nineteenth century. Kuroiwa was known for his aggressive and sensational articles and editorials. He once stated: "Newspapers should be antigovernment during peacetime, and chauvinistic during wartime." Kakegawa (1972) also concluded, after her thorough content analysis of Japanese newspapers from 1931 to 1941, that the Japanese press was heavily responsible for the expansion of the Manchurian Incident into the Pacific War (1941-45).

Toriumi (1973) compared the journalism immediately before and during the Russo-Japanese War in 1904-5 and that at the time of the Manchurian Incident. The newspapers that carried chauvinistic and sensational articles and editorials at the time of the Russo-Japanese War greatly expanded their circulation after the war, whereas those newspapers that were consistently critical of the war suffered a drastic reduction of their circulation. One of the major newspapers at that time which had been critical of the Russo-Japanese War, *Kokumin Shimbun*, was attacked by angry mobs, set fire to, and eventually went bankrupt. Toriumi (1973) suggested that those experiences at the time of the Russo-Japanese War might have caused the chauvinistic attitudes of the Japanese press at the time of the Manchurian Incident. For whatever reason, Japanese newspapers did something at the time of the Manchurian Incident which would eventually cause them problems.

According to Seiryu Hata, a former chief editorial writer of the *Assahi Shimbun* and a leading journalist with prewar experience:

> Newspapers at that time did not necessarily try to flatter those in power. Rather, they wrote to please readers. I may sound evasive, but *there certainly existed some kind of mechanism that aggravated the situation through subtle interactions* [between newspapers and the public]. . . . Readers were waiting for articles reporting the victorious Imperial Forces. Newspapers indulged themselves in competition for stronger patriotism and more victorious articles. Newspaper companies cooperated through the dispatch of comfort groups, call for patriotic songs, contribution campaigns for

more airplanes, and in various other ways. . . . The responsibility of newspapers is the second heaviest after the government. However, I disagree with the claim that "the general masses were victims." Newspapers form public opinion, but public opinion also influences newspapers. . . . The general masses are not like horses that can be tamed and trained in any way. ("*Senso to Shimbun,*" 1987)

The present writer agrees with this view. Prewar journalists received constant pressures from not only the police and the military, but also the fanatic public. Journalists were constantly threatened, their offices and printing plants were attacked, and some newspaper company executives were killed or seriously injured for being too liberal, Western, or un-Japanese. If their newspapers carried chauvinistic headlines and editorials, they sold well. While some newspapers agitated the masses, other newspaper companies which took the opposite position were attacked or threatened by angry mobs.

The theory that the imperialistic and totalitarian government mobilized the Japanese public for invasion and wars through a controlled mass media is too simplistic. Since their experiences before and during the Second World War were traumatic for the Japanese, Japanese social scientists must be able to elaborate on the "mechanism" pointed out above by Mr. Hata "that aggravated the situation through subtle interactions" between the mass media and the masses.

A Tripolar Model

As mentioned earlier, the tripolar model on social consensus formation proposed here is based on three kinds of studies by Japanese scholars. This model assumes that government leaders, journalists, and the general public have different interests, motivations, thought-patterns, and worldviews, as well as different levels of education and information. Therefore, their perception of and attitudes toward social issues often differ from each other. Let us see how they are different and how the differences are resolved.

Why Does Disagreement Occur between Government Policies and the Mass Media? While the government has a responsibility to plan and implement specific policies, the mass media have no such responsibility. In this sense, the mass media are similar to opposition parties. Their role and function is also similar to opposition parties, that is, to monitor government policies and the behavior of government officials. The relationship between the government and the mass media is also like that between performers or composers and critics. If critics always praise performers, the *raison d'être* of critics will be lost. Critics are expected to be sensitive and knowledgeable enough to be able to point out defects or mistakes of performers or composers that ordinary people do not notice. In a sense, they are expected to be always critical, even if they themselves cannot perform or compose as well as those they criticize. The author was amused to hear on the radio a music critic criticize (although with modest hesitation) Mozart's work. The mass media are somewhat similar to this music critic.

For whatever cause, the mass media are always looking for defects and mistakes in government policies and government officials, just like opposition parties and critics. Therefore, disagreements naturally occur between government policies and the mass media.

Why Does Disagreement Occur between Government Policies and Public Attitudes? The general public is very sensitive to private economic interests. As long as they are secure, it tends to leave policy-making to professional policy-makers, that is, politicians and bureaucrats. Also, it usually supports government policies when the issues are not familiar to them (despite opposition by the mass media and opposition parties). This means that the general public tends to "internalize" and thus support the worldview and policies expressed by political leaders as long as their private economic interests are secure, and especially when the issue is not familiar to them.

However, the public revolts against the government when they feel that their private economic interests are infringed upon by government policies, such as tax increases, construction of an airport near their homes, and so forth. Also, the public, together with the mass media, is usually very strict about corruption of government officials, as in money and sex scandals. The public revolts against the government when such scandals occur. As for issues familiar to the public, such as inflation, workers' strikes, and women's social roles, the public often shows independent judgment, often different from government policies or mass media contents.

Why Does Disagreement Occur between the Mass Media and the General Public? The mass media transmit not only their own views and opinions, but also those of government leaders. As mentioned earlier, when the issue is not familiar, the general public tends to "internalize" or incorporate views and opinions expressed by political leaders, leaving policy-making to politicians and bureaucrats. When the mass media are critical of the government under these circumstances, disagreement naturally occurs between the mass media and the general public which follows government leaders.

As mentioned earlier, however, the general public makes independent judgments in areas that it thinks it knows well. On issues like tax increases and government scandals, the mass media and the public agree, but in cases like women's social participation and workers' strikes, the mass media and the public often disagree. As for women's social participation, the Japanese public is far more conservative than the mass media. While the mass media tend to be sympathetic to workers' strikes, the public is usually more critical.

A major reason for these disagreements is that the journalists' education levels are much higher than the general public's average level of education. Moreover, journalists tend to be more idealistic, more rational, and have far more information, whereas the masses are less idealistic, less rational, and have less information. While journalists analyze the present situation based on abundant information, make rational judgments, and make suggestions for the future, the masses are more concerned with private economic profits and security and their judgments are often based upon naive emotions. As far as the educational level and the amount of information are concerned, journalists are more similar to government leaders than to the masses. Therefore, they sometimes agree with each other and try to change the general public, which tends to stick to traditional ways of thinking and doing things and existing privileges. "Democratization" at all levels after the Second World War, liberalization of the domestic market, and women's social participation may be examples in Japan, while the fight against racism and discrimination may be examples in North America and Western Europe.

How Are These Disagreements Resolved? Ito (1990) argued that when one of the the components disagree with the other two, it receives strong pressure for compliance from the other two, leading to its gradual concession and change. Japanese prewar experiences indicate that it was the mass media, public attitudes, and a part of the government such as the military that first created the chauvinistic *kuuki*. Due to international and domestic political and economic situations at that time, the chauvinistic *kuuki* was reinforced and helped militarists take over the government.

Many documents and records indicate that Emperor Hirohito consistently had wanted peace. As early as the time of the Manchurian

Incident, he was unhappy about the actions of his military. Although Emperor Hirohito expressed his wishes and "grave concerns" on many occasions, his expressions were too indirect, roundabout, ambiguous, weak, and were made more ambiguous by court bureaucrats around him. Court bureaucrats often advised the emperor not to be too direct or straightforward, not necessarily because they were militarists but because they wanted to protect the emperor and the imperial system. It means that even the emperor could not resist the *kuuki* at that time.

In subjects where these three components all agree, such as the imperial system or the Northern territories issue between Japan and Russia, the pressure of *kuuki* is extremely strong. It has become almost a taboo in Japan to criticize the imperial system in public, although there is no law to restrict or punish it. People used to criticize the imperial system more openly soon after the war and until around the mid-1960s.

When the three components are divided into one versus two, the majority opinions and attitudes may become *kuuki* that functions as a social pressure for compliance. Thus, the minority receives pressure for compliance through voting, demonstrations, and verbal attacks, protests and criticisms not only through the major mass media, but also through all kinds of communication channels including small magazines and books, letters, and telephone calls. Under these circumstances, the minority cannot help but concede to the majority, and a national consensus is gradually formed.

When Tsujimura (1976a, 1981) and Ito (1990) discussed agreements and disagreements among the mass media, government policies, and public attitudes, they ignored disagreement *within* each component. This, however, is too simplistic. There always exist minority opinions in public opinion survey results, disagreements among different mass media, different "factions" in the ruling party, or different top government leaders. When each component has a relatively large internal opposition, the power of *kuuki* cannot become strong even if two of the three components agree.

In other words, the power of *kuuki* is influenced by the degree of homogeneity within each component, that is, the mass media, the government, and the public. When more than two-thirds of the Diet members and more than two-thirds of the mass media eagerly support and propagate some idea, intense *kuuki* is created, functioning as a strong pressure on the third component, public attitudes. Similarly, when more than two-thirds of respondents in public opinion polls and more than two-thirds of Diet members (or more than two-thirds of the major mass media) support and propagate some idea, intense *kuuki* is created, functioning as a strong pressure on the third component, the mass media (or the government). However, when the difference between proponents and opponents within each component is small, the power of *kuuki* becomes weaker.

The reason for compliance with *kuuki* is not only psychological but also practical and reasonable. Resistance to *kuuki* can cause not only embarrassment or psychological discomfort but also actual practical damage such as defeat in election, loss of newspaper circulation, verbal or physical attack. One of the reasons why civilian leaders in the prewar Japanese government failed to control the military was the threat of terrorism. If the mass media and the public had supported civilian leaders and been more critical of the military and terrorism, civilian leaders would have been able to better control the military.

CASE STUDIES

Revision of the Consumption Tax Law

Government. The Japanese tax system traditionally had been dependent upon direct tax (e.g., income tax) and indirect tax had not existed until 1988 when the government introduced the consumption tax. The government, however, had always wanted to introduce large-scale indirect tax as practiced in many other countries in order to increase revenues and diversify tax sources. The first attempt to introduce a large-scale indirect tax was made in 1948 under the Ashida government. This government, however, was defeated soundly in the general election in the following year, and the attempt was canceled.

The second attempt was made years later in 1979 by the Ohira government. Prime Minister Ohira attempted to introduce the "general consumption tax," but this was also canceled due to the strong opposition movements by the masses especially merchants and small businesses and the defeat in the following general election for the House of Representatives (lower house).

The third attempt was made by the Nakasone government in 1987. In February 1987 Prime Minister Nakasone proposed a tax package including the introduction of a new type of indirect tax called "sales tax" and a reduction in income tax. This third attempt, however, also provoked strong opposition not only from opposition parties but also from department stores, supermarkets, medium- and small-scale industries, and Diet members representing the interests of these industries.

Prime Minister Takeshita, who succeeded Prime Minister Nakasone in November 1987, was determined to introduce the general consumption tax because it was anticipated that as the Japanese population became aged, pension, medical, and welfare expenditures would steadily increase whereas the revenues from income tax would decrease. Thus, a package of six bills to introduce a new consumption law was proposed in September of the same year. This package included reduction in income, corporate, and inheritance taxes and the introduction of a new tax on capital gains such as profits from stock dealings. Opposition parties strongly opposed these bills, and the ruling party, the Liberal Democratic Party (LDP), had to resort to *kyokoh saiketsu* (forced vote or vote by force)[2] in some Diet committees. In the process, Finance Minister Miyazawa resigned on 9 December, assuming responsibility for the *kyokoh saiketsu*. Thus, the National Diet passed the unpopular consumption tax law on 24 December 1988 as a "Christmas present" to the Japanese nation, and the law became effective on 1 April 1989.

Mass Media. The mass media had a good understanding of the need for new revenue sources to cover increasing expenditures for pension and welfare in an aging society. As *Asahi Shimbun* (1989) stated in its editorial, "We are not against the idea of taxing consumption, but . . ." (*Shohizei wa Sakkyu na min ooshi o,*" 1989). Then, it criticized the process by which it was decided, the lack of discussions on the bill, and many detailed shortcomings in the law. The *Nihon Keizai Shimbun* (1989) criticized opposition parties stating that if they "demand the withdrawal of the bill, they should propose alternative measures for new revenue sources" ("*Shin zeisei no fubi wo tadashi wo mezase,*" 1989). Most other mass media took similar positions and carried similar editorials. However, as they report opposition movements on the mass level and see public opinion survey results, they seemed to be influenced by the "anti-tax-increase *kuuki* among the public."

This irritated government leaders because they thought that the mass media understood the need for a new tax on the rational level but were influenced by the masses on the emotional level. The minister of posts and telecommunications, for example, criticized the Japan Broadcasting Corporation (NHK) for carrying programs emphasizing negative aspects of the new law and not publicizing the background of the law or the reduction of income tax enacted at the same time. This was taken as government intervention in mass media and criticized by the mass media, and the Minister withdrew this statement (*Hatsugen keisotsu datta,* 1989; *NHK hohdo hihan,* 1989).

Public Attitudes. According to the public opinion survey conducted two months after the introduction of the new law, 90 percent of respondents answered that they had complaints (53 percent "strong complaints" and 37 percent "some complaints") about the consumption tax law. Major complaints were (multiple answer): "Even daily necessities are taxed" (56 percent) and "many shops are raising prices taking advantage of the tax" (53 percent). As a result, the percentage of non-support of the government rose to as high as 84 percent.

Unfortunately for the government, the "Recruit" bribery scandal[3] was revealed in June 1988, and two leading members of the ruling party were arrested and indicted in early 1989. As a result, Prime Minister Takeshita resigned on 3 June 1989 and was replaced by Mr. Uno. Then, only a week later, Mr. Uno's "geisha girl scandal" was revealed. At the election for the Tokyo Metropolitan Congress held on 4 July, the number of seats held by the Liberal Democratic Party decreased from 63 to 43 and the number of seats held by the Japan Socialist Party tripled from 12 to 36.

In the same months, there was a national election for the House of Councillors (upper house), and the number of seats held by the Liberal Democratic Party drastically decreased from 142 to 109, losing them their majority. On the other hand, the largest opposition party, the Japan Socialist Party, increased its number of seats from 42 to 66. Thus, the opposition parties altogether won a majority in the upper house. The consumption tax law was the most important issue that affected voters' decisions.

According to the public opinion survey conducted after the upper house election, 60 percent of the respondents thought that the most important reason for LDP's defeat was the consumption tax and the most important reason for the victory of the Japan Socialist Party (JSP) was its promise to abolish the consumption law.

Thus, Prime Minister Uno announced his decision to resign immediately after the election, assuming responsibility for the defeat, and Prime Minister Kaifu, who succeeded Uno on 10 August, promised to revise the consumption tax law. The basic policies for the revision of the consumption law were announced by the government on 1 December of the same year.

Discussion. Tax increase is one of the easiest subjects for the general public to understand. Even if they do not understand the complicated tax system, they understand the meaning of the introduction of a new tax. The "anti-tax-increase *kuuki*" developed mainly among the general masses. As mentioned before, one of the criteria for the existence of *kuuki* is that those who are against it feel that it is difficult to express their opinions in public (Yamamoto, 1977, pp. 7-19). In this case, most LDP candidates avoided the subject in their campaigns for the elections held soon after the bill was passed. In local level elections, many LDP candidates claimed that they "personally opposed" the bill.

As mentioned earlier, the mass media understood the need for finding new revenue sources for the "aging society." They, therefore, could not be as "irresponsible" or "emotional" as the general public or some opposition parties who tried to take advantage of the "anti-tax-increase *kuuki*." Apparently, however, the mass media were affected by the "anti-tax-increase *kuuki*" on the mass level especially after the upper house election in July 1989, and became gradually more critical of the new tax. But most of the mass media, except for the *Asahi Shimbun*, which claimed the need for *denaoshi* (return to the starting point), could not be as extreme as the Japan Socialist Party (JSP) or the Japan Communist Party (JCP), which demanded the abolishment of the consumption tax law. Instead, most of them suggested that the law be amended. Thus, Prime Minister Kaifu promised in August 1989 to amend the consumption tax law. Japan had three prime ministers within eleven months from 24 December 1988, when the consumption tax law passed the Diet, to 1 December 1989, when the amendment of the consumption tax law was announced formally.

The content of amendment to the tax law was not drastic. The government only exempted taxation on several items about which public complaints were the strongest. The "anti-tax-increase *kuuki*" certainly existed, as shown in many public opinion surveys, and the fact that many LDP candidates claimed in their election campaigns that they were "personally against" the new tax. Unlike the prewar Japanese case discussed above, the mass media were not responsible for the creation of this *kuuki*. Although affected by the *kuuki*, the mass media as a whole seemed to have functioned as moderators between the government and the masses in this case.

Withdrawal of the United Nations Peace Cooperation Bill

Government. The so-called Gulf crisis broke out with the Iraqi invasion of Kuwait on 2 August 1990. Considering Japan's heavy dependence on Middle Eastern oil, huge economic profit from that area, and Japan's economic strength and military capabilities, it was inconceivable that Japan could avoid involvement. On 14 August, President Bush of the United States telephoned Prime Minister Kaifu asking for Japan's contribution to the solution of the crisis. The government already had determined that Japan would make economic contributions, but the question was what else should and could be done.

The dispatch of Japan's military troops to troubled areas has been a delicate issue since the Korean War in 1950. Because of bitter experiences before and during the Second World War, Japan soon after the war completely rewrote the prewar constitution and enacted in November 1946 a highly idealistic constitution under the guidance of the American occupation authority. For example, Article 9 of the present Japanese Constitution proclaims:

> Aspiring sincerely to an international peace based on justice and order, the Japanese people forever renounce war as a sovereign right of the nation and the threat or use of force as means of settling international disputes.
>
> In order to accomplish the aim of the preceding paragraph, land, sea, and air forces, as well as other war potential, will never be maintained. The right of belligerency of the state will not be recognized.

This idealism was challenged only four years later by the outbreak of the Korean War (1950-53). Faced with military threats from Communist forces, the Japanese government and the American occupation authority decided that Japan should build armed forces for pure self defense against direct attack by other nations. This idealistic constitution, however, was extremely difficult to amend. The support of more than two-thirds of Diet members *and* more than half of voters in referendum are required to make any change in the constitution. It has been impossible for any government in postwar Japan to overcome these two strict conditions.

The Police Reserve, the forerunner of the present Self-Defense Force, was thus built in 1950 without amending the constitution. The present Self Defense Force, therefore, has been opposed by leftist opposition parties such as the Japan Socialist Party and the Japan Communist Party as unconstitutional. Although public opinion surveys have indicated repeatedly that the general public acknowledged the necessity of the Self-Defense Force (see, for example, Nishihira, 1987, pp. 265-98; Public Opinion Research Institute, NHK, 1975, pp. 174-77), the Self Defense Force has suffered from low prestige and hostility occasionally shown by leftists and opposition party supporters.

In addition to the sensitive attitudes of the Japanese public, concerns of neighboring Asian countries complicate this issue. Although China, Korea, and Southeast Asian countries have approved of Japan's military capabilities necessary for pure self-defense against direct attack from outside, they occasionally cautioned not to expand it beyond the necessary minimum level. Considering the scale of Japan's gross national product (GNP), which exceeds the sum of those of all other East and Southeast Asian countries, Japanese military capability is a matter about which they cannot help having a grave concern.

During the Korean War, several Japanese ships belonging to the Maritime Safety Agency were dispatched to the Korean coast for mine sweeping. This, however, was an exception because Japan was still under occupation by the Allied Forces at that time and some of the mines on the Korean coast had been laid by the Japanese Navy during the Second World War. Since Japan's independence was restored in 1952, there has been no actual dispatch of Japanese military troops outside of Japan.

The dispatch of Japan's Self Defense Forces to troubled waters, however, had been considered several times during the period between the Korean War in 1950 and the Gulf crisis in 1990. The most recent case was the plan to dispatch mine sweepers to the Persian Gulf to secure marine routes for oil tankers during the Iran-Iraq War (1980-88). This plan, however, did not materialize due to strong oppositions from not only opposition parties, but even some leaders of the ruling party (LDP).

Discussions also have occurred regarding whether Japan could participate in the United Nations Forces organized based on the United Nations Charter, Chapter 7, Article 43. Japanese cabinets traditionally have taken the view that the activities of the Japanese Self-Defense Force is limited to pure self-defense against direct attack and participation in the UN Forces is not allowed in the light of Article 9 of the Constitution.

Thus, Prime Minister Kaifu announced on 29 August an intention to make a new law tentatively entitled "United Nations Peace Cooperation Law" to enable Japan's prompt aid and peacekeeping activities outside Japan at times of international crisis. It was emphasized at the same that the purpose of this law was to assist the United Nations' peacekeeping activities and did not contradict the spirit of the Japanese Constitution.

On 26 September, Prime Minister Kaifu presented an outline of the "United Nations Peace Cooperation Law" to LDP leaders and obtained their approval. According to this outline, the "United Nations Peace

Cooperation Corps" was to be created under the Prime Minister's Office. Members of the corps were to be recruited from government employees as well as private volunteers. It was made clear that the purpose of this law was to assist United Nations' peacekeeping activities such as transportation, communication, supply, medical and public health activities, and surveillance, and the corps would not be engaged in coercion by force or use of force. However, the relationship between this new "cooperation corps" and the Self Defense Force, the most delicate point of this bill, was not clear. It was understood that "government employees" to be recruited for this "cooperation corps" could include officers and soldiers in the Self Defense Force. In fact, President Bush of the United States expressed his expectation on 29 September that the dispatch of Japan's Self Defense Force would become possible by this law.

Answering questions at a press conference held on 8 October, Prime Minister Kaifu stated, "When we use vessels and aircraft owned by the Self-Defense Force (SDF) for the peace cooperation we must ask SDF personnel to operate them otherwise effective use of them is impossible" ("*Raigetsu kara nitcho seifukan kohsho*," 1990). In the revised outline proposed to LDP leaders on 8 October, it was made clear that the head of the "peace cooperation corps" would be the prime minister and the corps would be placed under strict civilian control. At the same time, it was suggested that the head of the corps could request outside organizations including the Self-Defense Force to provide the corps with their equipment and personnel.

The bill was approved at the cabinet meeting and was sent to the National Diet on 16 October. Major points of discussion at the Diet were: (1) Whether the dispatch of SDF equipment and employees under the name of "cooperation with the United Nations" is justifiable in the light of Article 9 of the Japanese Constitution; (2) to what extent and under what conditions the carriage and use of weapons are allowed; (3) how to guarantee that this attempt will not eventually lead to unrestricted expansion of military commitment outside Japan; and (4) how to cope with the concern in neighboring Asian countries.

The most difficult was the first question. As mentioned earlier, Japanese cabinets traditionally have taken the view that the SDF's participation in the UN Forces was unconstitutional. Then, opposition parties asked, what was the difference between "participation" and "cooperation"? According to the foreign minister's reply to the Diet on 26 October, "cooperation" is more independent and autonomous than "participation" because "cooperation corps" will voluntarily "cooperate," but will not automatically obey orders from UN Force commanders.

Regarding this point, Prime Minister Kaifu already had stated at the press conference held on 15 October that although postwar Japan traditionally had prohibited the Self Defense Force from participating in the UN Forces, it should be allowed in the future. This meant a new interpretation of article 9 of the Constitution and caused negative reactions even among LDP Diet members and government bureaucrats. For example, the Director of the Bureau of Legal Affairs in the Prime Minister's Office stated in his remarks to the Diet on 24 October that the Self-Defense Force's participation in the UN Forces is questionable in the light of the Constitution, contradicting Prime Minister Kaifu's new interpretation of the Constitution.

The Asahi Shimbun sent questionnaires to all 510 members of the House of Representatives (lower house) and obtained responses from 397. According to this survey, 11 percent of LDP members opposed the bill and none of opposition party members supported it (*"Jimin ka huha baratsuku san'i,"* 1990). In addition, public attitudes were strongly unfavorable to the bill and the mass media were divided. Thus, Prime Minister Kaifu and other LDP leaders decided to give up. They decided on 5 November to drop the bill, to the great disappointment of President Bush and the American leadership.

Mass Media. Four Japanese major newspapers, that is, the *Yomiuri Shimbun* (Approximately 10 million circulation), the *Asahi Shimbun* (approximately 8 million circulation), the *Mainichi Shimbun* (approximately 4 million circulation), and the *Nihon Keizai Shimbun* (approximately 2 million circulation) were investigated. While the *Asahi* and the *Mainichi* are close to leftist opposition parties such as the Japan Socialist Part and the Japan Communist Party, the *Nihon Keizai Shimbun* and the *Yomiuri* are close to the conservative ruling party (LDP). This difference clearly appeared in their attitudes toward the "United Nations Peace Cooperation Bill."

In the special article dated 26 August featuring Japan's contribution to the Gulf crisis, the *Asahi* expressed concern with LDP's inclination to dispatch the Self-Defense Force. In the editorial of 28 September, the *Asahi* maintained that Prime Minister Kaifu's attempt to dispatch a part of the Self-Defense Force contradicted LDP governments' traditional basic policy according to which an amendment of the Self-Defense Force Law was necessary to dispatch the Self-Defense Force overseas. The editorial also argued that even if the dispatch is limited to noncombat personnel at first, it may pave the way for the dispatch of combat troops in the future.

The *Asahi* created a special column entitled "Military Dispatch Overseas" on 17 October featuring opposition movements all over Japan and introducing grass-roots level opinions. It also encouraged readers to send their opinions to the editor by letter, telephone, or fax. Although this special feature ended on 31 October, the *Asahi* created another special column entitled "Choice After 45 Years" on 1 November to carry letters from the general public opposing the bill. In the editorial dated 29 October, the *Asahi* criticized Prime Minister Kaifu's foreign policy for paying too much attention to the United States and ignoring the serious concerns held by neighboring Asian countries regarding this issue. The *Asahi's* "Choice After 45 Years" continued until 10 November, five days after Prime Minister Kaifu's decision to drop the bill.

The *Mainichi's* attitudes were not as clear as the *Asahi's*, especially during the early stages. The *Mainichi's* editorial dated 26 August was ambivalent and ambiguous; it could not tolerate Saddam Hussein, but wanted to respect the pacifism of the Japanese Constitution. The *Mainichi*, however, seemed to gradually become influenced by the results of public opinion polls. In its editorial of 17 October, the *Mainichi* emphasized the necessity to pay more attention to *min'i* (the public will) regarding this matter. It also claimed in its editorial of 24 October that the "United Nations Peace Cooperation Bill" should be withdrawn because more than half of respondents in many public opinion surveys opposed the bill and the percentage of support for the Kaifu government had been declining ("*Kahansu 'hantai' wo chokushi,*" 1990).

On the other hand, the *Yomiuri*, which has the largest circulation (approximately 10 million) not only clearly supported the government, but also criticized the attitudes of the other mass media. It claimed that the military dispatch to cooperate with the United Nation's peacekeeping activities was justified despite Article 9 of the Constitution. In its editorial of 27 October, it claimed: "Japan can enjoy enormous profit from the restoration of order in he Gulf area. That is why the world is watching Japan's response. Japan, therefore, should contribute to the multinational force as much as possible" ("*Takokusekigen eno kyohryoku ga heiwa wo mamoru,*" 1990).

The logic used by the *Yomiuri* is easy to understand for non-Japanese, especially Westerners. The Japanese public, however, were not so simple and naive as to fully accept this logic, chiefly due to their bitter experiences before and during the Second World War. The stance of the *Nihon Keizai Shimbun* was between the *Asahi* and the *Yomiuri*. In its editorial, it emphasized the importance of international cooperation but was cautious about the reinterpretation of the Constitution (*"Jieiken no kem pou kaishaku de min'i wo toe,"* 1990).

Public Attitudes. As soon as Prime Minister Kaifu expressed his intention to enact the United Nations Peace Cooperation Bill on 29 August 1990, some Japanese strongly reacted against it. They were members of the older generation rather than younger people, and women rather than men. As mentioned in one of the previous sections, the Second World War was traumatic for the Japanese. The idea of being involved in the war outside Japan reminded them of their experiences in the past and they sent hundreds of thousands of letters to newspaper companies describing their devastating experiences.

Not many of the letters seriously discussed the situation in the Middle East. Their typical logic was that they had terrible experiences during the Second World War so they didn't want their children and grandchildren to have the same experiences. The government's plan was to send a part of the Self-Defense Force for noncombat missions such as transportation, supply, communication, and medical and public health activities. The idea of sending noncombat troops to the Middle East under the aegis of the United Nations had little to do with their experiences in Manchuria during the Second World War. For those who had really miserable experiences in the past, however, such "small differences" did not matter. The idea of "being involved in a war outside Japan" horrified them.

According to the public opinion survey conducted by the Prime Minister's Office in 1989 before the Gulf crisis, 46.5 percent of respondents opposed the Self Defense Force's "participating in" the UN Force. After the outbreak of the Gulf crisis, however, the percentage of those objecting increased to 53 percent in the *Yomiuri* survey and 58 percent in the *Asahi* survey. The outbreak of the war may have made the public more serious and negative, and the reactions of the older generation mentioned above may have affected younger generations. Technical differences between these three surveys such as those in the nuance of question and the number of alternatives may also be a factor. There were large differences between men and women in reactions to these answers. The percentage of those who opposed the idea of dispatching the SDF to overseas was always much higher among women than men.

The trend of support for the government also indicates the unpopularity of the "United Nations Peace Cooperation Bill." According to monthly surveys conducted by the Yomiuri Shimbun Company, supporters of the Kaifu government accounted for 60 percent in July and 62.5 percent in August, but the figure decreased in September and October, reaching 48.3 percent in November. Supporters of the ruling party (LDP) decreased similarly during this period. On the other hand, the percentage of nonsupporters increased from 22.8% in July and 21.8% in August to 35.8% in November. Although the popularity of the Kaifu government did not recover after the withdrawal of the bill, that of the LDP did.

Discussion. The Japanese who lost their families, friends, and relatives during World War II felt that they were deceived or misled by prewar leaders. Chiefly due to this strong resentment, the "antiwar and antimilitary *kuuki*" has always existed among the masses in postwar Japan. The Self Defense Force (SDF) has suffered from low prestige and even occasional hostility from leftists and opposition party supporters. Negative attitudes toward the SDF is usually referred to as *jieitai arerugi* (SDF allergy). Even some top government leaders, including Prime Minister Kaifu, pointed out that they had an "SDF allergy."

Generally speaking, the general public tends to feel "unfamiliar" with defense and foreign policies. In fact, the percentage of ambiguous answers such as "it depends" and "don't know" exceeded 30 percent in surveys regarding the dispatch of the Self Defense Force overseas conducted before the Gulf War and in the early stages of the war. The continuance of the war in the Middle East, however, made this problem more familiar and realistic to the masses. Accordingly, the percentage of ambiguous answers decreased. At the same time, the experiences during the Second World War were remembered, especially among the older generation and women.

Some mass media, for example, the *Asahi Shimbun*, that supported the "antiwar and antimilitary *kuuki*" in the 1950s and 1960s created special columns and departments to carry memories from the Second World War and conducted an "anti-UN Peace Cooperation Bill" campaign. This combination together with the fear of involvement in the ongoing war created the "anti-UN Peace Cooperation Bill *kuuki*."

As mentioned earlier, the mass media were divided because two major national newspapers, the *Yomiuri Shimbun* and the *Sankei Shimbun*, supported the bill. On the other hand, the ruling party, the LDP, also was divided because some LDP members (probably those who had bitter experiences or memories from the Second World War) were reluctant to pass the bill as indicated in the *Asahi's* survey of Diet members. After all, the government had to give up the enactment of the bill due to the *kuuki* based on the memories of miserable experiences during the Second World War and the fear of being involved in the ongoing war.

SUMMARY AND CONCLUSIONS

This chapter critically overviewed bipolar models on mass-media effects and proposed a tripolar model in which the government, the mass media, and public attitudes interact each other to reach a consensus. Two case studies were provided to show how the tripolar model on consensus formation actually work in the Japanese situation. In the case of the tax increase case, the mass media had a good understanding of the government policy, but were influenced by the "anti-tax-increase *kuuki*" among the masses. Ultimately, the mass media functioned like a moderator and brought a concession from the government (an amendment) and the masses (acceptance of the amended law).

The pattern of *kuuki* in the case of the United Nations Peace Cooperation Bill was more complicated. The mass media were divided between proponents (the *Yomiuri* and the *Sankei*) and enthusiastic opponents (the *Asahi* and the *Mainichi*). Public opinion was generally critical of the bill. Some ruling party Diet members were reluctant to pass the bill. Memories of miserable experiences during the Second World War and the fear of being involved in the ongoing war intensified the "antiwar *kuuki*" among the masses.

The *Asahi Shimbun* obviously reinforced this antiwar *kuuki* by creating special columns and departments devoted to the reports of mass movements and letters to the editor opposing the UN Peace Cooperation Bill. The government leaders had to withdraw the bill because they judged that the *kuuki* against the UN Peace Cooperation Bill was too strong at that time.

These cases challenge some bipolar models that assume the manipulation of the masses by the government through the control of the mass media. These case studies, however, need to be further refined. For example, more rigorous methods should used be to content analyze the mass media. Also, more case studies are needed to clarify the entire picture of this model.

The tripolar model proposed in this chapter cannot be applied to the countries where the mass media are placed under strict govern-

ment control or where mass media are all small and are not independent of the masses, but it should be applicable to most modern democracies.

NOTES

I would like to thank William B. Gudykunst for helpful comments on an earlier
draft and Alex Edelstein, Denis McQuail, and David Weaver for helpful comments on my recent oral presentations on this subject.

1. Since around the time of the Manchurian Incident of 1931, the Japanese
government and military began to feel a strong need for international as well as
domestic propaganda. A new government organization for propaganda, the
Information Commission, was jointly established in 1931 by the Army, Navy
and Ministry of Foreign Affairs. This commission later promoted studies of
propaganda and psychological warfare. For example, in the late 1930s this
department translated and published fifteen books on propaganda and psychological warfare previously published in the West (see Ikeda, 1981, for
details). Major tasks of this department were to assess accurately the effects of
psychological warfare and create effective programs.

2. "*Kyokoh saiketsu*," forced vote or vote by force, refers to the vote at the
National Diet under opposition party members' strong verbal or physical resistance. "Verbal or physical resistance" includes rushing to the chairperson and
shouting at him or her, beating chairperson's desk, physical intervention by
guards, pushing, kicking, etc.

3. "Recruit" is a relatively young information providing company that
grew large in a short period of time. In the process of its expansion, the company presented its stock to politicians, government bureaucrats and executives
of the Nippon Telegraph and Telephone Corporation (NTT). Twenty people
including two LDP (the ruling party) Diet members were arrested and indicted
in 1989.

REFERENCES

Aono, S. (1926, July). *Musan kaikyu no shimbun ni tsuite* (Newspapers for the
    proletariat), *Kaiho*, pp. 73-77.

Arai, N. (1989). *Media no Showa shi* (Showa history of the media). Tokyo:
    Iwanami Shoten.

Bryce, J. (1888-89). *The American commonwealth* (2 vols.). London: Macmillan.

Brucker, H. (1949). *Freedom of information.* New York: MacMillan.

Cooley, C. (1956). *Social organization.* Glencoe, IL: The Free Press.

DeFleur, M. S., & Ball-Rokeach, S. (1966). *Theories of mass communication* (3rd ed.). New York: David McKay.

Doob, L. W. (1935). *Propaganda: Its psychology and technique.* New York: Henry Holt.

Edelstein, A. S. (1973). An alternative approach to the study of source effects in mass communication. *Studies of Communication, 9,* 5-29.

Edelstein, A. S., Ito, Y., & Kepplinger, H. M. (1989). *Communication & culture: A comparative approach.* White Plains, NY: Longman.

Fujitake, A. (1967). Tokyo olympics and the Japanese public. *Studies of Broadcasting, 5,* 49-109.

Fujitake, A. (1968). *Gendai masu komyunikeishon no riron* (Contemporary mass communication theories). Tokyo: Nihon Hoso Shuppan Kyokai.

Fujitake, A., & Akiyama, T. (1967). *Tokyo orinpikku* (Tokyo olympics). Tokyo: NHK Hoso Yoron Chosa-jo.

Fukumoto, K. (1926). *Zen musan kaikyu no tame no shimbun* (Newspaper for the entire proletariat), *Marukusu Shugi,* 102-112.

"Funso kanyo" ni teikohkan: Kokuren kyouroku hoan denwa chosa (Resistance against "involvement in the conflict": Telephone survey on the UN Cooperation Bill). (1990, November 6). *Asahi Shimbun,* pp. 2-3.

Garnham, N. (1990). *Capitalism and communication: Global culture and the economics of information.* London: Sage.

Gerbner, G., & Gross, L. (1976). Living with television: The violence profile. *Journal of Communication, 26*(2), 173-199.

Gerbner, G., Gross, L., Jackson-Beeck, M., Jeffries-Fox, S., & Signorielli, N. (1978). Cultural indicators: Violence profile No. 9. *Journal of Communication, 28*(3), 176-207.

Gerbner, G., Gross, L., Signorielli, N., & Morgan, M. (1980). Aging with television: Images on television drama and conceptions of social reality. *Journal of Communication, 30*(1), 37-47.

Gerbner, G., Gross, L., Morgan, M., & Signorielli, N. (1980). The "mainstreaming" of America: Violence profile No. 11. *Journal of Communication, 30*(4), 10-29.

Gitlin, T. (1980). *The whole world is watching: Mass media in the making and unmaking of the new left.* Berkeley, CA: University of California Press.

Hall, S. (1982). The rediscovery of "ideology": Return of the repressed in media studies. In M. Gurevitch, T. Bennett, J. Curran & J. Woollacott (Eds.), *Culture, society and the media.* London: Methuen.

Hatsugen seisotsu datta (The remarks were careless). (1989, April 7, evening ed.). *Asahi Shimbun.*

Hayasaka, J. (1926). *Shakai soshiki to shimbun zasshi* (Social organizations and the press), *Shakai Mondai Kohza, 6*(15), 1-48.

Hirose, H. (1990). The development of discussions on journalism in postwar Japan, *Media, Culture & Society, 12*(4), 465-476.

Hume, D. (1963/1741). *Essays moral, political, & literary.* London: Oxford University Press.

Ikei, M. (1981). *1930-nendai no masumedia: Manshu jihen eno taio o chuhshin to shite* (Mass media in the 1930s: Focussing on their reports on the Manchurian Incident). In K. Miwa (Ed.), *Saiko: Taiheiyo senso zenya: Nihon no 1930-nendai ron to she.* Tokyo: Sohseiki.

Ikei, M. (1988). *Nitchu senso to Nihon no masumedia no taiou* (The Sino-Japanese war and the Japanese mass media). *Keio Gijuku Daigaku Hogaku Kenkyu, 61*(1), 41-65.

Inaba, M. (1987). *Masukomi no sogo riron* (Comprehensive theories on mass communication). Tokyo: Sohfu-sha.

Ito, Y. (1981). The *"johoka shakai"* approach to the study of communication in Japan. In G. C. Wilhoit, & H. de Bock (Eds.), *Mass communication review yearbook* (Vol. 2). Beverly Hills, CA: Sage.

Ito, Y. (1987). Mass communication research in Japan: History and present state. In M. L. McLaughlin (Ed.), *Communication yearbook 10.* Beverly Hills, CA: Sage.

Ito, Y. (1990). Mass communication theories from a Japanese perspective. *Media, Culture and Society, 12*(4), 423-464.

Ito, Y. (1991). *Johoka* as a driving force of social change, *Keio Communication Review, 12,* 33-58.

Jieiken no kempou kaishaku de min'i wo toe (Let the public judge regarding the interpretation of the self-defense right in the Constitution). (1990, October 17). *Nihon Keizai Shimbun,* p. 2.

Jimin kakuha baratsuku san'i (LDP factions differ in the degree of support). (1990, November 1). *Asahi Shimbun,* pp. 2-3.

Kadoya, H. (1929). *Puroretaria shimbun-ron* (Proletariat Journalism). In Seiji Hihan-sha (Ed.), *Marukusushugi Kohza* (Vol. 1). Tokyo: Marukusushugi Kohza Kanko-kai.

Kahansu "hantai" wo chokushi seyo (Face that more than half "oppose"). (1990, October 24). *Mainichi Shimbun*, p. 2.

Kakegawa, T. (1972). *Masu media no tohsei to taibei roncho* (Control of mass media and editorials on the United States). In C. Hosoya, M. Saito, S. Imai, & M. Royama (Eds.), *Nichibei kankei-shi 4: Kaisen ni itaru 10 nen (1931-1941)*. Tokyo: Tokyo Daigaku Shuppankai.

Katz, E. (1980). Media events: The sense of occasion. *Studies in Visual Communication, 6*, 84-89.

Katz, E. (1983). Publicity and pluralistic ignorance: Notes on "the spiral of silence." In E. Wartella, D. C. Whitney, & S. Windahl (Eds.), *Mass communication review yearbook* (Vol. 4). Beverly Hills, CA: Sage.

Katz, E., Gurevitch, M. & Haas, H. (1973). On the use of the mass media for important things. *Studies of Communication, 9*, 31-65.

Katz, E., Dayan, D., & Motyl P. (1981). In defense of media events. In R. W. Haigh, G. Gerbner, & R. B. Byrne (Eds.), *Communications in the twenty-first century*. New York: John Wiley.

Katz, E., & Lazarsfeld, P. F. (1955). *Personal influence*. Glencoe, IL: The Free Press.

Kuroda, H. (1966). *Showa genronshi eno shohgen* (A testimony on the history of journalism during the Showa period). Tokyo: Kohbun-do.

Lang, K., & Lang, G. E. (1960). The unique perspective of television and its effect: A pilot study. In W. Schramm (Ed.), *Mass communications*. Urbana, IL: University of Illinois Press.

Lasswell, H. (1927). *Propaganda technique in the world war*. New York: Knopf.

Lerner, D. (Ed.). (1951). *Propaganda in war and crisis: Materials for American policy*. New York: G. W. Stewart.

Lippmann, W. (1927/1919). *Liberty and the news*. New York: Macmillan.

Lippmann, W. (1922). *Public opinion*. New York: Harcourt.

McCombs, M. E., & Shaw, D. (1972). The agenda-setting function of mass media. *Public Opinion Quarterly, 36*(2), 176-187.

McCombs, M. E. (1976). Elaborating the agenda-setting influence of mass communication. *The Bulletin of the Institute for Communications Research, Keio University, 7*, 15-35.

Merton, R. (1946). *The social psychology of a war bond drive.* New York: Harper.

Merton, R. (1957/1949). *Social theory and social structure: Toward the codification of theory and research.* Glencoe, IL: The Free Press.

Mills, C. W. (1956). *The power elite.* Oxford University Press.

Nakano, O. *Shimbun to yoron* (Newspapers and public opinion). In M. Inaba & N. Arai (Eds.), *Shimbungaku.* Tokyo: Nihon Hyoron-sha.

Nishida, T. (1991, March). *Topics of conversation in initial interactions in Japan and the United States.* Paper presented at "Communication in Japan and the United States" held at the California State University, Fullerton.

Nishihira, S. (1987). *Yoron chohsa ni yoru dohjidaishi* (Chronology by public opinion polls). Tokyo: Brehn Shuppan.

NHK *hodo hihan* (Criticism of NHK news reports). (1989, April 4, evening ed.). *Asahi Shimbun.*

Noelle-Neumann, E. (1973). Return to the concept of powerful mass media. *Studies of Broadcasting, 9,* 67-112.

Noelle-Neumann, E. (1984). *The spiral of silence: Public opinion—our social skin.* Chicago, IL: The University of Chicago Press.

Noelle-Neumann, E. (1989). Advances in spiral of silence research. *Keio Communication Review, 10,* 3-34.

Novosel, P. (1991). *Komyunikeishon no tessoku matawa shihai kaisou eno saigo no shimban: Tohou-sobieto "kakumei" to masu media taishu* (Principles of communication or the Last Judgment: The Soviet/Eastern European "revolution," mass media and the masses). *Masu Komyunikeishon to Kohkoku, 19,* 22-24.

Peterson, T. (1956). The social responsibility theory. In F. S. Siebert, T. Peterson, & W. Schramm (Eds.), *Four theories of the press.* Urbana, IL: University of Illinois Press.

Prime Minister's Office, Public Relations Office of the Cabinet Secretariat (Ed.). (1990). *Heisei gannendoban yoron chohsa nenkan* (Public opinion polls yearbook, 1989 edition). Tokyo: Ministry of Finance, Printing Bureau.

Prime Minister's Office, Public Relations Office of the Cabinet Secretariat (Ed.). (1991). *Heisei 2 nendoban yoron chohsa nenkan* (Public opinion polls yearbook, 1990 edition). Tokyo: Ministry of Finance, Printing Bureau.

Prime Minister's Office, Public Relations Office of the Cabinet Secretariat (Ed.). (1992). *Heisei 3 nendoban yoron chohsa nenkan* (Public opinion polls yearbook, 1991 edition). Tokyo: Ministry of Finance, Printing Bureau.

Public Opinion Research Institute, NHK (Ed.). (1975). *Zusetsu sengo yoronshi* (Illustrated History of Public Opinion in Postwar Japan). Tokyo: Nihon Hoso Shuppan Kyokai.

Raigetsu kara nitcho seifukan kohsho (Japan-North Korea inter-governmental negotiations start next month). (1990, October 9). *Mainichi Shimbun*, p. 1.

Riesman, D. (1961). *The lonely crowd: A study of the changing American character.* New Haven, CT: Yale University Press.

Rosengren, K. E. (1974). Uses and gratifications: A paradigm outlined. In J. G. Blumler & E. Katz (Eds.), *The uses of mass communications.* Beverly Hills, CA: Sage.

Ross, E. A. (1969/1901). *Social control: A survey of the foundations of order.* Cleveland, OH: The Press of Case Western Reserve University.

Schiller, H. I. (1973). *The mind managers.* Boston, MA: Beacon.

Schramm, W. (1957). *Responsibility in mass communication.* New York: Harper.

Schramm, W. (1965/1954). How communication works. In W. Schramm (Eds.), *The process and effects of mass communication.* Urbana, IL: University of Illinois Press.

Senso to shimbun (War and newspapers). (1987, August 29). *Asahi Shimbun*, p. 4.

Shimizu, I. (1951). *Shakai shinrigaku* (Social psychology). Tokyo: Iwanami Shoten.

Shin zeisei no fubi wo tadashi kohei wo mezase (Defects of the new tax system should be removed to make it fair). (1989, April 1). *Nihon Keizai Shimbun*, p. 2.

Shohizei wa sakkyu na minaoshi wo (Consumption tax should be amended soon). (1989, March 30). *Asahi Shimbun*, p. 2.

Takokusekigun eno kyohryoku ga heiwa wo mamoru (Cooperation with the multinational forces keeps peace). (1990, October 27). *Yomiuri Shimbun*, p. 2.

Tarde, G. (1901). *L'opinion et la foule.* Paris: Alcan.

Tokinoya, H. (1970). *Manshu Jihen zengo no masukomi kai* (Manchurian Incident and mass media). In F. Yamamoto (Ed.), *Nihon no masu komyunikeishon shi.* Tokyo: Tokai Daigaku Shuppan Kai.

Toriumi, Y. (1973). *Taigai kiki ni okeru shimbun roncho* (Newspaper editorials at national crises). In Nihon Bunka Kaigi (Ed.), *Nihon ni okeru jahnarizumu no tokushitsu.* Tokyo: Kenkyu-sha.

Tsujimura, A. (1976a). *Yoron to seiji rikigaku* (Public opinion and political dynamics). In Nihonjin Kenkyu Kai (Ed.), *Nihonjin kenkyu, No. 4: Yoron towa nanika*. Tokyo: Shiseido.

Tsujimura, A. (1976b). *Shimbun yo ogoru nakare* (Warnings to arrogant newspapers). Tokyo: Takagi Shobo.

Tsujimura, A. (1981). *Sengo Nihon no taishu shinri* (Social psychology in postwar Japan). TOkyo: Tokyo Daigaku Shuppankai.

Uemai, J. (1977). *Shitencho wa naze shinda ka* (Why did the branch manager die?). Tokyo: Bungei Shunju-sha.

Wakamono hodo heiwa kaiketsu nozomu: Kyoryoku hoan yoron chosa (Younger generations want peaceful solution: Public opinion poll on the UN Cooperation Bill). (1990, October 23). *Mainichi Shimbun*, pp. 2-3.

Wallas, G. (1948/1908). *Human nature in politics* (4th ed.). London: Constable.

Weaver, D., Graber, D., McCombs, M. E., & Eyal, C. H. (1981). *Media agenda-setting in a presidential election: Issues, images and interest*. New York: Praeger.

Yamamoto, S. (1977). *"Kuuki" no kenkyu* (A study of "kuuki"). Tokyo: Bungei Shunju-sha.

Yamamoto, A. (1980). *Ideorogi* (Ideology). In Y. Wada (Ed.), *Shimbungaku wo manabu hito no tameni*. Kyoto, Japan: Sekai Shiso-sha.

PART IV
CONCLUSION

Chapter 9

ISSUES FOR FUTURE RESEARCH ON
COMMUNICATION IN JAPAN
AND THE UNITED STATES

*William B. Gudykunst,
Ruth M. Guzley, and Hiroshi Ota*

The authors of the chapters in this volume examined a wide variety of topics of research on communication in Japan and the United States. Taken together, the chapters provide a summary of the state of knowledge regarding communication in Japan and the United States. Most authors provided suggestions for the type of research that needs to be conducted in their specific areas. We, therefore, do not focus on the content of future research in this chapter. Rather, our focus is on general issues that need to be systematically addressed across the various areas of research.

One theme that was mentioned consistently by all of the authors in one form or another is that the United States is an individualistic culture and independent self construals predominate, while Japan is a collectivistic culture and interdependent self construals predominate. Differences in individualism-collectivism were reported to influence language usage, communication in interpersonal/intergroup and organizational communication, as well as how the mass media, government, and public interrelate. Gudykunst and Nishida, for example, linked cultural differences in individualism-collectivism to differences in interpersonal and intergroup communication. To illustrate, they argued that because Japan is a collectivistic culture there is a greater difference in how Japanese communicate with members of their ingroups and their outgroups than there is in the individualistic culture of the United States. They also linked differences in encoding behavior to individualism-collectivism arguing that staking claims to who they are verbally is more important in individualistic cultures like the United States than in collectivistic cultures like Japan. Similarly, Stewart linked individualism-collectivism to selected cultural differences in organizational communication in Japan and the United States.

Independent versus interdependent self construals also were linked to communication by several authors. Lebra, for example, linked self construals to selected aspects of communication. To illustrate, she argued that an independent self construal (which predominates in the United States) leads to a focus on self-disclosure as a means for individuals to let others know who they are. When an interdependent self construal predominates (like in Japan), however, individuals are known by members of their ingroup and need to protect themselves from outsiders and, therefore, do not self-disclose at a high level. Akasu and Asao also link self construals to language usage in English and Japanese.

As several authors also pointed out, it is important to recognize that not all Japanese are collectivistic and not all people in the United States are individualists. Similarly, people use an interdependent self construal in the United States and people in Japan use an independent self construal. Within cultural variations in individualism-collectivism and self construals, therefore, must be taken into consideration in future research if we are going to understand communication in Japan and the United States. Individual variations in individualism-collectivism involve personality differences within cultures (e.g., Triandis et al.'s, 1986, idio-centrism-allocentrism). Individualistic personality orientations (e.g., idio-centrism) cannot be equated with using an independent self construal, nor can a collectivistic personality orientation (e.g., allocentrism, contextualism) be equated with an interdependent self construal. They are related, but each can have a separate influence on communication.

Lack of equivalence in past research is the other issue that was mentioned by virtually all authors. Much of the early research and some of the current research on communication in Japan has involved the imposition of concepts derived in one culture (usually the United States) to study communication in the other culture. While this approach can provide insight into cultural differences (Triandis & Marin 1983), it also can distort our understanding of cultural differences if not used carefully.

To illustrate, consider research on organizational commitment in Japan and the United States. Several researchers (e.g., Lincoln & Kalleberg, 1985; Luthans, McCaul, & Dodd, 1985) have used Porter, Steers, Mowday, and Boulian's (1974) organizational commitment questionnaire (OCQ) in Japan. These researchers found that workers in the United States are more committed to their organizations than workers in Japan. Even though these findings are inconsistent with the vast majority of studies on Japanese organizations, the researchers do not question the validity of their findings. Given that there is no direct translation of the English word *commitment* into Japanese (*katakana* must be used), it would be reasonable to question the meaning of the items on the OCQ to Japanese. Rather than questioning their findings, these researchers conclude that "organizational commitment is not based on culture-specific norms and values" (Luthans et al., 1985, p. 218). A close examination of the OCQ clearly reveals an individualistic culture bias. Part of the explanation for the conclusions these researchers draw is that there are not Japanese collaborators on the research team. To draw valid conclusions in cross-cultural research, there must be conceptual, meaning, and linguistic equivalence (discussed below) of questions asked. This usually requires close collaboration with a native researcher (Brislin, 1980).

Our purpose in this chapter is to suggest how within cultural variations in individualism-collectivism, independent and interdependent self construals (for another recent discussion of Japanese self, see Rosenberger, 1992), and issues of equivalence can be addressed in future research (for a recent discussion of other issues, see Ito & Kohei, 1990). We begin with within cultural variations in individualism-collectivism.

INDIVIDUALISM-COLLECTIVISM

Several of the authors referred to the United States as an individualistic culture and Japan as a collectivistic culture. While these patterns tend to provide accurate descriptions of the general cultural tendencies, it is important in future research to recognize that there is variability in individual tendencies within Japan and the United States. These individual tendencies must be incorporated in future research.

Within Cultural Variations in Individualism-Collectivism

One way to study within cultural variations is to look at personality differences. Triandis and his associates (1985) point out that everyone has individualistic and collectivistic thoughts. They argue that there are personality level equivalents of individualism and collectivism, idiocentrism and allocentrism, respectively. Building on Hui's (1984) research, Triandis and his colleagues found that allocentric tendencies involve three factors: subordinating individual goals to group goals, viewing the ingroup as an extension of the self, and having a strong ingroup identity. They also discovered that idiocentrics report being more lonely and achievement-oriented than allocentrics, while allocentrics report receiving more social support, as well as less alienation and anomie than idiocentrics.

Triandis and his associates (1986) extended their earlier work by examining idiocentric and allocentric tendencies in nine cultures. They isolated four factors associated with idiocentrism and allocentrism: self-reliance with hedonism, separation from ingroups, family integrity, and interdependence and sociability. Collectivism country scores were computed by aggregating and combining the four scores. Triandis and his associates' scores were significantly correlated with Hofstede's (1980) individualism scores for the nine countries, suggesting convergent validity of measurement.

A second way to study within cultural variations is to focus on values. Schwartz and Bilsky (1987, 1990) present a theory of the psychological content and structure of human values. They argue there are three facets to the content of values: type of goal, interests served, and motivational concern. With respect to type of goals, Schwartz and Bilsky instrumental and terminal values following Rokeach (1973). The values people hold can serve individualistic, collective, or mixed interests in a culture. Schwartz and Bilsky (1990) isolated seven motivational domains of values. Specific terminal and instrumental values fall in each of the domains [example values are given in brackets below]:

Prosocial. Active protection or enhancement of the welfare of others. [world at peace, equality, helpful]

Restrictive conformity. Restraint of actions and impulses likely to harm others and to violate the sanctioned norms. [obedient, polite, self-controlled]

Enjoyment. Pleasure, sensuous and emotional gratification. [comfortable life, pleasure, cheerful]

Achievement. Personal success through demonstrated competence. [social recognition, capable, ambitious]

Maturity. Appreciation understanding, and acceptance of oneself, others, and the surrounding world. [world of beauty, wisdom, courageous]

Self-direction. Independent thought and action—choosing, creating, and exploring. [independent, logical, imaginative]

Security. Safety, harmony, and stability of society, of groups with whom one identifies, of relationships, and of self. [family security, inner harmony, salvation] (pp. 879-80)

With respect to the structure of human values, Schwartz and Bilsky (1987, 1990) argue that some of the seven domains are compatible and some are incompatible. Prosocial, restrictive conformity, and security, for example, are compatible because they promote "smooth" social relations. Achievement and enjoyment are compatible because they deal with self-expression. Maturity and self-direction are compatible because they express "comfort." They suggest that several pairs of the motivational domains are not compatible: self-direction and restrictive conformity, prosocial and achievement, enjoyment and prosocial, and achievement and security.

Schwartz and Bilsky's (1987, 1990) research in Australia, Finland, Germany, Israel, Hong Kong, Spain, and the United States supports their theory. They found that instrumental and terminal values can be separated across cultures. Their study also revealed that values serve individualistic, collectivistic, or mixed interests. Specifically, enjoyment, achievement, and self-direction serve individual interests; prosocial, restrictive conformity, and security serve collectivistic interests; and maturity serves mixed interests. Finally, they discovered that the domains they predicted were compatible and incompatible were generally consistent across cultures (there were some minor variations which are not important here). Schwartz and Bilsky's research suggests that the distinction between individual and collective interests is universally meaningful and that the motivational domains defined as individualistic and collectivistic appear to generalize across cultures.

Schwartz (1990) argues that individualistic and collectivistic values do not necessarily conflict. With respect to individualistic values, he points out that "hedonism (enjoyment), achievement, self-direction, social power, and stimulation values all serve self interests of the individual, but not necessarily at the expense of any collectivity. . . . These same values might be promoted by leaders or members of collectivities as goals for their ingroup" (p. 143). With respect to collectivistic tendencies, Schwartz indicates that "prosocial, restrictive conformity, security, and tradition values all focus on promoting the interests of others. It is other people, constituting a collective, who benefit from the actor's [or actress'] concern for them, self-restraint, care for their security, and respect for shared traditions. But this does not necessarily occur at the expense of the actor [or actress]" p. 143). Individuals and cultures, therefore, can have both individualistic and collectivistic tendencies.

Japan and the United States

Triandis, Bontempo, Villareal, Asai, and Lucca (1988) examined idiocentric and allocentric tendencies in Japan and the United States. In general, they found few cultural differences in self-ingroup relationships attributable to individualism-collectivism. There were, however, a few specific findings consistent with their predictions. They discovered, for example, that Japanese students report paying more attention to the views of coworkers than students in the United States. These included items such as co-workers views on "deciding where to shop and what to buy," "choosing an intimate friend (including a spouse)," and "deciding what kind of work to do." Given that the vast majority of the findings did not support the predictions, Triandis and colleagues concluded that Japanese students may not be allocentric and that using student samples may be inappropriate for studying Japanese collectivism.

Yamaguchi (in press) examined collectivism in Japanese students. In earlier research (Yamaguchi, 1990), he developed and validated a ten-item scale to assess collectivism in Japan. The scale focuses on the degree to which individuals subordinate their identity to their ingroups. Using his scale, Yamaguchi (in press) found that collectivism is correlated positively with sensitivity to rejection, affiliative tendency, and self-monitoring, while it is correlated negatively with need for uniqueness and internal locus of control. These findings appear consistent with Triandis' (1988, 1990) conceptualization of individualism-collectivism.

Hamaguchi (cited in Befu, 1990) developed a scale to assess Japanese contextualism (see Gudykunst & San Antonio's chapter for a description of contextualism).[1] He wrote his items as dichotomous choice pairs of statements. One choice represented a contextualized response and one choice represented an individualized response. The first pair of items, for example, reads:

(a) Since we owe what we are to others, we should try to get along with others and help each other.
(b) As much as possible we should not depend on others. Instead we should develop a strong and independent self, do everything on the basis of our own judgment and take responsibility for our own action. (Befu, 1990, p. 189)

In his study of face in Japan and the United States, Morisaki (1992) modified Hamaguchi's items using a Likert type response format. He also incorporated Triandis and colleagues' (1986) separation from ingroup scale. Morisaki discovered that two reliable factors emerge in the United States and the Japan samples.[2] These two factors represented individualism and collectivism at the individual level. His Japanese sample was more individualistic and more collectivistic than the United States sample.

Gudykunst, Nishida, Chung, and Sudweeks (1992) examined the extent to which perceived typicality and strength of cultural identity interact with culture to influence idiocentrism-allocentrism and individualistic and collectivistic values. In their first study, culture and strength of cultural identity interacted to influence four values (freedom, pleasure, social recognition, and self-sacrifice), but the interaction did not influence idiocentrism-allocentrism. Culture had an independent effect on three values (self-reliance, self-sacrifice, social recognition), as well as three of Triandis and colleagues' (1986) idiocentrism-allocentrism scales (separation from ingroups, family integrity, and interdependence and sociability). Strength of cultural identity did not have an independent effect on values, but it did influence two idiocentrism-allocentrism scales (separation from ingroups, interdependence and sociability). No pattern emerged when the values were correlated with idiocentrism-allocentrism.

In Gudykunst and colleagues' (1992) second study, culture and strength of cultural identity interacted to influence three values (being independent, harmony, and accepting traditions), while culture had an independent effect on six values (pleasure, enhancing others' welfare, being independent, safety, exciting life, accepting traditions). Strength of cultural identity influenced four values (being successful, being independent, obtaining status, accepting traditions). Perceived typicality did not influence the values examined in the second study.

The data from Gudykunst and colleagues' (1992) studies indicate that culture interacts with strength of cultural identity to influence individualistic and collectivistic values. Specifically, their data suggest that if the values of freedom, pleasure, social recognition, self-sacrifice, being independent, harmony, and accepting traditions are used to assess individualism-collectivism of a sample at the individual level, strength of cultural identity must be taken into consideration. All of the interaction effects that emerged in the studies were consistent with expectations based on the individualistic and collectivistic tendencies of the two cultures.

With the exception of three values (social recognition, being independent, and exciting life), Gudykunst and colleagues' (1992) results
for the main effect of culture on values in the two studies generally
were not consistent with expectations based on the individualistic and
collectivistic tendencies of the two cultures. The data indicate that the
Japanese respondents were more self-reliant, more pleasure-seeking,
less self-sacrificing, less interested in preserving others' welfare, less
accepting of traditions, and less safety-oriented than the United States
respondents. The patterns for social recognition, being independent,
and exciting life, however, were consistent with expectations (i.e. scores
for United States respondents were higher than scores for Japan
respondents on these three values). Gudykunst and colleagues' data,
therefore, clearly suggest that students in the United States and Japan
simultaneously hold individualistic and collectivistic values.

Triandis and his associates (1988) suggest that college students in
Japan may not provide an adequate sample if researchers are trying to
test the effects of collectivism on individuals' behavior. Gudykunst and
colleagues' (1992) research, however, suggests that demonstrating
whether samples are individualistic or collectivistic cannot not be
accomplished by simply assessing the students' values. Their data indicate that individuals' strength of cultural identity interacts with their
cultural background to influence individualistic and collectivistic values. If values are to be used to demonstrate the idiocentrism-allocentrism levels in samples, strength of cultural identity must also be taken
into consideration.

Future research must take into consideration that individualism-
collectivism appears to be a dialectic. That is, individualism and collectivism exist in all cultures and individuals hold both individualistic
and collectivistic values. This position is consistent with Schwartz's
(1990) contention that individualistic and collectivistic values are not
necessarily incompatible; they can coexist. It also is compatible with
earlier research on value orientations (e.g., Caudill & Scarr, 1961;
Nishida, 1981) which revealed that individualistic and collectivistic
value orientations both exist in the United States and Japan. As indicated earlier, the data suggest that students in Japan and the United
States simultaneously hold individualistic and collectivistic values. The
data are compatible with several recent discussions of individualism
and collectivism in Japan and the United States. Miyanaga (1991), for
example, points out that there are individualistic tendencies in Japan
due to the process of modernization (see also Mito, 1991; Yamazaki,
1990). Research (e.g., Schwind & Peterson, 1985) also suggests that

Japanese managers are becoming less collectivistic.[3] Several recent studies (e.g., Bellah et al., 1985; Wuthnow, 1991) also suggest that people in the United States consistently try to balance their individualistic and collectivistic tendencies.

If individualism-collectivism is a dialectic at both the cultural and individual level as it appears, then it is critical that future research hypotheses involve very specific predictions regarding the linkages between the various aspects of individualism-collectivism and individuals' behavior (e.g., the more individuals in a culture value being independent, the more they will self-disclose with members of outgroups). Isolating very specific relationships between particular aspects of individualism-collectivism at the cultural level and idiocentrism-allocentrism at the individual level to individuals' behavior is necessary to understand the individualism-collectivism dialectic and differentiate the influence of culture and personality on behavior.

Another way to approach this issue is to look at subdivisions within Japan and the United States. Sugimoto and Mouer (1989), for example, suggest social class as an important area for future research. Communication research, however, is more likely to be influenced by individual variations in individualism-collectivism (i.e., idiocentrism-allocentrism to use Triandis et al.'s, 1986, terms). Table 9.1 illustrates potential groups which could be compared in studying communication in Japan and the United States. To understand the influence of individualism-collectivism on communication we must isolate idiocentrics and allocentrics in Japan and the United States.

There are at least six comparisons that must be made. For the pur-

TABLE 9.1
Example Groups Which Need to be Compared in
Studying Communication in Japan and the United States

		Culture	
		Japan	*United States*
Personality Types	Idiocentrics	Japanese Idiocentrics	United States Idiocentrics
	Allocentrics	Japanese Allocentrics	United States Allocentrics

* The idea for this table is adapted from Sugimoto and Mouer (1989).

pose of illustration, assume that the topic of research is the difference between the way individuals communicate with members of their ingroups and their outgroups. This is one area where individualism-collectivism should have an identifiable influence (Triandis et al., 1988). To fully understand the differences in communication with members of ingroups and outgroups, it is necessary to compare how idiocentrics are different from allocentrics within cultures (comparisons 1 and 2 in Table 9.2), how idocentrics differ across cultures (comparison 3 in Table 9.2), and how allocentrics differ between the two cultures (comparison 4 in Table 9.2). It also is necessary to compare the findings for comparisons 1 and 2 across cultures (comparison 5 in Table 9.2) and to compare the results for the cross-cultural differences in idiocentrism and allocentrism (comparison 6 in Table 9.2). These six comparisons will provide a in-depth picture of how culture (e.g., differences in individualism-collec-tivism) and personality (e.g., differences in idiocentrism-allocentrism) influence communication in ingroup and outgroup relationships.

TABLE 9.2
Example Comparisons Which Need to be Made in
Studying Communication in Japan and the United States

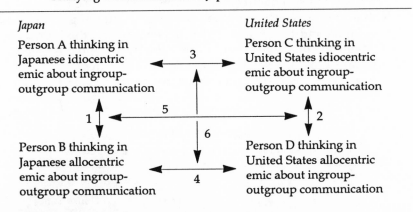

Comparison 1 = Idiocentrics vs. allocentrics in Japan.
Comparison 2 = Idiocentrics vs. allocentrics in the United States.
Comparison 3 = Idiocentrics in Japan and the United States.
Comparison 4 = Allocentrics in Japan and the United States.
Comparison 5 = Integrating results from comparisons 1 and 2.
Comparison 6 = Integrating results from comparisons 3 and 4.

* The idea for this table is adapted from Sugimoto and Mouer (1989).

Comparisons like the ones suggested also can be made using other dimensions of cultural variability and other personality level equivalents. If power distance is the dimension of comparability being used, then the personality equivalent of egalitarianism (Gudykunst, in press) could be used. If uncertainty avoidance is the dimension of comparability being used, then the personality equivalent uncertainty orientation (e.g., Sorrentio & Short, 1986) could be used. Finally, if masculinity-femininity is the dimension of cultural variability being used, then the personality equivalent of sex-roles (Bem, 1984) could be used.

In constructing Tables 9.1 and 9.2, we assumed that idiocentrism-allocentrism falls along one continuum, not two separate continuums as Morisaki (1992) discovered. If individualism-collectivism is a dialectic, there could be either one dimension with both poles existing in all cultures or two separate continuums that exist in all cultures. Future researchers need to develop measures of idiocentrism and allocentrism that are reliable and valid in Japan and the United States. A beginning attempt can be made in developing such a measure by combining Triandis and colleagues' (1986) measures, Hamaguchi's items, Yamaguchi's (1990) scale, items from Verma's (1992) allocentrism scales, and additional items (e.g., the individualistic equivalents of Yamaguchi's items) focusing on individualism at the individual level (e.g., idiocentrism).

INDEPENDENT AND INTERDEPENDENT SELF CONSTRUALS

Markus and Kitayama (1991) contend that people in different cultures use different construals of the self: the independent and the interdependent construal of the self.[4] While Markus and Kitayama draw on work in which the authors discuss individualism-collectivism (e.g., Hofstede, 1980; Schwartz & Bilsky, 1990), they do not link independent and interdependent construals of the self directly to individualism-collectivism. Morisaki and Gudykunst (in press), however, argue that there is a direct relationship: the independent construal of self *predominates* in individualistic cultures and the interdependent construal of self *predominates* in collectivistic cultures.

People in most Western (individualistic) cultures use an independent construal of the self. The independent construal of self involves the view that an individual's self is a unique, independent entity. Geertz (1975), for example, illustrates this view when he describes the Western self "as a bounded, unique, more or less integrated motivational and cognitive universe, a dynamic center of awareness, emotion, judgment, and action organized into a distinctive whole and set contrastively both against other such wholes and against a social and natural background" (p. 48; see Johnson, 1985; Sampson, 1988; Waterman, 1981; for more detailed discussions).

Markus and Kitayama (1991) argue that in the independent view of self, the self is separated from others. The self-representations "usually have as their referent the individual desire, preference, attribute, or ability" (p. 226); i.e., core conceptions, salient identities, self schemata, personal identity, or personal self-esteem. The Westerner's cultural "goal of independence requires construing oneself as an individual whose behavior is organized and made meaningful primarily by reference to one's own internal repertoire of thoughts, feelings, and action, rather than by reference to the thoughts, feelings, and actions of others" (p. 226). Johnson (1985), for example, defines the Western concept of self:

> as a *unitary phenomenon*; it is used to refer to a particular, individual person (or person-system) and not to a "personality" or to an aggregate of factors which "add up"—to a person. The concept of self is typically separated into a nominative ("I") *self-as-subject*, and an accusative ("me") *self-as-object*. *Self-as-object* includes both the idea of *self as a social object to others and that of the self as a social (and psychological) object unto itself.* (p. 93; emphasis in original)

The important tasks of a person with an independent self construal are to be unique, strive for her or his own goals, express self, and be direct (e.g., "say what you mean"; Markus & Kitayama, 1991). An individual's self-esteem is based in his or her ability to express him- or herself, and in her or his ability to validate her or his internal attributes (Markus & Kitayama, 1991).

Markus and Kitayama (1991) contend that people in many non-Western cultures such as Japan (collectivistic cultures) use an interdependent construal of the self. "Experiencing interdependence entails seeing oneself as part of an encompassing social relationship and recognizing that one's behavior is determined, contingent on, and, to a large extent organized by what the actor [actress] perceives to be the thoughts, feelings, and actions of *others* in the relationship" (p. 227).[5] Hsu (1985) illustrates the importance of relations to others when he discusses why he uses the Chinese concept of *jen* instead of the Western concept of personality.

I suggest the term *jen* advisedly because the Chinese conception of [hu]man (also shared by Japanese who pronounce the
same Chinese word *jin*) is based on the *individual's transactions
with his [her] fellow human beings.* When the Chinese say so-and-
so "*ta pu shih jen*" (he [she] is not a *jen*), they do not mean this
person is not a human animal; instead they mean that his [her]
behavior in relation to other human beings is not acceptable.
(pp. 32-33)

The interdependent construal of self involves a self-in-relation to
others. The relationship between the self and others, however, is not
stable. The self-in-relation to specific others guides behavior in specific
social situations.[6] Depending on the situation, different aspects of the
interdependent self guide people's behavior. If the behavior is taking
place at home, the family aspects of the interdependent self guide
behavior; if the behavior is taking place on the job, the coworker interdependent self guide behavior.

The important tasks of a person with an interdependent self construal are to "fit in" with the group, act in an appropriate fashion, promote other's goals, "occupy one's proper place," to be indirect, and
"read other's mind" (Markus & Kitayama, 1991). The importance of fit-
ting-in is illustrated by White and LeVine's (1986) discussion of *sunao*, a
characteristic Japanese parents value in children:

A child that is *sunao* has not yielded his or her personal autonomy for the sake of cooperation; cooperation does not suggest
giving up the self, as it may in the West; it implies that working
with others is the appropriate way of expressing and enhancing
the self. Engagement and harmony with others is, then, a positively valued goal and the bridge—to open hearted cooperation, as
in *sunao*—is through sensitivity. (p. 58)

Markus and Kitayama (1991) also point out that "giving is not a sign of
weakness, rather it reflects tolerance, self-control, flexibility, and maturity" (p. 229).

Self-esteem is based on one's ability to adjust to others, and one's
ability to maintain harmony in the social context when an interdependent self construal predominates (Markus & Kitayama, 1991).
Miyanaga's (1991) description of interaction rituals in Japan illustrates
this pattern. She points out that communicators'

body movements, tone of voice, degree of avoidance of eye contact, laughter, smiles, serious expressions, and even the degree of body tension are, to a certain extent, carefully controlled to constitute cues.

At the same time, a person tries as much as possible to catch the cues given by others. If a person keeps missing the given cues, he [she] will be judged "blunt" or "dull" (because he [she] is unreceptive), "impolite" (when it is judged that he [she] is deliberately choosing to miss cues), or *gaijin mitai* (like a foreigner). High receptivity is admired. The Japanese word generally used to indicate such receptivity is *sasshi*, which literally means "to guess." It implies that one guesses the real intention of others in spite of their surface disguise. (p. 85)

Miyanaga goes on to point out that when ingroup memberships are shared (i.e., there are interdependent self construals), each partner understands when the other will follow behavioral norms and when the other will violate the behavioral norms.

Hamaguchi's (1983) summary of the ways individuals view themselves in Japan and the United States is consistent with Markus and Kitayama's (1991) conceptualization of independent and interdependent self construals.[7] In the United states,

an "individual" . . . holds a conviction that he [she] is a firmly established substance which is solely independent, and, therefore, cannot be invalidated by others. Also, he [she] is convinced that he [she] is the master of himself [herself], but at the same time he [she] is liable for his [her] own deeds. The individual objectifies such an assertion (that he [she] is undoubtedly himself [herself]) and the sense of autonomy. (pp. 140-41)

Japanese, in contrast, view themselves contextually:

For the Japanese, "self" means the portion which is distributed to him [her], according to the situation he [she] is in, from the living space shared between himself [herself] and the other person with whom he [she] had developed a mutually dependent relationship.

A reason why this self-consciousness of the Japanese is formed this way is probably that self and others are in a symbiotic relationship, and that they believe that their beings depend largely on other being. . . . This relativistic "self" can easily be mistaken for being unindependent. . . . However, here, selves are "mutually dependent," and their spontaneous fulfillment of the needs are intentionally controlled. (p. 142)

While Hamaguchi does not use the terms, his descriptions of how individuals view themselves also is compatible with cultural differences in individualism-collectivism in Japan and the United States.

There is extensive evidence to support Markus and Kitayama's (1991) claim that independent self construal predominates in the United States and interdependent self construal predominates in Japan (e.g., Hess et al., 1986; Shikanai, 1978; Takata, 1987; Yoshida, Kojo, & Kaku, 1982). One important issue, for example, is that of conformity. Given Markus and Kitayama's conceptualization, greater conformity would be expected in Japan when the interdependent self construal is activated than when it is not activated, and greater conformity would be expected in Japan when the interdependent self is activated than in the United States when the independent self is activated. The research supports this speculation. Williams and Sogon (1984) discovered that when confederates are members of Japanese respondents' ingroups, conformity is much higher than in Asch's (1956) original study. Frager (1970) also found that when the confederates are strangers to Japanese respondents (i.e., a situation that should not activate the interdependent self construal), conformity is lower than in Asch's study.

Markus and Kitayama's (1991) conceptualization further suggests that Japanese should be more concerned with engaging in socially appropriate behavior and modifying their behavior based on their relationships to others than North Americans. A recent study (Gudykunst, Gao, Nishida, Nadamitsu, & Sakai, 1992) designed to develop a measure of self-monitoring appropriate in Japan supports this speculation. Gudykunst and colleagues found that when monitoring their behavior, people in the United States focus on how they can change their behavior to meet generalized expectations of others in the situation (i.e., how a prototypic person would behave). Japanese, in contrast, focus on how they can behave appropriately given their relationship to specific people in the situation.

The nature of the self construal also influences the way individuals manage topics and take turns in conversations. Yamada (1990), for example, found that Japanese "take short turns, distribute their turns relatively evenly, and continue to distribute their turns evenly regardless of who initiates a topic" (p. 291). North Americans, in contrast, "take long monologic turns, distribute their turns unevenly, and the participant who initiates the topic characteristically takes the highest proportion of turns in that topic" (p. 291). Yamada also discovered that Japanese organize topics in conversations interdependently, while North American organize their topics independently.

Earlier we pointed that independent construals of the self *predominate* in individualistic cultures and interdependent construals of the self *predominate* in collectivistic cultures. It is important to recognize, however, that everyone has both an independent and interdependent construal of the self.[8] Further, people with predominately interdependent construals of the self exist in individualistic cultures like the United States and people with predominately independent construals of the self exist in collectivistic cultures like Japan. We believe that the critical issue is which self construal individuals use in guiding their behavior in a particular situation.

To illustrate how this affects communication it is necessary to briefly discuss the self-concept. The self-concept involves "the set of cognitive representations of the self available to a person" (Turner et al., 1987, p. 44). Turner and his associates argue that everyone uses three basic selfcategorizations to define him- or herself: human identity, social identity, and personal identity. Our human identity involves those features that we share with all other humans (in contrast to other forms of life). Social identity is based on our ingroup-outgroup categorizations and includes those self-representations we share with members of our ingroups. More formally, Tajfel (1981) defines social identity as "that aspect of the individuals' self-concept which derives from their knowledge of their membership in a social group (or groups) together with the value and emotional significance attached to that membership" (p. 255). Our personal identity involves those aspects of the self that define us as unique individuals. We believe that personal identity is comparable to an independent construal of the self, while social identity is comparable to social identity.[9] Trafimow, Triandis, and Goto's (1991) research suggests that everyone has private self and collective self cognitions and that these cognitions are stored in different locations in memory.

In individualistic cultures like the United States, an independent construal of the self and personal identity predominate to influence behavior.[10] In intergroup situations, however, behavior is based mainly on social identity and individuals' interdependent construal of the self guides their behavior. The interdependent construal of the self also is a theme in some religious groups (e.g., Quakers), in small towns, and in rural areas (Bellah et al., 1985). Further, Gilligan (1982) argues that women in the United States are socialized to be interdependent, while men are socialized to be independent. In addition, there appears to be a trend in social science to view the self in relational terms (e.g., Curtis, 1991; Elias, 1991).

In collectivistic cultures like Japan, an interdependent construal of self and social identity predominate to influence behavior.[11] In some situations, however, behavior can be based on personal identity and individuals' independent construal of self will guide their behavior. To illustrate, Befu (1977), for example, argues that there is a strong sense of "personhood" in Japan:

> A reexamination of empirical cases of the so-called "group orientation" in Japan would probably reveal that group orientation is more apparent than real, and that behind the appearance of group solidarity one will find each member being motivated more by personal ambition than by his [her] blind loyalty top the group. Put another way, in many cases Japanese are [or anyone else is, for that matter] loyal to their groups because it pays to be loyal. (1977, p. 87)

Mouer and Sugimoto (1986) also argue that there are numerous ways that the autonomous individual (i.e., independent self construal) is manifested in Japanese society. They also point out that there is a gravitation toward individual activity during leisure time.[12]

Cousins' (1989) research suggests that Japanese independent self may be highly contextualized. When asked to describe themselves without a context, Japanese used more social role descriptors than North Americans, and the North Americans used more psychological attributes than the Japanese. When asked to describe themselves in a specific context (i.e., at home), however, the Japanese used more unique psychological attributes than the North Americans. We believe that the independent self construal will guide behavior in Japan when individuals are dealing with outgroup members with whom they do not have ongoing relationships (e.g., strangers) and in very intimate relationships (e.g., close friendships).

Before proceeding, it is important to make an additional point about independent and interdependent self construals (or personal and social identity) Deaux (1991) argues that identities vary along at least two dimensions: desirable-undesirable and voluntary-involuntary. Voluntary identities require "more effort to maintain" (p. 79) than involuntary ones. Also Deaux suggests that the desirability dimension "influences the degree to which that identity will be proclaimed or hidden—will serve as a source of self-esteem or be a cause of shame" (p. 79). Deaux points out that some people have a "master" identity with other identities subsumed under it, while others may give equal importance to their identities. Members of collectivistic cultures in general, and Japanese in particular, are likely to treat their social identity associated with their major ingroup as a master identity that is desirable and involuntary.

When the independent self construal predominates, individuals base their personal self-esteem on their ability to express themselves and in the validation of their internal attributes (Markus & Kitayama, 1991). When the interdependent self construal predominates, individuals base their collective self-esteem on their ability to adjust and maintain harmony with others (Markus & Kitayama, 1991). Self-esteem can be derived from both personal and social identities (Crocker & Luhtanent, 1990). It is important to recognize, however, that an individual's self-esteem is a combination of both personal and collective self-esteem. As Josephs (1991) points out:

> On the one hand, self-esteem is based on fitting in, being accepted, pleasing others, and gaining approval for meeting the expectations of others. On the other hand, self-esteem is based upon realizing one's unique potentialities; being an individual in one's own right; and having others recognize, respect, affirm, support, and encourage one's personal talents and individual uniqueness. (pp. 8-9)

He goes on to point out that is self-esteem is based only on fitting in, it can lead to "mindless conformity"; if it is based only on uniqueness, it can lead to "social alienation." "A balance must be achieved between fitting in and being an individual in one's own right" (Josephs, 1991, p. 9). The balance, however, will be different in individualistic and collectivistic cultures.

While the predominate locus of self-esteem differs in Japan and the United States, the general process of managing threats to self-esteem appears to be similar. When individuals perceive a threat to their self-esteem, they respond emotionally by feeling shame or some emotion associated with shame (e.g., embarrassment, humiliation; Scheff, 1990). Scheff argues that the feelings of pride and shame are the fundamental emotions, and they "signal" the state of our social bonds. Feeling pride indicates an intact, secure social bond. Feeling shame, in contrast, indicates a severed or threatened social bond.[13] While the general process of managing threats to self-esteem is similar, the conditions under which Japanese and North Americans experience threats to their self-esteem differ. In the United States, shame is felt most frequently when there is a threat to personal self-esteem. In Japan, shame is felt most frequently when there is a threat to collective self-esteem.

Future research must examine the self construal that is activated in specific situations. Personality orientation (i.e., idiocentrism-allocentrism) alone cannot explain within cultural variations. Individuals who are idiocentric, for example, may activate interdependent self construals in some situations and, therefore, act more like allocentrics. This line of reasoning suggests that a productive area for future research involves the situational activation of self construals. It is critical, however, that the situations that are examined are equivalent.

Issues of Equivalence

Gudykunst and San Antonio (chapter 2, this volume) pointed out that there are two basic approaches to studying culture and communication: emic and etic. Both approaches require that issues of equivalence be addressed. In this section, we first overview general issues of equivalence, then we apply them to studying communication in Japan and the United States.[14]

Types of Equivalence

"If comparisons are to be legitimately made across cultural boundaries, it is first necessary to establish equivalent bases upon which to make comparisons" (Lonner, 1979, p. 27). Equivalence refers to equality in quantity, value, meaning, and so forth. Five types of equivalence must be addressed: functional, conceptual, linguistic, metric, and sample equivalence.

Functional equivalence involves the relationship between specific observations and the inferences that are made from the observations. Goldschmidt (1966) argues that activities must have similar functions if they are to be used for purposes of comparison. Berry (1969) elaborated:

> Functional equivalence of behavior exists when the behavior in question has developed in response to a problem shared by two or more societal/cultural groups, even though the behavior in one

society does not appear to be related to its counterpart in another society. These functional equivalences must pre-exist as naturally occurring phenomena; they are discovered and cannot be created or manipulated. (p. 122)

To illustrate, one area of research in communication in which functional equivalence is of concern is research on communication apprehension (e.g., Klopf & Cambra, 1979). While communication apprehension is viewed as undesirable in the United States where the concept originated, this view is not shared in Japan where reticence is valued. Any comparisons of this phenomenon must take these differences into account.

Functional equivalence involves equivalence at the macro or cultural level. Conceptual equivalence, in contrast, "focuses upon the presence (or absence) of meanings that individuals attach to specific stimuli" (Lonner, 1979, p. 27). Sears (1961) argues that researchers must discover the meaning of concepts to individuals within the cognitive systems of the members of the culture(s) being examined.

Linguistic (or translation) equivalence focuses on the language used in questionnaires, interviews, field observations, or instructions used in research (see Brislin, 1976, for a discussion of translation issues). Administration of research instruments in a language of one culture to people in another culture for whom this language is not a native language or who are not bilingual in the language yields data that are not equivalent. Research instruments must be administered in the respondents' native language and the forms used in different cultures must be linguistically equivalent. The most widely used method to establish linguistic equivalence is back-translation. This procedure generally involves one bilingual translating the instrument from the first language into the second and another bilingual back-translating the instrument into the first language. Variations in original wording and the back-translation must then be reconciled.

Closely related to linguistic equivalence is the issue of metric equivalence, establishing that the score levels obtained in one culture are equivalent to score levels obtained in another culture. Poortinga (1975) argues that there are at least three alternative interpretations of differences in scores between two cultures: (1) the differences exist and are real, (2) the test measures qualitatively different aspects of the concept, and (3) the test measures quantitatively different aspects of the concept. Without establishing metric equivalence, the second and third interpretations become rival hypotheses to explain differences observed across cultures. Minimally both raw and standardized scores should be examined in cross-cultural studies to ensure metric equivalence.

The final equivalence is sample equivalence. It is important that comparable samples are used when cross-cultural comparisons are made between Japan and the United States. Brislin and Baumgardner (1971) point out that most cross-cultural studies use samples of convenience, rather than random samples. Since random samples generally are not feasible in cross-cultural research, steps need to be taken to ensure that samples are as equivalent as possible.

Related to sample equivalence is the issue of whether the samples used actually represent the dimensions of cultural variability being studied. Samples from Japan, for example, should be checked to ensure that the respondents are collectivistic and samples from the United States need to be checked to ensure they are individualistic. As indicated earlier, Gudykunst, Nishida, Chung, and Sudweeks (1992) argue that this often is problematic since Japanese college students demonstrate high levels of individualism and when selected "manipulation check" items are used Japanese samples may be more individualistic than United States samples. Researchers using etic approaches must be careful to ensure that their samples are indeed representative of the dimensions they are studying.

Equivalence in Research in Japan and the United States

There are many concepts that *nihonjinron* writers argue are unique to Japan. Doi (1973), for example, argues that *amae* (dependence) is a unique Japanese concept used to describe relations between mothers and their children, as well as other social relations in Japan. This "fact," however, does not negate the need for studying "dependency" across cultures. As Befu (1989) points out, the issue of dependency is a universal phenomenon. Isolating the commonalities and differences in how dependency is manifested across cultures contributes to better understanding Japan, and it also contributes to the development of social theory.

In his discussion of the relevance of the emic and etic approaches for Japanese studies, Befu (1989) argues that

> neither the *etic* nor *emic* approach is foolproof: both have inescapable methodological shortcomings, which might persuade one not to engage in either purely *etic* or in purely *emic* activities. Such methodological straight-jacketing, however, will not help

advance knowledge. Imperfection in any method is as commonly accepted in empirical science as inevitable. As long as we are not engaged in the impossible task of pursuing "ultimate truths", and as long as we are aware of the imperfections in each approach, we are in a good position to take advantage of both approaches. (p. 339)

Befu goes on to point out that isolating specific patterns within cultures, does not negate the need for cross-cultural comparisons.

Issues of equivalence must be addressed explicitly in future cross-cultural research in Japan and the United States. Frequently equivalence is established by translations of research instruments. Back-translations of research instruments. Brislin (1976), for example, argues that research instruments need to be de-centered where "material in one language is changed so that there will be a smooth, natural sounding version in the second language. The result of de-centering contrasts with the awkward, stilted versions common when material in one language is taken as the final content that must be translated with minimal change into another language" (p. 222). Befu (1989), however, points out that this is not always possible when multiple cultures are involved.

Before questionnaires are constructed, the concepts must be fully understood in each culture. When studying concepts that first appear unique to Japan (e.g., *amae, sasshi, ishin denshin, enryo, tatemae-honne, omote-ura*) or the United States (e.g., assertiveness, communication apprehension, empathy, rhetorical sensitivity), for example, it is necessary to begin by looking at emic conceptualizations of the concepts. Once the concepts have been studied emically, cross-cultural studies can begin. In terms of generating theory, however, it is critical to take one additional step and to generate etic conceptualizations of concepts that are compatible with culturally specific emic conceptualizations (i.e., derived etic conceptualizations).

To illustrate the process being suggested here, consider the concept of face. Some writers suggest that face is a universal construct (e.g., Brown & Levinson, 1978; Ho, 1976) while others argue that the conceptualization of face is culture specific (e.g., Hofstede, 1984; Morisaki & Gudykunst, in press). Morisaki and Gudykunst, for example, argue that face is based on interdependent self construal in Japan and based on independent self construal in the United States. Hofstede also points out that "preserving face—that is, preserving the respect from one's reference groups—is the collectivistic alternative to preserving self-respect in the individualistic culture" (p. 394). Given the differences in conceptualizing face, one must be careful in studying face in Japan and the United States. Since the referents are different, simple translations cannot be used to study cultural differences in face.

To study face across cultures, a derived etic conceptualization is needed. To capture the conceptualization of face that is shared in different cultures it is necessary to isolate the emic conceptualizations and look for commonalities. For face, the commonality is that both Japanese and North American conceptualizations involve claimed public images. The referents and who is included in the public image differ, but there are sufficient commonalities on which to base etic research. Table 9.3 illustrates one potential derived etic conceptualization.

TABLE 9.3
Example Derived Etic Conceptualization: Claimed Public Identity

Japanese emic conceptualization:	Claimed public identity involves interdependent self-construal, "face," reputation, and collective self-esteem. Failure to maintain the claimed identity leads to feeling shame.
United States emic conceptualization:	Claimed public identity involves independent self-construal, personal self-esteem, credibility, reputation, and "face." Failure to maintain the claimed public identity leads to feeling shame.
Derived etic conceptualization:	Claimed public identity involves the image a person wants to present to others and wants others to support in interaction. Failure to maintain the claimed public identity leads to feeling shame.

An alternative approach is to use emic operationalizations of concepts to test etic models. Triandis, Malpass, and Davidson (1973), for example, suggest that a three-stage process be used in cross-cultural studies. First, researchers develop etic constructs that appear to be universal. Second, researchers develop emic measures of the constructs and validate them. Third, they use the emic operationalizations to study the etic constructs across cultures. This procedure works well for constructs that are "universal," but it does not work as well in studying constructs that at first glance appear to be culturally specific. For these constructs, the procedure outlined earlier (i.e., developing derived etic conceptualizations) is needed.

CONCLUSION

There often is a tendency for scholars who use one approach to research on Japan and the United States (e.g., emic versus etic, qualitative versus quantitative) to view their own approach to research as superior to other approaches and to downgrade other approaches. While such evaluation is "natural" to some extent, it hinders our ability to increase our understanding of communication in Japan and the United States. To increase our understanding, methodological pluralism (i.e., valuing different approaches to research) is needed. Researchers need to recognize that all types of research can contribute to our understanding. Further, research teams that use multiple approaches to the study of communication in Japan and the United States are needed.

In addition to being methodologically pluralistic, research teams need to be bicultural. Many studies of communication in Japan and the United States are carried out by researchers from the United States who have Japanese translate their research instruments into Japanese, but do not include the Japanese as true collaborators in their research. This approach is problematic (e.g., generally these studies do not have conceptual equivalence) and it leads to ethnocentric research.[15] To maximize our understanding of communication in Japan and the United States, bicultural research teams are needed. These bicultural research teams need to be truly collaborative efforts; that is, the teams need to make joint decisions about the problems to be studied, how to study them, and how to disseminate their research findings. Ideally, there will be numerous bicultural research teams studying different aspects of communication in Japan and the United States from different perspectives.[16]

NOTES

1. Befu's citation as to the source of the items is incorrect. Correspondence with Befu suggests that the items were originally published in Hamaguchi's university research annual. The original citation for the items has been requested from Hamaguchi, but as of this writing it has not been received.

2. There were only minor differences in the items that loaded on the factors across cultures.

3. This tendency is supported by writing in the popular press. Helm (1992) reports, for example, that many Japanese businessmen are hiring private detectives to conduct "self-investigations." The purpose of these investi-

gations is to determine the individual's chance of being promoted within his organization. If something turns up in the report that might stop the individual from being promoted (e.g., to section chief), he would consider moving to another organization while his chances to move forward in his career are still high.

4. This section is adapted from material Gudykunst wrote for Morisaki and Gudykunst (in press).

5. Yamaguchi (1991) concurs that Markus and Kitayama's (1991) conceptualization applies in Japan.

6. Plath (1989) suggests that self construals differ across the lifespan. He discusses different "schedules" for selfhood in Japan.

7. The following translations of Hamaguchi's writing were presented by Miyanaga (1991, pp. 18-19).

8. Triandis (personal communication) has argued that everyone has both individualistic and collectivistic thoughts. This position also is supported by recent writings on the United States (e.g., Bellah et al., 1985; Wuthnow, 1991) and Japan (e.g., Miyanaga, 1991). Japanese writers of the *nihonjinron* (literally discussions of the Japanese) tradition (e.g., Hamaguchi), however, would argue that Japanese are unique in their self-conceptions and that they only have an interdependent self construal. While we agree that the interdependent (contextual) predominates, we believe there also is an independent construal as discussed below. For a critique of the *nihonjinron* approach, see Dale (1986).

9. It should be noted that we believe that the personal and social identity operate in every encounter, but one tends to predominate at any given moment.

10. There also are individuals whose interdependent construal of self predominates (see Bellah et al., 1985; Wuthnow, 1991).

11. There are, of course, specific individuals whose independent construal of self predominates (see Miyanaga, 1991; Valentine, 1990).

12. Mouer and Sugimoto also given several examples of proverbs that reflect an independent self construal; e.g., *seishin itto nanigotoka narazaran* ("where there is a will, there is a way"), *jigo jitoku* ("one must pay the consequences for one's misdeeds"). They also point out that "the phrase *karasu no katte desho* (literally "as the crow pleases") which can indicate that one can have one's own reason for doing things" (p. 195) has come into use in recent years.

13. Scheff also argues that in the United States individuals are socialized to repress feelings of pride and shame. He also contends that individualism is a myth that is a defense against the loss of secure social bonds.

14. The discussion of equivalence is drawn from Gudykunst and Ting-Toomey (1988).

15. Many early writers in cross-cultural psychology argued that not including a collaborator from the cultures being studied is unethical (e.g., Berrien, 1970).

16. Bicultural research teams are useful for studying communication in Japan and the United States. If the ultimate goal is to test theories across cultures, however, multicultural research teams are needed. To illustrate, if a research team is interested in testing predictions based on individualism-collectivism at least four cultures are needed: two individualistic cultures and two collectivistic cultures. For research to be productive, the same researchers need to work together over a period of time.

REFERENCES

Asch, S. (1956). Studies of independence and conformity. *Psychological Monographs, 70*, No. 9 (whole No. 416).

Befu, H. (1977). Power in the great white tower. In R. Fogelson & R. Adams (Eds.), *The anthropology of power*. New York: Academic Press.

Befu, H. (1989). The emic-etic distinction and its significance for Japanese studies. In Y. Sugimoto & R. E. Mouer (Eds.), *Constructs for understanding Japan*. London: Kegan Paul.

Befu, H. (1990). Conflict and non-Weberian bureaucracy in Japan. In S. N. Eisenstadt & E. Ben-Ari (Eds.), *Japanese models of conflict resolution*. London: Kegan Paul.

Bellah, R., Madsen, R., Sullivan, W., Swidler, A., & Tipton, S. (1985). *Habits of the heart: Individualism and commitment in American life*. Berkeley: University of California Press.

Bem, S. (1984). Androgeny and gender theory. In T. B. Sonderegger (Ed.), *Psychology and gender: Nebraska symposium on motivation*. Lincoln: University of Nebraska Press.

Berrien, F. (1970). A super-ego for cross-cultural research. *International Journal of Psychology, 5*, 1-9.

Berry, J. (1969). On cross-cultural comparability. *International Journal of Sociology, 4*, 119-128.

Brewer, M. B. (1991). The social self: On being the same and different at the same time. *Personality and Social Psychology Bulletin, 17*, 475-482.

Brislin, R. (1976). *Translation: Application and research*. New York: Gardner.

Brislin, R. (1980). Translation and content analysis of oral and written material.

In H. Triandis & J. Berry (Eds.), *Handbook of cross-cultural psychology* (Vol. 2). Boston: Allyn & Bacon.

Brislin, R., & Baumgardner, S. (1971). Non-random sampling of individuals in cross-cultural research. *Journal of Cross-Cultural Psychology, 2,* 397-400.

Brown, P., & Levinson, S. (1978). Universals in language usage. In E. Goody (Ed.), *Questions and politeness.* Cambridge: Cambridge University Press.

Caudill, W., & Scarr, H. (1961). Japanese value orientations and culture change. *Ethnology, 1,* 53-91.

Cousins, S. D. (1989). Culture and self-perception in Japan and the United States. *Journal of Personality and Social Psychology, 56,* 124-131.

Crocker, J., & Luhtanen, R. (1990). Collective self-esteem and ingroup bias. *Journal of Personality and Social Psychology, 58,* 60-67.

Curtis, R. C. (Ed.). (1991). *The relational self.* New York: Guilford.

Deaux, K. (1991). Social identities: Thoughts on structure and change. In R. Curtis (Ed.), *The relational self.* New York: Guilford.

Doi, T. (1973). *The anatomy of dependence.* Tokyo: Kodansha.

Elias, N. (1991). *The society of individuals* (E. Jephcott trans.). London: Blackwell.

Frager, R. (1970). Conformity and anticonformity in Japan. *Journal of Personality and Social Psychology, 15,* 203-210.

Geertz, C. (1975). On the nature of anthropological understanding. *American Scientist, 63,* 47-53.

Gilligan, C. (1982). *In a different voice: Psychological theory and women's development.* Cambridge, MA: Harvard University Press.

Goldschmidt, W. (1966). *Comparative functionalism.* Berkeley: University of California Press.

Gudykunst, W. B. (in press). Toward a theory of effective interpersonal and intergroup communication: An anxiety/uncertainty management perspective. In R. Wiseman & J. Koester (Eds.), *Intercultural communication competence.* Newbury Park, CA: Sage.

Gudykunst, W. B., Gao, G., Nishida, T., Nadamitsu, Y., & Sakai, J. (1992). Self-monitoring in Japan and the United States. In S. Iwaki, Y. Kashima, & K. Leung (Eds.), *Innovations in cross-cultural psychology.* Lisse, Netherlands: Swets & Zeitlinger.

Gudykunst, W. B., Nishida, T., Chung, L., & Sudweeks, S. (1992). *The influence of strength of cultural identity and perceived typicality on individualistic and col-*

lectivistic values in Japan and the United States. Paper presented at the Asian Regional Congress of the International Association for Cross-Cultural Psychology, Kathmandu, Nepal.

Gudykunst, W. B., & Ting-Toomey, S., with Chua, E. (1988). *Culture and interpersonal communication.* Beverly Hills, CA: Sage.

Hamaguchi, E. (1982). *Nihonteki shuhdanshugi towa nanika* (What is Japanese groupism?). In E. Hamaguchi & S. Kumon (Eds.), *Nihonteki shuhdanshugi* (Japanese groupism). Tokyo: Sensho.

Hamaguchi, E. (1983). *Kanjin-shugi no shakai Nihon* (Japan, society of contextual men). Tokyo: Touyou Keizai.

Hamaguchi, E. (1985). A contextual model of the Japanese. *Journal of Japanese Studies, 11,* 289-321.

Helm, L. (1992, July 6). Private eye to I. *Los Angeles Times,* pp. D1-2.

Hess, R., Azuma, H., Kashiwagi, K., Dickson, W., Nagano, S., Holloway, S., Miyake, K., Price, G., Hatano, G., & McDevitt, T. (1986). Family influences on school readiness in Japan and the United States. In H. Stevenson, H. Azuma, & K. Hakuta (Eds.), *Child development and education in Japan.* New York: Freeman.

Ho, D. (1976). On the concept of face. *American Journal of Sociology, 81,* 867-884.

Hofstede, G. (1980). *Culture's consequences.* Beverly Hills, CA: Sage.

Hofstede, G. (1984). The cultural relativity of the quality of life concept. *Academy of Management Review, 9,* 389-398.

Hsu, F. L. K. (1985). The self in cross-cultural perspective. In A. Marsella, G. DeVos, & F. Hsu (Eds.), *Culture and self.* London: Tavistock.

Hui, C. H. (1984). *Individualism-collectivism: Theory, measurement, and its relation to reward allocation.* Unpublished doctoral dissertation, University of Illinois, Urbana.

Ito, Y., & Kohei, S. (1990). Practical problems of field research in Japan. In U. Narula & W. B. Pearce (Eds.), *Cultures, politics, and research programs.* Hillsdale, NJ: Erlbaum.

Johnson, F. (1985). The western concept of self. In A. Marsella, G. DeVos, & F. Hsu (Eds.), *Culture and self.* London: Tavistock.

Josephs, L. (1991). Character, structure, self-esteem, regulation, and the principle of identity maintenance. In R. Curtis (Ed.), *The relational self.* New York: Guilford.

Klopf, D., & Cambra, R. (1979). Communication apprehension among college students in America, Australia, Japan, and Korea. *Journal of Psychology, 102*, 27-31.

Kluckhohn, F., & Strodtbeck, F. (1961). *Variations in value orientations.* New York: Row, Petersen.

Lincoln, J. R., & Kalleberg, A. L. (1985). Work organization and workforce commitment: A study of plants and employees in the U.S. and Japan. *American Sociological Review, 50*, 738-760.

Lonner, W. (1979). Issues in cross-cultural psychology. In A. Marsella, A. Tharp, & T. Cibrowski (Eds.), *Perspectives in cross-cultural psychology.* New York: Academic Press.

Luthans, R., McCaul, H., & Dodd, N. (1985). Organizational commitment: A comparison of American, Japanese, and Korean employees. *Academy of Management Journal, 28*, 213-219.

Markus, H. R., & Kitayama, S. (1991). Culture and the self: Implications for cognition, emotion, and motivation. *Psychological Review, 98*, 224-253.

Mito, T. (1991). *Ie no ronri* (The theory of *ie*) (two vols.). Tokyo: Bunshindo.

Miyanaga, K. (1991). *The creative edge: Emerging individualism in Japan.* New Brunswick, NJ: Transaction Books.

Morisaki, S. (1992). *Face in Japan and the United States: Independent and interdependent face.* Unpublished M.A. thesis, California State University, Fullerton.

Morisaki, S., & Gudykunst, W. B. (in press). Face in Japan and the United States. In S. Ting-Toomey (Ed.), *The challenge of facework.* Albany: State University of New York Press.

Mouer, R., & Sugimoto, Y. (1986). *Images of Japanese society.* London: Kegan Paul.

Nishida, H. (1981). Value orientations and value changes in Japan and the United States. In T. Nishida & W. Gudykunst (Eds.), *Readings on intercultural communication.* Tokyo: Geirinshobo.

Plath, D. (1989). Arc, circle and sphere: Schedules for selfhood in Japan. In Y. Sugimoto & R. Mouer (Eds.), *Constructs for understanding Japan.* London: Kegan Paul.

Poortinga, Y. (1975). Limitations on intercultural comparisons of psychological data. *Netherlands Tijdschrift voor de Psychologie, 30*, 23-39.

Porter, L., Steers, R., Mowday, R., & Boulian, P. (1974). Organizational commitment, job satisfaction, and turnover among psychiatric technicians. *Journal of Applied Psychology, 59,* 603-609.

Rokeach, M. (1973). *The nature of human values.* New York: Free Press.

Rosenberger, N. R. (Ed.). (1992). *Japanese sense of self.* Cambridge: Cambridge University Press.

Sampson, E. E. (1988). The debate on individualism. *American Psychologist, 43,* 15-22.

Scheff, T. J. (1990). *Microsociology: Discourse, emotion, and social structure.* Chicago: University of Chicago Press.

Schwartz, S. (1990). Individualism-collectivism: Critique and proposed refinements. *Journal of Cross-Cultural Psychology, 21,* 139-157.

Schwartz, S., & Bilsky, W. (1987). Toward a universal psychological structure of human values. *Journal of Personality and Social Psychology, 53,* 550-562.

Schwartz, S., & Bilsky, W. (1990). Toward a theory of the universal content and structure of values. *Journal of Personality and Social Psychology, 58,* 878-891.

Schwind, H. F., & Peterson, R. B. (1985). Shifting personal values in the Japanese management system. *International Studies of Management & Organization, 2,* 60-74.

Sears, R. (1961). Transcultural variables and conceptual equivalence. In B. Kaplan (Ed.), *Studying personality cross-culturally.* New York: Harper.

Shikanai, K. (1978). Effects of self-esteem on attributions for success and failure. *Japanese Journal of Experimental Social Psychology, 18,* 47-55.

Sorrentino, R., & Short, J. (1986). Uncertainty orientation, motivation, and cognition. In R. Sorrentino & E. Higgins (Eds.), *Handbook of motivation and cognition.* New York: Guilford.

Sugimoto, S., & Mouer, R. (1989). Cross-currents in the study of Japanese society. In Y. Sugimoto & R. Mouer (Eds.), *Constructs for understanding Japan.* London: Kegan Paul.

Tajfel, H. (1981). *Human groups and social categories: Studies in social psychology.* Cambridge: Cambridge University Press.

Tajfel, H. (1982). Social psychology of intergroup relations. *Annual Review of Psychology, 33,* 1-39.

Tajfel, H., & Turner, J. C. (1979). An integrative theory of intergroup conflict. In W. G. Austin & S. Worchel (Eds.), *The social psychology of intergroup relations.* Monterey, CA: Brook/Cole.

Takata, T. (1987). Self-depreciative tendencies in self-evaluation through social comparison. *Japanese Journal of Experimental Social Psychology, 27,* 27-36.

Trafimow, D. M., Triandis, H. C., & Goto, S. G. (1991). Some tests of the distinction between the private self and the collective self. *Journal of Personality and Social Psychology, 60,* 649-655.

Triandis, H. C. (1988). Collectivism vs. individualism. In G. Verma & C. Bagley (Eds.), *Cross-cultural studies of personality, attitudes and cognition.* London: MacMillan.

Triandis, H. C. (1989). The self and social behavior in differing cultural contexts. *Psychological Review, 96,* 506-517.

Triandis, H. C. (1990). Cross-cultural studies of individualism-collectivism. In J. Berman (Ed.), *Nebraska Symposium on Motivation* (Vol. 37). Lincoln: University of Nebraska Press.

Triandis, H. C., Bontempo, R., Betancourt, H., Bond, M., Leung, K., Brenes, A., Georgas, J., Hui, C. H., Marin, G., Setiadi, B., Sinha, J., Verma, J., Spangenberg, J., Touzard, H., & Montemollin, G. (1986). The measurement of the etic aspects of individualism and collectivism across cultures. *Australian Journal of Psychology, 38,* 257-267.

Triandis, H. C., Bontempo, R., Villareal, M., Asai, M., & Lucca, N. (1988). Individualism-collectivism: Cross-cultural perspectives on self-ingroup relationships. *Journal of Personality and Social Psychology, 54,* 323-338.

Triandis, H. C., Leung, K., Villareal, M., & Clack, F. (1985). Allocentric versus idiocentric tendencies: Convergent and discriminant validation. *Journal of Research in Personality, 19,* 395-415.

Triandis, H. C., Malpass, R., & Davidson, A. (1973). Cross-cultural psychology. In P. Mussen & M. Rosenzweig (Eds.), *Annual review of psychology* (Vol. 24). Palo Alto, CA: Annual Reviews.

Triandis, H. C., & Marin, G. (1983). Etic plus emic versus pseudoetic. *Journal of Cross-Cultural Psychology, 14,* 489-500.

Turner, J. C., Hogg, M., Oakes, P., Reicher, S., & Wetherell, M. (1987). *Rediscovering the social group: A self-categorization theory.* Oxford: Blackwell.

Valentine, J. (1990). On the borderline: The significance of marginality in Japanese society. In E. Ben-Ari, B. Moeran, & J. Valentine (Eds.), *Unwrapping Japan.* Manchester: Manchester University Press.

Verma, J. (1992). Allocentrism and relationship orientation. In S. Iwawaki, Y. Kashima, & K. Leung (Eds.), *Innovations in cross-cultural psychology.* Amsterdam: Swets & Zeitlinger.

Waterman, A. S. (1981). Individualism and interdependence. *American Psychologist, 36,* 762-773.

White, M., & LeVine, R. (1986). What is an *Ii ko* (good child)? In H. Stevenson, H. Azuma, & K. Hakuta (Eds.), *Child development and education in Japan.* New York: Freeman.

Wierzbica, A. (1991). Japanese key words and core cultural values. *Language in Society, 20,* 333-385.

Williams, T., & Sogon, S. (1984). *Nihonjin daigakusei ni okeru shudankeisei to tekio kodo* (Group composition and conforming behavior in Japanese students). *Nihon Shinrigaku Kenkyu* (Japanese Psychological Research), *126,* 231-234.

Wuthnow, R. (1991). *Acts of compassion: Caring for others and helping ourselves.* Princenton: Princenton University Press.

Yamada, H. (1990). Topic management and turn distributions in business meetings: American versus Japanese strategies. *Text, 10,* 271-295.

Yamaguchi, S. (1990). *Personality and cognitive correlates of collectivism among the Japanese: Validation of collectivism scale.* Paper presented at the International Congress of Applied Psychology, Kyoto, Japan.

Yamaguchi, S. (1991). *"Jiko" no shitenkara no shudan oyobi bunkasa eno aprochi* (Approaches to group processes and cultural differences from the perspective of the self). *Shakaishinrigaku Kenkyu* (Research in Social Psychology), *6,* 138-147.

Yamaguchi, S. (in press). Collectivism among the Japanese: A perspective from the self. In U. Kim, H. C. Triandis, & G. Yoon (Eds.), *Individualism and collectivism: Theoretical and methodological issues.* Newbury Park, CA: Sage.

Yamazaki, M. (1990). *Nihonbunnka to kojinshugi* (Japanese culture and individualism). Tokyo: Chukoronsha.

Yoshida, T., Kojo, K., & Kaku, H. (1982). A study on the development of self-presentations in children. *Japanese Journal of Educational Psychology, 30,* 30-37.

Author Index

A

Abegglan, J., 21, 39
Adler, N., 215, 217, 242
Akasu, K., 11, 88
Altman, I., 31, 39, 155, 158, 159, 177, 184, 191, 192, 211
Asao, K., 11, 88
Barnlund, D., 8, 15, 75, 78, 109, 118, 152, 154, 157, 159, 164, 165, 192
Atsumi, R., 157, 186, 192

B

Befu, H., 25, 30, 39, 40, 138, 144, 193, 220, 242, 296, 311, 312, 316
Bellah, R., 31, 40, 57, 59, 84, 193, 299, 306, 316
Benedict, R., 20, 40, 55, 128, 144
Berger, C. R., 6, 15, 150, 184, 186, 194
Berry, J., 19, 40
Bilsky, A., 294, 295, 320
Bond, M. H., 8, 15, 35, 37, 40, 162, 187, 188, 194
Brislin, R., 19, 40, 293, 310-312, 316, 317

C

Caudill, W., 38, 41, 195, 298, 317
Chinese Culture Connection, 29, 35, 41
Clancy, P., 70, 71, 84
Clark, R., 21, 41, 242
Condon, J., 7, 100, 119
Cousins, S., 37, 41, 63, 65, 78, 195, 307
Cronen, V., 6, 15
Cupach, W., 165, 201

D

Dale, P. N., 24-28, 36, 37, 41
Deaux, K., 307, 317
DeVos, G., 22, 36, 41
Doi, T., 31, 36, 41, 55, 93, 112, 113, 184, 311
Dore, R., 21, 41
Dulles, F., 3, 15

E

Ekman, P., 170-172, 196
Embree, J., 20, 42

SUBJCT INDEX

A

Address terms, 97
Affect orientation, 167
Agenda setting model of
    communication, 258
Aggressiveness, 167
Aizuchi, 69, 70, 101-104
Allocentrism. *See* idiocentrism-
    allocentrism
Amae, 55, 112, 156, 184
American organizations in Japan,
    237, 238
Americans' views of Japanese, 3-5
Apologies, 165
Assertiveness, 167
Awase-erabi worldviews, 168

C

Collectivism. *See* Individualism-
    collectivism
Communication apprehension. *See*
    Social anxiety
Communication satisfaction, 179-181

Communicator style, 163, 164
Compliments, 165
Conflict, 173-175
Confucian work dynamism, 35, 36
Consumption tax law (case study),
    269-272
Context: low- versus high-context
    communication, 31-32; context
    dependence in language usage,
    109-115
Conversations: differences between
    Japan and United States, 68-71;
    topic management, 168-170;
    conversational logics, 153
Coordinated management of
    meaning, 6
Criticism, 164, 165
Cross-cultural research: approaches
    to study of organizations, 215,
    216; emic versus etic
    approaches, 19; criticisms of,
    216; issues of equivalence, 309-
    313; limitations of, 238-240;
    types of, 7-10
Cultivation model of
    communication, 256, 257